THE **TESTING** SERIES
POLICE SPECIAL CONSTABLE
TESTS

THE **TESTING** SERIES
expert advice on test prepar...

how2become

Orders: Please contact How2become Ltd, Suite 2, 50 Churchill Square Business Centre, Kings Hill, Kent ME19 4YU.

You can also order via the e mail address info@how2become.co.uk.

ISBN: 9781907558603

First published 2012

Typeset for How2become Ltd by Molly Hill, Canada.

Printed in Great Britain for How2become Ltd by Bell & Bain Ltd, 303 Burnfield Road, Thornliebank, Glasgow G46 7UQ.

INTRODUCTION AND WELCOME

Welcome to your new guide, Police Special Constable Tests. This guide has been designed to help you prepare for and pass the Police Special Constable test that forms part of the selection process in England and Wales. The questions and answers contained within this guide are relevant for the Situational Judgement Test (SJT) that forms part of the Police Special Constable selection process.

The selection process to join the police is highly competitive. Approximately 65,000 people apply to join the police every year. But what is even more staggering is that only approximately 7,000 of those applicants will be successful. You could view this as a worrying statistic, or alternatively you could view it that you are determined to be one of the 7,000 who are successful. Armed with this testing guide you have certainly taken the first step to passing the selection process.

The guide contains a large number of sample test questions and answers which are designed to make it easier for you to prepare. Read the questions and answers carefully and take notes as you progress. After each sample question we have provided you with a small box section so that you can take down notes. You will not be able to do this during the actual selection test; however, we would encourage you to do his during the practice tests as it will help you to gain an understanding of the nature of the questions as you progress.

The questions that form part of the Situational Judgement Test require no prior knowledge of police policies or operational procedures. They do, however, require a level of common sense. Think carefully about each question and write down notes in the boxes provided as to why you have chosen each answer. Then, when you check your answers, you will be able to cross-check your reasoning with the descriptions provided at the rear of the book.

ABOUT THE SITUATIONAL JUDGEMENT TEST

The Situational Judgment Test is a multiple-choice test based on common situations that you may come across as a Special Constable. During the actual SJT assessment you will be required to answer 50 questions within a 65 minute time-frame. Take a look at the following sample SJT question:

SAMPLE SITUATIONAL JUDGEMENT TEST QUESTION 1

Whilst on foot patrol in your local High Street you are approached by a woman who informs you that she has just found a purse on the pavement. Upon inspection there is no money in the purse but you do notice personal details relating to the owner.

Please pick the best option (most effective option) and the worst option (least effective option) in terms of what you should do:

A. Challenge the woman as to why there is no money in the purse.

B. Immediately take the purse back to the station and record the lost property.

C. Ask the woman to hand the purse in at the local police station.

D. Immediately try to contact the owner of the purse in order to hand it back to them.

ANSWERS

BEST: OPTION: D

This option allows you to reunite the owner with the purse quickly and also allows you to stay out on patrol.

WORST: OPTION: A

This option could potentially damage relations with the public. You have no reason to suspect the woman has taken money from the purse.

Now take a look at the next sample question.

SAMPLE SITUATIONAL JUDGEMENT TEST QUESTION 2

It is 2200hrs and you are on duty at a music festival. You have not had a break for eight hours and you are feeling very tired and hungry. The festival is very busy and the revellers have been drinking heavily. There is potential for disruption. All other units in the area are busy as it is a Saturday evening and there is nobody to discuss the situation with face to face. There is a mobile food unit at the entrance to the festival where you could discretely take a well-earned break without many people noticing.

Please pick the best option (most effective option) and the worst option (least effective option) in terms of what you should do:

A. Take a break at the mobile food unit and leave your post without anyone knowing. After all, you deserve a rest.

B. Work through your tiredness and hunger and maintain position at your post.

C. Contact your Police Sergeant by radio and inform him/her that you have not had a break for eight hours and request a relief.

D. Buy a takeaway cup of tea and some food and eat it at your post.

ANSWERS

BEST: OPTION: C

You must contact your Police Sergeant or supervisor and inform them that you need a break. If you are tired and hungry then you are unlikely to perform to the best of your ability.

WORST: OPTION: A

This could lead to potential disorder with nobody being aware that assistance is needed in the area at the festival.

You will notice that you need no prior knowledge of police procedures in order to answer the questions. All you need is a good level of sensible thinking.

During the next chapter we have provided you with 60 test question to help you prepare. Work through the questions carefully and learn as you progress. Do not worry if you get some questions wrong. This is all part of the learning process and is only natural. The important thing is to learn from your mistakes and to understand how the answers are reached.

Finally, don't ever give up on your dreams; if you really want to become a Police Officer Special Constable then you can do it. The way to approach the selection test is to embark on a programme of 'in-depth' preparation, and this guide will help you to do just that.

If you need any further help with any elements of the selection process, including role play, fitness and interview, then we offer a wide range of products to assist you. These are all available through our online shop www. how2become.co.uk. We also run a 1-day intensive Police Special Constable Training Course. Details are available at the website

WWW.POLICECOURSE.CO.UK

Once again, thank you for your custom and we wish you every success in your pursuit to becoming a Police Special Constable.

Work hard, stay focused and be what you want…

Best wishes,

The how2become team

The How2become Team

60 SAMPLE
SITUATIONAL JUDGEMENT TEST QUESTIONS

Now work through the following 60 test questions. You have 60 minutes in which to complete the test. Once you have completed the entire test, take the time to work through the answers at the rear of the workbook carefully. Good luck and remember to take notes.

SAMPLE QUESTION 1

A work colleague at your station has been absent due to sickness and she has missed an important operational incident debrief that has highlighted a number of important changes to police procedures. What would you do?

Please pick the best option (most effective option) and the worst option (least effective option) in terms of what you should do.

A. Immediately explain to her what the changes are and clarify that she fully understands them.

B. Inform your line manager of her absence so that he can tell her what they are.

C. Do nothing. She will probably find out about the changes through other work colleagues or whilst she is on the job.

D. Wait until tea break before you inform her. There'll be more time then to explain what the changes are.

NOTES:

SAMPLE QUESTION 2

Whilst attending a Road Traffic Collision you notice a member of the public trying to help out the Firefighters by handing them items of equipment. What would you do?

Please pick the best option (most effective option) and the worst option (least effective option) in terms of what you should do.

A. Allow them to carry on as they probably know what they are doing.

B. Approach the person and offer to help them pass over the equipment.

C. Politely thank the person for their assistance but ask them to stay back behind the cordon where they will be safe.

D. Ask your supervisory officer what they think you should do.

NOTES:

SAMPLE QUESTION 3

Special Constables are often required to enter people's homes in order to carry out door to door enquiries. Whilst attending someone's home they offer you £50 as a thank you for the good work that you do. What would you do?

Please pick the best option (most effective option) and the worst option (least effective option) in terms of what you should do.

A. Thank them for the money, put it in my pocket, and leave a happy person.

B. Thank them for the money, put it in my pocket, and share it with the rest of the team when I get back to the police station.

C. Thank them for their kind offer but explain that you are unable to accept gifts of this nature.

D. Walk away and ignore them.

NOTES:

SAMPLE QUESTION 4

During an operational incident the Police Sergeant gives you instructions to immediately stop what you are doing and request more resources via the control centre. Once you have received the instructions, what would you do?

Please pick the best option (most effective option) and the worst option (least effective option) in terms of what you should do.

A. Finish off the job that I am doing before contacting the control centre to request more resources.

B. Immediately stop what I am doing if safe to do so before contacting the control centre to request more resources. Once I have requested the resources, and confirmed that the control centre fully understands my request, I will then inform the Sergeant that the message has been sent and that the resources are on their way. I would then return to my previous task.

C. Because I am already involved in another task, I will pass the message onto another Police Officer so that he/she can request the resources.

D. Immediately stop what I am doing if safe to do so before contacting the control centre to request more resources. Once I have requested the resources, and confirmed that the control centre fully understands my request, I will then go back to what I was doing before.

NOTES:

POLICE SPECIAL CONSTABLE TESTS

SAMPLE QUESTION 5

You are the first on the scene to a fire in a block of flats. Which of the following tasks would you carry out first?

Please pick the best option (most effective option) and the worst option (least effective option) in terms of what you should do.

A. Look for fire extinguishers.

B. Fight the fire.

C. Search the building for casualties.

D. Raise the fire alarm in order to start the evacuation process and then contact the control centre to ask for the attendance of the Fire Service and more police resources.

NOTES:

SAMPLE QUESTION 6

Whilst patrolling the streets a man runs up to you and tells you that a bank around the corner is in the process of being robbed by an armed gang. Which of the following would you do?

Please pick the best option (most effective option) and the worst option (least effective option) in terms of what you should do.

A. Ask the man to take you to the shop where the robbery is taking place. Once you get there you can decide what action to take.

B. Immediately contact control to inform them of the location of the incident and the circumstances surrounding it, i.e. that the robbers are armed. This will enable the control centre to deploy the correct resources.

C. Gather as much information from the man as possible about the incident and its location before making your way to the scene.

D. Immediately run to the location of the robbery and attempt to tackle the armed robbers.

NOTES:

SAMPLE QUESTION 7

You are responsible for the outer cordon at a serious incident when a man approaches you saying that he is from the local press and that he wants to take some pictures of the incident from within the inner cordon. What would you do?

Please pick the best option (most effective option) and the worst option (least effective option) in terms of what you should do.

A. Allow him into the inner cordon.

B. Tell him to go away.

C. Politely inform him that he is not permitted within the inner cordon and ask him respectfully to stay back away from the danger area.

D. Ask your supervisor what he/she thinks you should do.

NOTES:

SAMPLE QUESTION 8

During a visit to a local school you notice that a number of the fire doors are wedged open illegally. What would you do?

Please pick the best option (most effective option) and the worst option (least effective option) in terms of what you should do.

A. Ignore it for the time being. You are at the school on a talk and it would be inappropriate to say anything there and then.

B. Report the situation to the local Fire Safety Officer when you return to the police station.

C. Inform the school Head teacher that he/she must remove the wedges immediately.

D. Inform the school Head teacher that he/she must remove the wedges immediately and explain why the fire doors must not be wedged open. In addition to this I would inform the local Fire Safety Officer upon returning to the police station so that he/she could carry out an inspection of the school.

NOTES:

SAMPLE QUESTION 9

You are attending an incident that involves anti-social behaviour when an elderly woman approaches you and tells you that there is another similar incident a few roads away. What would you do?

Please pick the best option (most effective option) and the worst option (least effective option) in terms of what you should do.

A. Quickly make my way to the new incident.

B. Immediately take further details from the woman before radioing police control to inform them of the new incident so that another patrol can make their way there.

C. Ignore it. The lady has probably mistaken the two incidents as the same one.

D. Ask your line manager what they think you should do.

NOTES:

SAMPLE QUESTION 10

You are attending a crime scene and your supervisory officer asks you to stand by the entrance to the building and not allow anyone to enter without her permission. It is important that the crime scene is preserved whilst they await the attendance of forensics. A regular Police Officer walks up to you and says he needs to enter the building. What do you do?

Please pick the best option (most effective option) and the worst option (least effective option) in terms of what you should do.

A. Let him enter.

B. Ask him to wait outside whilst you contact your supervisory officer by radio to ask for permission for him to enter.

C. Tell him to leave. Nobody is allowed to enter under any circumstances.

D. Check his identification before allowing him to enter.

NOTES:

SAMPLE QUESTION 11

It is a Tuesday morning and a police officer colleague who normally works in the front office at the police station is away on sick leave, leaving it short-staffed. At 11am you are on your way to the staff room to take a quick tea break when, passing through the police station front office, you notice that it is in a reasonable amount of disarray as the staff who are there are busy attending to telephone calls.

Please pick the best option (most effective option) and the worst option (least effective option) in terms of what you should do.

A. Take your tea break and then on the way back quickly tidy up a few bits and pieces if it's still in a state.

B. Go back to your section and ask your supervisory officer whether you can be spared for 10 or 15 minutes to help out in front office. If agreed, offer your help to the front office team leader to quickly tidy up the area and take your tea break at 11.30am.

C. Do nothing. It is not your responsibility and does not fall under your job description as a police special constable.

D. Inform the front office team leader that there is a problem with the presentation of the front office.

NOTES:

SAMPLE QUESTION 12

A rural road has been closed because of a tree that has fallen and slightly blocked the road. Access to the road is only available for the emergency services. A diversion has been put in place and your supervisor has asked you to stand at one of the road closure to make sure that no one gets through. A line of traffic is building up behind you and one driver winds down his window stating that she is very late for an important appointment, and needs to get through.

Please pick the best option (most effective option) and the worst option (least effective option) in terms of what you should do.

A. Ignore her. There is no way you are going to let her through.

B. Apologise for the inconvenience, explaining that there has been a road traffic incident and no one can pass.

C. Say to the woman that you can let her through but nobody else.

D. Ask the woman to pull over and then radio your supervisor to see if he'll allow her through on this occasion.

NOTES:

SAMPLE QUESTION 13

You are attending an incident which involves a woman who has been assaulted. You have been instructed to write down eye witness accounts at the scene. Whilst talking to one eye witness you are struggling to write down his account of events.

Please pick the best option (most effective option) and the worst option (least effective option) in terms of what you should do.

A. Politely ask him to slow down so that you can take accurate notes.

B. Use shorthand and abbreviations so that you can take down the information quickly.

C. Listen to what he has to say and then write it down later when you return to the station.

D. Move on to the next person. Hopefully they will be able to give a better account of the incident.

NOTES:

SAMPLE QUESTION 14

Whilst patrolling the streets of your local community you become aware of a defect with your personal radio that means you are unable to contact control.

Please pick the best option (most effective option) and the worst option (least effective option) in terms of what you should do.

A. Carry on with the rest of my patrol without communications.

B. Spend time looking for a public telephone box in order to tell control that you won't be able to contact them for a while.

C. Immediately return to the police station in order to obtain a serviceable radio.

D. Try to fix the radio yourself whilst walking back to the station.

NOTES:

SAMPLE QUESTION 15

You are sent to an intruder alarm at an office building on an industrial estate outside the town centre with a regular police officer. On arrival the place appears to be deserted as it's a weekend. You check the rear of the premises whilst your colleague checks the front door. You notice that the access door to the rear of the premise is unlocked. You advise control, then go inside together and start a systematic search of the offices. Whilst checking the offices you come across the cleaner who apologises and says he set the alarm off when he came in earlier.

Please pick the best option (most effective option) and the worst option (least effective option) in terms of what you should do.

A. Thank him for his honesty and leave the building to continue with your duties.

B. Contact your supervisory officer by radio and ask him/her what they want you to do about the cleaner.

C. Check his identification in order to confirm that he is in fact the cleaner before continuing with your duties.

NOTES:

SAMPLE QUESTION 16

You are sent to an RTC (Road Traffic Collision) on one of the roads near to the town centre of your patch. On arrival you notice that the RTC is not too serious. One car has gone into the back of another at the traffic lights but nobody is injured. The collision is blocking one lane.

Please pick the best option (most effective option) and the worst option (least effective option) in terms of what you should do.

A. Breath-test both drivers and take down details of the incident before calling for a recovery vehicle for the most badly damaged car(s). Finally, cone-off the affected lane and direct traffic where necessary.

B. Contact your supervisory officer by radio and ask him/her what they want you to do about the incident.

C. Because the incident is minor it is the responsibility of the drivers and their insurance companies to sort out any recovery/liability. We can leave the scene without taking any action as there have been no injuries.

D. Take down details of the incident and direct traffic where necessary.

NOTES:

SAMPLE QUESTION 17

Working with a community policing team you are asked to attend a local neighbourhood watch meeting. You have a 15 minute designated time slot to talk about policing in the local area. You attend with a colleague who is a police constable with responsibility for the neighbourhood watch meeting as it is on his beat area. You begin your address and a few minutes in an anonymous member of the audience loudly shouts "get lost coppers".

Please pick the best option (most effective option) and the worst option (least effective option) in terms of what you should do:

A. Refuse to speak further until the person identifies themselves and apologises to you and your colleague.

B. Carry on with your talk as if nothing had happened.

C. Ask your police constable colleague to identify and arrest the offender.

D. Tell the meeting that you found the remark disappointing and continue with your address.

NOTES:

SAMPLE QUESTION 18

You are the first Officer to the scene of a fight between two males outside a pub. They have both been drinking heavily. Both men have bad facial injuries. You sense that there is still plenty of tension between them and that you must handle the situation correctly to prevent any further fighting.

Please pick the best option (most effective option) and the worst option (least effective option) in terms of what you should do.

A. Instruct both males to go separate ways before making a note of the incident in your notebook.

B. Immediately arrest both males on suspicion of assault.

C. Speak with both men calmly, separating them and call for back up.

D. Because they are no longer fighting it would be best to ignore the incident so as to prevent it from escalating further.

NOTES:

SAMPLE QUESTION 19

A motorway has been closed because a motorcyclist has been knocked over and killed. You have been asked by your Sergeant to only allow emergency vehicles on to the motorway access route. Whilst standing at the access route an angry lorry driver pulls up and informs you that he must get onto the motorway as he has a very important delivery to drop off at his destination. If he is late he will lose him job.

Please pick the best option (most effective option) and the worst option (least effective option) in terms of what you should do.

A. Allow him through. It would not be good 'customer focus' to prevent him from delivering his goods.

B. Ignore him.

C. Speak with your Sergeant on the radio and ask him what you should do.

D. Explain to the lorry driver in a polite manner that you are not permitted to allow him access and that he will need to use the diversion that has been put in place.

NOTES:

SAMPLE QUESTION 20

You are the first Officer on the scene at a report of a Domestic Incident where a young lady in her early twenties is alleging that she has been punched in the face by her boyfriend. On arrival at the scene you speak to both the lady and her boyfriend. She is very upset about the incident but there are no visible signs of injury to her face or otherwise. Her boyfriend informs you that he has not hit her.

Please pick the best option (most effective option) and the worst option (least effective option) in terms of what you should do.

A. Start off by separating both the lady and her boyfriend. Speak to them both calmly as individuals; gather as many facts about the incident as possible whilst waiting for backup to arrive.

B. Inform the lady that because there are no visible signs of injury you are unable to take the matter further. Leave and go back to the station.

C. Wait outside for the backup to arrive before speaking to both of them.

D. Immediately arrest the man on suspicion of assault.

NOTES:

SAMPLE QUESTION 21

Whilst sitting in the staffroom at the local police station one of your police officer colleagues is talking about a member of the public he had to deal with earlier in the day. He starts to openly criticise them in front of the entire staff room and proceeds to call the member of the public 'an idiot' and 'waste of space'.

Please pick the best option (most effective option) and the worst option (least effective option) in terms of what you should do.

A. Agree with your colleague and join in with the banter.

B. Ignore the comments as it's just police humour.

C. Challenge your colleague about the inappropriate remarks in front of everyone in the staff room telling him that his comments are unwelcome and inappropriate.

D. Challenge your colleague about the inappropriate remarks in private later, telling him that his comments are unwelcome and inappropriate.

NOTES:

SAMPLE QUESTION 22

Whilst in the police station locker room you accidentally spill your cup of coffee over a colleague's shirt that is hanging up, cleaned and pressed.

Please pick the best option (most effective option) and the worst option (least effective option) in terms of what you should do.

A. Immediately find your colleague and apologise for the accident.

B. Nobody has seen the accident so there is no need to tell anyone.

C. Immediately find your colleague and tell him about the accident but deny that it was you who spilled the drink.

D. Throw the shirt away in the bin.

NOTES:

SAMPLE QUESTION 23

It is late at night and you are called to a report of a burglary at a house located in the suburbs. The occupier of the house has dialled 999 and reported that she can hear someone downstairs whilst she is sleeping upstairs. You are the Officer to arrive at the incident and the time is 0114hrs. When you arrive at the house you notice that the front door is slightly opened and a person is lying down slumped at the foot of the stairs. Upon further investigation it is apparent that the person at the foot of the stairs is a female who is wearing her nightgown. She appears to be unconscious and has a head wound that needs immediate attention. At this point a figure appears out of the dark and pushes by you running out of the door and into the street.

A. Immediately run after the suspect.

B. Radio for an ambulance and backup, then carry out first aid to the female.

C. Carry out first aid to the female.

D. Immediately run after the suspect remembering to close the house door to prevent any further persons breaking in.

NOTES:

SAMPLE QUESTION 24

You are patrolling the crowds at a rugby match when you notice a spectator throw a glass bottle into the opposing crowd.

Please pick the best option (most effective option) and the worst option (least effective option) in terms of what you should do.

A. Deploy your CS gas spray on the offender.

B. Enter the crowd and arrest the suspect who threw the glass bottle.

C. Call for assistance/backup on your radio

D. Give the offender a warning and issue a fine.

NOTES:

SAMPLE QUESTION 25

Whilst carrying out a patrol you decide to visit the local park where youths are known to hang around. Members of the local community have complained to the police about youths in the park drinking, urinating and causing anti-social behaviour. When you approach the park you notice that a group of six youths are sitting on benches near to the public toilets.

Please pick the best option (most effective option) and the worst option (least effective option) in terms of what you should do.

A. Ignore the group as they are not causing any problems.

B. Ask them to move on and away from the park.

C. Take their names and addresses and inform their parents.

D. Speak to them regarding their presence in the park.

NOTES:

SAMPLE QUESTION 26

You are attending a serious fire in the High Street and you have been tasked with keeping people away from the outer cordon. Fire, Police and Ambulance crews are at full stretch due to the incident. Whilst you are standing on duty you notice a group of males leave the pub opposite and start staring at the incident. All of a sudden, one of the men walks over to a shop front and urinates in door entrance.

Please pick the best option (most effective option) and the worst option (least effective option) in terms of what you should do.

A. Use your radio and ask for assistance in order that you can leave your cordon point and deal with the male

B. Immediately leave your cordon and approach the male so that you can arrest him.

C. Stand on your cordon and do nothing about the male.

D. Use your radio to ask other units to deal with the offender.

NOTES:

SAMPLE QUESTION 27

You are tasked with patrolling the local High Street on a busy Saturday morning. Whilst walking along the High Street you notice a large group of people gathering around a street charity stall. Whilst you approach the stall a local shop keeper comes out from his shop to complain to you that the stall and crowds are having a negative effect on his trade.

He informs you that the stall is illegal as it does not have permission from the local authority. You check this with your control centre and the stall is in fact illegal.

Please pick the best option (most effective option) and the worst option (least effective option) in terms of what you should do.

A. Speak to the charity stall staff and ask them to move on as they are having an effect on the shop trade in the area. Inform then that they are also not permitted to operate in this area without local authority authorisation.

B. Inform the shop manager you cannot do anything but you will take steps to prevent them from appearing in the future.

C. Ask the shop owner to ask the charity stall to move on.

D. Call for assistance to deal with the entertainer and the crowd.

NOTES:

SAMPLE QUESTION 28

You attend a pub with three other colleagues where there is a report of violent disorder. When you arrive at the scene you notice that five males are involved in a fight. As one of your colleagues try to arrest the men they begin to resist. Another police officer colleague then uses his baton and strikes one of the males on his leg. He then arrests the male. You assist your colleague in restraining the male. The male, however, continues to be vocal and aggressive and he demands to make a complaint about being struck with the baton.

Please pick the best option (most effective option) and the worst option (least effective option) in terms of what you should do.

A. Attempt to calm down the male and explain to him that his complaint will be dealt with once the situation has abated.

B. Totally ignore the offender before escorting him to the waiting police van.

C. Immediately ask your colleague who struck him to explain his actions.

D. Tell the offender to calm down.

NOTES:

SAMPLE QUESTION 29

You are patrolling the High Street on a busy Saturday afternoon when you notice a car mount the pavement and knock down an elderly woman walking home with her shopping before driving off.

A passing motorist pulls up and offers you to jump into his car and give chase to the suspect vehicle.

Please pick the best option (most effective option) and the worst option (least effective option) in terms of what you should do.

A. Jump in the car and go after the offending vehicle.

B. Contact control and ask them for permission to chase after the offending vehicle.

C. Politely decline the offer and attend to the woman who has been knocked down.

D. Politely decline the offer and wait for back up.

NOTES:

SAMPLE QUESTION 30

You are on patrol with a police officer when he starts making sexist remarks about a work colleague.

Please pick the best option (most effective option) and the worst option (least effective option) in terms of what you should do.

A. Politely tell him that his remarks are inappropriate and ask him to stop.

B. Join in with the remarks; it is all part and parcel of Police Force banter.

C. Do not say anything.

D. Report the comments to your supervisory officer when you return to station.

NOTES:

SAMPLE QUESTION 31

At 21:45hrs you are about to leave the police station to go on a scheduled patrol. As you leave the office the telephone begins to ring.

Please pick the best option (most effective option) and the worst option (least effective option) in terms of what you should do.

A. Ignore the phone and go to your patrol. Another officer can answer it.

B. Answer the phone.

C. Ask a colleague to answer the phone as you need to go on your scheduled patrol.

D. Divert the call to answerphone in order that you can go on patrol. You can deal with it when you return.

NOTES:

SAMPLE QUESTION 32

You are called to a dispute between two neighbours in your local community. One of the neighbours has called the police to say that her neighbour is having a party and the music is too loud. As you arrive the male neighbour who is holding the party, notices you and approaches you asking if the "the nosy old bag" next door has complained about the noise. You note that the level of music coming from his house is excessive.

Please pick the best option (most effective option) and the worst option (least effective option) in terms of what you should do.

A. Issue the male with a warning as to his language.

B. Inform him that you cannot speak to him as you need to speak the neighbour first as she called the police.

C. Ask him politely to turn down the level of his music down. Also inform him that both he and his neighbour will both have their chance to put across their side of the argument.

D. Tell him to turn his music down and then leave.

NOTES:

SAMPLE QUESTION 33

You are attending an incident of alleged assault with a police officer colleague where a woman has complained she has been hit in the face by her partner. There is sufficient evidence to arrest the suspect. You decide to arrest the male, but as you do so, he tells you that he is "not going to be arrested by a fucking special copper!" and demands to be arrested by a regular police officer.

Please pick the best option (most effective option) and the worst option (least effective option) in terms of what you should do.

A. Carry on with the arrest regardless.

B. Warn the suspect regarding his language and continue with the arrest.

C. Give in to his request and ask your colleague to take over and make the arrest.

D. Radio for further assistance in case the suspect gets violent.

NOTES:

SAMPLE QUESTION 34

You are attending an incident of suspected shoplifting at a local supermarket. You have arrested the suspect and are about to escort her back to the station for questioning when the shop manager runs up to you and informs you that he suspects someone else in the store is shoplifting also.

Please pick the best option (most effective option) and the worst option (least effective option) in terms of what you should do.

A. Tell him to dial 999 and request the attendance of the police.

B. Tell him that you will come back after you have dealt with the first incident.

C. Radio for assistance and request that another unit deals with the incident.

D. Tell the offender to stay where they are whilst you go and deal with the new incident.

NOTES:

SAMPLE QUESTION 35

You are called to an incident at a domestic dwelling where the occupier has reported an attempted burglary. When you arrive at the house, the gentleman, who is of Muslim religion, asks you to take off your shoes before you enter.

Please pick the best option (most effective option) and the worst option (least effective option) in terms of what you should do.

A. Inform the gentleman that you will not remove your shoes as they form part of your personal protective equipment and that he must let you enter.

B. Remove your shoes on entering.

C. Politely inform the gentleman that you are unable to remove your shoes and ask him to reconsider.

NOTES:

SAMPLE QUESTION 36

You are on foot patrol in the local park when you see an older woman who is crying, shaking and clearly in distress.

Please pick the best option (most effective option) and the worst option (least effective option) in terms of what you should do.

A. Walk past the female and ignore her as this is not a police matter.

B. Speak to the female and try and ascertain what is wrong and why she is crying.

C. Call the control room and ask for assistance.

D. Speak to passers-by in the park and ask anyone nearby if they know the female.

NOTES:

SAMPLE QUESTION 37

Whilst walking along the High Street at 0100hrs a taxi driver pulls up next to you and winds down his window. He tells you that he has just found a purse in the back of his taxi that must have been left by a customer earlier on in the evening. Upon inspection of the purse, you notice that there is no money inside it.

Please pick the best option (most effective option) and the worst option (least effective option) in terms of what you should do.

A. Ask the driver to take the wallet to the station as you are busy on patrol.

B. Thank him for the purse and take it back to the station immediately so that you can log down the incident.

C. Try to contact the owner of the purse immediately.

D. Challenge the driver as to why there is no money in the purse.

NOTES:

SAMPLE QUESTION 38

It is a sunny summer's day and you are patrolling the High Street when you notice a car parked (legally) at the side of the road. There are four males sat in the car and the driver is revving his engine. You approach the driver and ask him politely to cease revving his car. His first reaction is to refuse and get angry with you.

Please pick the best option (most effective option) and the worst option (least effective option) in terms of what you should do.

A. Call for assistance as there are four males in the car.

B. Accept his decision and carry on with your patrol.

C. Demand in a forceful manner that the driver ceases to rev his engine.

D. Explain that the driver is causing a disturbance in public and that you insist he ceases to rev his vehicle.

NOTES:

SAMPLE QUESTION 39

You are attending a briefing at the police station prior to a planned raid on the property of a suspected drugs dealer. At the briefing you all of sudden realise that the property you are raiding is well known to you in your private life.

Please pick the best option (most effective option) and the worst option (least effective option) in terms of what you should do.

A. Don't tell the Police Sergeant that you know the individual concerned.

B. Interrupt the briefing immediately and inform the Police Sergeant of your connection with the individual concerned.

C. Wait until the end of the briefing before privately declaring your connection with the individual concerned to the Police Sergeant.

D. Wait until the end of the briefing and declare to everyone in the room that you are connected to the individual concerned.

NOTES:

SAMPLE QUESTION 40

At the commencement of duty briefing you are tasked with carrying out reassurance patrols from 1800-2100hrs in a local park when a man has been indecently exposing himself. You are also required to attend a serious domestic assault in order to take witness statements. You cannot do both tasks.

Please pick the best option (most effective option) and the worst option (least effective option) in terms of what you should do.

A. Try to write down the report as quickly as possible and then carry out the patrols.

B. Inform the Police Sergeant and then carry out the patrols.

C. Inform the Police Sergeant and then write down the report.

D. Carry out the patrols and ask someone else to write down your report.

NOTES:

SAMPLE QUESTION 41

You receive a complaint from a parent at a local primary school that some parents are parking illegally to drop children off in the morning. When you attend the school to observe, you notice a car parked illegally in a disabled parking space. You approach the car and speak to the driver.

Please pick the best option (most effective option) and the worst option (least effective option) in terms of what you should do.

A. Ask the driver to get out and join you on the pavement whilst you explain the problem.

B. Tell the driver to move on immediately.

C. Ask the driver to move on pointing out that the designated parking space is for disabled drivers only and that he is not to park there in the future.

D. Issue the driver with a fine.

NOTES:

SAMPLE QUESTION 42

The police control centre receives a 999 call. When the operator speaks the person hangs up without saying anything. The call is traced to a house on your area. When you arrive at the house you are met by a mother and her 6 year old daughter. The woman explains that the child must have dialled 999 in error and apologises.

Please pick the best option (most effective option) and the worst option (least effective option) in terms of what you should do.

A. Tell the woman that it is fine and then leave.

B. Tell the woman not to worry about it, but that her child must learn to behave.

C. Warn the child in front of her mother that this kind of behaviour will not be tolerated.

D. Ask the woman to try and ensure it does not happen again.

NOTES:

SAMPLE QUESTION 43

You are on foot patrol in your local High Street when you witness two youths arguing on the pavement. Their argument is becoming so heated that members of the public are crossing over the road to get away from them.

Please pick the best option (most effective option) and the worst option (least effective option) in terms of what you should do.

A. Ignore them as incidents of this nature usually blow over once the air is cleared.

B. Go up to the youths and inform them that their behaviour is causing a disturbance.

C. Approach them and tell them to quieten down or they could arrested.

D. Speak to any members of public in the High Street if they are intimidated before acting.

NOTES:

SAMPLE QUESTION 44

You are on duty at the front desk of the police station. You are dealing with one member of the public and there are also four other people sat patiently waiting. A man walks into the police station, slams his hand on the counter and demands that you see him immediately.

Please pick the best option (most effective option) and the worst option (least effective option) in terms of what you should do.

A. Ask him what the issue is and then decide the priority.

B. Ask him to sit down and wait patiently with the other people.

C. Ask the people waiting if they object to you dealing with this man first.

D. Tell him to sit down, wait his turn and you will speak to him then.

NOTES:

SAMPLE QUESTION 45

You are called to a quiet residential street where a member of the public has complained that two youths are kicking a ball against his wall. When you arrive you see the youths playing football against the man's garden wall.

Please pick the best option (most effective option) and the worst option (least effective option) in terms of what you should do.

A. Tell them, in a forceful manner, to stop kicking the ball against the wall or they will be arrested.

B. Explain to the youths that they are causing a nuisance by kicking the ball against the wall and ask them to stop.

C. Go to the caller's house first.

D. Confiscate the football.

NOTES:

SAMPLE QUESTION 46

You are carrying out reassurance patrols in the town centre following an important derby football match between the two local teams. The pubs have been full all day and people have been drinking excessively. As you walk along the High Street you witness a man lying on the ground next to a group of commercial dustbins wearing a football shirt and scarf. As you approach him he awakens and says "What's happened, where am I?"

Please pick the best option (most effective option) and the worst option (least effective option) in terms of what you should do.

A. Warn him for being drunken disorderly.

B. Just ignore him; he's conscious and has obviously had a good time.

C. Ask if he is okay.

D. Tell him to get up.

NOTES:

SAMPLE QUESTION 47

You have been asked to attend a member of the public's home to offer them advice on how to keep their property secure following an attempted burglary. When you are talking to the elderly lady you notice that there are a large number of cigarette burns on the carpet and that the property does not have a smoke detector.

Please pick the best option (most effective option) and the worst option (least effective option) in terms of what you should do.

A. Do nothing. You are only there to offer advice on security matters. This is the responsibility of the Fire Service.

B. Tell the lady she needs to stop smoking.

C. Provide the lady with fire safety advice and recommend that she gets a smoke detector.

D. Provide the lady with fire safety advice and recommend that she gets a smoke detector. When you return to the station contact the local Fire Safety Officer and recommend they offer her a Home Fire Safety visit due to the risk factors involved.

NOTES:

SAMPLE QUESTION 48

At 01:00hrs on a Monday morning you are on foot patrol with a police officer colleague in an area where CID have informed you illegal immigrants congregate. You see a male acting suspiciously and decide to speak to him. You both approach the male. As you do so he suddenly pushes your police officer colleague to the ground before running off. Your colleague falls badly on his hand and it appears to be sprained.

Please pick the best option (most effective option) and the worst option (least effective option) in terms of what you should do.

A. Chase after the suspect.

B. Stay with your colleague and give him basic first aid.

C. Note the description of the suspect as he runs off and remain with your colleague.

D. Chase after the suspect and radio for assistance for your colleague.

NOTES:

SAMPLE QUESTION 49

You are driving along a rural road when you see a woman up ahead trying to wave you down. You stop your car and wind down your window. She tells you that a young girl has been badly bitten by a dog in the nearby park. You park your car and make your way over to the park. When you arrive you notice the child and it is clear that it has been attacked. You also see the dog, it looks like it is out of control and you cannot spot its owner.

Please pick the best option (most effective option) and the worst option (least effective option) in terms of what you should do.

A. Go after the dog and try to bring it under control.

B. Stay with the girl and ask a member of public to chase after the dog.

C. Request immediate back up before calmly clearing the area giving first aid to the child.

D. Go back to your car and wait for back up to arrive.

NOTES:

SAMPLE QUESTION 50

You are attending a scene of serious public disorder and you have been asked by your Police Sergeant to assist regular police officers with the arrest of suspected looters. Whilst carrying out your duties you witness a youth trying to smash a window approximately 100 yards away.

Please pick the best option (most effective option) and the worst option (least effective option) in terms of what you should do.

A. Make a note of the youth's appearance and location of the incident.

B. Run over to the scene and arrest the youth.

C. Inform your Police Sergeant of the incident.

D. Do thing and stay at your current position.

NOTES:

SAMPLE QUESTION 51

You are on patrol in a police vehicle with a police officer colleague. You notice a driver up ahead swaying all over the road, so you decide to stop him on suspicion of driving under the influence of alcohol. When you pull over the car you get out of your vehicle and walk over to the driver. He winds down the window and immediately you can smell alcohol. All of a sudden he restarts his engine and puts the car in gear.

Please pick the best option (most effective option) and the worst option (least effective option) in terms of what you should do.

A. Stand in front of the car and tell him to stop.

B. Shout over to your police officer colleague that the driver might speed off.

C. Run back to the police car in preparation for the chase.

D. Instruct the driver to switch off the engine immediately.

NOTES:

SAMPLE QUESTION 52

You are attending a local primary school to discuss the problems with parking in the adjacent roads to the school. Whilst at the school you receive a call from control to attend an incident approximately one mile away. Just as you prepare to leave the Head Teacher approaches you and asks you to speak to two young pupils who have been setting off the fire alarm.

Please pick the best option (most effective option) and the worst option (least effective option) in terms of what you should do.

A. Ask the control centre to dispatch another officer and then go and speak to the pupils.

B. Quickly speak to the pupils and then attend the incident.

C. Inform the control centre you will attend the incident after you have spoken to the pupils.

D. Arrange a time with the Head Teacher to come back and speak to the pupils.

NOTES:

SAMPLE QUESTION 53

You are attending the scene of a road traffic collision involving a car and a motorcyclist. The paramedics are treating the motorcyclist who is suffering from serious injuries. They remove his watch and ask you to take care of it.

Please pick the best option (most effective option) and the worst option (least effective option) in terms of what you should do.

A. Take the watch from the paramedics and give it to the casualty at hospital later on.

B. Accept the watch and note down in your pocket book the circumstances it was given to you for later return.

C. Tell the paramedics that it is not your responsibility. Refuse the watch as she is the paramedic's responsibility.

D. Accept the watch and ask the paramedic who gave it to you for his name and a signature.

NOTES:

SAMPLE QUESTION 54

You are on foot patrol in the local High Street dealing with a man for possible theft from a shop when a young girl approaches crying, saying that she is lost and doesn't know what to do. She tells you that she last saw her parents in the Debenhams store.

Please pick the best option (most effective option) and the worst option (least effective option) in terms of what you should do.

A. Ask the child to go back to the Debenhams store to look for her parents.

B. Let the suspected offender off and take the child back to Debenhams to search for her parents.

C. Contact the control centre and ask for assistance to deal with the child so that you can continue with the alleged offender.

D. Escort the child to Debenhams, taking the offender with you.

NOTES:

SAMPLE QUESTION 55

Whilst carrying out reassurance patrols in a local park you come across a large bag of white powder which you suspect to be class A drugs.

Please pick the best option (most effective option) and the worst option (least effective option) in terms of what you should do.

A. Take the bag over to the nearest bin and dispose of it.

B. Take it with you and complete your control before disposing of it at the station.

C. Ask people in the park if it belongs to them.

D. Call for assistance in dealing with the matter whilst taking possession of the white powder.

NOTES:

SAMPLE QUESTION 56

You are attending the scene of a burglary at a domestic dwelling. The offenders have broken the rear door window during their break-in. You notice a small amount of blood on the window but are aware that it is starting to rain heavily. The blood is exposed to the elements.

Please pick the best option (most effective option) and the worst option (least effective option) in terms of what you should do.

A. Use a tissue to recover the evidence to prevent it from being washed away.

B. Take no action in case you spoil the chance of forensic recovery.

C. Contact control and request urgent forensic assistance.

D. Protect the glass and evidence from the elements until forensics arrive.

NOTES:

SAMPLE QUESTION 57

You are called to a multi-storey car park where a man is threatening to jump from the top storey. A large crowd has gathered at the bottom of the car park.

Please pick the best option (most effective option) and the worst option (least effective option) in terms of what you should do.

A. Try to talk the man down.

B. Do nothing and walk away from the scene. If he sees a police officer he may jump.

C. Contact control and request urgent assistance before moving the public away from the scene.

D. Make your way to the top storey of the car park so that you can speak to the man.

NOTES:

SAMPLE QUESTION 58

Whilst on patrol in a suburban area a man runs up to you and tells you that he has just passed a man who he believes to be holding a gun. He points out the man to you from a distance.

Please pick the best option (most effective option) and the worst option (least effective option) in terms of what you should do.

A. Make your way over to the man and search him for the firearm.

B. Shout to the man from a distance and ask him if he is in possession of a firearm.

C. Observe the man from a safe distance and inform the police control centre so that they can dispatch the appropriate response units.

D. Ask the man to go back and double-check that he has got a firearm.

NOTES:

SAMPLE QUESTION 59

You are carrying out foot patrols in an area that is known for anti-social behaviour. There have already been several complaints to the police by members of the public. You notice a group of eight youths standing by the entrance to a park.

Please pick the best option (most effective option) and the worst option (least effective option) in terms of what you should do.

A. Walk past them, they are not doing anything wrong.

B. Go over to them and speak to them.

C. Go over to them and warn them that they could be arrested if they carry out any anti-social behaviour.

D. Go over to them and tell them to move on to a different area.

NOTES:

SAMPLE QUESTION 60

You are carrying out foot patrols with a regular police officer when he starts making sexist comments about a fellow work colleague.

Please pick the best option (most effective option) and the worst option (least effective option) in terms of what you should do.

A. Do nothing.

B. Agree with him and join in with the comments.

C. Inform him that his comments are inappropriate and not acceptable in his role as a police officer.

D. Go back to the station and inform the person about the comments.

NOTES:

Now that you have completed the test, please work through the following answers carefully. For any that you have scored incorrectly, take the time to read the explanations as this will help you to improve for the real test.

ANSWERS TO SITUATIONAL JUDGEMENT TEST

QUESTION 1

BEST: A

It is important that all members of staff are kept up-to-date with issues that affect their role. It is good practice to inform your colleague of details of the meeting that she missed.

WORST: C

This option is not taking responsibility and is poor practice. You should never assume that your colleague will find out the information from someone else. Take action yourself and inform them of the information.

QUESTION 2

BEST: C

Although the member of public is trying to help, there is a danger they could become injured whilst handling the equipment. Health and safety rules and regulations dictate that this kind of practice should not be permitted.

WORST: A or B

Either of these responses would be the worst. By helping the person you would be condoning their actions. By ignoring it, you would also be condoning it.

QUESTION 3

BEST: C

You are not permitted to accept gifts of any nature whilst on duty or otherwise for working as a police special constable. Politely refusing is the best option.

WORST: A or B

You must never accept gifts of any description for your work in a public office.

QUESTION 4

BEST: B

This is clearly the most effective option. Not only are you carrying out a direct order but you are also confirming with the control centre that they have received the message and you are also confirming with the Police Sergeant that you have carried out the request successfully.

WORST: A

The danger with this option is that you might forget to send the message once you have completed the task. In addition to this you are failing to carry out a direct order by a senior officer by not 'immediately' stopping what you are doing in order to carry out the requested task.

QUESTION 5

BEST: D

In any incident of this nature you need to raise the alarm in order to start the evacuation process. You must then make provision for the relevant services and backup to be deployed.

WORST: B

If you start an attempt to fight the fire, without either raising the alarm or using the correct personal protective equipment, then you will be placing your life and the lives of others in danger.

QUESTION 6

BEST: B

During an incident of this nature it is imperative that the correct resources are deployed. If the robbers are armed then the lives could be in serious danger. Therefore, it is imperative that the control centre is informed so that the relevant response can be deployed.

WORST: D

Running to the incident, without sufficient information and resources, could place lives in danger.

QUESTION 7

BEST: C

Part of the role of a police special constable involves providing excellent customer service. Therefore, you should be polite to the individual, but inform them that it is not possible for him to enter.

WORST: A

You should never allow anyone into the inner cordon of an incident without the permission of the officer-in-charge. This is primarily for health and safety reasons.

QUESTION 8

BEST: D

The correct answer here is to inform the school Head teacher that he/she must remove the wedges immediately. This will hopefully reduce any risk of fire spread in the case of a fire. You should also take the opportunity to educate them and explain why the fire doors must not be wedged open. You should also follow up your actions by informing the local Fire Safety Officer upon returning to the police station so that he/she could carry out an inspection of the school, just in case there are any further contraventions.

WORST: A

The worst thing you can do is ignore it. You have a duty of care whilst at the school and therefore you should take action immediately.

QUESTION 9

BEST: B

Whilst attending the first incident you have a duty of care; therefore, you should stay at the scene unless the other incident involves a danger to life. The correct answer is to inform the control centre so that they can deploy the relevant response.

WORST: C

You must never ignore a report of an incident.

QUESTION 10

BEST: B

Although he is a serving police officer you have been told not to let anyone into the crime scene area; therefore, you should obey the instruction. The best option is to inform the officer-in-charge of the request to enter so that they can decide on the best course of action.

WORST: A

By allowing the officer to enter you are effectively disobeying a direct order.

QUESTION 11

BEST: B

By taking this action you are taking personal responsibility, one of the core competencies relevant to the role of a police special constable: takes personal responsibility for making things happen and achieving results. Displays motivation, commitment, perseverance and conscientiousness. Acts with a high degree of integrity.

WORST: C

It is your responsibility; therefore, you should take action and not ignore it.

QUESTION 12

BEST: B

One of the core competencies relevant to the role of a police officer is that of customer focus: Responds quickly to customer requests. It is important that you inform them of the fact that they are unable to enter in a polite manner. The reason why they are unable to enter the scene is due to health and safety reasons; the road/access is not safe.

WORST: C

By letting her through, you are not only potentially endangering her life, but also disobeying a direct order.

QUESTION 13

BEST: A

By asking the witness to slow down you will be able to take accurate notes. One of the core competencies relevant to the role is that of effective communication. In particular the competency states:

- Uses correct spelling, punctuation and grammar.
- Listens carefully to understand.

It is pointless writing down inaccurate or abbreviated details of the case, as these could be deemed inadmissible in court. Accurate note taking is an important aspect of the role.

WORST: D

By moving on to the next person you are effectively missing vital information that relates to the case.

QUESTION 14

BEST: C

Without communications you are unable to request backup if required or inform control of your whereabouts. Therefore, you must return to the station in order to obtain a new serviceable radio.

WORST: A

Without communications you are placing yourself in a vulnerable position. It is important that you have communications with you at all times.

QUESTION 15

BEST: C

It is imperative that you check the cleaner for identification. After all, they could be a burglar in disguise!

WORST: A

If you do not check their identification, how do you know that they are not a burglar?

QUESTION 16

BEST: A

It is important to breathalyse each driver before taking down details of the incident. You then have a duty to make the scene safe before diverting/directing traffic.

WORST: C

Because you have attended the incident you have a duty of care and therefore are required to take appropriate action to make the scene safe.

QUESTION 17

BEST: D

This option allows you to make your point about the incident without over-reacting.

WORST: C

This option would be a gross over-reaction and could do more harm than good.

QUESTION 18

BEST: C

You will need assistance to deal with the incident and to make the necessary arrests. You will also need backup in order to take down any witness details/accounts.

WORST: D

If you ignore the incident then it is likely that the males will continue to fight and further harm could be caused to them and/or others.

QUESTION 19

BEST: D

This is clearly the most effective option. It is important that you are both polite and resilient.

WORST: A

You must not allow him through because:

1. You would be disobeying a direct order.

2. You would be potentially endangering his life and the lives of others by allowing him access to the motorway.

QUESTION 20

BEST: A

It is essential that you speak to both parties as individuals in a calm manner. It will be your responsibility to gather as many facts about the alleged incident as possible whilst waiting for backup to arrive.

WORST: B

Just because there are no visible signs of an assault, it does not mean one has not taken place. You must not leave the scene until you have gathered all of the facts about the alleged incident and waited for backup to arrive.

QUESTION 21

BEST: D

It is essential that you challenge your colleague as this form of behaviour is unacceptable. It is also advisable that you do it in private, so as to not exacerbate the situation.

WORST: A

Ignoring the incident is bad enough, but joining in is even worse!

QUESTION 22

BEST: A

Honesty and integrity are two very important aspects of the police special constable role. It is important that you inform your colleague of the accident.

WORST: C

Telling lies to your colleague is not acceptable. The Police Force cannot operate effectively if there is dishonesty in the ranks. Having said that, options B and D are also just as bad!

QUESTION 23

BEST: B

It is important to request an Ambulance and backup immediately. You can then carry out first aid to the casualty. Because the casualty is unconscious it is imperative that you check their airway, breathing and circulation. Whilst it will be tempting to run after the suspect, your priority here is the life of the casualty.

WORST: D

If you run after the suspect and close the door behind you, how will the ambulance crews be able to gain access to treat the casualty?

QUESTION 24

BEST: C

The only option you have here is to call for assistance. You will need to keep a note of the offender who threw the glass bottle but it would be dangerous to either enter the crowd or deploy your CS spray.

WORST: A

This is not the type of incident where you should deploy the use of your CS gas. Remain calm and wait for assistance.

QUESTION 25

BEST: D

This is the most effective option. It is common sense to go over and speak to the youths to ascertain why they are in the park.

WORST: C

There is no reason to take their names and addresses and inform their parents as you have not ascertained why they are in the park. After all, it is not illegal for youths to sit on a park bench!

QUESTION 26

BEST: C

The most effective option is to simply stand on your cordon and do nothing about the male. All crews are at full stretch and this is a minor incident.

WORST: B

If you arrest the male or the minor offence then you will have to take him to the Police Station, thus leaving your post. The safety of the public at the fire is paramount; therefore, this would be the worst option to choose.

QUESTION 27

BEST: A

This is a relatively minor issue that you should have the confidence to deal with yourself.

WORST: D

You do not need to involve other units in this relatively trivial matter.

QUESTION 28

BEST: A

The offender has the right to complain; however, now is not the time to deal with it. If you take this course of action it will probably calm down the situation.

WORST: C

The priority in this case is to deal with the violent conduct, not the complaint.

QUESTION 29

BEST: C

The priority of life here is paramount.

WORST: B

Not only are you wasting controls time with this request, you are also failing to attend to the casualty.

QUESTION 30

BEST: A

Comments and remarks of this nature are not welcome within the Police Force. It is important that you challenge them.

WORST: B

These remarks are certainly not part of Police Force life. By joining in you are as bad as the person making the remarks.

QUESTION 31

BEST: B

The call may be urgent so you should answer it.

WORST: A

The call may be urgent so you should answer it.

QUESTION 32

BEST: C

You have to solve the issue of the loud music and also be fair to both parties.

WORST: B

You cannot show favouritism to either party.

QUESTION 33

BEST: A

You must have the confidence in your own abilities and the decision you have taken.

WORST: C

You have the same powers are a regular Police Officer and therefore should continue with the arrest.

QUESTION 34

BEST: C

You must remain with the suspected offender as you have arrested them, therefore, you will need to call for assistance so that another unit can deal with the new incident.

WORST: D

The suspect is under arrest and therefore you cannot leave them.

QUESTION 35

BEST: B

This is a good opportunity to build strong relations with the community.

WORST: A

This would cause extreme offence and could damage the relationship the police have with the local community.

QUESTION 36

BEST: B

You do not know if the female has been a victim of crime or not. She may also suffer from mental health problems.

WORST: A

This would demonstrate to the community that the police are an uncaring service.

QUESTION 37

BEST: C

There is no need to go back to the station. You should first of all try to contact the owner of the purse as this will enable you to stay out on patrol where you are needed most.

WORST: D

You have no grounds to suspect the driver has taken money from the purse.

QUESTION 38

BEST: D

It is important to be calm, confident and resilient ion this situation.

WORST: B

By failing to take any action the public would lose confidence in the Police Force.

QUESTION 39

BEST: B

It is important to inform the Police Sergeant immediately so that he/she can change plans for the raid if required.

WORST: A

By not declaring your connection could jeopardise the raid at the scene.

QUESTION 40

BEST: C

You do not have the time to carry out both; therefore, you should write down the report as this is priority. The Police sergeant can arrange for someone else to carry out the reassurance patrols.

WORST: D

You are the only person who has the knowledge of the case. Therefore, you must write down the report, not someone else.

QUESTION 41

BEST: C

You need to make driver aware of the fact that he is parked illegally. There is no need to issue a fine or make an example of the driver.

WORST: D

This is over the top for a minor offence and could cause poor relations between the school and the Police Force.

QUESTION 42

BEST: D

This is the most effective resolution and you are making an effort to try and ensure it does not happen again.

WORST: C

This is over the top considering the child's age.

QUESTION 43

BEST: B

This is the most effective option as you are not escalating the matter.

WORST: A

Because their behaviour is causing people to move away from them you must act swiftly.

QUESTION 44

BEST: A

Once you have gathered the information you can then make an appropriate decision based on the facts.

WORST: D

You need to ascertain what the problem is first. It could be a genuine emergency.

QUESTION 45

BEST: B

This is an effective first stage option and it allows you to escalate if required.

WORST: C

You could expose the man to unnecessary risk as the youths will see you attending his house before you speak to them about the incident.

QUESTION 46

BEST: C

You cannot assume that he is drunk. You need to check his welfare.

WORST: B

There could be a negative public perception if you did not ascertain if the man was OK.

QUESTION 47

BEST: D

You should offer advice at the scene before informing the local Fire Safety Officer. The Fire Service can fit some detectors free of charge to people at risk.

WORST: A

Doing nothing is not an option. The lady is potentially at risk due to the smoking hazards, her age and the fact that she does not have a smoke detector.

QUESTION 48

BEST: D

Your colleague is not seriously hurt; therefore, you can attempt to arrest the suspect whilst still providing care for your colleague by requesting assistance.

WORST: B

Your colleague is not seriously hurt and therefore does not require first aid.

QUESTION 49

BEST: C

In this type of situation it is important to remain calm. You must request back up, clear the area and then give first aid to the child.

WORST: B

This could place the member of public in danger.

QUESTION 50

BEST: C

Your Police Sergeant can make a decision on the best course of action.

WORST: B

This could place you and your colleagues in danger.

QUESTION 51

BEST: D

This should be your first course of action. If he fails to turn off his engine the you will be right to suspect that he may drive off.

WORST: A

You are placing yourself in serious danger.

QUESTION 52

BEST: D

The talk is not serious so it can be done later.

WORST: A

You have been asked to attend an incident and therefore you should attend. You should not tie up other resources and time.

QUESTION 53

BEST: B

This request is acceptable and, due to the nature of the incident, perfectly reasonable.

WORST: C

It is your responsibility and refusing to do so could damage relationships with the Ambulance Service and also hinder their care of the motorcyclist.

QUESTION 54

BEST: C

You have a duty of care to deal with the incident of alleged shoplifting. This option allows you to deal with both incidents.

WORST: A

This could place the child in serious danger.

QUESTION 55

BEST: D

This could be a serious offence if it is proven to be drugs. It is important that a thorough investigation is carried out.

WORST: A

This will place the public in danger and could also prevent a proper investigation being conducted.

QUESTION 56

BEST: D

This is the only practical solution to the problem and will allow you to try and save vital evidence.

WORST: A

The evidence you gather would be inadmissible due to the method used to collecting it and your lack of qualifications and expertise in the matter.

QUESTION 57

BEST: C

It is important that you request backup so that the relevant resources can be dispatched. It is also your responsibility to keep the scene safe by moving the crowd away from the scene.

WORST: B

You have a duty of car and doing nothing is not an option.

QUESTION 58

BEST: C

It is important not to approach the man, but instead keep a safe distance and arrange for the appropriate response to be despatched.

WORST: D

This would place the man in serious danger.

QUESTION 59

BEST: B

Although they are not doing anything wrong, it is an opportunity to engage with the youths and emphasise your presence.

WORST: A

This is an opportunity to engage with the youths so that they are aware of your presence. It will also give you the chance to identify who they are in case of future incidents.

QUESTION 60

BEST: C

Comments of this nature are not acceptable within the Police Force or society in general. This is your opportunity to express your dissatisfaction about the comments and to put a stop to them.

WORST: B

You are just as bad as the person making the comments and this type of behaviour is not acceptable.

how2become

Visit www.how2become.co.uk to find more titles and courses that will help you to pass the police special constable selection process, including:

- How to pass the police special constable interview DVD.

- 1-day police special constable training courses.

- Online testing.

- Psychometric testing books and CD's

www.how2become.co.uk

Sally Child SRN, HV, DIP ION is a qualified nurse and worked as a health visitor for several years. To consolidate her interest in nutrition she completed a 3 year diploma course at the renowned Institute for Optimum Nutrition in London.

She now practises as a nutritional therapist in Chandler's Ford and Fareham, Hampshire, seeing a wide range of problems. She runs two nutrition groups for weight control and is the local representative for Foresight and the Hyperactive Children's Support Group with a special interest in children's health and sub-fertility.

She also lectures on babies and children and on weight control to nutrition students and has written for various journals and newsletters.

She is married with three daughters (aged 24, 21 and 15) and lives in Hampshire.

AN A–Z
OF CHILDREN'S HEALTH

a nutritional approach

Sally K Child

Argyll
publishing

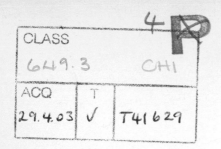
Argyll Publishing
Glendaruel
Argyll PA22 3AE
www.skoobe.biz

Sally K Child can be contacted at
email:
nutrition.sally@virgin.net

This book is dedicated to my
youngest daughter Rosie whose
early problems inspired me to
retrain as a nutritionist and
whose ambition to become an
author will be realised.

Acknowledgements are due to
all the children I have had the
pleasure of working with over
the last 30 years.
   To my family for supporting
me through the months of
research and writing.
   To Wendy and Ruth for typing
the manuscript.
   To Debbie for her
administrative help.

Typeset & Origination
Cordfall Ltd, Glasgow

Printing
Mackays of Chatham

"Love and good nutrition are two of
the greatest gifts you can give a child."
Sally Child

"Let your food be your medicine"
Hippocrates

PUBLISHER'S NOTE

**The advice in this book offers
a <u>complementary</u> approach to
children's health rather than
an alternative approach to
medical care.**

**It is not intended in any way
to replace appropriate
medical intervention.**

**Nutritional therapy is most
effective under the
supervision of a qualified
practitioner. This also applies
to other complementary
therapies mentioned.**

CONTENTS

HOW TO USE THIS BOOK

A-Z

Conditions occur in alphabetical order with a cross-reference in each section for further information. In the index, bracketed items are included elsewhere. A brief description of the condition, its conventional treatment and symptoms is included prior to nutritional recommendations.

FACTORS TO CONSIDER

This section suggests possible underlying causes in the condition. Not all will apply, but some may be relevant and addressing these can bring about a more sustainable recovery than treating symptoms alone. The body works like an orchestra; if one section is out of tune, others will be too.

DIET ADVICE

Bullet points are given to increase, decrease or avoid foods and when food groups are mentioned, eg vitamin C foods, protein, fibre or dairy products, these will be included in the beneficial foods. Comprehensive lists are included in the appendix for sources of vitamins, minerals, salicylates etc and alternatives suggested.

There are contacts for specific companies (including mail order supplies). Some foods do not appeal to children so wherever possible I have chosen acceptable ones. However, some imagination in preparation may be required, eg soups, juices, stews, shakes.

NUTRIENTS TO CONSIDER

Includes suggested nutritional supplements. I cannot mention all the available products and many will need a qualified practitioner's supervision with some only being available from them.

The letters at the end of each recommendation are companies selling that particular product and a full key is included. Supplementation for children is complicated. Please see Supplements section for more information on nutrients for children.

GENERAL ADVICE

Includes miscellaneous information not necessarily appropriate for other sections. In many cases it holds a wealth of hints, extra help and reassurance.

CONTACTS/READING

these are usually only included in the individual section when they would only be relevant to that condition. If universally useful, books and contacts are included in the reading list or Useful Information sections of the Appendix.

APPENDIX

Sometimes the appendix can be as big as the book. I have attempted to include as many items as is useful. Inevitably some are left out but one contact will often lead you to another. Mainly telephone numbers are included as you can then obtain the address, fax, email address or website but occasionally these details are included in the main text, eg websites for teenagers.

FOREWORD

I decided to write this book during my nutrition training when it became apparent that there were no books specifically aimed at children's health from an holistic viewpoint. There seemed to be lots of recipe books but nothing addressing a therapeutic role for food.

Gathering knowledge from adult sources is unsatisfactory for children. You cannot just scale it down. Children experience many of the same conditions as adults but some are unique and all respond to a different approach. Symptoms, bodily reactions and healing are very different in children.

The aim of the book is to provide a quick reference guide to childhood health problems from birth to 16 years. Teenagers are so often left out and they have their own specific health problems. It is primarily for parents but also to provide a basis from which nutritionists can work.

The approach is one of a nutritional therapist, looking at possible underlying causes, dietary changes and suggested supplements for correction of imbalances. There is extensive information in the appendix including some suggestions for other alternative therapies. Reference to gender is random and applies to both sexes in most cases.

Nutrition is at last receiving more attention as a fundamental way to ensure health and correct 'dis-ease' in the body. Many adults who consult a nutritionist have years of problems to correct, but children are less complicated and respond quickly to quite minor alterations in diet and lifestyle.

> NB:
> The recommendations in this book are not intended to replace appropriate medical intervention but to relieve symptoms by addressing the causes and to support healing and recovery.

WHY IS CHILDREN'S HEALTH AFFECTED?

Media coverage can be confusing as contradictions frequently occur. How do you decide what is right or wrong for your child? Dietary and supplementary suggestions often fail to take into account a child's age. Most children fail to eat 2 portions of fruit and vegetables daily when 5 are recommended. What does 5 portions of fruit and vegetables mean?

Most children eat about 60% 'junk' food which lacks vitamins and minerals and affects appetite control.

Many diets are low in protein and essential fatty acids, whilst high in sugar, salt, saturated fats and refined carbohydrates. Young children need lots of energy for growth, play and learning. Most get this from 'short burst' refined foods, eg cola and crisps rather than sustainable sources like fruit and wholegrains.

FOOD PRODUCTION

Modern, intensive farming methods and food manufacture have altered so rapidly in the last 50-60 years that our bodies cannot adjust quickly enough.

Wheat for bread is very different from then with different grain, vast fields and extensive spraying of crops with pesticides and fertilisers and much wheat imported. Genetically modified crops have entered the food chain. Home-made bread from wholegrain, natural spelt wheat is a thing of the past.

Dairy products, once fresh from the cow are now produced so intensively that the cows are pumped full of artificial hormones to increase production and antibiotics to reduce the subsequent mastitis. The cattle feed is often contaminated with chemicals and even animal products. Our milk can contain these chemicals. Eggs are similarly affected and fruit is often sprayed many times and picked unripe resulting in low levels of vitamins.

As society 'progresses' we are in danger of losing access to 'real' food, becoming swamped in a sea of artificially produced foods that the body metabolism has difficulty recognising. No wonder the immune system overreacts to these apparently foreign substances and develops food allergies and intolerances and auto-immune diseases like diabetes, arthritis and cancer.

Immunity is a finely tuned, complex system of protection in danger of becoming overwhelmed by unfamiliar, toxic foods and artificial additives and chemicals.

CHANGING DIETS

In the 1950s bread and milk were the mainstays providing fibre and calcium.

Then energy derived from sugar was 15%. Today it is 28%.

Vitamin C was derived from fruit and vegetables. Today it comes mainly from sugary fruit juices with no fibre. Daily iron intake was 8mgs from red meat mainly. Today it is 6mgs (chicken is a poor source of iron).

MARKETING /ADVERTISING

The marketing of foods to children raises serious ethical and moral issues. It is not easy for any parent to resist the 'pester power' that the advertising companies exploit so well.

Obesity is increasing rapidly leading to ill-health and low self-esteem. We are rapidly catching up with the USA. In one study 21% of 6 year old girls were found to be overweight. By 15 years old nearly half the male population were overweight.

By the time a child born in 2002 is 20 years old, the health risks associated with obesity will be far greater than from an eating disorder. Major diseases like diabetes, heart disease and cancer occur earlier, eg arterial disease in junior school children. It is possible to be malnourished and overweight!

With 20% of all women constantly fighting weight problems and many more actually dieting, children are getting the wrong messages about food.

According to the Food Commission, a child will have eaten its own weight in food additives (by 17 years of age). The *National Diet and Nutrition Survey: Young People 14-18 years* by HMSO highlighted the risks of malnutrition in teenagers, partly due to inadequate semi-vegetarian diets.

Stress amongst children is increasing with childhood getting shorter. Stress affects the endocrine (hormonal), digestive and immune systems and imbalances the body mentally and physically.

ORTHODOX APPROACH

Doctors are ill-equipped to address patients' requests for nutritional advice. They have received very little nutrition training and most relates to specific diseases. General practice does not allow for in-depth discussions. Through no fault of their own, responses by the orthodox medical community to obesity for example are often too little too late.

I have not included recipes, menus or specific ideas (apart from a few specific items in Helpful Information/Recipes), as there are plenty of recipe books available. My aim is to identify foods and nutrients, beneficial for certain conditions and the rest is up to you. Each condition will have specific food suggestions but a common theme becomes obvious. Nuts, seeds, wholegrains, oily fish, water, garlic, onions, fresh fruit and vegetables occur in most sections. This is a good starting point for rebalancing children's diets.

I have only included those health conditions which may benefit from nutritional therapy. I have left out childhood infectious diseases, apart from chicken pox, as the sections on bacterial/viral infections, fever or rashes cover these.

I hope the extensive contents of this reference book will provide parents and practitioners with some much needed guidance into taking control of your children's health in a natural, holistic way to allow the body to heal itself and prevent some of our modern diseases which often start in childhood, many of which have increased since processed foods were introduced. Take control and follow your instincts.

Sally K Child
July 2002

Acid-forming foods Coffee, animal protein, dairy produce, wheat, prunes, lentils, brown rice. Eat in moderation with alkaline forming foods.

Alkaline-forming foods Millet, all vegetables especially green leafy vegetables, all fruit except rhubarb, oranges and plums. Cherries are particularly helpful in reducing inflammation.

Allergy An immune response to substances outside the body ie eaten or inhaled. Usually involves rapid response of Ig E antibodies. Tends to be lifelong.

Amaranth A nutritious alkaline grain rich in the minerals, iron, calcium, zinc and potassium and vitamins E and B. Contains 16% protein. Used as a cereal or in bread making, sprinkled on salads, mixed with vegetables in casseroles or lightly roasted to use as a seasoning.

Anti-oxidants are vitamins and minerals which protect cell membranes from damage and inflammation. They can protect from allergies, heart disease and cancer. They include vitamins A, C and E and beta-carotene and the minerals zinc and selenium.

Atopic A family history of allergy such as migraine, hayfever, asthma or eczema can indicate that a childhood allergic disease is linked to a faulty enzyme needed for the metabolism of EFAs. This leads to inflammatory responses in the body like eczema, asthma or food allergies, but the allergy may not be the same as the parents.

Beans One type of legume. High in fibre and B vitamins. Source of protein and beneficial for digestive problems, including constipation and for regulating blood sugar. Kidney, pinto, soy, haricot. If sprouted, protein is even higher. Dried beans are preferable but can use tinned beans when well rinsed.

Beta-carotene An anti-oxidant giving yellow-orange pigment to foods, eg carrots, apricots and cantaloupe melon. It can be converted into vitamin A in the body as required (except in diabetics) and is safer than vitamin A. It belongs to the group known as carotenoids which also includes lycopene, quercetin, glutathione and lutein.

Bio-flavonoids are anti-oxidant compounds found in some fruits, eg citrus, cherries, and blackcurrants and in buckwheat, garlic and onions. They are sometimes known as vitamin P and are often accompanied by vitamin C. There are about 500 varieties including rutin, hesperidine and flavones.

Blackstrap Molasses is the last extraction in the refining of sugar. Sugar beet is actually a nutrient rich food until refinement. Blackstrap molasses is rich in B vitamins and vitamin E and has excellent levels of minerals, eg more iron than some eggs, more calcium than milk and the best source of potassium available. 1-2 tsps daily in warm milk, on cereals, in yoghurt or stewed fruit. Not suitable for candida sufferers.

Caffeine is present in coffee, tea, cola and similar fizzy drinks, chocolate and chocolate beverages.

Cereals A variety of grains including corn, barley, oats, wheats, rice and rye. See wholegrains

Complex Carbohydrates are starches and fibre which are healthier carbohydrate options than simple carbohydrates (sugars).

Dysbiosis an imbalance of intestinal bacteria with inadequate levels of beneficial bacteria (flora) increasing risks of potentially harmful bacteria, yeast or parasites taking over. Babies are born with a sterile gut and develop balanced flora over the early months of their lives

EFAs Essential fatty acids which are fats vital for health that cannot be made in the body, and need to be eaten daily. Involved in many reactions including hormone balance, metabolic rate, skin, hair and nail health, immunity, controlling inflammation, healing, brain function and many more. In fact they are essential to every function. 2 main groups: omega 3 and omega 6.
    Omega 3 includes oily fish, seeds, nuts, green leafy vegetables, flax seed oil. Within this group there is DHA (docosahexaenoic acid) and EPA (eicosapentaenoic acid).
    Omega 6 – sunflower, sesame and sunflower oils and their seeds, breast milk, soya, walnuts, evening primrose and starflower oils. Within the group there is GLA (gamma-linolenic acid).

Fibre Not a food and not absorbed, but vital to many functions. Wheat fibre is an irritant for some people and can impair absorption of vitamins and minerals. A balance of soluble and insoluble fibre is required. Can help with IBS, constipation, blood sugar imbalances, PMS, fatigue, IBD, obesity, dysbiosis.

Soluble fibre sources are fresh fruit and vegetables, seeds, beans, peas and lentils, dried fruit, popcorn and wholegrains.

Insoluble fibre sources are nuts, cereals such as rye, wheat and rice foods with skins, husks and peel, fruit and vegetables with pips and peel.

Food Combining is a method of separating certain food groups to enhance digestion. Fruit alone, protein with vegetables but not starches, vegetables with starches. It is not easy to manage and not usually an option for children but in some cases it may be beneficial in rebalancing acid/alkaline balance. See Reading list.

Food Intolerance An immune response to substances outside the body ie usually food, involving a slower response of Ig G antibodies. Much more common than an allergy. Offending food is less easy to identify as symptoms are more insidious and not immediate. Not permanent but need to heal gut and rebalance the immune system.

FOS Short for fructo-oligosaccarides. They act as a prebiotic and can also be used as a natural sweetener. Supplemented usually as a powder and suitable for candida sufferers.

Gluten is a protein found in wheat and rye and to a lesser extent, in oats and barley.

Green leafy Vegetables include broccoli, cabbage, spinach, various lettuce leaves, kale etc.

Inflammation is a normal bodily response to injury or infection, but many conditions are actually a result of too much inflammation in the cells. This can upset the pH of the tissues ie the acid/alkaline balance. Many nutritional approaches are aimed at reducing inflammation by correcting the pH.

Lecithin is naturally present in every cell. It helps the liver to use fats and 'feeds' the brain. Available in eggs, wholewheat, soya, nuts and corn and also as capsules or granules which can be sprinkled onto cereals, yoghurt or soups. 1-2 tsps daily is sufficient for children. Available in health stores. Keep refrigerated. Usually soya derived.

Legumes are plants that have edible seeds within a pod. They include beans, lentils, chickpeas, peas and peanuts and contain iron and B vitamins and incomplete protein.

Manuka honey comes from New Zealand tea tree pollen and as such carries valuable immune boosting properties. All honey is good for immunity but manuka is the king! One tsp daily is sufficient for a child to keep bugs at bay. Also good for clearing sinuses and congestion. NB Do not give any honey to children under one year due to small risk of botulism.

MSG Mono-Sodium Glutamate (E621) is an artificial flavouring derived from sugar, wheat and other grains which are rich in the protein glutamate. Unfortunately the processing can have adverse health effects, eg migraine, impaired brain function, insomnia and hyperactivity. Present in many processed foods and chinese cooking and is best avoided. NB – May contain gluten.

MVM Multi-vitamin and mineral supplement. Choices are listed separately.

Nuts The dry fruit or seeds of some plants, usually trees, eg hazelnut. Others include Brazils, walnuts, pecan, almonds, cashews and pine nuts. Technically peanuts are a legume. Supply protein, EFAs, B vitamins, vitamin E and several minerals. Can be eaten whole, ground or as oils. Care with children for choking and occasionally allergy, especially to peanuts. Keep refrigerated.

Oily fish Halibut, sardines, trout, tuna, salmon, pilchards, mackerel and herring.

Organic Naturally reared or grown food without use of artificial aids. Unlikely to contain anti- biotic or hormone residues or chemicals from pesticides, fertilizers and fungicides. Free from artificial additives but may contain sugar. Available in many supermarkets, local farmers markets, health shops and by mail order box schemes. Remember – an organic bag of crisps is still a bag of crisps!
Non-organic fruit and vegetables can be improved by washing in a weak solution of either washing up liquid, citricidal (HN), one tablespoon vinegar to large bowl filtered water or in Veggie Wash from Food Safe Ltd (Tel: 01788 51045).

Phytonutrients Naturally occurring plant substances including bioflavonoids and natural phyto- oestrogens.

Prebiotics Carbohydrates which encourage the growth of beneficial bacteria in the colon/ intestines. Some foods are good sources, eg artichokes, garlic, onions, bananas, cottage cheese, soya, asparagus, chicory. Supplements of prebiotics are available as FOS.

Probiotics The 'good guys' (beneficial bacteria) that colonise specific areas of the intestines and colon, depending on oxygen levels and acidity. They play a vital role in protecting from infection, supporting digestion, preventing allergy, boosting immunity, producing B vitamins, correcting diarrhoea, digesting lactose, controlling yeast and producing natural antibiotics. Deficiency creates symptoms including tummy ache, bowel changes, infections, poor digestion, fatigue and many more. Probiotics can correct dysbiosis. Regular live sugar-free yoghurt can prevent dysbiosis and boost immunity, but some products marketed contain a lot of sugar which feeds the 'bad guys'! Choices of supplements are listed separately.

Proteins consist of 22 amino acids of which 8 are essential needing to be obtained daily from food. They are required for growth, repair and maintenance of health by every single body cell. See separate list.

Quinoa (pronounced keen-wah) is a marvellous vegetarian/vegan source of protein, being the only grain to do this. It is an ancient alkaline grain providing good levels of calcium, iron and B vitamins with a slightly nutty taste which can be used as you would rice, add to soups, or as a cereal or milk pudding. Contains 20% protein. Good for immunity.

Sea Vegetables are a good source of minerals especially fibre, iodine, folic acid and other minerals. A rare source of vegan B12. They include nori, arame, wakami and dulse. Good for cold sores, arthritis, thyroid problems, constipation and skin irritations. Available from health stores, delicatessen and some supermarkets, dried or salted. Use as a flavouring or salt substitute in cooking. Can also supplement. Not for young children due to salt levels.

Seeds are the powerhouse of flowering plants. Rich in protein, calcium and other minerals, EFAs and B vitamins. Varieties include sunflower, sesame, pumpkin, flax (linseeds). Also poppy, hemp, celery and dill seeds as seasonings. Eaten raw as snacks or added to salads, soups, cereals. Seed oils such as sesame or sunflower can be used as salad dressings. Keep all seeds refrigerated

Tahini is a spread made from sesame seeds and is rich in GLA, an omega 6 EFA. Can replace butter, be used as a dip, in stir fry sauces or in baking.

Topical Applied to the skin. Not for internal use

Wholegrains Brown rice, oats, rye, barley, wholewheat, corn, bulgar wheat, millet, amaranth, quinoa, buckwheat, wholemeal pasta, wholegrain bread, cereals. Rich in protein, carbohydrate, vitamins B and E, the minerals, selenium, iron, zinc and copper, and phyto nutrients and fibre.

A TO Z OF HEALTH CONDITIONS

ACNE

There are two types of acne: *Rosacea* – mainly superficial on the face; and *Vulgaricus* – more widespread and chronic.

The usual onset is at puberty but may persist through adulthood with 15% of adults affected. The most common sites are the face, back and chest where the majority of the sebaceous glands are situated.

The male hormone, testosterone, is over produced in males and females resulting in increased sebaceous secretions especially at puberty, with blocked pores and secondary infections. In addition a small percentage of female acne sufferers may be linked to polycystic ovary syndrome.

Acne may also be triggered by stress due to hormonal fluctuations and liver congestion.

Some causes are hereditary.

Medical treatments usually consist of long term antibiotics or contraceptive pill for girls.

Key approach is to prevent accumulation of toxicity and correct dysbiosis.

GENERAL ADVICE

Avoid constipation and anti-biotics. Probiotics can help both.

Mash ripe avocado with a little olive oil and apply as a face mask for 15 minutes.

Wash in tea tree and calendula solution.

Twice daily washing with warm water and soap (special ones with increased detergent) to remove excess grease.

Cleanse with lemon juice in water for antiseptic effect.

Avoid steam as high humidity aggravates spots.

Apply the following daily; crushed cloves of garlic in 100ml of surgical spirit. Keep solution in sealed bottle in the fridge.

Exercise in fresh air and sunshine 15 minutes daily is helpful.

Avoid electric razors, shave in the direction of hairs to protect follicles.

Sunshine daily for 15 minutes.

Surgical spirit and acne soaps are available in chemists.

Dietary Advice

- Steam, grill or bake instead of frying or roasting.
- Avoid: coffee, tea, cola, alcohol, sugar, spicy foods, citrus fruits, eggs, cheese, salt, nuts, chocolate, processed 'junk' foods, saturated fats, seaweed (iodine can make it worse,) and very hot drinks as flushing can increase secretions. Yeast avoidance may also help.
- Dairy products contain hormones which are antagonistic to vitamin E. Avoid or reduce. Replace with rice, soya, nut, goat or sheep milk products.
- Increase: fibre from wholegrains and fruit and vegetables, EFAs for healing.
- Drink minimum of 4-5 glasses of water per day.
- Juices: papaya, cucumber, tomato, pineapple and radish together to help balance sebum secretions.
- Snack on seeds, unsalted nuts, dried apricots and dates.
- Ginger tea daily helps to cleanse the digestion.
- Anti-oxidant foods, ie vitamins A, C and E and minerals, zinc and selenium should be increased to reduce inflammation and promote healing.
- Increase sulphur foods for cleansing, eg eggs, onions, garlic.
- BENEFICIAL FOODS: Green vegetables, pumpkin, sesame and sunflower seeds, ground and sprinkled onto vegetables, cereal,

soups and yoghurt, seafood, pecans, rye, oats, berries, peppers, kiwi, non-citrus fruits and papaya, carrots and sweet potatoes, avocado and wheatgerm, onions and garlic and eggs, fish, and white meat.

If antibiotics or contraceptive pill have been prescribed, probiotics are extra important.

NB: Skin takes a while to heal and regenerate so be patient. It may get worse before it improves.

Contacts:

Sher System – Tel: 020 7499 4022

Acne Support Group – Tel: 020 8841 4747 ■

To be applied topically

● Rosa Mosqueta for scars – Tel: 01273 570987.

● Fresh pineapple to the scars for 15 minutes. Rinse in cool water. Do this twice daily.

● Tea tree oil – 2 drops in bath or as a facial wash (is antiseptic).

● Wheatgrass juice powders (X)– make a paste and apply overnight with warm water.

● MSM cream (HN) – cleansing, moisturising.

● Aloe skin gel (HN) is anti inflammatory and healing.

● Living Nature Acne Kit contains purifying gel, deep cleansing day mask/peel, manuka antiseptic gel, balancing pH cream and teenage skincare guide. Costs £30. Tel: 01489 556144.

● BPT Formula (N) for teenage and problem skin aims to purify blood.

● Skin Treatments range. (BM)

● Vitamin E cream. (X,L)

Nutrients to consider

(doses are adult, as sufferers are usually over age 12)

● Research suggests zinc is low in acne sufferers, take 30mg daily with evening meal. (BC,BM,AR)

● Acidophilus 1gm twice daily in a little water can help rebalance bacteria in the intestines to improve absorption and immunity whilst correcting acidity. (BC, BM)

● BPT Formula is a herbal complex for teenage skin: $^1/_2$tsp thrice daily. (N)

● Vitamin A (if not pregnant or at risk of) one drop daily (BC) or betacarotene 15mg. Caution is required with Vitamin A as can be toxic. (HP, L)

● Vitamin E – 300ius daily for healing and reducing scars. Especially good if combined with selenium. (L)

● Vitamin C 1g daily (BC, L). Ester C 500mgs – 1000mgs and grape seed extract 200mgs, thrice daily. (R) NB: if on the contraceptive pill maximum Vitamin C is 500mg per day, as 1gm can convert a low oestrogen pill into a high dose.

● B Complex (over 5 years) and extra B6. (BC)

● ZBM Complex contains Vit A, B6, and zinc, manganese and magnesium. Take one per day. (BM)

● Sulphur compound as MSM in powder or capsules. Contains natural vitamins and minerals to detox, cleanse and heal scars, use with MSM cream. (HN)

● Fish oils – Max EPA /GLA softgels one per day (S) or Flax oil as Udos Choice (Sa) are anti-inflammatory.

● Dandelion for liver support, 10 drops 6-8 times per day for first month then twice daily. (N)

● Red Clover is antibacterial, 10 drops 6-8 drops per day. (N)

● Great Burdock to decongest the liver and improve digestion. (N)

● Bromelain for scars. (S, NO)

● Agnus Castus tincture (BF). Avoid if on contraceptive pill.

SEE ALSO: FOOD INTOLERANCES, BLOOD SUGAR, EATING DISORDERS, CANDIDA, ANXIETY, DEPRESSION, SMOKING, SOLVENT ABUSE

Many teenagers try drugs in one form or another. Alcohol is often linked. There is no evidence to state that smoking will lead to use of hard drugs but is a common factor in most drug abuse. This may involve caffeine, sugar, tobacco, alcohol, glue, marijuana, cocaine or heroin.

Stimulants ('uppers'): sugar, caffeine, nicotine, cocaine, amphetamines

Dependants ('downers'): alcohol, nicotine, heroine, and tranquilisers

Also includes food and food additives.

FACTORS TO CONSIDER

Blood sugar imbalances, nutrient deficiencies, refined/processed diet, anxiety, depression, food intolerance and candidiasis. These have a stimulant effect on the body with a subsequent fall in mood and energy levels so that another 'fix' is required.

Cravings for certain foods can indicate food intolerances, eg wheat.

Sugar, wheat and alcohol cravings can indicate candida.

Low blood sugar results in the need for a quick stimulant. Caffeine and sugar are the most common stimulants available. Teenagers may think its 'cool' to drink coffee and cola. Cola has sugar (about 10 tsp per can!) and caffeine, not to mention chemicals.

Signs to look for include poor memory, poor concentration, depression, insomnia, lack of appetite, fatigue, mood swings, skin and hair deterioration, cravings, sore lips, nose and mouth, recurrent infections.

GENERAL ADVICE

Main aim is to keep blood sugar levels stable.

Exercise can help but a reluctant teenager is not always compliant.

Try to offer wholesome, regular, small meals when at home and trust to luck when they're out!

Education on diet and lifestyle is likely to be rejected by this stage!

Supplements can help to provide dietary shortcomings and support specific factors like blood sugar regulation, taste and appetite.

Dietary advice

- Encourage small meals 3 hourly.
- Include good protein for lunch, eg tuna or egg with a seed bar. Have protein with every meal/snack.
- Always encourage breakfast for teenagers or a piece of fruit and nuts on the way to school.
- Identify any allergies/intolerances as these create cravings. Milk is sometimes linked.
- Soluble fibre.
- Live yoghurt most days.
- Increase water to redress dehydration from caffeine, alcohol.
- BENEFICIAL FOODS: Sunflower seeds, sesame seeds, oats, eggs, wholegrains, honey, fresh fruit and vegetables, cheese and pulses.

Nutrients to consider
● (may reduce withdrawal and food intolerance. All doses are adult, as most sufferers will be over age 12.)
● Probiotics, eg bioacidophilus one capsule twice daily.(BC)
● MVM, eg Supernutrition Plus x 2 daily. (HN)
● Zinc (15-30mg) for appetite, mood, immunity and blood sugar or one capsule daily (BC). Solgar do Ca/Mg/Zn combined, one daily in evening.
● Chromium for cravings and blood sugar 200mcgs daily. (HN)
● B vitamins to include 50-100mg for anxiety, cravings and mood. (therapy with higher doses and of individual B vitamins needs a qualified nutritionist)
● Calcium and magnesium to calm and improve sleep one daily in ratio 1:1. (HN, S, AR). Bio magnesium 2 per day also has calcium, B6 and minerals. (BM)
● L-Glutamine for cravings especially for sugar and alcohol, also heals gut lining. One tsp or 2 capsules twice daily. (HN)

Alcohol is empty calories which leads to addiction and a vicious cycle

Caffeine may be used as a way to manage weight. Be alert to eating disorders but remember nicotine, alcohol and drugs will depress appetite.

If addictions are causing secondary health problems such as poor skin, hair, nails, frequent infections, weight fluctuations and mood problems, these need to be addressed and may be a way into the real problem. Vanity usually wins!

Encourage development of other interests

Address anxiety or depression if involved

Only attempt giving up one thing at a time. This is more manageable and gives less toxic reactions. Withdrawal can result in fatigue and headaches. ■

ADENOIDS

SEE ALSO: SORE THROATS, IMMUNE FUNCTION, EARS.

Situated near the tonsils at the back of the throat, they are lymph nodes whose function is to fight upper respiratory infections to protect the lungs. They swell and produce white blood cells during infection and they are often enlarged in children under age 5. They reduce in size from 5 years old and disappear by puberty.

Symptoms include: snoring, mouth breathing, frequent ear infections and speech problems.

GENERAL ADVICE

See GP if recurrent but surgical removal is rare under age 5.

Boost immune function.

Reduce dairy foods if mucous is a problem.

Have hearing tested. ■

Allergic Rhinitis

SEE ALSO: HAYFEVER, ASTHMA, IMMUNE FUNCTION, BRONCHITIS, ALLERGIES

Rhinitis is inflammation of the nasal mucous membranes. Can be caused by an infection (cold) or an allergy. Unlike hayfever it is usually non-seasonal. The child often appears to have a constant cold (perennial allergic rhinitis).

Allergic rhinitis is often caused by inhalant allergens such as moulds, pet fur/ dander, dried cat saliva, house dust mite, feathers, but can also be linked to foods.

Excess histamine is released resulting in red, sore eyes, runny nose and sneezing. May also result in asthma and hayfever.

General Advice

Use a room ioniser to reduce airbourne allergens and dust.

Boost immune function.

Identify food allergens.

Skin prick testing may identify allergen, but will not address the imbalances in the body.

Eucalyptus or peppermint oil on a tissue – not for babies.

Use special vacuum cleaner to reduce house dust mite. ∎

Dietary Advice

- Avoid dairy foods as they increases mucous production. Replace with soya (if over 6 months old,) rice, goats' or oat milks.
- Wheat can trigger inflammation. Substitute with rice, rye, oats, amaranth.
- Refined foods lack nutrients so avoid.
- Bromelain, found in pineapple, is anti-inflammatory.
- BENEFICIAL FOODS: Pineapple, garlic, onions, ginger, fresh fruit and vegetable juices.

Nutrients to Consider

- If there is a family history of allergies (atopy) this may necessitate GLA supplements (see allergies.) Evening primrose (EPO) or starflower oil may help reduce inflammation. Try EPO 1-3 daily 4-12 years (L) or Essential Balance Junior which also includes flax oil and has butterscotch flavouring from herbs not sugar; $1/2$-3 tsps from weaning. (HN)
- NB: do not give GLA if child has had fits or non-febrile convulsions or if there is a family history of epilepsy.
- For immunity:
- Vitamin C – Immune C one daily over 8 years (HN) or Bio C $1/8$tsp over 4 years which includes minerals or Mg Ascorbate $1/4$gm (BC, L)
- Children's B Complex one daily (over 5 years) (BC)
- Zinc 10 drops daily (BC) or $1/2$level measure under tongue of sherbet powder alternate days for over age 8. (HN)
- E-Kid-Nacea 2-4 years $1/8$- $1/2$tsp or E-Kid-Nacea Plus over 4 years which is especially good for catarrh (K)
- Probiotics, eg ABC Dophillus up to 4 years (S) or strawberry or banana acidophilus (BC)
- Oralmat one drop. An extract of rye grass which may help support respiratory function and reduce allergic reactions (AR)
- Cytolog – one spray twice daily to increase immunity (AR)

ALLERGIES

SEE ALSO: SINUSITIS, FOOD INTOLERANCES, ASTHMA, ECZEMA, HAYFEVER, RHINITIS, LEAKY GUT, TOXICITY

(Food allergies and intolerance are discussed under F. Inhalant allergies are in this section.)

Many childhood conditions are linked to allergic responses. These include asthma, hayfever, eczema, sinusitis and allergic rhinitis. The environment is full of potential toxins from traffic, hormones, pollens, pesticides, food additives, animal dander, perfumes and chemicals. As society 'progresses' the body appears to be becoming overloaded by environmental pollutants and the normal detoxification pathways overwhelmed. The immune system becomes hypersensitive and can react inappropriately. Stress and anxiety create inflammation in the body and leaky gut and irritable airways can result.

GENERAL ADVICE

Reduce the load on the body by:

Eating organic and exclusively for babies.

Filtering water to reduce fluoride, oestrogens and other hormones, antibiotic residues from farm animals and heavy metals. Plumbed in systems are best but expensive. Otherwise a jug filter or bottled water should help. Always change filters at least monthly.

Most high street cosmetics, toothpaste, soaps, shampoos and perfumes contain potentially harmful chemicals including sodium laurel sulphate (SLS). Try Green People or Xynergy.

Use special vacuum cleaner to reduce house dust mite.

When decorating or DIY take extra care with products used and ventilation. Avoid in presence of young children and babies as their lungs are more susceptible to chemicals.

Keep children away from cigarette smoke.

Washing powders, fabric conditioners and household cleaning products contain detergents and chemicals. Wash with E-cover or Eco-balls.

Consider hair mineral analysis test to identify any imbalances and presence of toxic metals like lead, aluminum and antimony.

Skin prick testing for IgE true allergy. Needs to be done at a hospital.

Nettle tea may restore respiration and support the sinuses.

Dietary advice

- Organic foods to reduce pollution.
- Filter your tap water. Increasing your water intake can dilute mucous secretions.
- Avoid additives.
- Increase soluble fibre to eliminate toxins.
- BENEFICIAL FOODS: Oatbran, non-citrus fruits, oily fish, wholegrain cereals, dark green leafy vegetables, bananas.

Nutrients to consider

- MVM, eg Ultra Care for Kids is a complete nutritional formula for up to age 12 (an adult product is available from 12 years). Acts as a low allergy MVM with probiotics to maintain nutrients when on restricted diet (under supervision only).
- Vitamin C and bioflavonoids (antihistamine); Bio-C $^1/_4$tsp daily includes minerals (AN, NC, R) or children's capsules one with breakfast or 4 drops. (BC)
- Apple pectin removes heavy metals. (S)
- Magnesium supports the airways. Try Bio-Mg $^1/_2$capsule sprinkled for 1-3 years (BC), or chewable lemon flavoured one daily over 4 years (L), or Mg solution $^1/_4$tsp 1-2 times daily. (AR)
- Vitamin A to reduce inflammation in airways; one drop daily. (BC)
- Super Gar one capsule daily over 8 years (HN) or liquid garlic. (N)
- Essential Balance Junior Oil is anti-inflammatory $^1/_2$-3 tsps from weaning. (HN)
- Calcium compound may reduce inflammation. (BM)
- Calcium phosphate is a constitutional strengthener. (BM)
- Oralmat – one drop under the tongue 3 times daily. Increases lung function and decreases allergic responses. (AR, NC, R)

ANAEMIA

SEE ALSO: FATIGUE, GROWTH

There are several different types of anaemia and correct medical diagnosis is essential for treatment. All types involve a lack of haemoglobin and poor oxygen transport. Most cases are mild and temporary, but some are chronic and severe, eg spherocytosis, arthritis, thalassemia and cancers.

Fussy eaters, late weaners, Asians, vegetarians and vegan children are most at risk.

Iron deficiency is the most common form of anaemia in childhood. Iron stores at birth are depleted by 6 months old, regardless of feeding method. If weaning is delayed risks are higher.

Effects include poor growth.

Symptoms of anaemia include loss of appetite, poor taste, pallor, tiredness, headaches, learning problems, poor concentration and dizziness. Breathlessness, brittle nails and sore tongue may occur in serious cases. Pica is a disease characterised by cravings for non-food items, eg soil, coal, chalk and is usually due to iron deficiency – occasionally it is linked to behavioural problems.

GENERAL ADVICE

Do not give iron supplements alone or without GP's advice as toxicity can occur and iron can feed bacteria during an infection. Iron ascorbate is better tolerated

Eating iron rich foods with Vitamin C foods improves absorption of iron, eg fish with iron rich vegetables, boiled egg with wholemeal soldiers and orange juice. Keep dairy foods away from iron foods. If breast-feeding attention to maternal diet is important after 6 months and introduction of solids if bottle fed use fortified infant formula.

Some types of anaemia actually contra-indicate iron supplements, eg thalosaemia (or sickle cell) which are most common in Afro-Asian communities.

If diarrhoea occurs, reduce vitamin C.

Pica is the name given to the habit of eating non-foods, eg coal or licking surfaces and can be linked to iron deficiency. ■

Dietary Advice

- Avoid sugar.
- Have fibre away from iron foods.
- Tea and coffee prevent iron absorption.
- Increase folic acid and vitamin C, B vitamins and iron foods.
- Shellfish improve absorption of iron. (not under 2 years)
- Quinoa is complete protein with iron.
- Broccoli has iron, vitamins, folic acid and vitamin B12.
- Blackstrap molasses in warm milk daily for iron and B vitamins.
- BENEFICIAL FOODS:
Blackstrap molasses, oily fish, beans and pulses, eg lentils, baked beans, kidney beans, dried fruits, strawberries, nuts and seeds for non-haem iron, fortified cereals and breads, broccoli, peas and cauliflower. Green vegetables, eggs, wholemeal bread, lean meat, lentils, fish, dried fruit, almonds, sesame/sunflower/pumpkin seeds, avocados, peas, beans, cereals, tomatoes, fortified formula, fruit/vegetable juices.

Nutrients to consider

- Vitamin C to improve iron absorption. Ascorbic acid $1/4$gm or chewable 100mgs (L)
- MVM to include vitamin A, C and B vitamins, eg Supernutrition Plus over 8 years x 2 daily also includes gentle iron.
- B vitamins needed for iron absorption are B12 and folic acid. Take as a children's B complex (over 5 years) (BC)
- Easy iron – 2 to 5 years one capsule every 3 days; 5-8 years alternate days; over 8 years daily (HN) (one tablet crushed) or Floridix by Salus House which is herbal iron with B vitamins and vitamin C (one drop per 6lbs body weight) (N) or Nutri-sorb iron ascorbate 10 drops. (BC)
- Iron phosphate is homeopathic. (one tablet crushed) (BM)
- Molybdenum helps iron conversion. One drop alt days or trace minerals 4 drops per day (BC) or Concentrace one drop per 6 lbs weight. (HN)

ANAL FISSURE

SEE ALSO: CONSTIPATION, DIARRHOEA, WORMS

Nutrients to consider

- Comfrey cream. (N)
- Witch Hazel Ointment for healing. (Ch or HS)
- Children's Vitamin C and bioflavonoids. (BC)
- Calcium fluoride for healing. (BM)

Usually linked to trauma during constipation, this is a tiny tear in the lower rectum/anal sphincter and can also be linked to worms or diarrhoea. It can lead to a leak from vagina to rectum.

Symptoms include itching, and streaks of blood on toilet tissue or pants. If bleeding persists and no obvious cause always seek medical advice.

GENERAL ADVICE

Bathe area in salty water after using the toilet.
Address constipation.
Increase zinc foods for healing.
Lubricate anus before passing a motion with
petroleum or KY Jelly.

SEE ALSO: WORMS, RASHES, BITES AND STINGS, ALLERGIC
RHINITIS, ASTHMA, ECZEMA, IMMUNE FUNCTION, HAYFEVER

Pets are very important for emotional well being.
Children also learn responsibility and loving care.
However there are some risks to health associated with
animals which can be overcome with simple
awareness.

RISKS

Toxoplasmosis, from animal excrement.
Lyme disease contracted from tic bites.
Worms and parasites.
Fleas.
Rashes and itching.
Asthma – house dust-mite/pet fur.
Eczema.
Allergic rhinitis.

ACTION

Boost child's immune system.
Regular treatment of pets for fleas, worms and mites
	with non-toxic products and herbal powders.
Avoid litter trays.
Look out for dog/ cat faeces when out playing.
Wear long cool trousers in countryside and long grass
	for summer months.
Non-furry pets and non-feathery pets for sufferers of
	asthma, allergic rhinitis, eczema, eg fish and
	reptiles.
Treat child for thread-worms regularly (chemist).
Regular live yoghurt and probiotics to rebalance gut-
	flora ('dysbiosis').

FOR ANIMAL TREATMENTS

Give $^1/_4$tsp nutritional yeast and $^1/_2$tsp garlic powder
sprinkled onto pets food 3 times a week helps to
protect against infestation of fleas and tics.
	50mg vitamin B1 daily to pets to prevent infestation.
	Rosemary, pennyroyal, eucalyptus and mint
sprinkled into animal's bedding.
	No tea tree oil on cats fur as toxic but it is okay for
dogs.
	Tea tree will kill a tick for easy removal.
	Lemon grass or citronella to carpets (put into
vacuum bag too).	■

ANOREXIA NERVOSA

SEE ALSO: EATING DISORDERS, BULIMIA NERVOSA, BLOOD SUGAR, EXERCISE, DEPRESSION

Anorexia Nervosa is an addiction to dieting as a means of control / willpower and is classed as a psychotic illness. A disorder self starvation with 20% of sufferers eventually dying of the consequences either by starvation or suicide. However with early intervention 50% will recover completely. An extreme aversion to food which can lead to psychological, gynaecological and endocrine imbalances. Incidence in females 12 – 18 year olds is 1–2%. May overlap with bulimia. It is not really a loss of appetite, but a denial of hunger. The person is often obsessively tidy and precise setting themselves very high often unattainable standards so they never actually achieve them.

FACTORS TO CONSIDER

There is no single cause and it is thought to be essentially a psychotic illness, but increasingly recent research is indicating several biochemical factors may be involved.

Glucose intolerance

Nutrient deficiencies, eg vitamin A (or toxicity), zinc, EFAs, B vitamins

Deep-seated psychological problems

Depression

Low self esteem

Media, peer, parental (perceived pressure of)

Low levels cholecystokinin which controls appetite

Low serotonin with possible inability to convert tryptophan to serotonin especially if deficiencies of certain minerals

Family or personal history of alcohol or drug abuse, depression or anxiety

Family stress (current or previous)

Food allergies

Nutrient deficiencies especially zinc

Malabsorption and poor digestion often result from starvation diets

SIGNS AND SYMPTOMS OF ANOREXIA

Loss of 15%-20% body weight, equivalent to 2 stones if original weight was 8 stone.

Continued dieting when not overweight.

Obsession with weight and food (shopping, cooking, recipes, but rarely eating).

Nutrients to Consider

(doses are adult as sufferers are usually age 12)

● Zinc is vital as it is usually very deficient and controls appetite, taste and food choices. Required in high doses in teenage years. Zinc deficiency symptoms mirror those of eating disorders and depression. Zinc citrate 30mgs one in evening. (S)

● All vitamins and minerals likely to be deficient Aqueous Multi Plus one tablespoon daily. (BR)

● Probiotics: acidophilus 1 gm or Bioacidophilus one capsule twice daily. (BC)

● Vitamin A x one drop for mucous membranes and growth. (BC)

● Calcium compound 2 daily to provide sodium, calcium and iron. (BM)

Rituals surrounding food, eg unable to eat in
company or slow precise eating and chewing.
Distorted body image.
Isolation (low social life).
Wearing loose baggy clothes.
Cessation of menstruation.
Constipation or diarrhoea.
Obsessive exercise.
Hyperactivity.
Denial of problem 'just not hungry' or 'i ate earlier'.
Feels nauseated or bloated after normal amounts of
food.
Intolerance to cold.
Hair loss.
Mood swings.
No desire to grow up.
Addictive behaviour.
Obsessive / compulsive disorder.
Anxiety and depression.

GENERAL ADVICE
Don't bully!
Dietary approaches often fail initially due to the fear
of gaining weight.
Anorexics will often accept supplements rather than
food and this approach should over time alter
appetite.
Supplements are best taken at least $1/2$ hour before
food.
Liquid or powdered forms are better absorbed as the
gut may be leaky leading to poor absorption.
Sublingual are even better.
Drinks are accepted when food is not. Offer shakes
and freshly squeezed juices in which you can
administer supplements as well if appropriate.
Seek advise for the family even if the sufferer will
not yet accept help. This will help you to
manage the problems more effectively.
Remember the other children and explain to them
that this is an illness and is not catching.
Address depression with a doctor and ask for a
referral to a psychiatrist as this is essentially a
mental illness.
If she becomes very underweight and ill she may
have to be compulsorily admitted.
Seek help from a qualified dietician or nutritionist as
well.

Best results are from a combination of nutritional and psychiatric treatment.

There is no ideal weight or shape; we are all individuals which is what makes us so special.

Avoid scales. Think health not weight.

Set realistic goals.

It is not your fault.

Help can support and speed recovery. We all need a little help sometimes. It does not mean we are failures.

Contacts:
Self Help and Psychology Magazine online: www.cybertowers.com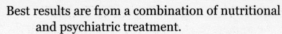

ANTIBIOTICS

SEE ALSO: FEVER, INFECTIONS, COLDS, IMMUNE FUNCTION, DYSBIOSIS, EARS, BACTERIAL INFECTIONS

ForewordForewordAlthough in some cases antibiotics can and do save lives, they are often over prescribed and resistant bacteria are increasing, eg only 10% instead of 95% of children respond to penicillin now. They only work for bacterial infections so viruses such as colds and flu and childhood infectious diseases such as measles, will be unaffected unless there is a secondary infection. Young children are most likely to be resistant to antibiotics as they are prescribed twice as often to under 5 years as over 5 years. Antibiotics actually suppress immunity leading to greater susceptibility to future infections.

GENERAL ADVICE
Do not pressurise your doctor for an antibiotic prescription.
Treat any 'fever' first.
Be aware that childhood illness helps build immunity.
Boost immune function.
See GP if fever is very high and not responding, stiff neck, sensitive to light with a rash or sore throat.
Reduce dairy if mucous is a problem.
Food is not required during acute infection, but plenty of clear fluids are.

EFFECTS OF REPEATED ANTIBIOTICS
Resistance.
Dysbiosis.
Reduced Immunity.

Reading:
Boost Your Child's Immune System (Chapter 3) Lucy Burney ■

Nutrients to consider
- Probiotics after any antibiotics. See Appendix for age specific probiotics.
- Immune nutrients: Immune C one daily over age 8. (HN)
- Sambucol one tsp twice daily. (HN)
- E-Kid- Nacea 1/8 – 2 tsps or Immuno-Kid from 2 years 2-3 times daily. (K)
- Echinacea and black elderberry 1-2 daily over 5 years. (HN)
- UltraCare for kids – up to 12 years provides a powdered MVM with probiotics to boost digestion following antibiotics.

ANXIETY

SEE ALSO: EATING DISORDERS, OCD, APPETITE, STRESS, ADDICTIONS, DEPRESSION, PANIC ATTACKS, SLEEP PROBLEMS, EXERCISE

Anxiety in children is a growing problem. The increase in family breakdown, stepfamilies, acrimonious access visits, school league tables and SATs exams all add pressure and insecurity for children. The influence of TV, videos, computer games and the Internet is a controversial one but children are exposed to life issues much earlier than ever before and the age of innocence gets ever shorter. Families are often so busy with their individual lives that joint activities, family meals and communication are all too rare. Children are also exposed to peer group and media pressure and feel they have to grow up quickly and fit in with the perceived norm.

All children worry and this is a natural part of coping with life and growing up. Anxiety is when these feelings get out of control and affect daily life and health. Symptoms include panic attacks, poor sleep, loss of appetite, headaches, apathy, diarrhoea, fatigue, low concentration, learning problems, bed wetting, tummy ache. In adolescence eating disorders may occur. Anxiety can be linked to depression in some cases.

Obsessive compulsive disorder is becoming more common as a means of managing anxiety. Adolescents may develop eating disorders or turn to drugs. Bullying at school or perceived pressure may be involved.

GENERAL ADVICE

Encourage breakfast or send a healthy snack like fruit or nuts to eat on the way. (Teenagers often get up too late for breakfast!)

Eat small frequent meals or snacks.

Exercise is important for stress especially swimming, walking, yoga or Tai Chi.

Neck rolls for 3 minutes twice daily.

Lavender oil in a room burner is relaxing.

Chamomile tea before a stressful event may help.

If the fear centres around bedtime or the night be calm and comforting. Some children still use comforters or suck thumbs into teens. Leave a night light on.

Dietary Advice

- Avoid:
Chocolate, cola and sugar as these are 'false crutches' leading to blood sugar irregularities and rebound fatigue.

- Artificial chemicals, eg eat organic and avoid additives as these may affect brain functioning.

- Alcohol which depresses nervous system and increases depression and dependence.

- Caffeine in cola, coffee, tea and chocolate stimulates the nervous system.

- Increase:
Magnesium and B vitamin foods for the nervous system.

- Tryptophan foods to increase serotonin production.

- EFAs for brain function.

- Minerals especially calcium and magnesium which are calming.

- Vitamin C foods as this is excreted more under stress.

- Celery and lettuce contain calming phyto chemicals.

- BENEFICIAL FOODS:
Oats and other wholegrains cereals, pasta, avocados, bananas, mangoes, strawberries, apricots, cottage cheese, yoghurt, turkey, oily fish, green vegetables, potatoes, sweet potatoes, celery, lettuce, yeast extract, blackstrap molasses, dried fruits, nuts and seeds, beans and brown rice.

Listen to your children. Stop what you are doing and use eye contact.

For over one year olds, add Children's Oil Blend which contains calming herbs to the bath or as a massage. (N)

Avoid adding pressure by nagging about minor things like untidy rooms or odd socks!

Praise the achievements however minor and don't emphasise the weaker points.

Seek professional counselling if the problem is persistent.

If appetite is affected or digestive problems, try a one month course of digestive enzymes. (see Appendix)

Herbs include vervain, valarian, wood betony, hops and chamomile which can be calming. See a herbalist and Appendix.

Reassess child's lifestyle. He may be doing too many after school activities, eg dancing or music lessons (with exam pressure). Do they really need to do so much?

Massage can help muscle tension.

Aromatherapy oils under supervision. (see Appendix)

Homeopathic natrum mur under supervision.

NB: Kava Kava is unavailable at time of writing. (summer 2002) ■

Nutrients to consider

● Children's B complex over 5 years, one daily (BC) or B vital with ginseng for stress, one per day over 5 years. (HN)

● Calcium and magnesium 1:1 ratio are calming minerals so give at bedtime sprinkled onto food or drink. (HN, S, AR)

● Bio magnesium $1/2$ capsule 1-3 years or one capsule 4-12 years. (BC)

● Magnesium Ultra Food Form two at bedtime over 8 years. (HN)

● Vitamin C: Bio-C $1/8$ tsp (AN, NC, R) or Magnesium Ascorbate $1/4$–$1/2$ gm. (BC)

● EFAs: a) Eye Q start with 2 daily building up to 6 daily for 3 months, then 2 daily maintenance (NC, HS) b) Eskimo 3 x 5 mls daily (Nu) c) Max EPA/GLA one daily over 12 years (S) d) Udo's Choice. (Sa)

● Stabilium one daily for a 50lb child to a maximum of 3 daily. Can be given to infants in graduated dose under supervision. (AR)

● Chromium deficiency can cause anxiety symptoms probably via blood sugar irregularities.one drop daily. (BC)

● Bach Flower Remedies and Australian Bush Remedies for emotional problems come as single tinctures or complexes. (Ch, HS for leaflets which give guidance on choosing correct one). Rescue Remedy is a good all rounder.

● Phytotherapies – various, contact the BM nutrition department, but incarnata, lavender, hops, valerian may help.

● Potassium phosphate and magnesium phosphate CP. (BM)

● Kid Chamomile (over 2 years) is calming. (K)

● Seretone 50mgs at bedtime alternate days over 5 years, daily over 8 years.

● Chill formula one daily over 12 years contains B vitamins herbs, amino acids and GABA. Studies show this can be helpful in anxiety and sleep disorders. (HN)

● Stabilium one daily for 50lb child. Can be given from infancy in graduated doses under supervision NB: contains fish extracts. (AR)

● Livecalm – Sleep Deep one at bedtime over 12 years (AR)

● Zen works in acute anxiety in 20-30 minutes one daily over 5 years. (AR)

ANXIETY

APPETITE

SEE ALSO: EATING DISORDERS, FUSSY EATERS, ANXIETY, CONSTIPATION, OBESITY, ANAEMIA AND ADDICTIONS

Anorexia literally means loss of appetite and is not in itself an eating disorder, (which is anorexia nervosa). Poor appetite is often a symptom of another problem. Psychological and emotional factors may be involved in poor appetite, but there are a few biochemical factors to consider as well. Compulsive eating is uncontrolled appetite, which leads to obesity (see Eating disorders)

FACTORS TO CONSIDER

Deficiencies of zinc for digestion, appetite, taste and growth; iron for appetite and energy and vitamin C for iron usage.

Dysbiosis leading to abdominal discomfort.

Constipation.

Anxiety/stress suppress digestion (from 'butterflies' to complete loss of appetite).

Blood sugar irregularities affect appetite and food choices.

In older children and teenagers smoking, drug and alcohol abuse may also be factors.

GENERAL ADVICE

Iron only if diagnosed as deficient by blood test with GP. Better to improve usage of iron.

Offer small meals and snacks at regular intervals.

Encourage drinks of fresh juices or shakes as well as water. ■

Dietary Advice

- Check list of iron rich foods.
- Take vitamin C with these foods.
- Zinc foods for taste.
- Avoid all junk foods.
- Freshly juiced fruit and vegetables for concentrated nutrients.
- Shakes with fruit and seeds added.
- BENEFICIAL FOODS: Meat, sardines, eggs, dried fruits, broccoli, beans, citrus fruits, avocados, fresh juices and smoothies.

Nutrients to consider

- MVM.
- Digestive enzymes.
- Zinc10 drops daily (BC) or $^1/_2$level measure under tongue of sherbert flavoured powder alternate days (HN) or zinc citrate 15mgs one daily over 8 years. (L)
- Calcium Compound tablets contains sodium, calcium and iron. Suitable for children. (BM)
- Iron – Easy iron – 2 to 5 years one capsule every 3 days; 5-8 years alternate days; over 8 years daily (HN) or Iron Phosphate one tablet crushed (BM) or Floridix by Salus House which is herbal iron with B vitamins and vitamin C. (N)
- Iron phosphate is homeopathic so does not feed bacteria. (BM)
- Mo helps conversion of iron. One drop alternate days or as trace minerals at 4 drops per day (BC) or Concentrace one drop per 6 lbs body weight. (HN)
- Citrus aurantium as a tea with peppermint before meals.

ARTHRITIS

SEE ALSO: *INFLAMMATION, FOOD INTOLERANCES, CANDIDA, DYSBIOSIS, LEAKY GUT*

Often known as juvenile chronic arthritis (JCA) of which Still's Disease is one form. There are various degrees with the severest form being quite devastating, but fortunately rare.50-70% resolve spontaneously around puberty, but prevention and limitation of abnormalities of bone development is vital. It often develops around 2-3 years old. Fever often accompanies the outbreaks of pain.

Early diagnosis is vital to identify the type of arthritis, initiate correct treatment and reduce the risks of abnormalities of bone growth and development. Typically one to four joints are affected, often in the hands and feet with periods of flare up and remission

FACTORS TO CONSIDER

It can be genetic, but often isolated case in the family as several, rather than one gene are thought to be involved.

Also linked to certain viruses or bacteria, eg chicken pox, influenza, rubella and throat infections which can all lead to joint pains. It is usually temporary, but some will become chronic if there is a genetic predisposition.

Magnesium deficiency can lead to calcium deposits in the joints.

Poor digestion often linked to zinc deficiencies and 'dysbiosis' of the gut.

Food intolerances which increase inflammation especially in the joints.

Copper toxicity resulting in zinc deficiency. Conversely some arthritis sufferers appear to need extra copper which like zinc acts as an anti-inflammatory. The correct ratio between zinc and copper of 10:1 is essential.

Iron levels in arthritics are often elevated indicating possibilities such as poor digestion or vitamin C deficiencies.

Candida.

Iron/selenium deficiencies can increase inflammation and free radical damage.

Dietary advice

- Minimise or avoid dairy products especially from cows, but also from sheep and goats in some cases.
- Avoid red meat as it too can promote inflammation. This means beef, pork and lamb.
- Reduce/avoid citrus fruits, rhubarb, aubergine, courgettes, peppers, gooseberries and tomatoes as these foods are from the nightshade family which can aggravate arthritis.
- Include pineapple for its bromelain which is an anti-inflammatory.
- Wheat may be a problem for some children with arthritis.
- Increase EFAs to reduce inflammation and ease joints.
- Sulphur foods can help detoxification and are good for joints.
- Increase vitamin C, E and betacarotene foods.
- Increase potassium and calcium foods.
- Specific foods include grapes which appear to affect an enzyme involved in bone and cartilage formation, celery which alkalizes the system and contains silicon for connective tissue and ginger and oily fish to reduce inflammation.
- BENEFICIAL FOODS: Oily fish, oatbran, flaxseeds, fresh vegetables (esp broccoli, kale and carrots), celery, non-acidic fruits (eg apricots, berries, apples, kiwis), grapes, pineapple, brown rice, onions, garlic, eggs, sunflower seeds, walnuts, chestnuts, almonds, hazelnuts, beans, lentils, wholegrains, sea vegetables.

Nutrients to consider

- Vitamin B5 is involved in calcium metabolism and control of inflammatory hormones. Vitamin B3 improves circulation and joint mobility; vitamin B6 reduces synovial membranes improving joint mobility. Take children's B Complex one daily over 5 years. (BC)

- Vitamin C for cartilage/bone formation and as an antioxidant. Children's capsule daily (BC) or chewable over 4 years (L) or Bio C $^1/_4$tsp daily. (AN)

- Vitamin E especially in rheumatoid arthritis one drop or capsule 100 ius (BC) or cream. (L)

- EFAs especially fish oils and blackcurrant seed oils, eg Eskimo 3 x 5 mls daily (Nu) or Max EPA / DHA one capsule over 12 years (S) Dricelle CLO powder. (BC)

- MVM.

- Probiotics.

- Aloe Gold one tsp daily over 5 years. (HN)

- MSM powder $^1/_4$tsp daily over 8 years or as professionally directed. (HN)

- Apply MSM cream or Boswellia joint and muscle balm 4 times daily in over 2 year olds. (HN)

Aims of a nutritional programme are to reduce inflammation, prevent flare ups and control joint damage. Supporting the immune system and identifying any food intolerances is important rather than addressing JCA directly and usually produces better results.

GENERAL ADVICE

Ask water board for free test for copper. Address source if elevated.

Drink only filtered or bottled water.

Hydrotherapy is important. Regular swimming in warm water preferably with guidance of a physiotherapist.

Elimination diets are sometimes very helpful, but require professional supervision.

Regular eye checks as some forms of JCA can affect vision.

Alka bath salts to eliminate toxins from the joints and alkalise the system. Add to bath water twice a week or during flare ups. Tel: 01342 410 303.

TESTS

Hair mineral analysis for mineral ratios and copper levels.

Contacts:
Chronic Children's Arthritis Association
Tel: 01905 763556.

Reading:
Diet and Arthritis by Gail Darlington and Linda Gamlin has a good section on types of JCA. ▪

ASTHMA

SEE ALSO: ALLERGIES, LEAKY GUT, FOOD INTOLERANCE,
IMMUNE FUNCTION, ECZEMA

Potentially life threatening. Always seek medical advice. Incidence is now 1 in 7 children. 50% of suffereres grow out of asthma by 7 years old, the majority by adolescence, but 10% of 10 year olds still have it.

Asthma is not easy to diagnose before 2 years old. 30% of children have wheezing in the first 5 years of life, but only half of these will go on to develop asthma.

The ratio of asthmatic boys to girls is 2:1. It can develop when steroids suppress eczema. Lots of children are prescribed inhalers for these wheezing attacks and labeled asthmatics when they may only have transient attacks. Long term use of steroids, eg for eczema, can damage gut bacteria and affect the intestinal membrane (leaky gut) and suppress immunity.

FACTORS TO CONSIDER

Infections.

Stress.

Changes of temperature.

Housedust.

Traffic pollution (incidence of attacks is less in school holidays when there is less traffic).

Mites.

Pests.

Pollen.

There is usually a family history of allergies. Most common food allergens are eggs, wheat, cows' milk, yeast and fish. Mucous secretions are often excessive. Dairy products aggravate this. Children need to strengthen their immune systems to ward off attacks and reduce allergic reactions.

GENERAL ADVICE

Teenagers have particular problems due to hormonal fluctuations. A new combination inhaler has recently been licensed for over 12 years of age allowing the child to be more in control of treatment and reduce frequency of 'puffs'. Called Symbicort Turbo inhaler it is still a steroid, but when medication is necessary

Dietary Advice
● Avoid: Milk products, eggs, strawberries, sugar, nuts, shellfish, peanuts, chocolate, MSG, vinegar, salt, all food additives but especially foods containing sulphites (E220 and E227), eg dried fruit, soft drinks, fruit juices and sausages.
● Limiting grains which are the grass family, eg wheat and rye can reduce cross reactions.
● Increase: Non-animal proteins, eg oily fish can reduce severity of attacks as it is anti-inflammatory.
● Bromelain (in pineapples and papaya) as it reduces mucous.
● Selenium foods.
● Vitamin C foods as often low in asthmatics and can neutralise pollutants in lungs.
● Vitamin B12 (from sea vegetables) may be deficient.
● Low levels of antioxidant foods in the diet may be linked to increasing asthma. Freshly juiced fruit and vegetables give concentrated levels of antioxidants, vitamins and minerals.
● Ellagic acid present in strawberries sits in lungs and neutralises chemical pollutants.
● BENEFICIAL FOODS: Brown rice, millet, quinoa, oatmeal, pineapple, papaya, non-citrus fruits, avocadoes, blackstrap molasses, tuna, sardines, oily fish, fresh juices, sea vegetables, beans, soya products and quorn are non-animal proteins, fresh raw organic fruits and green leafy vegetables and brazil nuts.

ASTHMA

may offer a more acceptable treatment for rebellious teenagers!

Peak flow meters can be provided for home use to predict an attack.

Avoid gluten until 9-12 months when weaning.

Need to monitor peak flow and may need to see GP to reduce medication.

Swimming, walking and cycling to encourage full use of lungs.

Several studies have shown the benefits of yoga breathing and stretching postures which can reduce attacks and doses of medication.

Room ioniser can counteract pollen and dust in the atmosphere.

Avoid carpets and feathers.

Applied kinesiology to indicate possible allergens (can be done through mother for small children) Not 100% accurate, but non-invasive and a good guide.

Skin prick testing at a hospital for inhalant allergens is useful but different to food intolerances.

During attack sit child straddling a dining chair with arms over the back and head on arms, to expand chest and open airways.

Keep a diary of attacks to correlate with situations/ triggers.

Avoid very hot or cold drinks as they may trigger a spasm.

Ventolin and Becotide inhalers can have side effects and may actually create bronchospasm.

Never stop medication without your doctor's consent.

Some vaccines contain egg which may initiate reactions.

Regular use of paracetamol has also been linked to asthma attacks.

Vitamin B12 deficiency is linked to some childhood asthma. Ask GP for a blood test.

Buteyko Breathing Centre can teach correct breathing Tel: 0116 277 2051.

Coleus Forksholli may help – See a homeopath and refer to Appendix.

Inhaling peppermint oil vapours may help in children over 5 years. NB: Be careful with hot water.

Contacts:
National Asthma Campaign Helpline
Tel: 08457 010203. Run by specialist
nurses, further information – Tel:
020 7226 2260 ∎

Nutrients to consider

● EFAs – If there is a family history of allergies (atopy) this may necessitate GLA supplements (see allergies.) Evening primrose (EPO) or starflower oil may help reduce inflammation. Try EPO 1-3 daily 4-12 years (L) or Essential Balance Junior which also include flax oil and is butterscotch flavoured from herbs not sugar; $^1/_2$-3 tsps from weaning (HN) NB: do not give GLA if child has had fits or non-febrile convulsions or if there is a family history of epilepsy.

● Vitamin C as an antihistamine; Vitasorb C x 4 drops daily or magnesium ascorbate $^1/_4$- $^1/_2$gm or children's C 100mgs (BC) or Bio C $^1/_4$tsp daily which includes minerals. (AN)

● Probiotics.

● Magnesium, involved in muscular actions. Deficiency can cause spasms. $^1/_2$Bio Mg 1-3 years (BC), or chewable lemon-flavoured one daily over 4 years (L), or Bio Mg one per day 6-12 years which also includes calcium B6, minerals (BM), or True Food Mg 1-2 daily over 8 years (HN), or Mg solution $^1/_2$tsp 1-2 times daily. (AR, NC, R)

● Vitamin B6 is involved in relaxation of bronchial muscles. Children's B complex one daily over 5 years. (BC)

● Oralmat can increase lung function and decrease allergic responses whilst boosting immune function. Oralmat is rye grass extract which contains tryptophan and zinc to strengthen immune system and magnesium to relax muscles. It may also have a de-sensitizing effect. 1 drop under tongue thrice daily held for 15 seconds and then swallowed. (HS)

● Cytolog one spray twice daily – boosts immunity. (AR)

● Selenium solution x 1 ml daily (AR, NC, R) or Trace Minerals x 4 drops (BC) or 200mcgs alternate days over 8 years. (HN)

● Calcium phosphate is a good constitutional for children or with magnesium phosphate. (BM)

● Euphorbia Complex twice per day. (BM)

● Milk thistle $^1/_2$tablet crushed daily for liver support esp if on medications. (BM)

● Gingko Complex $^1/_2$tablet twice daily (BM) or as a tincture in older children. (N)

● Quercetin can reduce allergic reactions. Quercetin 300 also has vitamin C and E – Give 1-2 per day per 50 lbs body weight (AR). Quercetin Plus one daily 50lb body weight (BC) to decrease inflammation and histamine.

ATHLETE'S FOOT

SEE ALSO: CANDIDA, DYSBIOSIS, RING WORM

An infectious fungal infection leading to itching and sore skin usually between the toes or on the soles. Check for connected symptoms such as thrush in mouth or vagina. Tends to be more common in older children who use swimming pools and school changing rooms. May be linked to intestinal overgrowth of yeast. (see candida)

GENERAL ADVICE

Cotton socks.

Plastic shoes (flip flops at public pools).

Encourage thorough drying of feet.

Separate towel and bath mat.

No bare feet.

Anti-fungal powder.

Finely shredded garlic in socks and shoes.

Soak feet daily in solution of vinegar, lemon juice, tea tree oil or citricidal. ▪

Dietary advice

- Avoid: sugar, yeast, cheese, mushrooms, marmite, grapes, peanuts.
- Sulphur foods are anti-fungal.
- BENEFICIAL FOODS: Live yoghurt, garlic, onion, eggs, fresh fruit and vegetables.

Nutrients to consider

- Tea tree oil diluted one drop in 100ml boiled and cooled water, use topically or add two drops to bath. (HS)
- Citricidal (grapefruit seed extract) 2-6 drops 1-3 times daily over 8 years. Can also be diluted and applied topically. Not for citrus allergies. (HN)
- Colloidal silver, topically, is 'nature's antibiotic'. (HN, AR, HS, NC)
- Probiotics.

Attention Deficit Disorder (ADD) & Attention Deficit Hyperactivity Disorder (ADHD)

SEE ALSO: HYPERACTIVITY, IMMUNE FUNCTION, TOXICITY, FOOD INTOLERANCE, LEAKY GUT, AUTISM, CANDIDA,

Does not always involve hyperactivity but may respond to the recommendations here. Thought to be part of the autism spectrum. This does not mean your child is autistic if labelled ADD hyperactive or ADD/ADHD, but merely that these conditions are linked by some common factors. Appears to be increasing in incidence. 3 in 100 children are affected, with 15,000 children affected in the UK. The sex ratio is 9:1 boys:girls.

As you will see from the following information and advice, the hyperactivity spectrum disorders are complex and professional help is often needed.

Factors to consider
Genetic.
Smoking in pregnancy triples the risk of ADHD.
Nutrient deficiencies especially zinc, magnesium, calicum, iron, EFAs.
Processed and refined diets are low in nutrients and high in phosphates. High carbohydrate and low protein may exacerbate problems.
Blood sugar imbalances.
Toxicity from chemicals/ food additives.
Toxic metal poisoning especially lead, copper and aluminum.
EFA deficiency – children with a family history of allergies may have an enzyme defect affecting metabolism of EFAs and creating a deficiency.
Leaky gut and dysbiosis (history of recurrent antibiotics likely).
Food intolerances.
Liver overload.
Gut infections.
Sulphation problems (liver).
Serotonin deficiency in the brain.
salicylates intolerance.
Thyroid hormone may be less active at cellular level.

Dietary advice
- Sugar and additives are often the main dietary problems.
- Eliminate all food additives.
- Identify food intolerances. Most likely is cows' milk, oranges and citrus, chocolate and wheat. Also yeast, soya, corn, salicylates and artificial sweeteners.
- Sugar causes blood sugar imbalances, mood swings and energy fluctuations. One small fruit juice and 2 pieces fruit daily should be the only sugar. When necessary use blackstrap molasses or honey to sweeten.
- Give a daily green salad or at least a token leaf and build up!
- Increase iron, calcium, magnesium and zinc foods.
- Use chopped nuts (no peanuts) on desserts instead of chocolate sauce etc (over 2 years old).
- Increased rate of metabolism necessitates increased protein – suggest 2:1 protein:carbohydrates.
- Small frequent meals of wholesome, natural foods.
- No fizzy drinks unless using a soda siphon and fruit juice.
- Iron and vitamin C foods together.

BENEFICIAL FOODS:
Soya products, wheatgerm, rice cakes, oatcakes, rye crispbreads, oily fish, free range poultry and vegetables, especially raw.

Medication should be a last resort. Severely hyperactive children may be given the controversial amphetamine-type drug Ritalin, which improves mental functioning. It is a classified, controlled drug in the same category as cocaine and should not be prescribed in under 6 year olds. It replaces dopamines in the brain. Dopamines occur naturally in normal children, helping them to focus attention. This symptomatic approach to ADHD does not address underlying causes.

A drug becomes a controlled substance when it has the potential for abuse and/or addiction and there are many potentially damaging side effects to Ritalin including addiction, seizures, insomnia, growth impairment and psychotic behaviour. Little is known about the long-term effects and yet most parents are desperate enough to give their child Ritalin, which is for some calming, increasing concentration. It eases the lives of those who are affected by ADD, whether or not they themselves are taking it. However there are other, non-medical ways to treat the symptoms.

Medications such as tranquillisers during pregnancy.

Frequent antibiotic use may indicate lowered immunity and lead to nutrient deficiencies and impaired brain function.

Inhalant allergies, eg cat fur, house dust mite.

CHARACTERISTICS OF ADHD

Include restlessness, lack of concentration, easily distracted, irritable, poor sleeper, learning difficulties, thirst, tummy ache, language disorder, clumsy, emotional instability, cries easily, aggression, impulsive, excitable, impatient, bed wetter, 'a holy terror,' demanding, unhappy, swearing. Other allergic symptoms such as sinusitis, rashes, headaches, asthma, eczema. May fight a lot, bully or be bullied and finds it hard to respond to discipline (may laugh, cry or become aggressive).

SUMMARY OF AIMS

Eliminate chemical additives and sugar

Eliminate allergens, test if necessary (York Lab or HN)

Test hair for toxic metals and mineral levels and detoxify any toxicity

Supplement EFAs (Omega 3 and 6)

Supplement Vitamin B6, B3, zinc and magnesium and a good multi vitamin and mineral complex.

GENERAL ADVICE

If simple dietary modification is ineffective consult a nutritionist for assessment.

Some research indicates sugar is actually calming and may not be the main culprit. However it is a non-nutrient source of calories which can disturb blood sugar and mood so is best avoided.

Undiagnosed and untreated ADHD sufferers may suffer more stress and depression, anxiety, teenage suicide and may become delinquent. Depression and anxiety are common in ADHD children with self esteem lower due to others' reactions to difficult behaviour.

ADHD may be linked with Asberger's Syndrome, substance abuse, dyspraxia, OCD and speech and learning delay. NB: Learning difficulties are not always caused by ADHD but can be missed due to ADHD.

Exclusion of salicylates eliminates many fruits. Cut out for 6-8 weeks as last dietary restriction, relying on vegetables for vitamin C and fibre. Then slowly re-introduce.

Resistance to thyroid hormone in the cells has been highlighted in research suggesting a possibility that T3 hormone replacement may help some hyperactive children. More research is needed.

Research suggests that zinc may become bound to artificial colouring speeding up excretion. Cut out colourings.

EFA deficiencies affect brain function and causes dry skin and excessive thirst. EFAs require vitamins and minerals to be utilised.

Promising research into SAMe which assists in detoxification and recycling of neurotransmitters, eg serotonin and dopamine.

HACSG can give advice on the Feingold diet and arrange a cheap hair test

Magnesium deficiency results in fidgeting, anxiety, insomnia, co-ordination problems and learning difficulties.

Add Children's Oil Blend which contains calming herbs to the bath. Add (over one year) or massage. (N)

Get some emotional support and day to day help for yourself. Contact HACSG for information.

Some severe cases need residential or respite help to relieve the other children and facilitate targeted, intensive help. Don't feel guilty about this.

Invest in a book about E numbers which are not all bad. Foresight does an excellent £2 booklet called

---

Suggested diet programme

One year old

- Gradually change follow on milk to soya or Nanny goat formula. Mix half-and-half until she gets used to the taste, gradually increasing soya / goats' until cows' milk is eliminated.
- Avoid baby foods containing cows' milk products.
- Reduce sugar / eliminate additives.
- Natural whole food diet.
- Offer more drinks of diluted fruit juice (not orange), preferably in a cup to reduce volume of milk taken. Aim for maximum of 2-3 cups / bottles of soya or goats' formula daily.

3 year olds+

- give a natural whole food diet, avoiding processed/refined foods such as white flour/rice.
- Remove all additives, especially colours/ preservatives.
- Reduce sugar; read all labels for; sorbitol, dextrose, fructose, maltose etc. Includes most processed foods and fizzy drinks. See appendix.
- Avoid smoked foods such as sausages, ham, bacon, as they contain preservatives and can affect an enzyme needed for brain function.
- Give small regular meals/snacks to maintain even blood sugar levels, vital for mood stabilization, sleep and energy production.
- Increase oily fish such as tuna, salmon, herring, and mackeral for essential fats, free-range poultry.
- Increase fresh fruit and vegetables. Children often prefer raw vegetables such as thin strips of carrots, baby sweetcorn or cucumber. NB: if salicylates are excluded, increasing vegetables should secure vitamin C levels.
- Wheat/dairy are sometimes a problem so reduce if possible. Introduce some wheat alternatives such as oatcakes, Ryvita or rice cakes to reduce wheat intake and moderate cows' milk intake.
- Consider Feingold diet, eg salicylates free.

Nutrients to consider

(need to be aware of additives, sugar and citrus flavourings)

● EFAs – 1g daily of fish or flax oil. Try these;

● 1)Eye Q start with 2 capsules per day building up to 6 per day for 3 months; then 2 per day maintainance. Contains preferable ratios of EPA / DHA /GLA (omega 3 and 6 oils) for memory and concentration (HS, NC) or use Eskimo 3 x 5 mls daily. (Nu)

● 2) Biocare do various combinations of omegas as Dricelle powders (contains citrus).

● 3) Einstein's DHA (omega 3 fish oils only) under 3 years take 1-2 daily squeezed onto food. 3-12 years 2-3 capsules daily. (HN)

● 4) Essential Balance Junior which provides Omega 3 and 6 in natural butterscotch flavour. Can be used when Omega 3 levels are improved: $^1/_2$–3 tsps from weaning. (HN)

● Mineral deficiencies are common.

● 1) Zinc for brain function, mood and EFA metabolism. Give as citrate You can open the capsule and sprinkle onto food. (BC, AR, R) BC also do drops. For over 8 years try $^1/_2$ level measure of sherbet flavoured powder directly under tongue on alternate days. Contains citrus. (HN)

● 2) Iron needed for brain function and energy levels often low in ADHD – Easy Iron is well tolerated (HN) NB: Do not give for more than one month without a blood test, for iron levels. Floridix by Salus House which is herbal iron with B vitamins and vitamin C.

● 3) Concentrace Minerals for good levels of magnesium and other minerals. (HN)

FINDOUT, which gives a traffic lights system to identifying the good, the bad and moderate additives. Or 'E for Additives'.

Avoid chemicals in household cleaners and personal hygiene products. Try pure toothpaste (BC) and Green People products.

Little Miracles are Bach Flower Remedies made up for your child. Tel: 020 7431 6153

Hyperactivity is multi-factorial. A systematic approach is required to facilitate evaluation and ensure minimum dietary restriction. Seek professional help.

Thought and deed are poorly connected. Try to praise the good and ignore the errors. He is rarely deliberately naughty.

Herbs include valerian, hops, passionflower. See Appendix.

Young offenders have responded well to dietary intervention and removal of toxic metals with nutritional supplements.

Your child is not naughty but frustrated and often bored. It is not your fault but you can affect the outcome. ▪

● 4) Magnesium /Calcium are calming minerals often deficient in ADD / ADHD. Give as 1:1 ratio at bedtime. Can be sprinkled onto food. (S, HN, AR). Bio magnesium one daily 6-12 years also contains calcium, minerals, B6. (BM)

● 5) Epsom salt (magnesium sulphate) 2 cups in a warm bath for 20 minutes every 3 nights has been shown to increase sulphur in blood, do not use soap etc. Pat dry and into bed. Sulphur is needed for toxins and sulphation.

● 6) Molybdenum can help sulphation. Trace minerals contain it. Give 4 drops daily (BC), or Concentrace. (HN)

● Celloid magnesium compound has potassium-phosphate to support nervous system and magnesium phosphate to help relaxation (BM) eg one twice daily 3 months to 3 years.

● MVM, eg Nutribalance Children's Formula (AR) which includes plenty of calcium/magnesium.

● B complex for the nervous system and stress especially B6 if serotonin is low or B3 if blood sugar is imbalanced (BC). Large doses of B vitamins under supervision have been successful in rebalancing brain chemicals.

● Vitamin C to help perceptual dysfunction and bioflavonoids (antihistamine); Bio-C $^1/_4$tsp daily includes minerals (AN, NC, R) or children's capsules one with breakfast or 4 drops. (BC)

● Brain Food Formula has a complex of nutrients to improve concentration and learning and reduce anxiety. One per day over 12 years. (HN)

● Liv Calm contains herb Stephania Rotunda that has been shown to produce a rapid calming effect with improved sleep, comprehension, anxiety and learning ability. Doses need to be tailored to the individual, some are better taking one capsule 3 times per day others all at night. For children under 5 years start with $^1/_3$ of a capsule 6 hourly building up to one capsule thrice daily. May need 2 for bedtime. Needs professional supervision.

● Probiotics.

● Seretone 5 HTP 50mg alternate days for 5-8 years; over 8 years one daily. Give at bedtime to help sleep and mood. (HN) Avoid if Ritalin taken.

● Kid Chamomile $^1/_8$-2 tsps for 2 years to 28lbs weight in graded doses 2-3 times daily. (K)

● Homeopathic Mg Compound contains Mg and Potassium for relaxation and the nervous system. For 3months–3 years give one twice daily. (BM)

● Siberian Ginseng 10-60 drops for 2 months only or 1-2 gms capsule (N) or B Vital which include B vitamins and Ginseng one daily over 5 years. (HN)

AUTISM

Dietary advice

● You must have professional help with diet exclusions. Autistic children often have heightened sensitivity to taste and smell and will reject anything unfamiliar. Dietary changes can be hard initially. Marilyn Lebretton's book is of great help here, but there are many complicated interactions which need the expert help of a nutritionist.

● Removal of potential allergens/toxins can relieve 'brain fog'.

● Casein in milk produces a peptide that has opioid effects and gluten in wheat, oats, barley and rye increases opioid load. Supervised elimination diet of all casein and/or gluten for at least 3 months Test first (ARU) and see a qualified nutritionist.

● Many will not eat protein as they have difficulty digesting it. Craving carbohydrates may indicate intolerance and opioid reactions.

● Eat organic.

● Avoid additives, MSG, citrus, sugar, corn and corn syrup, nuts and apples.

● Dr Rosemary Waring's research also advises exclusion of salicylates, cheese, chocolate, bananas, citrus.

● Increase vitamin E, C, A and calcium foods.

● Filtered and bottled water not tap. A plumbed in filter so all household water is pure including bathing, showering and laundry.

● Anti-candida diet if tested positive.

SE ALSO: *HYPERACTIVITY, ADHD, LEARNING DIFFICULTIES, TOXICITY, CANDIDA, FOOD INTOLERANCE, OCD, 'LEAKY' GUT, VACCINATION*

A brain disorder which affects behaviour especially communication and social interaction with variable learning ability. Incidence is 2 per 1000 children, approximately 76,000 in the UK. Some recent figures suggest as many as one in 86 children show signs of autism. Boys are affected four times more than girls. Autism Spectrum Disorders (ASD) cover a wide range of behaviour and learning difficulties from mild hyperactivity to severe autism. In between there are many degrees of autistic tendencies.

Autism is very topical and many theories and controversies abound. ASDs are apparently increasing. This may be partly due to increased awareness and alterations in diagnostic procedures. ASD has been linked to some ADD/ ADHD cases.

Recent exciting research has indicated that rather than a mental illness, autism may well be a metabolic disorder. Dr Paul Shattock OBE of the Autism Rearch Unit in Sunderland is a leader in this field and believes there is a gut/ brain connection. The use of a casein and gluten free diet is proving very effective in some cases. Milk contains casomorphins which are natural opiates and can exert a drug-like effect.

Media coverage has discussed injections of Secretin to affect improvement in ASD. The mechanisms by which this work appear to be very similar to Dr Shattock's opioid theory. Dr Rosemary Waring at Birmingham University has also conducted a lot of useful research.

Dr Mary Megson is studying autistic children and Vitamin A therapy. Vitamin A is thought to be malabsorbed due to intestinal damage and digestive disturbances.

One type of autism is called Asberger's Syndrome characterised by normal or above average intelligence with some autistic features such as obsessive interest in one item or hobby, difficulty with abstract thought/ concepts and excelling in one field, eg music. Speech is often normal. Diagnosis is more difficult and may not be made until the teens or adult life.

POSSIBLE CHARACTERISTICS OF ASD

Unresponsive to people and environment.
    Withdrawn and indifferent to affection.
Delayed speech or monologues.
Repetitive behaviour, eg spinning, tapping and
    kicking.
Poor social skills/few friends/plays alone.
Literal interpretation.
Special ability in one thing.
Inability to cope with change of routine.
Precise and tidy.
Disturbed sleep patterns.
Lack of eye contact.
Poor or absence of imaginative play (no pointing,
    hide and seek, building bricks).
Rocking/head banging.
Restlessness or total apathy.
Bursts of hyperactivity and aggression, eg kicking
    and biting.
Sticking up hair or red ears.
Bowel irregularities.
One of the first signs presented is often delayed
    speech at 2 years.

THEORIES AS TO ITS CAUSES

Genetic.
Pre natal exposure to aspartame.
Male with family history of alcoholism or diabetes is
    seen to be more at risk.
Toxic overload pesticides, chemicals and additives in
    foods, toxic metals and possibly vaccines for
    some. (Professor Paul Shattock feels toxic
    rather than immunological reactions are
    involved).
Organophosphates can block serotonin synthesis
    and increase IAG present in 80% of autistic
    urine.
Neurological imbalance resulting in hypersensitivity
    to environmental input, eg noise, visual
    overload. This may partly explain 'switching
    off' from people.
Sympathetic dominant nervous system is usually
    present and results in hormonal and enzymatic
    deficiencies.
Digestive enzyme abnormalities combined with
    'leaky' gut, occurring in most autistics can lead

● BENEFICIAL FOODS:
Fresh fruit and vegetables,
eg carrots, beetroot,
broccoli, parsley, swede,
sea vegetables, apricots,
bananas, papaya, cherries,
mangoes (not in candida),
tuna, sardines, salmon,
chicken, brown rice, millet,
quinoa, FOS, gluten/casein-
free cereals and breads.

AUTISM

43

Nutrients to consider

- (all need supervision of a qualified practitioner)
- Supplements need to be tasteless and able to be administered in food and drink. Autistic children are sensitive to change and will detect the slightest difference. Build up very slowly.
- Aim to improve sulphation in the liver.
- EFAs – 1g daily of fish or flax oil. Try these:
- a) Eye Q start with 2 capsules per day building up to 6 per day for 3 months: then 2 per day maintenance. Contains preferable ratios of EPA / DHA /GLA (omega 3 and 6 oils) for memory, sleep and concentration. (HS, NC, R) Alternatively Eskimo 3 has similar ratios. Give 5mls daily. (Nu)
- b) Biocare do various combinations of omegas as Dricelle powders (contains citrus).
- c) Einstein's DHA (omega 3 fish oils only) under 3 years take 1-2 daily squeezed onto food. 3-12 years 2-3 capsules daily. (HN)
- Essential Balance Junior which provides Omega 3 and 6 in natural butterscotch flavour. Can be used when Omega 3 levels are improved: $^1/_2$-3 tsps from weaning. (HN)
- Flax oil is also omega 3 but may not be as effective as fish oils. Higher doses may be needed to convert it in the body.

to brain cell destruction and misfiring of nerve impulses.

History of repeated antibiotics.

Allergies, inhalant and/or food.

A predominantly sympathetic dominance in the nervous system can result in hormonal and enzyme deficiency.

Gut infestation of yeast, parasites or bacteria can release opioid peptides. I have found several ASD children with gut infestation.

Vaccinations are probably safe for the majority but linked with genetic predisposition and other environmental factors may be the last straw for some children in terms of toxic overload. Preservatives originating from mercury in vaccines may be linked. The jury is still out on vaccination and autism.

Contact www.cdc.gov/nip/vacsafe/concerns/thinerosal.htm and refer to vaccination.

Problems with sulphation in the liver affecting detoxification and digestion (eg more affected by heavy metal toxicity due to inability to detoxify.

Low/high stomach acid leading to inadequate enzyme secretion and food allergies. Generally, low acid applies to withdrawn, children with low appetite and high acid to aggressive, hungry children.

Serotonin function may be impaired, with too much in autistics.

Abnormalities of secretin production. Secretin is needed with sulphated cholecystokinin (CCK) from intestinal secretions to release digestive enzymes from the pancreas. Secretin is not legally available in the UK. Secretin supplementation can cause severe problems in some individuals. Ainsworth do a homeopathic secretin combination. Addressing gut problems seems to act in a similar way to improve secretin production. There is, however, little research on this.

SUMMARY OF NUTRITIONAL VIEW

Incorrect stomach acid levels means that enzymes are low and certain undigested food particles can cross the damaged gut creating an opioid (drug like) effect in the brain. Neurotransmitters mis-fire and repetitive, obsessive behaviour, such as in autism, can result. Removal of the offending foods often results in the removal of the 'shroud' around the brain. Then new play/learning techniques can begin.

Nutritional therapy aims to:

advise, support and guide you through the maze of information;
identify underlying factors;
interpret and advise on tests;
recommend a balanced supplement programme
ensure a safe, balanced diet when excluding foods
support digestion;
monitor progress and adjust the programme accordingly.

GENERAL ADVICE

Auditory Integration Training (AIT) involves assessment and possibly a 10 day course of specific musical frequencies to stimulate the brain into paying attention to sounds including speech.

National Autistic's Society runs courses called 'Early Bird Programme' for parents to educate them on managing behaviour pre-school once diagnosed Tel: 0870 600 8585 for details and location of courses. Much behaviour is thought to be due to communication problems and learning to identify causes and intervene/react appropriately can reduce autistic symptoms, though not a cure. There are only 3000 places in specialist units or schools including private ones

In America, Facilitated Communication (FC) is often used. Child uses a keyboard to communicate. FC workshops are run to train parents and teachers to become FCs – Telephone – FC Institute in New York, USA – 315 443 9657

Maintain fairly strict routines to provide security.
Kneel down and make eye contact even if it is not returned.
Speak simply. Don't ramble but repeat to reinforce
Anxiety is a major underlying factor in autism
Perception of time is poor. Watches with timers and alarms may help.
Circadian rhythm can be upset by opioid reactions.

Vitamins and minerals

● Nutribalance is a good multi vitamin/mineral powder containing nutrients to heal the gut, lots of Ca / Mg some beneficial bacteria and flax oil. Best in mashed potato, cereals, dairy free yoghurt as it does not mix in liquids.(AR)

● Vitamin A may improve leaky gut, speech and eye contact. Vitamin A is also anti-viral. Dricelle Cod Liver Oil has vitamin A and EFAs or give one drop vitasorb A.(both BC)

● Buffered vitamin C to improve protein digestion. Bio-C $^1/_8$–$^1/_4$tsp daily. (AN,NC)

● B Vitamins for nervous system and anxiety. Include B6, 10mg per kilo of body weight as requirements are high; drops (BC) or Children's B complex (over 5 years). (BC)

● P5P as vitamin B6 with calcium carbonate if high stomach acid, or with ascorbic acid if low stomach acid.

● Epsom salts (magnesium sulphate) 2 cups in a warm bath for 20 minutes every 3 nights has been shown to increase sulphur in blood, do not use soap etc. Pat dry and into bed. Sulphur is needed for toxins and sulphation.

● Selenium as Trace Minerals 4 drops daily (BC) or solution x 1 ml daily (AR, NC, R) both for sulphation.

● Molybdenum as Trace Minerals 4 drops daily (BC, AR). Needed for liver function and sulphation. Extra Mo is available at one drop daily. (BC, AR)

● Magnesium for anxiety and sulphation 15mg per kilo of body weight. $^1/_2$capsule daily for 1-3 year olds then one daily or chewable lemon one daily (L) or True Food Mg 1-2 tablets daily for over 8 years (HN) or magnesium solution x $^1/_2$tsp 1-2 times daily (2.5mls). (AR, NC, R) Bio Magnesium one daily 6-12 years also contains calcium, magnesium and vitamin C. (BM)

Others

● Liv Calm contains herb Stephania Rotunda which has been shown to produce a rapid calming effect with less anxiety, improved sleep, focus comprehension, and learning ability. It appears to inhibit dopamine and serotonin in autistics. Doses need to be tailored to the individual, some are better taking one capsule 3 times per day others all at night. For children under 5 years start with $^1/_3$ of a capsule 6 hourly building up to one capsule thrice daily. May need 2 for bedtime. Needs professional supervision.

● Quercetin and vitamin C $1^1/_2$ tablets daily over 12 years (R) or Quercetin Plus vitamin C; $1^1/_2$ tablets daily for 5-12 years (R) or Quercetin Plus one daily for 50lbs body weight to reduce inflammation and histamine reactions. (BC)

● Probiotics – especially Sacromycees Boullardii if suffering with diarrhoea and to increase gut immunity. (AR, NC, R))

● Slippery Elm as Kiddy Tum (K) or Aloe Gold 1tsp daily over 5 years for digestive support.(HN)

Children may have a half to one hour difference in their daily rhythm, which builds up to a three weekly crisis. Sleep problems may be linked to this

Temper tantrums give the child an opioid 'fix' similar to morphine, which may explain repetitive behaviour like spinning; it's like an addiction, to get the good feeling.

Obtaining a diagnosis can be complicated

Exercise in a structured form can increase body awareness and balance chemicals

Educational needs assessment should be offered on diagnosis. Local authority has to 'statement' children with special needs preferably by 3-4 years of age. Independent Panel for Special Educational Advice Tel: 0800 0184016 if dissatisfied

The younger the child the more likely that the dietary intervention will succeed. Pre-schoolers usually respond best

Identify any gut infections prior to healing leaky gut

Aim to reduce toxic load on the body (may be an increased risk of toxic metals especially mercury and aluminum. Do hair test. Avoid environmental toxins, eg detergents, personal hygiene products, chemicals. Eliminate allergens

NB: some medicines contain gluten

Various educational initiatives are currently in progress including a government funded school in London called Rosemary. There are various private units such as Treehouse (pre-school) and Honormead. Contact National Autism Society

Acupuncture and yoga breathing may be helpful

Various homeopathic remedies and alternative vaccinations available from a qualified homeopath. It can also clear residual antibiotics and vaccinations from the system.

Australian Bush Fuchsia may help focus. See Appendix

AUTISM

Remember autism is just a label. Your child is individual. He is just as special as any other child is. Look at the child not the label. He could amaze you with his knowledge. For a moving biographical read *Child of Eternity* by Adriana Rocha and Kristi Jorde

TESTS TO CONSIDER

There are many useful tests and Dr Goldbergs who works with ASD in California recommends a huge list of tests prior to consultation. Here are some of my most commonly used tests.

These four will need a practitioner to refer, interpret and act upon:

Digestive and infection test – stool;

Intestinal permeability/leaky gut – urine;

Hair analysis for toxic metals and mineral levels – hair;

Organic Acids Urine Test – urine;

Standard Liver Detoxification Profile – urine and saliva;

These two can be arranged by parent/patient:

Polypepide Urine Test (via ARU) – urine;

Kinesiology – muscle testing (for allergies);

Blood tests via GP for iron, serum ferritin, zinc and magnesium.

Contacts:
Buteyko Breathing Centre Tel 0116 2772051
Hanen System owns *More than Words* for ASD children –
Tel: 0141 946 5433 www.honormead-school.co.uk
See appendix. ■.

- Appropriate supervised treatments if positive tests for gut infections.
- TMG / DMG often advised by specialists.
- Thiodox can support liver detoxification often faulty in autism. One per day 50-60 lbs body weight. (AR)
- Milk thistle $1/2$ tablet crushed daily for liver support (BM) or Liv Detox Support one daily over 4 years. (BR, R)
- Sulphur as MSM to increase CCK and digestive enzymes. (HN)
- Digestive enzymes. (See appendix)

BACTERIAL INFECTION

SEE ALSO: BRONCHITIS, ANTIBIOTICS, IMMUNE
FUNCTION, COLDS, COUGHS, CONJCTIVITIS, OTITIS
MEDIA, DIGESTIVE PROBLEMS, GASTRO-ENTERITIS,
TONSILITIS

Bacteria can live independently of the body, eg in soil or foods. Generally bacterial infections are common in the upper respiratory tract (URT) of young children. Boils, meningitis and tetanus are bacterial. They also occur in gastro-intestinal tract. Gastro-enteritis is an acute potentially serious condition. Dehydration can occur quickly especially in very young children and if diarrhoea and vomiting are present.

Avoidance of antibiotics is preferable but always seek medical advice if in doubt.

GENERAL ADVICE

The body withholds iron when bacteria are present as they feed on it. Do not give iron supplements during any acute stages.

Boost immune system.

Following antibiotics always give probiotics. ■

Dietary advice

- Increase Vitamin C and zinc foods.

- Cabbage contains glucosinolates thought to be anti-bacterial.

- Leeks, garlic and onions contain allicin which is antibiotic. Garlic can be given crushed raw in honey.

Nutrients to consider

- For immunity:

- Vitamin C: Immune C one daily over 8 years (HN) or Bio C $^1/_8$ tsp over 4 years which includes minerals or Mg Ascorbate $^1/_4$gm. (BC,L)

- Children's B Complex one daily (over 5 years). (BC)

- Zinc 10 drops daily (BC) or $^1/_2$level measure under tongue of sherbet powder alternate days for over 8 years alternate days. (HN)

- Echinacea: E-Kid-Nacea 2-4 years $^1/_8$-$^1/_2$tsp or E-Kid-Nacea Plus over 4 years. This one is esp good for catarrh. (K)

- Super Gar one daily from 8 years. (HN)

- Probiotics.

- Oralmat can increase lung function and decrease allergic responses (HS) whilst boosting immune function. Oralmat is rye grass extract which contains tryptophan and zinc to strengthen immune system and magnesium to relax muscles. It may also have a desensitising effect. 1 drop under tongue thrice daily held for 15 seconds and then swallowed. (HS)

BED-WETTING

SEE ALSO: SOILING, ANXIETY, CANDIDA, UTI, FOOD INTOLERANCES, SOILING, DIABETES, CONSTIPATION, ALLERGIES

The medical name is eneuresis. There are two types of eneuresis. 30% caused by a weak bladder which may be helped medically or by bladder training. 70% caused by an imbalance of the hormone vasopressin which results in excess nocturnal production of urine. Usually treated with synthetic hormone, but often recurs when drug stopped. New hormonal medication, Minirin, which reduce urinary output at night is now available as tablets on prescription from spring 2002 and work on a wafer for children is underway. Of course it is not addressing the causes and relapse may occur on cessation of the drug.

Alarm systems may help by conditioning the child.

Age of bladder control varies, with night control later than daytime and boys slower than girls. Normally attained by 4 years but this varies a lot. If control is gained and then lost or still not gained by 5 years seek medical advice. Approximate incidence: 30% at 4 years, 20% at 6 years, 3% at puberty and 1% in adulthood.

FACTORS TO CONSIDER
Genetics; recent research indicates one of two genes is involved in 50% of cases.
Emotional problems (anxiety).
Urinary infections.
Yeast overgrowth (candidiasis/thrush).
Constipation.
Food intolerances/ allergies.
Diabetes.
If any of these factors are suspected refer to relevant section.

GENERAL ADVICE
GP can refer for alarm system to condition the child to wake when urination commences. Often long waiting lists. Speak to your health visitor or GP.
Alarm systems can create more stress if family already under pressure.
Snoozy Night Time Training Pad £16.99 + £2.95

B

Dietary advice
- Reduce animal protein.
- Identify food allergies/ intolerances. Suspect yeast, wheat, dairy and sugar.
- Filter water (fluoride can aggravate incontinence)
- Increase potassium rich foods.
- Acidify urine and reduce chance of infections with cranberry juice.
- Avoid all 'junk' foods, additives, sugar and fizzy drinks encouraging whole, natural foods.
- BENEFICIAL FOODS: Cranberries, bananas, melons, vegetables, potatoes, tomatoes.

Nutrients to consider

- Probiotics.
- MVM to contain 10mgs zinc.
- Vitamin E 100ius for 6-12 year olds. one drop vitasorb or one capsule (BC) or vitamin E cream for absorption through the skin. (L, X)
- Calcium and magnesium for muscle control and anxiety 500mgs Ca / 250mgs Mg for 6-12 year olds or chewable Ca and Mg (L) or Ca/Mg. (S)
- Potassium 100mgs for over 12 years (BC) to alkalise the system.
- Ca phosphate and Mg phosphate celloid one daily. (BM)
- Sodium phosphate and sodium sulphate to lower acidity of urine and kidneys. (BM)
- St Johns Wort found to be effective over 12 years under supervision.
- Vitamins B2 and B5 with magnesium have been found to help children. As a children's complex or drops. (BC)

p&p, for Fledglings Tel: 0845 458 1125. Also have waterproof duvets and pillows.

Homeopathy (eg causticum 6 c and equisetum 6 c), herbs, acupuncture and hypnotherapy have helped some cases.

Daytime wetting can also be extended into school years and beyond. Some children with special needs may never attain continence.

'Lifting' your child in his sleep may discourage him from responding to bladder signals and prevent the bladder from developing and stretching.

Daytime toileting should occur about 6 times in a 4 year old. Any less often may indicate inadequate emptying. Any more could mean infection or 'irritable' bladder. See GP.

Your child cannot control this. It is not wilful. Eneuresis can be helped.

Contacts:
Eneuresis Resource and Information Centre (ERIC) Helpline Tel: 0117 090 3060. They produce a booklet and leaflets and sell aids and equipment including alarms. ▨

BEREAVEMENT

SEE ALSO: ANXIETY, STRESS, DEPRESSION, IMMUNE SYSTEM

This may be from the death of a family member, pet or friend but could also be experienced when families break up as in separation and divorce. Children are the innocent by-standers and may feel guilt, confusion, fear, anxiety or despair. ▓

B

Dietary advice

● Do not force food, but offer small healthy snacks frequently.

● Avoid sugar, chocolate and cola as these are stimulants which stress the adrenal glands.

● Support immune system as stress lowers its function.

● BENEFICIAL FOODS: Eggs, cottage cheese, salad, jacket potatoes, wholegrains, pasta, yoghurts, fruit and fish.

Nutrients to consider

● Calcium and magnesium for anxiety, tension and insomnia. Chewable Ca/Mg over 4 years (L) or capsules (S, HN) or solution $^1/_2$tsp 1-2 times daily. (AR, NC, R)

● For 5-12 years give children's B Complex for the nervous system take one daily. (BC)

● Bach Flower Remedies; Rescue Remedy contains Star of Bethlehem for shock and grief. Sweet chestnut, gorse, agrimony may also help. (HS)

● Red Suva Frangipani is an Australian Bush Flower Remedy from Ancient Roots for grief and despair.

● Homeopathic ignatia for grief. (A, HS)

BITES AND STINGS

SEE ALSO: ANIMALS, ALLERGIES

B

● Prior to a holiday or walk especially near water avoid banana, nuts, avocadoes, chicken, potatoes, fish, cottage cheese, as they are serotonin foods which attract insects.

● Avoid sugar.

● Garlic when eaten regularly is excreted through the skin deterring insects.

Nutrients to consider

● Vitamin C is anti-histamine to reduce allergic reactions – Immune C 1 daily over 8 years (HN), or Bio C $^1/_8$tsp over 4 years which includes minerals or Mg Ascor-bate $^1/_4$gm. (BC, L)

● Neem oil deters mosquitoes. Bioforce produce a range of products including oil, shampoo, cream.

● Tea tree oil deters and cleanses bites. (HS)

● Super Gar over 8 years one daily. (HN)

● B vitamins especially B1 when excreted through skin can deter insects. Always take a vitamin B complex with individual B vitamins (over 5 years). 10 drops or children's complex. (BC)

● Aloe gel soothes and reduces inflammation. (HN)

● Alfresco anti-insect moisturiser is herbal. Tel: 020 8348 6704

● Quassia shampoo (N) (over 3 years) contains tea tree, lavender and quassia for nits, lice and fleas.

Young children commonly go through a phase of biting each other or adults. Unless the skin is broken this is not a health risk although it may become a behavioural and social issue. **Animal bites** especially dogs, cats and rabbits can be a problem as a secondary infection is common. Clean the wound well with a solution of tea tree oil. Seek urgent advice if rabies is a risk.

Insect bites and stings are less likely to cause severe reactions in children than in those over 40 years old.

Bees leave their sting in. Remove with fingernail not tweezers to avoid squeezing the poison into the skin.

Tics require great care and speed when removing as legs and mouthpiece can remain in the skin and cause infection. Apply tea tree oil or surgical spirit initially to kill it before removing with tweezers as close to the skin as possible. Vaseline can immobilise. NB: tics can carry Lyme disease, a serious illness.

Mosquitoes are a serious problem in some countries. Avoid sugar for a week prior to and during a stay in affected regions to deter them. Use Neem oil or vinegar.

Fleas are common in small children, who play on the floor, as they live in carpets. Make sure all pets are treated regularly with non-toxic repellents. Pennyroyal repels fleas but do not use if pregnant.

Ant bites can be treated with vinegar or baking soda paste.

GENERAL ADVICE

Lemon oil in a burner or citronella.

Rescue Remedy Cream. (HS, Ch)

Mosiguard is a natural non-toxic insect repellant. (Ch)

Ainsworths homeopathic pharmacy sell a travel kit.

Homeopathic aconite immediately for shock. (HS, Ch)

Antihistamine creams are readily available.

Calendula cream is a deterrent and soother. (N)

Apply baking soda and water to ant or mosquito bites after washing the area with soap and water.

Calamine lotion is still a good remedy.

Citronella oil is a natural insect repellant.

A raw slice of onion or potato to wasp stings.

Honey with one drop of peppermint oil can ease pain.

Toothpaste seems to help!

Many aromatherapy oils deter insects. (A)

Protect the house from insects by sprinkling vanilla water, dried tomato leaves, talc, garlic or eucalyptus powder around doors, cracks and windows. ▪

BLOATING

SEE ALSO: CANDIDA, CONSTIPATION, FOOD INTOLERANCES, FLATULENCE, LEAKY GUT, IBS, TUMMY ACHE, DIGESTIVE PROBLEMS, COLIC, ANXIETY

Bloating is a symptom not a condition. Children may find this difficult to describe. It may manifest itself as wind, tummy ache, constipation or lack of appetite. Although there are various medical conditions that have this symptom some simple actions can often relieve it, but always see a GP if it persists. Refer to other sections. Some bloating is emotionally linked as digestion is suppressed by anxiety.

GENERAL ADVICE

Encourage regular bowel habits.

Exercise like cycling or swimming helps relieve trapped wind.

If persistent see a qualified practitioner to address the following:

Identify and eliminate the cause;

Support digestion;

Replace beneficial bacteria;

Heal the gut lining.

B

Dietary advice

- Keep foods light and easy.
- Avoid and reduce yeast, sugar, pulses, cabbage family, fizzy drinks and salt which increases water retention.
- Reduce wheat – try rice bread, oatcakes, ricecakes rye and wheatfree cereals and pasta.
- Soluble fibre from oats and vegetables rather than wheat bran.
- Reduce dairy products.
- If lactose intolerance is suspected use alternative milks or enzymes. (BC)
- Lightly cooked / steamed vegetables may be better tolerated than raw.
- BENEFICIAL FOODS: Oats, fruit and vegetables, soya, rice, oat milk, sheep/goats' milk, small amounts of live yoghurt.

Nutrients to consider

- Probiotics.
- FOS on cereals, yoghurt or fruit as a prebiotic. Start slowly with $1/2$– 1tsp to encourage the growth of beneficial bacteria in the gut.
- Windy Pops is a herbal tincture safe from birth. (K)
- Kiddy Tum from 2 years. (K)
- Digestive enzymes. (see Appendix)

BLOOD SUGAR IMBALANCES (BSI)

SEE ALSO: DIABETES, EATING DISORDERS, OBESITY, ANXIETY, FATIGUE

Low = hypoglycaemia
High = hyperglycaemia (eg Diabetes)

Blood sugar imbalances are common in many people and children are no exception. Who hasn't brought an irritable child home from school, given a snack and had a transformation! Smaller tummies need smaller, more frequent meals. Certain conditions often have BSI as a factor so if these recommendations don't work seek medical advice. Occasionally may indicate candida, diabetes, immune deficiency and kidney problems.

Symptoms include: hyperactivity, insomnia, irritability, aggression, fatigue, poor concentration, learning difficulties, cravings for sweet foods, trembling, erratic behaviour, dizziness and fainting.

GENERAL ADVICE

Brain function depends on a constant flow of glucose so poor memory, concentration and learning may be linked to BSI.

BSI can lead to diabetes later in life if not addressed. The age of non-insulin dependent diabetes is lowering all the time with more children suffering.

Spirolight bars make a useful energy snack. (X) ▪

Dietary advice

● Encourage small meals 3 hourly.

● Have protein with every meal/ snack esp. for lunch, eg tuna or egg sandwich with a seed bar.

● Always encourage breakfast. For teenagers a piece of fruit with nuts on the way to school.

● Identify any allergies/ intolerances as these create cravings. Milk is sometimes linked.

● Increase complex carbohydrates. These help to sustain glucose in the blood as the fibre slows down the rise in glucose levels.

● Reduce sugar and white flour because these cause a sudden rise in glucose levels in the blood and a subsequent drop.

● The beneficial foods encourage the liver to release glucagon to raise glucose levels. BSIs are often caused by too many refined foods, which triggers insulin too often.

● BENEFICIAL FOODS: Beans, pulses, vegetables, carrot, wholegrains, brown rice, cereals, houmous, yoghurt, almonds.

Nutrients to consider

● Chromium one drop daily (BC) or Bio-Chromium one daily for over 8 years contains Mg, Zn, Mn and B 3. (BM)

● B complex with B3; drops or one capsule daily for 5-12 years. (BC)

● Magnesium: Bio Mg $^1/_2$capsule daily 1-3 years or one chewable daily (L) or one capsule daily over 3 years (BC) or solution $^1/_2$tsp 1-2 daily. (AR, NC, R)

● Bio magnesium (BM) contains calcium, B6 and minerals as well. One per day 6-12 years.

● Vitamin E 100ius as one drop or capsule. (BC)

● Magnesium phosphate. (BM)

● L Glutamine $^1/_4$tsp or 1-2 capsules over 8 years before meals 1-3 per day or on cold food. (HN)

Body Odour

SEE ALSO: CANDIDA, INDIGESTION, HALITOSIS

Rarely occurs in young children, but from puberty, hormonal changes increase perspiration and teenagers need to be more aware. Smelly feet are common in teenagers esp. boys.

FACTORS TO CONSIDER

Toxicity in the rest of the body.

Check for other signs such as constipation, fatigue and headaches.

Poor fluid intake concentrates toxins and low fibre slows their excretion.

Constipation means toxins are eliminated through the skin.

May indicate yeast overgrowth.

GENERAL ADVICE

Use natural deodorants as many others contain chemicals such as Aluminium, eg Pitrok, is a crystal. (HS or try Green People)

Bathe feet in tea tree solution or bicarbonate of soda. ■

B

Dietary advice

● Detox diets are not recommended for children but older teenagers can clean up their diet under supervision. All children will benefit from fewer processed foods, including sugar.

● Avoid yeast, marmite and too much fruit and sugar to reduce fermentation in the digestive tract.

● Increase fibre to speed elimination (add one tsp cracked golden linseeds to yoghurt or soup).

● Increase water to 5 – 6 glasses per day.

● Support digestion with pineapple or papaya.

● BENEFICIAL FOODS: Linseeds, vegetable juices, raspberries, pineapple, papaya, flax oil, live yoghurt.

Nutrients to consider

● Doses for over 12 years as not usually a problem under 12 years.

● Silica reduces body odour 2 daily. (L)

● Zinc as deficiency increases perspiration. Zinc citrate 15mgs (L) or 25 mgs. (AR)

● Probiotics, eg Acidophilus Extra one daily. (L)

● Flax Oil, linseed capsules (BC) or flaxseed oil as salad dressings or in shakes. (HN)

BODY ODOUR

BOILS

SEE ALSO:
IMMUNE FUNCTION

Blocked hair follicles create boils which are pus (staphylococcus aureus) filled lumps. Frequent boils may, rarely, indicate underlying conditions so seek medical advice if recurrent or larger than a 2p piece (carbuncle or collection of boils).

The most common sites are the face, buttocks and scalp.

FACTORS TO CONSIDER
Depressed immunity .
Poor diet.
Infected acne.
Rarely diabetes, anaemia and kidney disorder may be involved.

GENERAL ADVICE
Warm epsom salt baths or 2 tsp in $1/2$pt hot water, applied directly.

Avoid over the counter antibiotic creams as most are ineffective on boils.

Warm compress using a new, sterile gauze pad each time to encourage release of pus.

Never syringe or prick. ■

Dietary advice
● See Immune function.

● Increase betacarotene, vitamin C and zinc foods.

● Reduce saturated fats, red meat, cheese, chocolate and 'fast' food.

● Avoid biscuits, cakes and crisps.

● Freshly juiced fruit to drink for antioxidants.

● Increase water intake 5-6 glasses daily minimum.

● BENEFICIAL FOODS: Live yoghurt, non-citrus orange coloured fruit, eg apricots, mangos, vegetables especially orange coloured, eg carrots, water, garlic, onions.

Nutrients to consider
● Silica – two daily. (L)

● Vitamin C; Bio-C $1/4$tsp daily (AN) or chewable 100mgs 4-8 years (L) or capsule. (BC)

● Zinc citrate 15mgs (L) or sherbet powder under tongue $1/2$measure alternate days over 8 years (HN) or 10 vitasorb drops. (BC)

● Vitamin A x one drop daily. (BC)

● Super Gar one daily over 8 years. (HN)

● E- Kid –Nacea Plus over 4 years. (K)

● Potassium chloride and iron phosphate for infection. (BM)

Topicals
● Tea tree oil.

● Colloidal silver. (HN, HS, NC)

● Apply honey.

Nutrients to consider – Bronchitis
● Vitamin C as drops or Mg ascorbate powder $1/4$– $1/2$gm (BC) or chewable C over 4 years. (L)

● Super Gar over 8 years one daily. (HN)

● Zinc lozenges for older children (L) or drops. (BC)

● Echinacea and Black Elderberry with Olive leaf extract 1-2 capsules over 5 years daily betw- een meals. (HN)

● Elderberry extract – Sambucol one tsp or capsule daily. (HN)

● Colloidal silver is natures antibiotic and promotes healing. (HN, AR)

● E-Kid-Nacea over 2 years or E-Kid-Nacea Plus over 4 years. The latter is esp good for catarrh.

● Vitamin E is an antioxidant which may protect against bronchitis; drops for 0-4 years (BC) or capsules. (L)

● Kiddy Tum contains slippery Elm and ginger, good for mucous membranes in the lungs. (K)

● Bromelain 100mgs per day is anti-inflammatory. (NO)

BRONCHITIS/BRONCHIOLITIS

SEE ALSO: FEVER, ASTHMA, IMMUNE FUNCTION

B

Bronchitis is inflammation of the bronchus and larger airways and is usually a complication of a viral or bacterial infection such as a cold or sore throat. Bronchiolitis is an inflammation of the bronchioles, the tiny airways and is often a bacterial or viral complication and affects babies and toddlers. Usually lasts 3-4 days. It may, if severe or unrecognised trigger an asthma attack in asthma sufferers due to bronchiole spasm.

Always seek medical help especially in tiny children as asphyxia can occur. If the child's lips are blue, call an ambulance, otherwise see a GP. Bronchial dilators are usually given to open the airways. Some children are given antibiotics, but viral infections will not respond to these.

Do not suppress coughing with cough medicines, as expectorating the phlegm is important. If recurrent attacks occur, identifying the triggers is useful (see asthma). For some children, food may be a factor.

GENERAL ADVICE

Inhalation of olbas oil in a bowl of steaming water.
NB: Always supervise and never use for small children due to risk of scalding.

Room burner with eucalyptus oil or add a drop to a tissue and put under the pillow (not babies).

Rest in the acute phase can speed recovery.

If antibiotics are prescribed, give acidophilus for 6 weeks when the course is finished to re-establish the healthy bacteria and immunity in the gut.

A humidifier can be helpful, but the same effect can be had from boiling kettles and running hot taps prior to taking the child into a room.

Sitting in a warm bath can relieve the spasms but if fever is present do not raise temperature further.

Tiger Balm to chest may relieve congestion. (HS)

Swimming when recovered improves lung function as can the blowing up of a balloon daily (older children only).

There are various herbs (which include mullein and thyme) that have a direct effect on the airways. Consult a qualified herbalist and see Appendix.■

Dietary advice

● In acute phase give plenty of fluids and liquid foods which are easy to digest.

● Food intolerances may exacerbate problems, eg cows' milk products and red meat which are mucous forming as well as inflammatory.

● To prevent attacks and boost immunity reduce dairy and refined foods, eg biscuits and cakes.

● Lemon juice, honey and root ginger in warm water can relieve congestion.

● Avoid sugar.

● Increase vitamin A foods.

● Pineapple juice or the fresh fruit in older children for bromelain which can improve lung function.

● Fresh vegetables best for bioflavonoids, but frozen a good second choice.

● Juicing fresh fruit and vegetables is an easier way to give the high requirements. Can be drunk as juices or in shakes.

● Fresh raw garlic in honey over one year.

● Strawberries contain ellagic acid which can protect lung membranes. Also present in raspberries and grapes.

● BENEFICIAL FOODS: Sweet potatoes, regular fish, lemon juice, honey (over one year), root ginger, pineapple, vegetables (minimum 7 portions each per week), avocados, leafy green vegetables, onions, garlic, chicken soup, strawberries, raspberries, grapes.

BRONCHITIS

BRUISING

SEE ALSO: HENOCH'S PURPURA

This is normal leaking of blood from the capillaries into the tissues on injury. Some children bruise very easily and this can be due to vitamin C deficiency, anaemia or incorrect body weight. If regular, unexplained bruising occurs seek medical advice as in rare cases it can be linked to leukeumia, HSP or haemophilia.

GENERAL ADVICE:
Check for iron deficiency or anaemia if persistent.
Avoid painkillers and steroids if possible.
Apply pineapple slice directly to bruise or orange or witch hazel to a black eye. ▪

Dietary advice

- Make sure all food is nutrient dense; no empty calories.
- Avoid processed foods
- Cook fruit and vegetables very lightly or eat raw to conserve vitamin C and fibres.
- Include vitamin C bioflavonoid and iron rich foods
- Increase vitamin K foods to assist blood clotting and healing.
- BENEFICIAL FOODS: Kiwi, cherries, citrus fruits, pineapple, strawberries, grapes, papaya, dark green leafy vegetables, peppers, broccoli, buckwheat, alfalfa sprouts.

Nutrients to consider

- Vitamin C drops 0-4 years; chewable 100mgs (L); Bio-C $^1/_4$tsp. (AN)
- Bromelain (500mg daily until bruise has gone). (S, NO)
- Homeopathic arnica cream.(HS, Ch)
- Witch hazel topically.

BULIMIA NERVOSA

SEE ALSO: EATING DISORDERS, ANOREXIA NERVOSA, BLOOD SUGAR, FOOD INTOLERANCES, DEPRESSION, ADDICTIONS, BSI

B

Bulimia Nervosa rarely involves significant weight loss and is often described as a lack of control over behaviour (compulsive behaviour). May be associated with self-harming, it is a compulsive cycle of bingeing and purging which may include laxative or diuretic abuse, excessive exercise and/or self-induced vomiting. The relief felt on purging may be partly guilt and partly removal of the opioid effect of allergens. Some sufferers eat 4000-10,000 calories daily!

This should be treated as an addiction with emphasis on identifying trigger foods and potential allergens and balancing blood sugar levels.

SIGNS AND SYMPTOMS OF BULIMIA

Secretive behaviour, normal or over weight with fluctuations, sore knuckles, sore lips, mouth ulcers and swollen glands from induced vomiting, poor dental health, hair loss, fainting, halitosis, depression, obsessive exercise, frequent visits to the bathroom, disappearance of food. SAD may be factor linked to serotonin levels. Mimics hibernation and food storage with obsessive interest in food and its attainment, inability to voluntarily stop eating.

Complications (some also apply to anorexia) include dehydration, cardiac irregularites, gastro-intestinal and metabolic disorders, dysbiosis due to purging, potassium deficiency due to purging, diarrhoea, dehydration which can affect heart function and fainting.

Longer term problems include infertility, liver malfunction, serotonin levels affect mood, but there may be other brain chemical imbalances such as dopamine, nor-epinephrine and endogenous opioids. The latter reinforces addictive behaviour. Depression may be result of starvation rather than its effect.

GENERAL ADVICE

Improving nutrition may help both body weight and mood. Very important to combine psychological support with
    nutritional therapy to effect the best recovery by
    addressing underlying issues with food and self-esteem.
Try to instigate healthy eating habits with food from a very
    young age without putting undue emphasis on it.
Don't diet!
Use any additional support available, eg college and school.
Do not comment on weight, but concentrate on appearance in
    general, effort in life and achievement. ■

Dietary Advice

● Minimal emphasis on food, but encourage natural wholefoods with plenty of nutrients.

● Balance blood sugar. (see BSI)

● Identify foods eaten frequently as these may be intolerances increasing cravings usually for carbohydrates.

Nutrients to consider

● MVM.

● Chromium. 1 drop daily. (BC)

● Zinc regulates appetite and taste. 10 drops or 15mg capsule BC or sherbet flavoured powder. $^1/_2$level measure under tongue alternate days over 8 years. (HN)

● Probiotics – see Eating Disorders for more details.

BURNS

SEE ALSO: SUNBURN

Dietary advice

- Avoid sugar and processed foods which are lacking in nutrients and slow healing
- Increase protein to speed repair of skin.
- Increase EFAs for skin health
- Vitamin C foods for healing
- Increase carotenoids for healing and prevention of scarring
- Lots of potassium foods to replace losses from fluid leakage
- Increase fluids especially water
- BENEFICIAL FOODS: Lentils, fish, chicken, eggs, wheatgerm, avocado, melon, carrots, apricots, sweet potatoes, green leafy vegetables.

Nutrients to consider

- (to support healing and repair)
- Zinc 10 drops daily (BC) or $1/2$ level measure under tongue of sherbet powder alternate days over 8 years. (HN)
- Vitamin C and bioflavonoids; Bio-C $1/8$ tsp over 4 years (AN, NC, R) or children's C one daily. (BC)
- Vitamin A, 1 drop daily. (BC)
- Children's B complex one daily over 5 years. (BC)
- Extra vitamin B3 in older children as drops. (BC)
- Vitamin E 100ius drops or capsule (BC). Vitamin E cream applied to burn can speed healing. (L)
- MSM is an anti inflammatory and aids the healing of wounds.(HN)

Burns commonly occur from, acids, solvents, chemicals, fire, sun and candlewax. If more than 10% of the body surface is affected, shock may occur. Signs of shock include pallor, sweating, cold clammy skin, shallow breathing. Action: lie child down, raise legs, cover and dial 999. Electrical burns should be medically supervised.

If the burns are large or deep get urgent medical assistance.

If minor immerse in cold running water for 10 minutes. Cover with a dry, clean dressing or cling film after choosing from the following:
Colloidal silver – nature's antibiotic;
Calendula cream;
Tea tree oil;
MSM cream; (HN)
Rescue Remedy cream from chemists;
Aloe Vera gel; (HN)
Honey is antiseptic, healing and soothing.

GENERAL ADVICE
Identify the risk and remove it.
Apply raw honey to minor burns appears to improve healing by absorbing moisture and preventing bacterial infection.
Bach Flower Rescue Remedy tincture for shock. (HS, Ch)
Homeopathic aconite for shock.
Lavender oil is cleansing and calming. Use as an inhalant or diluted with tea tree to cleanse wound. (N, HS)

CANCER

(protection and prevention)

SEE ALSO: TOXICITY, IMMUNE FUNCTION

Treatment of cancer by anyone other than a medical practitioner is illegal in the UK, but there are nutritional strategies to support chemotherapy and radiotherapy, replace nutrient deficiencies and reduce the risk of recurrence. Prevention is better than cure. Intestinal cancer may take 20 years to develop. There are simple dietary and lifestyle guidelines to reduce the risk.

Children most commonly get leukaemia (blood cancer) or lymphoma (cancer of the lymphatic system, eg non-Hodgkin's and Hodgkin's disease). Symptoms of leukaemia may include easy bruising, pale skin, fever, pain in limbs and joints, fatigue, gum bleeding, recurrent infections. Sarcomas (cancer of the bones, muscles and connective tissues) and carcinoma (cancer of the organs, skin, glands and mucous membranes) are less common in children.

Environmental factors including diet are believed to be important factors in the development of cancer. It therefore seems logical that addressing these should help to prevent and maybe alleviate its effects of free radicals ('rogue' cells) which may lead to cancer and immune impairment. The disease process involved in cancer has a marked nutritional effect including deficiencies, weight loss and anorexia and nutritional therapy may have a re-balancing and supportive role as well as preventative.

GENERAL ADVICE

Boost immune function

Children have high fat requirements for energy and growth. Do not put them on low fat regimes. However reducing saturated fats in favour of essential fatty acids is beneficial, eg fish instead of red meat; seeds instead of cheese.

Maintain correct weight as obesity increases the risk of cancer.

Regular exercise.

Beware of radiation from TVs, microwaves, x-rays and overhead and underground cables.

Identify potential carcinogens in the home – see *Safe Shoppers Bible*.

Dietary advice

- Eat organic to avoid potentially carcinogenic chemicals.
- Increase soluble fibre from fruits, vegetables and oats.
- Increase antioxidants, (especially beta-carotene and vitamin A foods which contain lycopene) which are mainly brightly coloured fruit and vegetables to protect cells from damage by free radicals .
- Increase vitamin C, potassium, zinc and selenium foods.
- Reduce saturated fats, eg dairy products, processed foods, meat, increase EFAs, eg fish, seeds, vegetables.
- Encourage red blood cell formation, especially important in leukaemia, by increasing vitamin A, potassium and selenium foods.
- Avoid burnt or barbecued foods as these create free radicals which damage cells.
- Excess caffeine can be toxic.
- Avoid sugar because it is an anti-nutrient.
- Avoid refined processed, smoked and salty foods.
- Juicing fresh fruit and vegetables is a good way to increase intake of relevant nutrients, as they are concentrated in their natural state.

CANCER

61

Breast fed infants appear to have a reduced risk of leukaemia.

Research is linking deficiencies of vitamin A and E, niacin (B3), calcium, iodine, phyto-oestrogens to cancer.

Children will enjoy sprouting their own seeds which contain minerals, protein and enzymes and are antioxidants protecting cells.

Avoid suspect carcinogens, eg food additives, chemicals such as pesticides, preservatives, fried or burned food, cigarette smoke, radiation including excess sun and fire retardants.

In rare cases bleeding gums can be a sign of leukaemia if accompanied by bruising, fatigue and pallor.

Lymphomas have been linked in some cases to mercury dental fillings, petro-chemicals and herbicide exposure.

Childhood leukaemia shown to be linked with parental smoking.

Malnutrition due to excessive refined foods is thought to be a contributory cause in some children.

Over-fluoridation of water may be a factor.

Acupuncture on wrist pressure points may relieve nausea from chemotherapy. Also ginger is helpful as capsules or in food. Try Kiddy Tum or Kid Chamomile for over 2 years. (K)

Lycopene (in tomatoes) is a very beneficial antioxidant. Oddly, it is better absorbed in cooked tomatoes which is just as well for most children! Organic tomato ketchup and puree can be useful. ■

Candida

SEE ALSO: IMMUNE FUNCTION, DIGESTIVE PROBLEMS,
FOOD INTOLERANCES, ANTIBIOTICS, GROWTH, PARASITES,
THRUSH, BLOATING, CRADLE CAP, UTI, LEAKY GUT,
FLATULENCE

Candidiasis refers to overgrowth of yeast in the mouth, vagina and intestines. Normally small amounts of yeast exist in the gut, but reduced levels of beneficial bacteria (flora) can allow yeast to multiply and convert to a fungal form, which can then cause damage and ill health. Some babies are born with the problem, having been infected during vaginal delivery.

FACTORS TO CONSIDER

The following may lead to an imbalance of gut flora:

Antibiotics;
Contraceptive pill in teenagers;
Food intolerances;
Stress/anxiety;
Refined, processed diet;
Steroid inhalers for asthma/hayfever;
Maternal candida in pregnancy/delivery;
Parasite or bacterial infections in gut;
Lowered immunity;
Incorrect weaning.

Symptoms in babies include recurrent cradle cap, oral thrush (white coated tongue and mouth), unresponsive nappy rash, vomiting and regurgitation, slow weight gain/failure to thrive, colic and irritability, diarrhoea or constipation.

Symptoms in children include poor concentration, recurrent ear infection, headaches, constant colds and infections, blocked nose/snoring, eczema/dermatitis, acne, digestive problems, food intolerances, bowel disturbances, cravings for cheese, bread or sugar, appetite disturbance, urine infections, diarrhoea or constipation, fatigue, hyperactivity, athletes foot, anal itching.

Other conditions which may be associated – leaky gut, autism, hyperactivity, eczema, asthma, obesity. Candida can increase the chances of other gut infections due to dysbiosis.

The aims of nutritional treatment are to identify the causes, starve the candida, boost immunity,

Dietary advice

- Always see a qualified practitioner as diet and supplements are extensive.
- The adult anti-candida diet is very strict and not suitable for young children. However a modified version is often effective.
- Avoid all yeast, sugar, MSG or refined foods. This is a small sentence with big implications! It means very few pre-packaged foods as most have sugar or yeast in them. Refined foods like white flour, rice or pasta converts into sugar rapidly. Sugar includes molasses, honey and malted products like Weetabix.
- Can use FOS powder as a sweetener; has the benefit of being a prebiotic.
- Cows' milk products are often not recommended due to milk sugars. If possible reduce or exclude replacing with soya, oat or rice milks, temporarily.
- Reduce saturated fats as they are converted to sugars. Children need fat for energy and growth so it is important to increase the healthy fats from nuts (over 3 years), seeds, green leafy vegetables, oily fish and flax oil. If your child will not eat these foods, supplementation may be necessary.
- No ham, bacon or smoked foods as they are cured – this means no sausages!
- No mushrooms, marmite, peanut butter or tomato ketchup.
- Initially (in the first month) no fruit due to fructose (fruit sugar) and later 1 or 2 per day carefully selected. Avoid melon, grapes, mango.

- Avoid malted products (have sugar compounds), eg Wheetabix, granary bread.
- Avoid dried fruit unless soaked first.
- Fruit juices are high in sugar and can carry mould if not organic and fresh.
- Dairy exclusion is preferable (cheese is fermented). Yoghurt and cottage cheese are allowed and have probiotic qualities.
- Increase fibre to assist detox and balance blood sugar.
- Increase iron, zinc and vitamin C foods.
- Add seed oils to cereals, cooked vegetables, rice or pasta and as salad dressings.

- BENEFICIAL FOODS: Olive, walnuts, sesame, flax seed, pumpkin/ sunflower seeds as oils or seeds, coconut is anti-fungal, organic meat and fish, wholemeal flour/ pasta (not white), brown rice, amaranth, millet, buckwheat (which are all grains), coriander, soda bread, original rye crispbreads, oatcakes, ricecakes, fresh vegetables and salad, onions, leeks and garlic (anti-fungal), jacket potatoes, kiwi/ pineapple after the first month, carrot and celery sticks, cherry tomatoes, live plain yoghurt – add coconut or organic berries, avocadoes, pulses and lentils.

address any nutrient deficiencies, identify food intolerances (which may be a cause or an effect of candida), eradicate remaining candida with specific supplementation, replace beneficial flora and heal intestinal lining (leaky gut).

Also stool testing for candida, yeast and parasites and levels of beneficial bacteria and treatment suggestions can be done via a nutritionist but is expensive.

GENERAL ADVICE

Wash all fruit and vegetables in citricidal as anti-fungal. Can also be used to clean toothbrushes and feeder cups. (HN)

Make pizza base from wholemeal flour, baking powder and egg (like a scone mix) to avoid yeast.

Prewitts make sesame biscuits which are sugar free. (HS)

Freshly squeeze vegetable juices and some fruit juices, after the first month, dilute by at least half.

Invest in an anti-candida book for recipe suggestions. There are some allergy-free books, which would also be helpful as they often cut out yeast and sugar.

Most stock cubes have yeast. Use yeast free Marigold Swiss Bouillon or Kallo stock cubes. (HS)

Organic foods tend to be more natural but may also have more mould due to lack of fungicides so it is a double edged sword!

Whisk yoghurt with sparkling mineral water; add mint or vanilla essence.

Make a vegetable soup with coriander.

Avoid tap water as fluoride may encourage candida growth.

Most breakfast cereals have sugar or its derivatives. Offer porridge, shredded wheat, muesli (without nuts or dried fruit), eggs, yoghurt or soda bread for breakfast or snacks.

Plain, low salt crisps a maximum of 2-3 times maximum per week, plain popcorn, and vegetable sticks or seeds as snacks or lunchbox fillers are okay.

Sprinkle raw, unsweetened, desiccated coconut onto cereals or into yoghurt as a sweetener and flavourer. It contains caprylic acid which as anti-fungal.

Garlic is nature's anti-fungal.

Pineapple is anti-inflammatory (not in the first month of the diet).

Australian Bush Fushia may help.

Initial weight loss is quite common in adults on a candida diet. Unless your child is overweight, this needs to be monitored. Increase meat, fish, eggs, seeds and their oils and wholegrains.

Reduce exposure to environmental pollutants (household or inhalant).

Mothers may also have candida especially if child still quite young and contracted candida via vagina at delivery or breast during feeding. Treat mum too! ■

Nutrients to consider

● (Candida can cause leaky gut and malabsorption so deficiencies are common.)

● Eliminex gently cleanses the bowel and acts as a prebiotic (L) 1-2 tsps.

● Vitamin C to boost immunity and decrease inflammation. Drops, powder or children's capsule (BC) or Immune C x one daily over 8 years. (HN)

MVM:

● Aqueous Plus Multivitamin and mineral one tsp daily. (BR, NC, R)

● Nutribalance has multi-nutrients, probiotics and mild gut healing properties. One 20gm scoop per 25lbs body weight mixed into food such as yoghurt, cereals or mashed potatoes. (AR, NC, R)

EFAs:

● Flax; capsule or dricelle powder. (BC)

● Udo's choice oil. (Sa, HS)

● Essential Balance Junior is 1:1 omega 3 and 6 oil. Junior version is butterscotch flavoured and sugar-free 1-3 tsp from weaning. (HN)

● Probiotics.

● Kiddy Tum from 2 years to soothe and protect gut lining (K) or Bromelain 100mgs as a digestive enzyme. (NO)

● Infant starflower cream for itchy bottom. (N)

Anti-candida nutrients: these are anti-fungal, often herbal and are required after one month of anti-candida diet to kill the remaining fungal yeast. Here are some choices, but children must see a qualified practitioner.

● Colloidal silver for anti-fungal, parasitic, bacterial properties. Tasteless, clear, golden liquid very easy for children ($^1/_2$tsp twice daily for 3 year olds for 3 −4 months). (HN, AR)

● Mycropryl Junior, 1 small capsule twice daily. (BC)

● Black Walnut tincture is anti-fungal 5 drops twice daily (age specific). (Nu)

● Citricidal is grapefruit seed extract – 2-6 drops 1-3 times daily for over 8 years between meals for one month.

● Probiotics.

● Milk thistle to support liver during detoxification of candidiasis. Give $^1/_2$tablet twice daily (BM) or Livotrit Plus $^1/_2$tablet over 6 years or Lipoic acid 1 capsule per day over 4 years. (AR)

● Sacromycees Boullardii is a probiotics formula, which helps to increase gut immunity to fight the infection and enhance colonisation of future beneficial bacteria. 1 capsule sprinkled onto food or drink for 3 year old. (AR)

● Permavite is a powder for leaky gut. May increase absorption during treatment. (AR)

CATARRH

SEE ALSO: RHINITIS, ASTHMA, COLDS, IMMUNE
FUNCTION, INFECTIONS, FOOD INTOLERANCES/
ALLERGIES, EARS

Factors to consider include infections, allergies to
inhalants and food intolerance especially cows'
milk products, but also wheat, citrus, eggs.

GENERAL ADVICE

Hot drinks may increase the mucous flow and
    relieve congestion.
Fresh air and exercise to improve oxygenation and
    circulation.
Golden seal may relieve catarrh.
See Aromatherapy in Appendix.
       ■

Dietary advice

- Elimination diets. (see Food intolerances)
- Dairy foods, even if not intolerant, can increase mucus congestion. Replace dairy with soya (over 6 months), Nanny Goat formula, rice or oat milk. Soya beans, seeds and fish will replace any calcium lost from dairy.
- Boost immunity.
- Increase potassium, zinc, vitamin C and betacarotene foods.
- Fresh garlic raw and crushed in honey (over 1 year)
- BENEFICIAL FOODS: Soya, rice or oat milk, pineapple, papaya, ginger, garlic, soya beans, sesame/ sunflower seeds and fish.

Nutrients to consider

- Bromelain 100mgs is anti-inflammatory. (NO)
- Super Gar one daily over 8 years. (HN)
- Vitamin C with bioflavonoids; drops, powder or children's capsule (BC) or chewable C over 4 years. (L)
- E-Kid-Nacea Plus over 4 years is especially good for catarrh. (K)

CHICKEN POX

Included as the only childhood infectious disease in the book because it is so common, incurable and no vaccination is given.

Very infectious viral disease caused by Herpes Zosta. Usually a mild illness in healthy children but newborns, those with suppressed immunity and adults who have not had chicken pox as a child may be more seriously affected. Transmitted via mouth, nose or direct contact with vesicles.

Symptoms are a mild fever and runny nose followed by small, itchy dark red spots appearing in crops over 3-4 days on the trunk and face. Spots turn to blisters (vesicles) and then crust over. It can affect the mouth too.

Infectious from 4 days prior to rash for approximately 7-10 days until the last crust has dried up. Incubation period 12-21 days from contact.

GENERAL ADVICE

Bathe in cool water with bicarbonate of soda to relieve itching.

Alternatively add lavender, calendula or chamomile oil (dispersed in baby oil first) to bath water. Aromatherapy. (see Appendix)

Isolate child until scabs have formed and fever gone.

Avoid soap or perfumed products.

Cool, wet towels may soothe.

Clean, short nails to prevent secondary infection due to scratching.

Serious damage can occur to an unborn child if contracted during first 3 months of pregnancy. Zoster immunoglobin can be administered to mother by GP.

Chicken pox virus as a child will be present in the body for life. It lies dormant and can be reactivated as shingles in adulthood. A shingles rash can infect others with chicken pox but not shingles.

NB: Never give aspirin to under 12 year olds and especially not during viral infections as risk of Reyes Syndrome is increased.

Homeopathic pulsatilla may help. ■

Dietary advice

- (See Viral infections)
- Appetite may be reduced initially.
- Maintain fluids.
- Avoid milk formula during fever.
- Catnip tea with blackstrap molasses for fever in infants and children.
- BENEFICIAL FOODS: Fruit juices, stewed apples, mashed bananas, avocado, live yoghurt.

Nutrients to consider

- (See Immune function/Viral infections)
- Echinacea complex. (BM)
- Bio C for vitamin C includes potassium to alkalise body and magnesium and calcium for immunity and calming effect.
- Anti-oxidants – vitamin C, E, A and zinc.
- MVM.

Topicals:

- Aloe vera gel.
- Infant starflower cream. (N)
- Combine one part each of bicarbonate of soda, zinc oxide and cornflour. Mix to a paste with water and apply to affected areas to reduce irritation.
- Vitamin E cream after itching has gone to reduce scarring. (L, X)
- Calamine lotion is still an effective remedy for itching. (Ch)
- Witch hazel compresses to specific sites.

C

CHILBLAINS

SEE ALSO: RAYNAUD'S SYNDROME

More common in adults but some school age children may suffer with these itchy painful areas on the hands or feet. Constriction of blood vessels causes loss of circulation and heat to the area. May indicate Raynaud's Disease if severe.

GENERAL ADVICE

Exercise for circulation.

Apply infant starflower cream or chamomile and peppermint cream to relieve irritation/ itching. (N)

Vitamin E cream. (L, X)

Wear socks in bed.

Keep feet warm and dry.

Homeopathic agaracus 3c orally or Tamus Cream (black bryony). (HS, A)

Massage area with one drop cinnamon oil in 2 tabsps of olive oil, or black pepper and rosemary oil. (N, HS)

Dietary advice

● Avoid red meat, dairy, sugar, vinegar to improve circulation and reduce inflammation.

● Increase fibre.

● Increase vitamin C and E foods, also for circulation.

● BENEFICIAL FOODS: Garlic, ginger, fresh fruit and green and orange vegetables, oats, linseeds, avocados, seed oil, oily fish.

Nutrients to consider

● Vitamin C and bioflavonoids to strengthen capillary blood vessels and reduce inflammation. Chewable C over 4 years (L) or powder or children's capsules. (BC)

● Vitamin E 100ius as drops or capsule. (BC)

● B complex especially niacin B3 for circulation (always take a B complex alongside individual B vitamins) 10 drops up to 5 years or children's capsule 5-12 years. (BC)

● Gingko Complex $^1/_2$ tablet twice daily (BM) or Gingko Biloba tincture in older children. (N)

● Udo's Choice (Sa, HS) or flax seed oil for circulation. Capsule (BC) or oil. (HN)

● Calcium phosphate can increase circulation. (BM)

C

CHRONIC FATIGUE SYNDROME (CFS)

SEE ALSO: GLANDULAR FEVER, DIABETES, ANXIETY, ANAEMIA, IMMUNE FUNCTION, BLOOD SUGAR, TOXICITY, THYROID PROBLEMS

Lack of energy need not be CFS but the symptoms here may help. In adults there are many underlying factors, but in children it is often less complicated. However a child with chronic fatigue is often labelled as lazy and not taken seriously. About one in 1000 teenagers are affected. It tends to occur in school aged children, but any child with a persistent lack of energy should be investigated by a doctor for such factors as diabetes, anaemia, thyroid insufficiency, viral infections or glandular fever.

Chronic fatigue syndrome is sometimes triggered by an infection, but if the 'normal' recovering period is extended, eg into months not weeks, then further investigations are required.

FACTORS TO CONSIDER

The above conditions, which may be linked;
Vitamin and mineral deficiencies;
Blood sugar imbalances;
Immune system abnormalities;
Food intolerances;
Candida;
Stress/anxiety/depression;
Epstein Barr Virus (glandular fever);
Intestinal parasites;
Leaky gut.

Symptoms may include headaches, aching muscles, reduced appetite, irritability, anxiety and poor concentration. Sleep often has little effect and the child wakes tired and fails to improve during the day.

GENERAL ADVICE

Seeking professional help is very important as the condition can be complex.

Ask GP or paediatrician for blood tests to eliminate anaemia, EPB virus, infectious processes, thyroid deficiency, diabetes etc.

Arrange to see a counsellor / therapist if psychological issues are a possibility.

Discuss with school as it may mask learning or

Dietary advice

- Encourage higher intake of clean water.
- Increase calcium and magnesium foods.
- Keep carbohydrates for later in the day; give jacket potatoes of whole-wheat pasta with some protein for dinner.
- Avoid stimulants like sugar and caffeine, eg no chocolate, tea or coffee.
- Increase immune boosting foods.
- Offer small regular meals which include some protein but are easy to digest.
- BENEFICIAL FOODS: Pulses, wholegrains, jacket potatoes, peas, bananas, apples, apricots, peaches with sesame seeds, dried fruits, shakes, yoghurt, cottage cheese, custards, milk puddings, vegetable or chicken soups and fresh juices, soya products.

Nutrients to consider

- Calcium and magnesium are calming minerals if anxiety or stress are involved and can improve sleep. Magnesium can also help muscle pains and fatigue. Often need magnesium to calcium ratio of 2:1. Try Bio-Mg $1/2$ capsule daily 1-3 years; chewable Mg or Ca over 4 years (L); 1:1 ratio over 8 years (HN); 2:1 ratio (S, BC) or Mg solution $1/4$ tsp 1-2 times daily (AR, NC, R). Bio magnesium by BM also has calcium, B6 and minerals.
- B vitamin complex for nervous system and energy levels; children's capsule for 5-12 years (BC) or B Vital with ginseng for energy/ stress. One daily over 5 years. (HN)

- Vitamin C with bioflavonoids; drops, powder or children's capsule. (BC)
- EFAs for brain function and hormone balance; Eye Q 2-6 capsules daily (can be pierced) or Eskimo 3 oil 5mls daily. (Nu)
- Milk thistle $^1/_2$ tablet twice daily for liver support. (BM)
- MSM sulphur $^1/_4$ tsp or 1-2 capsules daily to alleviate toxicity.

social difficulties. If a lot of school is missed ask for an assessment for a home tutor and a phased return to school.

Encourage deep breathing into tummy at regular intervals.

Gentle exercise can help, although if energy levels are very low this may not be possible initially. Prolonged inactivity can weaken bones.

Fresh air daily.

Increase fluids as dehydration can cause energy depletion and toxicity

Support liver by balancing sugar levels and eating organic foods to reduce toxic load.

Homeopathic flower remedies and aromatherapy approaches can help some children. See Appendix.

COELIAC DISEASE

SEE ALSO: GROWTH, DIGESTION, LEAKY GUT, FOOD INTOLERANCE, ALLERGIES

This is gluten allergy which damages the gut lining. Research is indicating that coeliacs may inherit a particular type of carbohydrate marker in the intestinal cells, which binds with lectins and appears to be foreign to the immune system. This results in antibody production against bound lectin and the ensuing 'war' causes the immune system to damage the intestinal villi. Vitamins A, D and E are fat-soluble and may become deficient due to impaired fat absorption. Research is ongoing.

Symptoms in babies and children are very specific and include pale, offensive stools, wind, bloating, colic and failure to thrive. These symptoms usually develop a few weeks after introducing cereals to the diet, ie after weaning.

Diagnosis is usually by biopsy of small intestine under paediatric supervision. Nutritionists may use a gluten antibody sensitivity test, but usually elimination of gluten is so effective the diagnosis is obvious.

GENERAL ADVICE

Occasionally the sensitivity is complicated by other factors such as leaky gut or dysbiosis.

Weak reactions to gluten may indicate that gluten is aggravating an underlying condition rather than causing it.

Always seek a medical opinion.

There are digestive enzymes to improve the breakdown of gluten, but is not advised for young children. May help if eating out or on holiday. (BC)

Some adults develop gluten sensitivity, but this is not necessarily coeliac disease. Unfortunately in children it usually is coeliac disease.

See appendix for gluten free sources. ■

Dietary advice

- Breast feeding reduces incidence.
- Avoid all gluten for life.
- Include alternative grains.
- Dairy alternative if appropriate.
- Increase calcium, magnesium, zinc foods.
- Cabbage is soothing on the digestive tract. Use its cooking water also.
- Reduce inflammation with anti-inflammatory diet (reduce red meat and dairy products plus lots fresh fruit and vegetables, oats and fish).
- Papain and pineapple contain bromelain which can reduce inflammation and support digestion.
- BENEFICIAL FOODS:
Wholegrain rice, quinoa, corn and buckwheat provide alternatives to wheat, oat, nut and rice milks, fish. Seed oils rather than the seeds provide EFAs without the irritation of whole seeds.

Nutrients to consider

- Damage to intestinal villi reduces absorption so although the following suggestions will not cure the disease they should address deficiencies caused by it and help to heal the leaky gut.
- Zinc citrate; drops (BC); 15mg capsules (L); or $1/2$level measure of sherbet flavoured powder alternate days over 8 years. (HN)
- MVM.
- Aqueous Multi Plus one tsp daily (BR, NC) is well absorbed as liquid. Also Vitamist, children's MVM is an oral spray so bypassing gut problems (NW) or Ultra Care for Kids.(Nu)
- Vitamin E for healing; drops or 100iu capsule. (BC)
- B Complex; Vitasorb B 10 drops under tongue or from 5-12 years one children's capsule. (BC)
- EFAs to help heal gut lining and reduce inflammation; Udo's Choice (Sa, HS) or Essential Balance Junior is butterscotch flavoured, $1/2$-3 tsps from weaning. (HN)
- Probiotics.
- Apple Pectin can soothe $1/4$tsp daily. (S)
- Kiddy Tum, from 2 years, contains slippery elm and papain to help soothe and support the gut. (K)
- Bromelain 100mgs daily decreases inflammation. (NO)

SEE ALSO: IMMUNE SYSTEM, FEVER, AND BRONCHITIS

Dietary advice

- 'Feed a cold and starve a fever' has some truth. Extra energy and nutrients are required to fight off the viruses. If fever is present then fluids are more important.
- Offer light, nutritious meals and juices. Reduce need for chewing as the child is congested.
- Avoid dairy food as it forms mucous.
- Garlic contains allicin for immunity and viral protection; add raw to honey.
- Beta-carotene, vitamin C, A, E and zinc are all antioxidants to fight off infections.
- EFAs to reduce respiratory inflammation.
- Drinking hot water with manuka honey, lemon and root ginger can be beneficial. Vitamin C powder could be added.
- Prevention involves adequate protein and folic acid and a healthy immune system.
- BENEFICIAL FOODS: Pumpkin, squash, courgette, oily fish, honey, lemon and ginger, water, brussel sprouts, fresh juices and dairy free shakes, chicken soup, garlic, onions, sea vegetables.

Common it is, but there are about 200 different viruses! The duration is usually 7 days without complications. Immature immune systems in under 5's and contact at nurseries and pre-schools means increased incidence in young children. Expect 4-5 colds per year.

Bacterial infection is sometimes a complication due to immune suppression by the virus. The main problem is fever, but bronchitis may develop. If temperature is above 102°C or chest symptoms occur, see a doctor.

GENERAL ADVICE

Honey not advisable for under one year due to small risk of botulism infection.

Manuka honey comes from the tea tree and can be very helpful in reducing sinus congestion and boosting immunity. Good during an infection and as a preventative. Not under one year. (HS)

Steam inhalation of eucalyptus. NB: take care with hot water.

Gargle 2-3 drops of tea tree oil in warm water (not recommended for small children as they may swallow).

Frequent hand washing as infection can live on the hands for several hours.

Parents and carers can boost own immunity at the time to prevent cross infection.

Humidify room by placing bowl of water on the radiator or burn eucalyptus oil (one drop) in an aromatherapy burner.

Sprouting seeds and pulses is fun and they are high in enzymes and minerals.

Lots of clean water.

Rest with gentle exercise to encourage lymphatic drainage of toxins. ■

Nutrients to consider

● Blackmores do two children's complexes.

  ● Cold Defense for Kids for prevention especially in winter. 1-2 tablets chewed with meals. Over 2 years.

  ● Bounceback Formula after a cold to boost recovery / immunity. 2-3 chewed with meals. Over 2 years.

● Vitamin C promotes interferon production which reduces viral effect. Drops, powder or children's capsule (BC) or chewable for over 4 years (L). Bio C $^1/_4$tsp daily has minerals as well. (AN, NC, R)

● Nat-Choo is a gentle herbal tincture to support the child, relieving symptoms through the early stages of a cold or 'flu – Kid Catnip can be used if frequent colds a problem. (K) (over 2 years)

● E-Kid-Nacea over 2 years or E-Kid-Nacea Plus over 4 years (latter is good for catarrh). (K)

● Zinc as drops (BC), 15mg capsule (L) or sherbet powder $^1/_2$level measure under tongue alternate days for over 8 years. Zinc lozenges if old enough to reduce duration of symptoms 2 hourly.

● Vitamin B5 (pantothenic acid) deficiency linked to respiratory infections. Always give a B Complex as well (BC) (over 5 years).

● To fight of infection at first sign give over-5s echinacea/ goldenseal tincture 8-10 drops into the mouth. Hold as long as possible before swallowing. Or add to drink, but best sublingually (under the tongue) 2 hourly for 3 days. Then daily for a maximum of one week. (N,A)

● Oralmat – rye grass extract which contains tryptophan and zinc to strengthen immune system and magnesium to relax muscles. It may also have a de-sensitizing effect. 1 drop under tongue thrice daily held for 15 seconds and then swallowed. (HS)

COLD SORES

SEE ALSO: HERPES, BLISTERS, IMMUNE SYSTEM

Caused by the herpes simplex virus it can follow a cold or flu virus initially. The virus lays dormant in the bodys' nerve cells for life and is triggered by sunlight, immune deficiency and anxiety. It is infectious in that the child may develop other lesions if scratching the sore. Looks like a small blister and is usually on the lips and when it breaks, cross-infection is likely. They can also erupt on the vulva or penis and can be transmitted sexually in these cases in teenagers.

The main course of action is to keep the immune system in optimal condition to prevent outbreaks, but there are certain foods, which encourage herpes activation.

GENERAL ADVICE

Manuka honey topically as it contains tea tree pollen. (HS)

Licrogel, a cream containing lysine. (HN)

Derma C cream.(BC)

Vitamin E capsule, pierced and applied to sore.

Rescue Remedy cream at first sign. (HS, Ch)

Colloidal silver solution sprayed or dabbed onto sore. (HN)

Homeopathic Rhus Tox may help. See also Appendix.

Melissa officinalis lip salve is a useful preventative. (N, A)

Use separate towels and flannels.

Homeopathic oscillococcinum 200 is a bestseller in France and available in the UK. (A)

See Aromatherapy in Appendix.

Dietary advice

- Reduce or avoid arginine rich foods such as lentils, citrus, oats, nuts, seeds, chocolate, white flour, coconut, dairy, raisins and wheat. Should be kept to a minimum and avoided in an outbreak and for one month as herpes simplex uses it to multiply.
- Increase lysine rich foods which opposes arginine
- Immunity boosting diet
- Avoid sugar and refined foods
- Identify any food intolerances which may depress immunity
- Increase zinc, bioflavonoids, selenium and vitamin C foods
- Manuka honey comes from the tea tree and can be very helpful in reduces sinus congestion and boosting immunity. Good during an infection and as a preventative. Use as sweetener or spread. Not under one year
- BENEFICIAL FOODS: Oily fish, turkey, chicken, vegetables, soya, potatoes, yeast, eggs, some cheese and berry fruits, manuka honey, brazil nuts, sea vegetables

Nutrients to consider

- L-lysine with vitamin C. Over 14years. (BC)
- Vitamin E 100ius as drops or capsule. (BC)
- Multi vitamin/ mineral.
- E-Kid-Nacea 2-4 years or E-Kid-Nacea Plus over 4 years. (K)
- Selenium can prevent an outbreak – Trace mins 4 drops. (BC), selenium with vitamin E, 1 daily over 12 years (L), selenium solution 1 ml daily. (AR)

Colic

SEE ALSO: FOOD INTOLERANCES, IRRITABLE BOWEL SYNDROME, DIGESTIVE PROBLEMS, WIND

Colic is common in babies. onein 10 suffer, mainly from 3 weeks–3 months old but age varies. Colic can occur in older children, but is usually known then as tummy ache or irritable bowel syndrome.

In babies the condition is very distressing with sudden severe spasms of apparent pain, which usually occur in the evening, with the baby crying loudly and continuously, frequently drawing the legs upwards towards the chest. The stomach is distended and tense. It may take several hours for the symptoms to abate – often after the baby passes wind or stools. Disturbances in smooth muscle function in gut is a more likely cause than just wind although this will make matters worse! Doctors may tell parents whose babies suffer from colic there is nothing wrong. They are left believing they cannot cope with their baby. Although normally there is no serious condition involved, there are strategies to relieve the symptoms.

Artificially fed babies may develop colic more often and this may be due to cows' milk intolerance.

It is likely that a combination of various factors is involved in most cases of infant colic.

FACTORS TO CONSIDER

Immature nervous system, which affects intestinal function.
Over feeding.
Incorrect mixing of formula feeds.
Wrong posture when feeding.
Poor metabolism of intestinal hormones.
Cows' milk or lactose intolerance.

GENERAL ADVICE

If fever is present take action.
Any high pitched piercing scream should be investigated further by a doctor.
Rarely a baby will have intersusception (a blockage in the intestines) which requires urgent medical help.
Camomile tea is a well-known soother and relaxant. A nursing mother should drink one cup, twice a day. Give a bottle-fed infant one tsp of tea, three times daily, in formula or water for 3 – 4 days. Then reduce the dosage to twice daily.

C

Dietary advice

For breast feeding mothers:

- Avoid dairy products, chocolate, caffeine, melons, cucumbers, peppers, citrus fruits and their juices, and spicy foods. Elimination or rotation diets may help. When nursing a colicky baby, try deleting all gas-forming foods from your diet, including cauliflower, broccoli, brussel sprouts, cucumbers, red and green peppers, onions, beans, legumes

- A mother nursing a colicky baby should minimise the amount of raw foods in her diet. Breast feeding mother's diet should consist of 70 to 80% cooked foods and only 20 to 30% raw foods. Keep the diet simple

- Keep an on-going food diary to help identify relationships between foods and symptoms, both in baby and mother. If an unsuspected sensitivity is discovered, simply avoiding that food may improve mother's health and alleviate baby's colic as well

For bottle fed infants:

- (See food intolerance section)

- Dilute the formula for 24 hours.

- Feed more often with smaller amounts.

- Offer bottled water in between.

- Only change milk as a last resort, trying an alternative cows' milk formula first.

- Soya milk is not ideal for infants under 6 months.

Nutrients to consider

- Probiotics:
  - 1) a breast-feeding mother should take Acidophilus $^1/_2$tsp, twice daily. (BC)
  - 2) give a bottle-fed baby Bifido Infantis $^1/_8$tsp dissolved in formula, twice daily (BC)
  - NB: It is vital to use a special infant formulation of probiotics, as the colonic environment is different.
- Windy Pops is a gentle herbal tincture suitable from birth for the relief of colic and wind(K) can also be applied directly to nipples of lactating mother before feeds 3-4 times daily.
- Kiddy Tum from 2 years old for tummy aches and irritable children. (K)
- Kid Catnip from 2 years if prone to recurrent colic. (K)
- Homeopathic Colocynthus 12c granules in liquid for new-born colic. (N)

Fennel can also be helpful in relieving colic. The nursing mother can drink one cup of fennel tea, three times a day. Or dilute one cup of fennel tea in 2 cups of water, and give your baby I teaspoon of the diluted tea, four times a day.

Ginger: a nursing mother can drink one cup of ginger tea, three times a day, to help relieve her baby's colic.

Peppermint tea helps to speed the emptying time of the stomach, enhances digestion, and acts as an anti flatulent. Give your child one tsp of peppermint tea, four to five times a day.

Try giving your baby a combination herbal tea. Israeli researchers gave a daily dose of about 1/2 cup of a tea made from camomile, liquorice, fennel, and balm-mint to babies who were experiencing episodes of colic, and found that symptoms were eased in more than half the children studied.

Holding baby upright during an attack or laying the infant across the knee, gently patting or rubbing the back may also have a soothing effect. This will make it easier for the baby to expel the air when he burps.

To control the amount of air baby swallows when feeding, limit actual drinking time to about ten minutes. After each two ounces of fluid, try to burp baby (but don't be discouraged if he doesn't burp).

Massage baby's belly with a non-alcohol-based lotion or oil. Following the natural path of the intestines, gently rub from the baby's lower right 'corner' of the abdomen up across the bottom of the rib cage, down to the lower left 'corner', and around again. Use Jurilique Baby's Colic Relief Massage Oil. (BM)

Some babies respond to cuddling and rocking. A drive in the car at 2 am is not uncommon!

Babies with sensitive nervous systems may respond better to a decrease in external stimulation. Try soft lighting, less touching, and a quiet atmosphere or soft, comforting music.

With the baby lying on his back on the floor, gently move his legs in a bicycle-pedalling motion. Practice this exercise several times daily.

These passive leg movements can be very comforting to the baby's digestive system.

Try to avoid overfeeding or underfeeding the baby, follow your child's lead As long as the baby is gaining weight and developing normally, you are probably doing just fine.

Gripe water is high in sugar and used to contain alcohol – a natural alternative is dill water.

Mix tsp dried dill seeds, one tsp dried peppermint and one cup of boiling water. Lactating mother can drink or cool and spoon feed baby. 2.5–5ml newborn, 10–20ml for 6 months – oneyear, 20–30ml over a year.

Cow & Gate have just introduced the first formula, Omneo Comfort, with beneficial bacteria added.

Colief drops may help if lactose intolerance is the problem. (Ch, HS, NC)

Caraway water in boiled water before a feed may help. ■

CONSTIPATION

SEE ALSO: THYROID PROBLEMS, COLIC, DIGESTIVE PROBLEMS, FOOD INTOLERANCES.

Can mean infrequency, difficulty in passing or incomplete motion/stool. Maintaining a soft, well-formed stool is more important than frequency.

EMOTIONAL INFLUENCES

Some children can create atypical constipation by retention, ie holding back or refusing to go. This may be due to various emotional reasons such as family tensions, nursery insecurities, potty training too early, or a previous episode of constipation leading to fear of discomfort. Depression in older children can be a factor.

PHYSICAL CAUSES

Low fibre, highly refined diet.
Food Intolerance (especially dairy foods in babies and wheat in children).
Dysbiosis.
Vitamin/mineral deficiencies especially vitamin C and magnesium.
Dehydration.
Digestive disturbances.
Intestinal infections, eg candidiasis.
A change of water supply (often temporary, eg whilst on holiday).
Low thyroid function.
More seriously, but rarely, anal fissure which should be checked by GP if problem persists.

GENERAL ADVICE

Increase exercise such as cycling or swimming.
Babies may respond to gentle abdominal massage (clockwise) and cycling movements of the legs.
Petroleum jelly applied to the anus can ease the initial stool.
Some prescription medications such as Fybogel contain aspartame (suspected cancer risks).
Read her a story on the loo or potty after meals to allow plenty of time and reduce anxiety but not if this causes co-operation problems.
Use bottled, boiled or filtered water rather than tap water. **All** babies' water should be boiled first.■

Dietary Advice

- Avoid wheat as it retains fluid, irritates the bowel and can congest and slow transit time.
- Avoid refined and processed foods such as ice cream, white flour and fizzy drinks.
- Excess milk can contribute.
- Identify potential food allergens such as dairy, replacing with soya (not under 6 months), rice or goats' milks. This is common in infants with constipation.
- Increase soluble fibre.
- Increase fluid intake – 6 cups water or juice daily and 5 portions of fruit and vegetables.
- Live yoghurt contains bifido bacteria which have the same effect as fibre, useful for babies where high fibre is difficult.
- Inulin, present in artichokes, is an indigestible carbohydrate can have laxative effect. Try including in freshly squeezed juice as children are unlikely to eat it alone!
- Blackstrap molasses in water may help whilst providing minerals.
- BENEFICIAL FOODS: Oats and oat bran, fruit, eg kiwi and plums, vegetables, eg carrots and cabbage, wholegrains, eg brown rice, pulses, dried fruit, especially prunes, figs, dates (try stewed, ready to eat or juice), water or diluted fruit juice for babies (never sugar water!), live yoghurt, lentils, baked beans, artichokes, sea vegetables.

Nutrients to consider – Constipation

- Vitamin C, as Mg ascorbate powder (BC), Mg helps muscular action / vitamin C is a laxative in good doses. (BC)

- Magnesium phosphate 65; $1/4$tab into expressed milk is very effective in infants. (BM)

- Probiotics.

- FOS as a sweetener on cereals adds soluble fibre and feeds beneficial bacteria too. (HN)

- Psyllium husks: powder or capsule can provide soluble fibre in older children if dietary changes inadequate. (HS)

- Slippery elm and psyllium seed powder; one pinch – $1/4$tsp, $1/2$tsp 5-10 years, 1 tsp over 10 years. Can add honey and nutmeg. (N)

- Eliminex can gently loosen and cleanses the bowel encouraging growth of beneficial bacteria. From 2 years. (L)

- Aloe Vera Gold one tsp daily as a maintenance. (HN, X)

- Flax oil onto cereals and rice. (HN, Sa, HS)

- Colon Fibre one tsp or one capsule daily over 4 years, with plenty of water. (BR, NC, R)

Coughs

Linked to infections, food intolerances, and inhalant allergens. Coughing fits often occur at night and disturb sleep.

GENERAL ADVICE

Elevate head of bed with large books or put a rolled blanket underneath the mattress. Never use a pillow for small children and babies.

Medicinal cough mixture can depress immunity due to added sugar and only mask the underlying cause.

Children's Cough Syrup is mainly wild cherry bark, but good all round. Use as a relaxant and expectorant. onetsp thrice daily over 2 years. (N)

Olbas oil or eucalyptus oil on a tissue near cot or under pillow in older children.

Herbal remedies such as mullein to increase clearance of mucous can help, but seek advice of a medical herbalist for children. Do not use if asthmatic. See also Appendices.

Vapourizer lamps can ease airways at night. (Ch)

Easily digested foods will help relax the vegas nerve, which stimulates cough reflex.

TYPES OF COUGHS AND THEIR REMEDIES

Productive coughs may respond to verbascum (mullein) but not in asthma. (BM)

Tickly coughs may respond to cherry bark. (BM)

Dry coughs may respond to marshmallow. (BM)

Broad spectrum remedies include garlic, mullein and elderflower.

Sore, painful cough – Farmacia Soothing Elixir also boosts immunity. (F)

Whooping cough has various stages and will need a changing programme. Contact BM for recommendations. ∎

Dietary advice

- Increase fluids.
- Avoid dairy/soya to reduce mucous congestion.
- Avoid sugar which lowers immune function.
- No fizzy drinks.
- Bromelain from pineapples is anti-inflammatory.
- Strawberries contain ellagic acid which lines the lungs and protects. Also in raspberries and grapes.
- BENEFICIAL FOODS: Water, pineapple, pears, garlic in honey, strawberries, grapes, raspberries.

Nutrients to consider

- Zinc; lozenges if old enough, 2 hourly for 1-2 days; drops (BC); 15mg capsule (L); sherbet flavoured powder $^1/_2$ level measure under tongue alternate days for over 8 years. (HN)
- E-Kid-Nacea 2-4 years or E-Kid-Nacea. (K)
- Vitamin C to ease tightness in the chest. Bio C $^1/_4$tsp daily alkalises system as it contains extra minerals (AN, NC, R); drops or children's capsules (BC); chewable from 4 years. (L)
- Magnesium aids muscular function and can relieve spasm of the airways. Bio Mg $^1/_2$capsule sprinkled on food or drink for 1-3 year olds; chewable one daily from 4 years (L); $^1/_4$tsp (1.5 mls) Mg solution in glass water daily over 4 years. (AR, NC)
- Kiddy Tum contains slippery elm and ginger, good for mucous membranes in respiratory tract. (K)
- Super Gar – 1 daily over 8 years to reduce mucous and fight bacteria. (HN)
- Bromelain 100mgs is anti-inflammatory. (NO)

CRADLE CAP

SEE ALSO: DERMATITIS, CANDIDA, CONJUNCTIVITIS, EARS

This is a form or seborrhoeic dermatitis, which results in thick, waxy encrustation on the scalp, eyebrows, eyelids, nose or ears. If persistent, secondary fungal infection may occur.
Complications include sticky eyes or conjunctivitis.

FACTORS TO CONSIDER
Dysbiosis.
Candida.
EFA deficiency.
Overactive sebaceous glands.
Biotin deficiency.

GENERAL ADVICE
Cradle cap is rarely seen after one year

Cradle cap can affect eyes causing sticky discharge and crusting. Bathe with saline and address cradle cap

If encrustations are thick apply baby oil mixed with a drop of tea tree oil overnight and wash off in the morning.

Massage mashed avocado into scalp and gently rinse. Rub skin over scalp to encourage healing

Vitamin E capsule pierced and applied to the affected area, topically. Not near the eyes. (HS)

Infant Starflower cream to reduce encrustations (N)

Avoid chemicals in shampoos. Even baby products can contain sodium laurel sulphate, which can lead to protein breakdown and exacerbation of cradle cap.

Try Jurilique range of baby products or (N)

Contacts:
Green People Tel: 01444 401444 ■

C

Dietary advice
- Lactating mothers should avoid sugar and yeast.
- Yeast and sugar may aggravate.
- Food intolerance sometimes involved.

Nutrients to consider
- Dricelle evening primrose oil powders. (BC)
- EFAs as flax oil in feeds or via mother if breast-fed. (HN, Sa, HS)
- Potassium sulphate to alkalise the system. (BM)
- Give probiotics in feed, solids or in boiled and cooled water; Bifido Infantis $1/8$tsp dissolved in formula or expressed breast milk twice daily or acidophilus $1/2$tsp daily to lactating mothers. (BC)
- Biotin – 1000mgs to lactating mothers (L) or in bottle fed infants B complex drops including biotin can be added to feeds. (BC)

CRAMP

SEE ALSO: BLOOD SUGAR, THYROID, PMS, PERIODS

Dietary advice

- Increase magnesium and potassium foods.

- Avoid refined and processed foods as they reduce potassium and magnesium levels in the body.

- Increase fluids as dehydration makes cramps worse.

- Include vitamin E foods for circulation.

- Absorbable calcium is found at good levels in watercress and fish.

- Avoid oxalates in rhubarb and phytates in bread especially pitta bread, which can block calcium absorption.

- Avoid spinach and beetroot, which may increase cramp.s

- BENEFICIAL FOODS: Fresh fruit and vegetables, beans, oily fish, brazil nuts, almonds, sesame seeds, water, watercress (make into a soup for younger children) and blackstrap molasses.

Nutrients to consider

- Magnesium: Bio Mg $^1/_2$capsule sprinkled on food or drink for 1-3 year olds; chewable one daily from 4 years (L); $^1/_4$tsp Mg solution in glass water daily over 4 years (AR). Bio magnesium also contains calcium, B6, minerals one per day 6-12 years. (BM)

- Trace minerals – 4 drops daily (BC) or Concentrace one drop per 6lbs body weight. (HN)

- Vitamin C to improve magnesium utilisation; powder or drops. (BC)

- Children's B complex Extra B3 for circulation over 5 years. (BC)

Common but not dangerous, however it may indicate mineral imbalances and blood sugar problems. If extensive, severe and frequent, consider thyroid problems as they can affect calcium metabolism

FACTORS TO CONSIDER

Exercise-induced cramp.

Magnesium deficiency.

Poor circulation.

Vitamin E deficiency.

Cramp may also be a result of diarrhoea or dehydration and the imbalance of tissue salts (Calcium, potassium, magnesium and sodium).

For abdominal cramps, see periods.

GENERAL ADVICE

Massage affected area.

Blackstrap molasses one tsp daily is high in minerals including magnesium, calcium and iron.

Warm up before exercise and encourage warm bath afterwards.   ■

CROHN'S DISEASE/ IRRITABLE BOWEL DISEASE (IBD)

SEE ALSO: CANDIDA, LEAKY GUT, FOOD INTOLERANCE, DIGESTIVE PROBLEMS

This is a potentially serious disease, which is mainly an inflammatory condition of the bowel, but sometimes from the mouth to the anus is all affected. It is usually linked to chronic food allergies with frequent thickening and ulceration of the intestinal wall and 'leaky' gut. Therefore it is less likely to manifest in young children, although incidence is rising. There appears to be an enzyme deficiency for detoxifying histamine, which results in inappropriate allergic reactions. Linked to candida in many cases.

Signs and symptoms include blood in stools, slow weight gain or weight loss, malabsorption, tummy ache, wind, diarrhoea, anaemia, lack of energy, dehydration, fatty stools, loss of appetite, nausea and intermittent fever.

GENERAL ADVICE

Gentle exercise helps lymphatic system
    drainage and encourages removal
    of toxins
Stress/anxiety can exacerbate. Teach
    correct breathing
Check for iron deficiency as chronic
    minor bleeding in the gut

Contacts:
Crohn's in Childhood Research Association
(CICRA) Tel: 020 8949 6209

Or HYPERLINK mailto:support@circra.org for
information and parental support ■.

Dietary advice

● Avoid sugar and refined foods as incidence has escalated since the 1950s when rationing ended and processed food production increased. Return to basics!

● Identify food allergens; most common are dairy and shellfish.

● Food combining may help ease digestion.

● Gluten may aggravate the bowel so avoid rye, oats, barley and wheat monitoring symptoms.

● Increase EFAs and fluids.

● Increase calcium, vitamin D and folic acid rich foods. Some cannot tolerate lots of vegetables, but they are an excellent source of calcium and folic acid. Try soup or fresh vegetable juices.

● Follow anti-candida diet if appropriate. See a practitioner.

● BENEFICIAL FOODS:
Lightly cooked fruit and vegetables, eggs, oily fish, nuts, wholegrains, brown rice (can increase diarrhoea and pain for some sufferers and decrease it for others) and fortified cereals, soya products, cottage cheese, live yoghurt.

Nutrients to consider

● Need to choose readily absorbable products especially liquid and powders.

● Fish oils; Dricelle Omega Plex powder (BC); Eskimo 3 oil x 5mls daily. (Nu)

● Aloe Gold one tsp daily to soothe digestion and reduce inflammation. (HS)

● Marshmallow to soothe. (BM)

● Kiddy Tum contains slippery elm and ginger to soothe gut. (K)

● Aqueous Multi Plus one tsp daily. (BR,NC,R)

● Folate (folic acid) deficiency is common in irritable bowel disease. Folic acid and B12 should be taken as a B complex; 10 drops in water or under tongue daily. (BC)

● Probiotics.

● Vitasorb zinc and vitamin A for the healing of the gut; 10 and one drop respectively daily. (BC)

● L- Glutamine powder to heal the gut lining $^1/_4$tsp 8-10 years then one tsp. (HN)

CROUP

SEE ALSO: BRONCHITIS/BRONCHIOLITIS, VIRAL INFECTIONS

Usually occurs 6 months – 4 years old and is an infection of the larynx (voicebox) which usually follows a cold and often occurs at night. It is an acute viral infection

Symptoms include a 'barking' cough, whistling sound on inhalation, hoarse voice or cry and laboured breathing.

Always call medical help first if breathing is laboured or there is a blue tinge to the lips.

FACTORS TO CONSIDER
Inflammation of the airways
Muscular spasm
Dehydration
Immune suppression
Magnesium deficiency.

GENERAL ADVICE
Acute action involves humidifying airways by running hot tap in the bathroom and holding child upright on your lap to improve oxygen supply.
Prevention includes boosting immunity.
Increase fluid intake to prevent dehydration and friction of airways.
See Appendix for suitable homeopathic, herbal, aromatherapy and flower essences. ▪

Nutrients to consider

● Bronchodilators include Euphorbia complex. (BM)

● Anti-viral horseradish and garlic complex. (BM)

● Magnesium to relax airways, aid muscular function relieving spasm of the airways.

● Bio Mg $^1/_2$capsule sprinkled on food or drink for 1-3 year olds; chewable one daily from 4 years (L); $^1/_4$tsp (1.5mls) Mg solution in glass water daily over 4 years. (AR,NC,R)

● Probiotics following any antibiotics needed.

CYSTIC FIBROSIS

SEE ALSO: IMMUNE FUNCTION

Cystic fibrosis is the most common genetic error of metabolism. It is an inherited disease of the exocrine glands, particularly those involving the lungs and digestive systems, causing damage to many organs including the pancreas, lungs, liver, digestive and reproductive systems. The viscosity of the mucous is too high causing thick, sticky mucous secretions with a high incidence of secondary infection and excessive inflammation.

It is due to an abnormality on chromosome 7, which controls transport of salts and water across cell membranes.

Life expectancy – before the advent of antibiotics the condition killed almost all sufferers in early childhood. In 1940s, 70% died usually as a result of infection during the first year of life. Now the outlook has improved dramatically with the average life expectancy at over 40 years, although it remains a potentially fatal disorder.

Incidence is about 5 babies born each week with onein 25 persons being an asymptomatic carrier of the gene. More common in Caucasians / much rarer in Asians and Afro-Caribbean children. Not always diagnosed until child is a little older.

MAIN FEATURES

At first the pancreas produces digestive enzymes normally and then gradually becomes a mass of scar tissue (abnormal cyst-forming tissues develop in the pancreas, from which the descriptive name cystic fibrosis is derived) and can't synthesise enzymes. Digestion and absorption gradually become so incomplete that a deficiency of all nutrients quickly occurs. Eventually most of the food eaten remains undigested causing persistent diarrhoea and bulky foul smelling stools.

8 out of 10 have a major loss of pancreatic function. This leads to deficiency or absence of pancreatic enzymes such as trypsin, amylase and lipase and other digestive factors.

The secretion of thick, sticky mucous in gut and lungs affects energy, respiration and absorption. Scarring also occurs.

Symptoms include constant coughs, recurrent chest

Dietary advice

- High proportion of raw foods.
- Increase fluid to account for high perspiration levels and prevent dehydration and mineral imbalances.
- Strawberries contain ellagic acid which lines the lungs and protects. Also in raspberries and grapes.
- Avoid or reduce mucous forming foods, eg dairy products, red meat and sugar to reduce inflammation.
- Lecithin granules 1-2 tsp to meals to help with fat metabolism.
- BENEFICAL FOODS: Raw fruit and vegetables, nuts, seeds, bio yoghurt, wheatgerm, rice, oat, goat or soya milk products, pulses and beans, fish, chicken, turkey.

infections, increased appetite, but poor growth, pale, oily, foul-smelling stools and/or blocked bowel at birth. Earliest symptom is respiratory, but malabsorption is a common result of pancreatic deficiency. Abnormally high levels of sodium and chlorine appear in the sweat and the diagnosis can be confirmed by the sweat test.

TREATMENT

Daily physiotherapy, postural drainage and other physiotherapeutic measures are essential to the relief of respiratory obstruction to clear the lungs of mucus and so aid breathing.

Treatment is with pancreatin preparations to improve intestinal digestion of food, but the use of high potency products requires care. Pancreatin preparations are used to promote the absorption of high-energy diets, but as they are protein and enzymatic in nature they are liable to inactivation by gastric acid. However, obstruction of the colon has been reported following the use of high active pancreatic preparations in young children.

In 1989, scientists identified the gene, which causes CF, and so it is now possible to offer prospective parents genetic screening, involving a simple mouthwash test, to see if they are carriers. Screening is particularly important for those related to someone with CF, or a known CF carrier.

CURRENT DIETARY APPROACH

Optimal nutrition is essential to help control the repeated infections. Diet needs to be high in calories, twice the theoretical calculation on actual weights.

There should be adequate fat and restricted starch intake due to incomplete digestion and infants should be breast-fed as long as possible.

Deficient enzymes should be replaced by pancreatic preparations and added to food in large amounts as gastric acidity destroys much of the powder.

When digestive enzymes and granular lecithin are given with each meal, the digestion and absorption of an extremely ill person can be

markedly improved and both should be
immediately increased if the digestion is still
faulty.

With those digestive aids, yeast, liver, and B
vitamin syrup can be taken. All these foods
should be started the minute a diagnosis of
cystic fibrosis is made.

GENERAL ADVICE

Supplementation should not interfere with
adequate dietary intake. It is additional.

8 out of 10 sufferers show signs of malnutrition.

As fat digestion is diminished, fat soluble vitamins
A, D, E are likely to be deficient. A and E are
anti-oxidants needed to protect the cells from
inflammation which is so prevalent in CF.

Recent research has shown that a new drug,
Pulmozyme, if given early can extend life by 2
years and reduce chest infections and
consequent antibiotics.

Regular exercise helps to clear the lungs of mucous,
eg running or walking,

Contact:
The Cystic Fibrosis Trust – Tel: 020 8464 7211   ■

Nutrients to consider

● **EFAs:**

1) Essential Balance Junior
$^1/_2$-3 tsps daily from
weaning (HN)

2) Dricelle Omega Plex or
linseed oil powders (BC)

● Aqueous Multi Plus one
tsp daily (BR,NC,R) or
drops (BC) or Vita mist
MVM for kids is absorbed
via mouth, avoiding gut
problems. (NW)

● Probiotics after any
courses of antibiotics which
are frequently needed.

● Selenium, vitamin A and
vitamin E are often deficient
in cystic fibrosis; combined
Se /E tablet one daily for
over 12 years (L) or 4 x
trace mineral drops and
Vitamin A and E drops x
one drop of each. (BC)

● Taurine can help support
respiratory function. Seek
professional advice.

● Kiddy Tum for mucous
membranes including lungs
from 2 years. (K)

C

DEPRESSION

SEE ALSO: ANXIETY, OCD, EATING DISORDERS, ALLERGIES, BSI

Incidence increasing in children and often unrecognised. one in 100 children under 12 years suffers and 2-3 teenagers in 100. Linked to wide variety of social/environmental factors, eg school, home and friendships. Also biochemical factors and illnesses such as diabetes

Symptoms include headaches, irritability, withdrawal, loss of appetite, fatigue, apathy, tummy ache, self-criticism, comfort eating, erratic sleep.

FACTORS TO CONSIDER

School – learning problems like dyslexia or high ability or bullying and socialisation difficulties.
Home – family tensions and sibling rivalry.
Family history of depression.
Biochemical imbalances– serotonin or dopamine deficiency (brain neuro-transmitters which affects mood).
Blood sugar imbalances (BSI).
Magnesium and calcium imbalances.
Zinc, selenium or folate deficiency.
Toxic metal poisoning, eg lead.
Allergies especially wheat, chocolate or yeast.
Lack of EFAs for brain function.
Low fat / high stimulant diets.
Faulty digestion, leading to nutrient deficiencies and food intolerances.

GENERAL ADVICE

Listen to your child, make time and opportunities to discuss feelings, initially you may be rejected but you must make yourself available.
Seek help via your GP for referral to a child psychologist/psychiatrist.
Praise the smallest achievements to boost self esteem.
Discuss with school to identify any social/learning problems.
Ask for psychometric assessment to diagnose cognitive imbalances and identify conditions such as dyslexia and dyspraxia. You may have to do this privately if no obvious learning difficulties at school.
Test hair for toxic metals and mineral imbalances.

Dietary advice

- Avoid cheese and marmite as tyramine can impair neuro-transmitter function.
- Small regular meals to balance blood sugar.
- Tryptophan foods to increase serotonin.
- Increase selenium, magnesium iron, vitamins C and B esp folic acid, foods.
- Tyrosine foods to increase dopamine for mood.
- Increase water intake to prevent dehydration.
- Avoid sugar as it depletes chromium, vitamin C and B complex vitamins needed for serotonin production.
- Add lecithin granules to cereals for choline needed for brain function.
- Natural licorice sticks may help.
- BENEFICIAL FOODS: Porridge oats, green vegetables especially broccoli and spinach, beetroot, black eye beans, peas, fortified breakfast cereals for folic acid, fish, bread, meat, cottage cheese, turkey, pumpkin/ sunflower seeds, baked potatoes including the skin, milk, brown rice, bananas, avocados, lentils, yeast extract for B vitamins, garlic, avocado, soya protein, licorice, tahini.

Try Bach Flower Remedies or
Australian Bush Flower
Remedies for emotional
problems. Get lists from the
health food store or Ancient
Roots – Tel: 020 8421 9877.
Also, see Appendix.

Encourage exercise and sunlight or
daylight.

If medication is needed some have
adverse dietary interactions.
Ask GP or pharmacist
especially with MAOI drugs.

Contacts:
Young Minds Tel: 020 7336 8445 for advice
and support on young people's mental
health problems.

Reading
So Young, So Sad, So Listen by Philip
Graham and Carol Hughes. Contact Book
Sales, Royal College of Psychiatrists, 17,
Belgrave Square, London SW1X 8PG ■

D

Nutrients to consider

● MVM.

● B complex especially B6 and B3 to
increase serotonin. Children's capsule for
5-12 years or adult for 12-16 years (BC,
AR).

● Zinc citrate 25mgs (BC, AR) or sherbet
flavoured powder $^1/_2$level measure under
tongue alternate days. For over 8 years.
(HN)

● Vitamin C for tryptophan conversion to
serotonin. Children's capsule or powder.
(BC)

● **EFAs**: esp EPA; 1g daily of fish or flax
oil. Choose from:

1) Eskimo 3 x 5mls daily (Nu) or Eye Q
(HS, NC); start with 2 capsules per day
building up to 6 per day for 3 months;
then 2 per day maintenance for memory,
sleep and concentration (HS, NC).

2) Biocare do various combinations of
omegas as Dricelle powders (contains
citrus).

3) Einstein's DHA (omega 3 fish oils only)
under 3 years take 1-2 daily squeezed
onto food. 3- 12 years 2-3 capsules daily.
(HN)

● Essential Balance Junior which provides
Omega 3 and 6 in natural butterscotch
flavour. Can be used when Omega 3 levels
are improved: $^1/_2$–3 tsps from weaning
(HN)

● Flax oil is also omega 3 but no research
on whether it is as effective as fish oils
higher doses may be needed to convert it
in the body.

● Seretone 5HTP 50mgs before bed
alternate days for 5-8 years or daily over 8
years. (HN)

● St John's Wort is not recommended in
children. Over 12 years with supervision
sometimes.

● Zen may alleviate anxiety related to
some types of depression. Works in acute
stress situation in 20-30 minutes. One
daily over 5 years. (AR)

● Stabilium 1 daily for 50lb child. Can be
given from infancy in graduated doses
under supervision. NB: contains fish
extracts. (AR)

● Connect Food Formula provides a variety
of nutrients for the brain to promote a
feeling of 'connectedness'. One daily over
12 years. (HN)

Diabetes

SEE ALSO BLOOD SUGAR, EXERCISE, IMMUNE SYSTEM AND OBESITY.

Diabetes Mellitus is an auto-immune disease in which insulin-producing cells are attacked by the body's own immune cells. It is the most common form of diabetes in children and is known as type 1 diabetes. Type 1 diabetes is insulin dependent and there is usually a genetic link. Usual treatment is insulin injections twice daily and some dietary modifications.

Diabetes Insipidus is a defect in fluid regulation either in the kidneys or the pituitary gland. It is not connected to insulin but leads to excessive thirst and urination. However the incidence of type 2 diabetes is increasing in adolescents and young adults and is thought to be due to refined processed foods with high sugar and fat and lack of exercise. Increasing obesity is probably linked.

1 in 500 children have diabetes and there are 20,000 sufferers amongst children and teenagers in the UK. 2 in 100,000 UK adolescents may have type 2 diabetes and there is a higher risk in Afro-Caribbean and Asian families. This may be connected to lactose intolerance. Research is indicating that diet and lifestyle changes in children can delay the onset of type 2 diabetes.

Symptoms in children include frequent urination, lack of energy, appetite disturbances esp. constant hunger, excessive thirst, recent weight loss, cravings for sweet foods, tummy ache

Linked conditions include obesity, polycystic ovaries, blood pressure rises. Children as young as 6 years old have been shown to have changes in blood fats, a marker for heart disease in *The Early Bird Research Study* by Professor Wilkin.

Treatment of diabetes by anyone other than a medical practitioner is illegal in the UK, but there are nutritional approaches and lifestyle advice to support good health and prevent complications.

GENERAL ADVICE

Exercise is vital for blood sugar regulation and control of obesity (see exercise section).

Medical professionals permit eating sweets and chocolate as part of a meal in diabetic children. As a nutritionist I prefer to alter

Dietary advice

- Mainly low saturated fats, refined foods and sugar
- Increased vegetarian proteins, wholegrains and EFAs
- Avoid processed meats, sausages, butter and cheese as all have high saturated fats which can increase blood sugar and blood fat levels
- Avoid sugar and refined foods including white flour and ready meals
- Fruit and vegetables are rich in potassium and fibre which is good for blood sugar regulation
- Follow the blood sugar guideline section.
- Increase B vitamins, chromium and zinc foods
- BENEFICIAL FOODS: Yoghurt, seeds, under-ripe bananas, apples, pears, cherries, apricots, citrus fruits, wholemeal bread and pasta, baked beans, vegetables, eg broccoli, cucumber, peas, jacket potatoes, beans, wholegrains, eg barley, oily fish, lentils esp. green and brown, oats, onions, garlic and eggs.

eating habits to include healthy snacks and
desserts like fruit, yoghurt and seeds.

Concentrate on starchy complex-carbohydrates
like bread, pasta, jacket potatoes and baked
beans for slow release of sugar into the blood

Impaired taste for sweet foods can occur, leading
to cravings.

Some research has linked cows' milk products with
diabetic autoimmune reactions (type 1
diabetes). Breast feeding for at least 3
months, weaning at 5-6months, no cows' milk
products until after 1 year old would be
advisable.

Avoid special diabetic foods as sorbitol, an
artificial sweetener is not healthy, encourages
a sweet tooth and may cause diarrhoea and
tummy ache.

Recurrent high blood sugar levels can cause
tummy ache due to ketosis.

Urinary infections are more common when blood
sugar is high.

Healthy eating and exercise for the whole family is
advisable.

Regular eye tests are important in older children.

Fenugreek seed powder has been shown in trials to
enable insulin dose reduction.

Sugar is often given if there is a sudden drop in
blood sugar which results in hypoglycaemic
attack (dizzy, fainting, pale, slurred speech)
This is good advice in an emergency. Try
concentrated fruit juice.

Contacts:
British Diabetic Association Tel: 020 7636 6112 ■

D

Nutrients to consider

● Beware chromium if on
medication as it improves
insulin function and
prescription doses may
need reducing under
medical supervision.

● MVM to provide broad
base of vitamins and
minerals for health.

● Flax oil added to cereals
daily; linseed capsules (BC)
oil (HN, Sa, HS)

● Apple pectin $^1/_4$tsp daily
as a source of soluble fibre
which slows glucose
absorption and can prevent
sudden rises in blood sugar
levels (S)

DIARRHOEA

Dietary advice

In babies:
- More boiled water, less milk.
- Stop solids.
- Breast feeding can often continue but careful attention to mother's diet, eg avoid below mentioned items to give bulk to infants stools.

In children & adolescents:
- Increase soluble fibre.
- Increase boiled or bottled water.
- Avoid wheat and dairy until settled replacing with goats', rice or soya milk.
- Avoid fizzy drinks as sugar can induce diarrhoea.
- Increase clear fluids to rehydrate.
- Coffee can aggravate.
- No fruit juice (or dilute 50-60% water).
- Avoid sugar and sorbitol (artificial sweeteners).
- Carob powder can halt diarrhoea (give in diluted apple juice or water, 3 hourly).
- Camomile tea or red raspberry tea in older children.
- Potassium foods can balance minerals lost through dehydration.
- Probiotic foods including soya, yoghurt and cottage cheese to rebalance gut bacteria.
- NB: If diarrhoea persists after dietary changes consult a GP. In rare cases can be due to Crohn's Disease.
- BENEFICIAL FOODS: Wholegrain cereals, brown rice, bananas for potassium, fruit and vegetable juices goats' or soya milk, small amounts of fish and brown rice, low fat live yoghurt, starchy soups, eg carrot, beans or potato, oatbran, cottage cheese, soya products.

SEE ALSO: WORMS, PARASITES, DIGESTIVE PROBLEMS, BACTERIAL INFECTIONS, CANDIDA, FOOD INTOLERANCES, GROWTH

May be frequent, unformed, incontinence or steatorrhoea (fatty stools). In babies loose frequent stools are normal in breast fed infants but any change should be reported to a GP or health visitor. Can rapidly become a medical emergency in babies and young children especially if vomiting too, due to dehydration and disturbance of minerals in blood.

Toddler diarrhoea is common is common and normal due to an immature gut. Loose nappies may occur up to 8 times daily. If growth is okay, don't worry just increase fluids to prevent dehydration and fibre.

FACTORS TO CONSIDER
Bacterial infection; diarrhoea often follows a course of antibiotics; maternal diet high in citrus, spices, caffeine, alcohol and certain fruit and vegetables; food allergy/intolerance, often dairy, but may be just lactose (milk sugar); coeliac disease, food poisoning especially if vomiting; cystic fibrosis; digestive disturbances; imbalanced intestinal bacteria (dysbiosis); yeast overgrowth (candida); excess vitamin C; stress in older children; teething.

GENERAL ADVICE
Stop any vitamin C supply temporarily.
Homeopathic camomilla can help especially if watery diarrhoea. See Appendix.
Probiotics can help prevent diarrhoea if travelling.
Electrolyte mixes are available, eg Dioralyte from GP or chemist.
Oatbran added to cereals for couple of days can clear diarrhoea as a good source of soluble fibre.
Increase fluids.

DIARRHOEA

D

DIGESTIVE PROBLEMS

SEE ALSO: ANXIETY, INDIGESTION, NAUSEA, DIARRHOEA, CONSTIPATION, BLOATING, GASTRO-ENTERITIS, IRRITABLE BOWEL SYNDROME, FOOD INTOLERANCES, GROWTH

These are common in children and range from 'butterflies' to gastro-enteritis. In between there may be nausea, bloating, wind, bowel disturbances and indigestion. Irritable bowel syndrome (IBS) in children should be taken seriously.

Identifying the underlying causes is vital to a sustained recovery. Many children suffer gastric disturbances when nervous or worried, eg examinations, new school, bullying, upsets at home. These are usually transient and related to a nervous system problem rather than digestive. Although symptomatic relief can be achieved the problem will recur in the same situation.

Gallstones are rare in children but there are some genetic links. Formation of stones in children is thought to be due to a faulty enzyme, which results in inadequate bile formation with excess cholesterol crystallising into stones. British Liver Trust: 01473 276 326.

Please refer to relevant section for more detail. ■

Nutrients to consider Diarrhoea

● Super Gar for antifungal/bacterial properties and immune system; one daily over 8 years (HN)

● Slippery Elm powder; a pinch – $^1/_4$tsp daily (N)

● Kiddy Tum for gentle herbal relief for over 2 years (K)

● Kid Chamomile for nervous diarrhoea in over 2 years (K)

● Zinc citrate 15-25mgs (L, BC, AR) or $^1/_2$level measure sherbet flavoured powder under tongue alternate days for over 8 years of age (HN) or drops (BC)

● Vitamin A x 1 drop daily (BC)

● Probiotics, eg acidophilus powder (BC) or sacromycees boullardii 1 twice daily or 2 twice daily short term (helps raise SigA immunity in gut and reduces diarrhoea), lacto bascillus acidophilus plus pectin as a capsule or opened to rebalance beneficial bacteria (AR, NC) can halt diarrhoea. Lacto G.G. in older children (AR,NC)

Dietary advice

● Increase fibre.

● Avoid refined white flour and grains.

● BENEFICIAL FOODS: Fruit especially apples, kiwis, bananas, nectarines, pineapple, papaya and pears, oats, pulses, live yoghurt, cabbage, pinch nutmeg, dried fruit and wholegrains.

Dizziness

SEE ALSO: ANOREXIA, ALLERGY, MIGRAINE, FAINTING, BLOOD SUGAR IMBALANCES.

This is usually a symptom of something else. There are many causes.

Factors to consider

Blood sugar imbalances, diabetes, anaemia, petit mal/epilepsy, food allergies, ear infection, anorexia, anxiety (adrenal stress), postural hypotension (low blood pressure on standing up), poor oxygen and circulation to the brain, drug side effects, too much computer!, migraine (nausea, but not necessarily headache).

General advice

Follow guidelines under blood sugar.

Consider cranial osteopathy as head and neck problems may be involved.

Check hearing and vision as the ears are linked to balance.

Ask GP to test iron levels.

In rare chronic cases brain tumour could be a factor. See GP.

DMG for increased oxygen to the brain (AR) needs professional supervision.

In an acute situation, eg fainting or trembling, eat something sweet, eg sugar in water or juice to raise blood sugar quickly. NB: this is not a long term solution so see GP for tests. ■

Dietary advice

● Reduce dairy foods as mucous congestion may affect ear balance.

● Ginger can help. Add to stir fries or to hot water and fresh lemon or in baking.

● Eat often.

● Reduce animal fats from meat and dairy.

● Avoid fizzy drinks and salty snacks.

● Include potassium and betacarotene foods.

● BENEFICIAL FOODS: Garlic, ginger, wholegrains, fruit and vegetables.

Nutrients to consider

● MVM for all round nutrients.

● B complex for nerves and blood sugar; 10 drops (BC)or B Vital x I daily over 5 years or 10 drops or children's capsules x one daily 5-12 years. (BC)

● Gingko Complex $^1/_2$tablet twice daily (BM) or Gingko biloba tincture in older children. (N)

● Chromium drops x one daily (BC, BR) or as Trace Minerals x 4 drops daily (BC)or as Cr GTF 1 alternate days over 8 years. (HN)

Down's Syndrome

SEE ALSO: LEARNING DIFFICULTIES, IMMUNE FUNCTION, THYROID PROBLEMS, OBESITY, BLOOD SUGAR

Affects about 1 in 800 births with a steep rise in incidence with pregnancies in women over 35 years. The statistics are altered by terminations. Approximately 92% of positively tested pregnancies are aborted.

Down's Syndrome increases the risk of heart disorders by 40% and thyroid disorders by 30%. There is male infertility in Down's syndrome sufferers and hearing problems in 50% and an increase in visual disturbances is common. Increased life-span means Alzheimer's and respiratory diseases are more common now.

There is an extra chromosome present. The extra chromosome results in increased super-oxide dismutase (SOD). Production of SOD, an anti-oxidant enzyme accelerates aging. There are three genes making SOD. Glutathione Peroxidase (GP) is also affected, but the reason is less clear. Glutathione Peroxidase is responsible for disarming hydrogen peroxide produced from SOD. It is the build up of hydrogen peroxide that is thought to cause the rapid ageing associated with Down's. Supplementing selenium theoretically should slow this process down. Other research has shown that supplementing high levels of B vitamins can improve performance.

Prognosis

Children with Down's syndrome frequently demonstrate friendly, affectionate and cheerful moods, which can make looking after them very rewarding. There are special schools for a child with Down's syndrome, but integration into mainstream schools is now often the norm.

However, mental stimulation before school age, which usually rests on the parents, has an important influence on the child's eventual level of intellectual development. Experience shows children such as these can integrate successfully into the family and society and make a valuable contribution. Most children with Down's syndrome learn to walk, and many learn to speak and read well with good education and many have jobs. There are varying degrees of disability/ IQ. Various research papers

---

Dietary advice

- Control weight as obesity is common (small frequent meals).
- Blood sugar management (obesity = more diabetes).
- Lots of brightly coloured fruit and vegetables for antioxidants to reduce the effects of rapid aging.
- Increase magnesium foods.
- Avoid dairy, refined foods and sugar.
- Reduce gluten grains (wheat, oats, barley and rye.) to reduce autoimmune reactions and improve absorption.
- Increase fish oils and lecithin for learning/brain function.
- BENEFICIAL FOODS: Sesame, sunflower, pumpkin seeds and their oils, tahini (sesame paste), seafood, yeast cereals cottage cheese, chicken, garlic, dairy produce, lean meat.

D

Nutrients to consider
●MVM, eg Vitamist MVM for kids. (NW)
●Chromium drops x one daily (BC) or GTF chromium one daily over 8 years (HP) or Bio Cr Complex one daily over 12 years. (BM)
●Selenium (for GP and SOD enzymes); Selenium and vitamin E combined as one daily over 12 years (L) or 4 drops trace minerals (BC) or 1 ml of selenium solution (AR,NC,R) for over 8 years or Selenium 2000 mcgs over 8 years – one tablet alternate days. (HN)
●Antioxidants, eg vitamins ACE, zinc and selenium one daily over 12 years. (L)
●B vitamins for performance; 10 drops or 1 x children's capsule 5-12 years (BC) or B Vital one daily over 5 years. (HN)
●Super Gar one daily over 8 years to protect the heart. (HN)

are showing that IQ and learning ability can be increased with nutritional supplementation.

GENERAL ADVICE

Massage dry skin with vitamin E cream (L) or Infant Starflower cream. (N)

Beware temperature fluctuations if thyroid is affected.

Boost immune function as respiratory infections are common.

Babies may have problems sucking initially. You may need to express breast milk for a week or two.

Development is progressive, but delayed.

Exercise and breathing exercises to improve oxygen to the brain.

MSB Formula contains garlic and other nutrients to protect the heart. Contact ; Ontario, Canada Tel: 613 820 9065 or 613 829 2226.

Stimulation is vital especially for 0-5 year olds.

Check internet for nutritional advice.

Contacts:
Down's Syndrome Association. Tel: 020 8682 4001

American based programmes :Warner Programme, California Tel: 714 441 2600

Institute for Achievement of Human Potential, Philadelphia have specialised programmes for Down's children, Pennsylvania Tel: 800 736 4663 ■

Dyslexia

SEE ALSO: LEARNING DIFFICULTIES, ADHD, HYPERACTIVITY, DYSPRAXIA, GLUE EAR, TOXICITY, ANXIETY, DEPRESSION

Sufferers of dyslexia usually have normal or above average intelligence, but have difficulties processing information especially in relation to letters. Spelling, reading and writing are the main areas affected. Children may have good creative, oral and numerical skills but auditory and visual perception, sequencing and organisational skills may be lacking. Instructions may need repeating and times and dates become muddled. This specific learning difficulty requires early diagnosis and implementation of educational and social strategies.

Incidence is 10% of school children with boys four times more likely than girls. Diagnosis is possible as young as 3 years old but most common age for identification is 6-7 years when reading may be delayed.

FACTORS TO CONSIDER

Genetics.

Research indicates cerebellum in the brain may be involved.

EFAs may be deficient in dyslexia. The brain is 60% fat and chemicals for neurotransmitter functions seem to be impaired, probably due to changes in neurons (nerve cells). EFAs help to build neurons.

Research is indicating that although a type of fatty acid called DHA is vital for brain formation and structure, it appears to be EPA which is more important for minute to minute functioning.

Insufficient choline, folic acid, B vitamins and glutamine.

Previous glue ear.

Toxic metals such as mercury, lead or aluminum can affect brain function.

SYMPTOMS

Slow to complete written work, reverses letters, eg b for d, confuses left and right, slow reader, short term memory loss, under-achievement, fatigue, problems with shoe laces, poor at sequencing (days of the week and alphabet). Some dyslexic children can

Dietary advice
● Lean red meat for iron once per week.
● Oily fish for EFAs and iron.
● Vitamin C and iron foods together.
● Avoid sugar, an anti-nutrient.
● No junk food as sugar and additives can confuse the brain.
● Add lecithin granules to cereals, soups or yoghurt. Contain choline vital for brain function esp. memory.
● BENEFICIAL FOODS: Oily fish, lean red meat, seeds, nuts, leafy green vegetables, flaxseeds, ginger.

D

Dyslexia

Nutrients to consider

● EFAs These are the best choices of EFAs researched for dyslexia at time of writing – Eye Q; start with 2 capsules per day building up to 6 per day for 3 months; then 2 per day maintenance. Contains preferable ratios of EPA/DHA/GLA (omega 3 and 6 oils) for memory, concentration and processing of information. (HS, NC, R) Alternatively Eskimo 3 has similar ratios. Give 5mls daily (Nu).

● Gingko Complex to improve circulation to the brain and short term memory $^1/_2$tablet twice daily (BM) or tincture in older children. (N)

● Iron is vital for brain function, concentration, memory and learning; Easy iron 5-8 years one alternate days or one daily over 8 years (HN) or herbal Floridix. (N)

● Calcium/magnesium in 1:1 ratio for most dyslexics. (HN, S)

● Zinc for brain function; Zn citrate 25mgs (BC) or sherbet flavoured powder $^1/_2$level measure under tongue alternate days over 8 years. (HN)

● B complex for nervous system; B Vital has ginseng for energy and anxiety, 1 daily over 5 years or children's capsule daily 5-12 years. (BC)

● ZEN has a relaxing calming effect in 20-30 minutes whilst maintaining and maybe improving mental alertness and concentration. One daily over 5 years. (AR)

● Brain Food Formula 1 daily over 12 years provides nutrients for optimal concentration, memory and learning. (HN)

● Chocolate Memory is a delicious chocolate drink containing phosphatidyl serine to boost brain chemicals for memory. 10gms in milk or water at bedtime. (HN)

become disruptive at school and at home due to frustration and boredom.

GENERAL ADVICE

EFA supplementation appears to be the most effective nutritional approach, but will work best for those with the signs and symptoms of deficiency such as rough, dry patches of skin, excessive thirst, poor sleep pattern and poor hair condition which are all signs of deficiency. Concentration and attentiveness usually improve. Avoid cod liver oil and other fish liver oils as levels of Vitamin A could be too high. Additionally liver oils can be polluted and toxic.

The Dyslexia Research Trust is researching the role of EFAs in learning. They are also conducting a trial on saliva tests to identify dyslexia in young children to enable early action.

More often linked to inner ear than visual problems but unstable eyes and visual function is common in dyslexia. Tinted glasses, computer guards and reading sheets can help. Eye function is also affected by EFA deficiency.

Simple computer games are being developed for pre-school children to identify dyslexia before normal reading age.

Genetic links are being discovered.

There are overlaps between dyslexia and ADHD and 50% overlap between dyslexia and dyspraxia.

Clear biological basis to dyslexia with brain scans showing asymmetry in the language areas and connections between neurons impaired, affecting rapid processing of information.

'Labels' of ADHD, dyslexia and dyspraxia are not necessarily helpful.

Self esteem is often low so regular praise and concentrating on non-academic skills as well is important.

Anxiety, depression and fatigue may be involved.

Computers can be very helpful for dyslexic children. However the screen can be difficult to see for some. You can use a blue screen in Word by going to tools/options/general and

ticking Blue background, white text. This should enable clear fixing of words on the screen. You can also get a natural keyboard, split so the right and left hands are kept separate enabling touch typing.
Australian Bush Flower Remedy – Bush Fuchsia. (An R)

Contacts:
Dyslexia Research Trust – Tel: 01865 271042

British Dyslexia Association – Tel: 0118 966 8271 ■

Nutrients to consider

(These are the best choices at time of writing.)

● Eye Q; start with 2 capsules per day building up to 6 per day for 3 months; then 2 per day maintainance. Contains preferable ratios of EPA / DHA / GLA (omega 3 and 6 oils) for memory, concentration and processing of information (HS, Ch, NC, R) Alternatively Eskimo 3 has similar ratios. Give 5mls daily (Nu).

● Magnesium for muscles and fatigue; Bio Mg capsule whole or sprinkled onto food or drink; chewable one daily from 4 years (L); or Bio magnesium with calcium, manganese, B6, 1 daily 6-12 years (BM), Bio Mg one daily over 3 years (BC) or solution $^1/_4$-$^1/_2$tsp (1.5mls) 1-2 times daily. (AR, NC,R) Magnesium phosphate is calming. (BM)

● B complex for nervous system; B vital has ginseng for energy x one daily over 5 years or children's capsule daily 5-12 years. (BC)

● Gingko Complex to improve circulation to the brain and short term memory $^1/_2$tablet twice daily (BM) or tincture in older children. (N)

● Iron is vital for brain function, concentration, memory and learning; Easy iron 5-8 years one alternate days or one daily over 8 years. (HN)

● Calcium in 1:1 ratio for most dyslexics. (HN, S)

● Zinc for brain function; Zn citrate 25mgs (BC) or sherbet flavoured powder $^1/_2$level measure under tongue alternate days over 8 years. (HN)

● ZEN alternate days. (see Dyslexia)

● Brain Food Formula one daily over 12 years provides nutrients for optimal concentration, memory and learning. (HN)

● Chocolate Memory. (see Dyslexia)

DYSPRAXIA

SEE ALSO: DYSLEXIA, LEARNING DIFFICULTIES, ADHD, HYPERACTIVITY, ANXIETY, DEPRESSION

Defined as an impairment or immaturity of the organisation of movement. Associated problems with perception, thought and language.

It affects:

Acquisition and maintenance of gross and fine motor skills;

Language may be inarticulate and late to develop;

Organisational skills.

Symptoms include poor handwriting, fatigue, poor at sport/ PE, poor memory, needs instructions repeated, poorly organised, impaired concept of time (often late), short attention span, easily distracted, does better one to one than in a group, poor balance, clumsy, (eg breaks and spills things, bumps into things, slips on the stairs), messy eating.

In older children anxiety, OCD, depression and fatigue may occur. Maybe, but not always, has a history of feeding problems, irritable baby, slow motor development and speech.

GENERAL ADVICE

The Dyspraxia Society believes 20-30% of all learning difficulties may be rooted in EFA deficiency.

Boost self-esteem by ignoring the errors, praising achievement, listening well. Provide non-spill cups and sauce bottles.

Exercise is important. Ball games are usually not a good idea as hand/eye co-ordination is poor. Concentrate on swimming and walking.

Aching legs are common. Magnesium and manganese may help.

Reading::

Dyspraxia: The Hidden Handicap – Dr Amanda Kirby – covers all ages, mainly for parents and sufferers.

Contacts:

The Dyslexia Research Trust – Tel: 01865 271042 also research dyspraxia and EFAs.

Dyspraxia Foundation Tel: 01462 454986, have a series of factsheets, a reading list and special pens. They also do research and offer help and support to parents, teachers and carers. ■

EARS

RED EARS

Sudden onset of red, hot external ear. Usually due to circulatory problems and often grown out of.

May indicate:

Erythromylalgia, but this usually only affects hands and feet;

Raynaud's disease, mainly hands and feet, fluctuates hot and cold, but mainly cold;

Migraine can trigger red ears but mainly in adults;

Autistic children suffer from this, but red ears do not necessarily mean your child is autistic.

Advice:

Cool with ice packs;

Keep diet alkaline so reduce acidic foods and animal protein to lower inflammation, eg milk, meat pulses, chocolate, oatmeal, pasta, eggs and fish. Increase alkaline foods, eg vegetables, fruit, honey (over one year), raisins, melon, millet, corn;

Give vitamin C with bioflavonoids for circulation and anti-inflammatory effect. Bio C also has minerals to alkalise the system $1/4$tsp daily (AN);

Avoid junk food.

DISCHARGE

Usually a sign of otitis media. There are various discharges, eg yellow and sticky, offensive, white and milky. Each responds to a different approach. Blackmores celloid minerals are good for this with different types for each.

DEAFNESS

Often linked to otitis media and sinus congestion. It is not usually total, but certain frequencies are missed leading to speech delay. Always get full testing.

SENSITIVITY TO NOISE

Some children appear to be afraid of certain noises, eg vacuum cleaner, aeroplanes, lawn mower, food mixer. This may have a psychological basis, but it is also important to eliminate hearing imbalances. Occasionally the hearing is over sensitive mainly to high pitched noises. Ask for a full audiometry test to check for hearing frequencies. Contact the Auditory Integration Training (AIT) Centre for advice. Although most children grow out of this phase if no cause can be found it can, rarely, be a sign of autism.

OTITIS MEDIA

Also known as **Glue Ear** occurs when the eustachian tube, linking the middle-ear to the back of the nose, becomes blocked, and a jelly-like fluid, naturally secreted by the ear, is unable to drain away becoming thicker and filling the middle-ear cavity. This can reduce hearing to a muffled roar. Can be acute as a result of a cold or measles or may be chronic (glue ear). 30% of under 6 year olds are affected, with 95% suffering at least one bout.

Grommets are often inserted under general anaesthetic for glue ear (rarely before 5 years and a long waiting list). The editors of *The New England Journal of Medicine* report 'the results of this study indicate that the procedure has little long term benefit with respect to hearing, behaviour or cognitive development'.

A link has also been discovered between glue ear and bottle feeding. Using ultrasound monitoring, researchers at the University of Southampton have found that the method of feeding a baby could be the key to understanding this common ailment. The action of sucking on the breast, which is pulled up into the mouth against the soft palate, exercises a muscle which effectively opens the Eustachian tube and this tube connecting the middle ear to the back of the throat, drains away the fluid. In bottle feeding, the teat does not reach up into the soft palate, so the muscle is not used in the same way.

Acute symptoms include pain, fever, discharge and nasal congestion, repeated ear infections (usually treated with antibiotics), behavioural problems, speech delay and poor social development.

Chronic symptoms: often painless, but may appear partially deaf in the affected ear, the ears feel full or blocked, behavioural problems, speech delay, lack of concentration and poor social development may be noticed. The condition can remain undiagnosed for some time.

Dietary advice for Otitis Media

- Stop dairy foods during an attack as it increases mucous formation. If it recurs on re-introduction, discontinue and replace with soya (over 6 months), rice milk or goats' milk including Nanny Goat formula.
- Also consider wheat and citrus allergies.
- Increase fluids.
- No sugar.
- Raw garlic in honey.
- Fresh lemon or cider vinegar and honey in water to clear mucous and boost immune system.
- BENEFICIAL FOODS: Soups, live yoghurt, rice, oat, goat or soya milks, sweet potatoes, berries, blackcurrants, kale, oily fish, garlic.

FACTORS TO CONSIDER

Recent or current infection of the respiratory tract and food allergy especially dairy are major causes of ear ache and glue ear. Inhalant allergy to dust mites, animal dander or smoke, immune suppression, foreign body, pollution, tooth decay, sinusitis and vaccination may also be involved.

GENERAL ADVICE

Always see a GP as a secondary infection and
   perforated eardrum are possibilities especially
   if there is a discharge of pus.
Chewing sugar free Xylitol gum can exercise the
   eustachian tube from throat to ear, coats the
   lining preventing bacteria from sticking and
   helps drainage. Sugar free chewing gum
   containing Xylitol has beenshown to reduce
   infections by inhibiting pneumococci which are
   bacteria with the ability to colonise the ear
   passages. Xylitol syrup for under 5 year olds.
   (HS, Ch)
Hopi Ear Candles can draw out the wax. Care is
   needed when using on small children. (HS,
   NC)
Cranial osteopathy may help in chronic cases, esp.
   glue ear.
Horseradish and garlic crushed in honey can ease.
Avoid swimming during an attack and use earplugs
   otherwise.
If antibiotics are prescribed give probiotics, eg
   acidophilus when the course is finished, eg
   ABC Dophillus. (S)
Boost immune system.
Steam inhalation/eucalyptus oil in a room burner
   can help congestion.
See aromatherapy etc in Appendix.

SUMMARY OF HOW TO KEEP EARS AND HEARING HEALTHY

Nutrients needed: EFAs, vitamin A, B vitamins,
   Vitamin C/bioflavonoids.
Avoid: cola, sugar, dairy, salicylates.
Maintaining even blood sugar/insulin levels reduces
   constriction of blood vessels.
Regular routine testing of hearing and
   development. ■

Nutrients to consider for Otitis Media

E

- Immune nutrients
- Cod liver oil $^1/_2$tsp twice daily. (HN) or dricelle CLO powder (BC). Ascertain an unpolluted source and beware dose as vitamin A toxicity is a risk in under 5 years.
- Herbal aloe ear drops for congestion, pain, deafness 2-6 drops. (HN)
- Mullein oil formula as ear drops. (N)
- MVM.
- 3 drops of warmed garlic and/or onion oil dropped into the ear for pain, healing and infection.
- Potassium Chloride (as PCIP) in homeopathic potency hourly to relieve congestion in the eustachian tube. (BM)
- Calcium Phosphate to boost immunity and act as a tonic. (BM)
- Sambucol Complex is immune boosting and contains anti-viral elderberry or elderflower. $1^1/_2$tsps twice daily. Contains elderflower for mucous membranes and acts as a decongestant (HN) or elderflower herbal compound from 2 years. (N)
- Nat-Choo contains eyebright for sinuses from 2 years. (K)

EARS

103

EATING DISORDERS

SEE ALSO: ANOREXIA NERVOSA, BULIMIA NERVOSA, EXERCISE, BLOOD SUGAR

Dietary advice

- A healthy balanced diet can prevent the start of an eating disorder by reducing cravings and providing the right nutrients.
- Avoid stimulants like tea, coffee, chocolate and sugar.
- Refined foods like pizza, white bread, sugar and fast foods are lacking nutrients and imbalance blood sugar.
- Increase fibre foods to satisfy and balance blood sugar. Fibre is not absorbed.
- Avoid common food allergens such as dairy and wheat
- Increase zinc foods.
- Include fish for EFAs which help control hormones.
- Adequate fluid intake is vital to offset dehydration caused by low food intake in anorexics and purging in bulimics. Need at least 8 glasses water daily.

Defined as an unnatural obsession with weight accompanied by distorted body image.

Increasingly, younger children are suffering from eating disorders. Some as young as infant school age are concerned about body image and weight. With 48% of 25-35 year old women 'dieting' and 20% of all women constantly fighting weight problems, children are getting the wrong messages about food. Picky eaters will not necessarily develop an eating disorder but many adults with eating disorders have childhood triggers. Girls more so than boys but do not overlook boys who also suffer from eating disorders and this appears to be increasing

The term covers a wide range of presentations including: Anorexia Nervosa; Bulimia Nervosa; binge eating; and compulsive over eating.

A typical pattern is yo-yo dieting leading to anorexia, then bulimia, then compulsive overeating, but there are often overlaps. Eating disorders are commonly linked to depression and anxiety and are more prevalent in middle class, high achievers. The effects of eating disorders can include infertility (as low weight stops periods), depression and osteoporosis.

The management of eating disorders is most effective when nutritional therapy is combined with psychotherapy or professional counselling.

FACTORS TO CONSIDER
Blood sugar imbalances.
Food allergies.
Nutrient deficiencies (especially zinc and chromium).
Depression.
Anxiety.
Family history of addictive behaviour.
Serotonin disturbances and low self-esteem. Some research suggests a genetic link.

HOW TO SPOT THE SIGNS OF AN EATING DISORDER
Preoccupation with weight, wearing baggy clothes constantly, trips to the bathroom straight after meals, laxative abuse, food disappearing, increase in exercise, social withdrawal.

Symptoms include fluctuations in mood and energy, depression, lack of self esteem, poor sleep patterns, night time fridge raiding, hoarding of food, poor performance at school.

E

Binge eating involves episodes of uncontrolled eating, but not necessarily accompanied by purging. May yo-yo from very little foods to very large amounts. It is possible to be a binge eater without being bulimic.

Compulsive overeating is when obese or overweight children have little control over their appetite. They may binge but not purge and then become oveweight. Foods used frequently include refined carbohydrates such as cakes, pizzas and biscuits and it is thought that comfort eating is more common as the pressures on children increase in the modern world. Nutrient deficiencies from processed foods may also be involved.

GENERAL ADVICE

Set a good example. Concentrate on healthy eating for the whole family with no actual dieting

Praise children for every achievement. Boost self-esteem. Discuss all qualities and reduce the emphasis on appearance

Don't use food as a reward as it reinforces the idea that food is a treat and therefore not to be enjoyed without guilt

Never impose calorie restricted diets on children

Children need fats for brain development and their high-energy requirements for growth. Just make sure they are essential fatty acids from fish, seeds and vegetables. What is healthy for an adult is not necessarily so for a child

Don't ban foods. Occasional sweets and crisps are okay. This discourages secret eating

Encourage children to help shop and cook, teaching them to make good choices.

Let her know she is loved no matter what!

Be prepared to listen at any time

Educate yourself so you can help her and be ready when she is, to initiate help

Leave information of helplines etc lying around. She may not speak to parents, but could cope initially with anonymous help

Contacts:
Eating Disorders Association: Tel: 01603 619090 or helpline Tel: 01603 621414

First Steps to Freedom Tel:01926 851 608 or helpline on 01926 851608

Overeaters Anonymous Tel: 07000 784 985 ■

Nutrients to consider

● Zinc at supervised high levels to address associated depression in anorexia and bulimia. See a qualified nutritionist.

● Chromium – one drop daily (BC) or GTF Cr one daily (HN) or special formula for regulating blood sugar, eg Sucroguard 1 daily (BC) or Normoglycaemia 1 daily (L), both over 12 years.

● EFAs – Essential Balance Junior 3 tsps daily. (HN)

● Aqueous Multi Plus 1 tablespoon daily (BR,NC,R) or spray MVM. (NW)

● Probiotics.

● See also Anorexia Nervosa and Bulimia Nervosa for more suggestions.

E

ECZEMA

Dietary advice

● Identify food intolerances/ allergies in following order: avoid cows' milk products, citrus, eggs, additives, wheat, tomatoes, beef, goats' products, and peanuts if found to be allergic. Cows' milk products are the commonest, but some may need to exclude all gluten grains, eg wheat, barley, rye and oats which should not be given to babies under a year old. See allergy section for details of exclusion diets. For skin disorders, exclusion for a minimum of 6 weeks is required to allow for healing.

● Walnut kernels contain polyphenolic compounds which appear to reduce allergic responses in specific cells.

● Increase EFAs and reduce saturated fats, eg from dairy products, crisps, chips.

● Vitamin E, A, chromium and zinc foods for healing.

● Pineapple and papaya can improve digestion and are anti-inflammatory.

● Quercetin is an anti-oxidant capable of reducing histamine and inflammation. Found in cauliflower and broccoli.

● Try a low allergenic diet and take special care on weaning.

● If breast feeding try a dairy free maternal diet and monitor the effect.

● BENEFICIAL FOODS:
Fish, green vegetables, carrots, seed oils, seeds (hemp, flax, sesame, sunflower and pumpkin) avocados, pineapple, papaya and other tropical fruits, vegetable soups, fresh fruit juices, red cherries, onions, garlic, broccoli and cauliflower, soya, rice, oat milks, pear or apple juice instead orange juice, brown rice and millet are anti-inflammatory, walnut kernels, lamb, turkey, turmeric, sea vegetables.

SEE ALSO: CANDIDA, ASTHMA, HAYFEVER, ALLERGIES, LEAKY GUT, CONSTIPATION

From the Greek word meaning 'to boil over', it is certainly an inflammatory condition. Also known as dermatitis, skin is inflamed, dry, itchy and weepy. Can appear in patches, often in creases such as elbows and back of knees which come and go. Identifying 'causes' may reduce likelihood of later asthma or hayfever.

Eczema's incidence is approximately 1 in 7 children under the age of 5 years. Usually appears in the first year of life, but most will resolve by five years. 4% of under 12 year olds have eczema. 50% of sufferers later develop asthma. In rare cases, onset can occur in adolescence often accompanied by other allergies, eg hayfever.

Dermatitis usually refers to contact irritation, eg washing powders etc. Eczema refers to more chronic skin irritation.

FACTORS TO CONSIDER

Contact irritants, eg washing powder, or inhalants, eg cat hair, but often linked to food allergies, candida, 'leaky gut' (damage to intestinal lining leading to allergies and malabsorption), anxiety, toxicity, nutrient deficiencies, eg essential fatty acids, zinc, vitamin A and early weaning, genetic or familial condition.

Research has shown that abnormal white blood cells from eczema sites result in a rise in histamine which increases allergic response.

There are 7 different kind of eczema with different causes and responses.

15% of cases are atopic, ie another close family member has an allergy. This is thought to be linked to poor metabolism of EFAs.

External skin health can reflect internal skin health. Leaky gut may be involved.

GENERAL ADVICE

Steroid creams may slow growth and may accumulate in body contributing to 'leaky gut' and spider veins in adulthood.

Secondary infection is a common cause of un-

responsive eczema. Ask for a
swab to be tested.

Avoid creams containing arachis
oil (a peanut derivative), eg
in zinc and caster oil cream,
as some research suggests a
link with peanut allergy as it
can be absorbed easily
through inflamed skin, ie
eczema sufferers may
develop peanut allergy if
using arachis oil.

Wear cotton clothes. Avoid wool
and man made fibres.

Keep nails short and clean.

Encourage exercise to reduce
stress and enhance
circulation.

Avoid constipation.

Beware secondary infections
especially staph aureous.
Avoid antibiotics as leaky gut
can be made worse. Treat
leaky gut when cause found,
eg allergy or infection.

Use vitamin E oil in bath with one
drop lavender and one drop
tea tree oil. Bathe at least
once daily in the solution and
moisturise afterwards. NB
always use a bath mat as oils
can make bath slippery.

No smoking in the house.

Non-bio washing powders or
preferably use Eco-balls
which are detergent free. No
fabric conditioner.

Use a water softener in hard water
areas.

Bottled or filtered water rather
than tap for drinking or
cooking. Fitting a plumbed in
systemic water filter can help
as toxic chemicals can be
absorbed through the skin as
well.

E

Nutrients to consider

● Evening primrose oil (HS), which is anti-allergenic (also 2-3gms topically daily) especially if family history of allergies or use Infant Starflower cream. (N)

● Fish or linseed oils – Essential Balance Junior is 1:1 ratio of omega 3 and 6 oils with a butterscotch flavour 1-3 tsps daily from weaning (HN); Dricelle CLO powder orally (BC) or one capsule daily for 4-12 year olds (L) or Udos Choice. (Sa, HS)

● Zinc – for EFA absorption and skin healing; 10 drops daily (BC) or sherbet flavoured powder $^1/_2$level measure under tongue alternate days for over 8 years on alternate days. (HN)

● Vitamin E helps prevent scarring and itching. 100ius taken orally or pierced onto sore area. (BC)

● Vitamin A x one drop daily for new skin growth. (BC)

● Biotin 25-100 mcgs has been helpful for childhood eczema. Add a B complex.

● Magnesium; Bio Mg $^1/_2$capsule whole or sprinkled onto food or drink 1-3 years or one daily over 3 years (BC); chewable one daily from 4 years (L); $^1/_4$tsp Mg solution in glass water daily over 4 years. (AR,NC,R)

● Calcium compound may provide temporary relief by reducing acidity and inflammation. (BM)

● Quercetin and vitamin C – (Quercetin can reduce allergic reactions) $1^1/_2$ tablets daily for under 12 years (R). Quercetin 300 also has vitamin C and E – 1-2 per day per 50 lbs body weight (AR). Quercetin Plus one daily 50lb body weight. (BC)

● MVM including B vitamins.

● Nettle tincture acts as an anti-histamine to reduce itching (one drop per 6 kgs body weight) Take orally in water or juice. (HS, A) Or nettle juice to lactating mothers.

● Aloe vera gel taken orally. (HN)

● FOS can potentiate growth of beneficial bacteria. Use as a sweetener on cereals, fruit etc. (HN)

● Acidophilus to improve digestion and reduce toxic load, eg ABC Dophillus. (S)

● BPT Formula is a herbal complex for teenage skin $^1/_2$tsp thrice daily. (N)

ECZEMA

Topical Remedies

- Best to identify causes of eczema. So use creams only when investigations completed. The following are some of the best;
- Allergenics cream. Tel: 0870 747 9131
- SK cream. Tel: 01526 832491 or from Green People.
- Golden Emu Oil. (Green People)
- Infant starflower cream. (N)
- Bach Flower Rescue Cream. (HS, Ch)
- Aloe Gel. (HN, X)
- Vitamin E cream. (L,X)
- Super Sensitive Skin Cream – blend of chamomile, rose otto and lavender, has antiseptic properties and addresses inflammation and healing. (Human Nature 020 7328 5452)
- Burdock, nettle and echinacea or goldenseal diluted and applied topically as a wash (anti-bacterial) or orally at one drop per 6 kgs body weight in water or juice. (HS,N,A)
- New pharmaceutical non-steroid cream is available from early 2002 on prescription as Protopic; contains tacrolinius, which is an immune suppressant to reduce allergic response. 90-100% of sufferers in 1000 patients had complete remission.

Avoid carpets. Small children spend a lot of time on the floor. Hard floors reduce house dust mites.

No feather pillows or duvets.

Use a hypo-allergenic mattress cover. (Healthy House)

May be worse in the winter due to low humidity, moisturising the skin can help.

Development of asthma is 3 times more likely in children with eczema.

More prone to herpes simplex virus so avoid anyone with cold sores as widespread infection is possible with fever.

Warts are more likely.

Furry pets can aggravate.

Jurilique do a range of baby products to help dermatitis-related conditions.

Sunlight and seawater are helpful, so go on holiday!

Calendula compresses may ease itching.

Aromatherapy oils can be helpful. Contact qualified practitioner for safety.

Homeopathy and herbs may help. See Appendix.

Contacts:
National Eczema Society – www.eczema.org or Tel: 0870 241 3604

Alternative Centre in London has holistic skin clinic. There is a long waiting list. Tel: 020 7381 2298 ∎

EXERCISE

Not a health condition, but rapidly becoming a health problem. Important for healthy hearts, digestion, diabetes, mood and weight. Modern life has made our children into sloths. Research shows that exercise increases academic performance. This is partly due to improved oxygen to the brain from the circulatory system.

SOME PRACTICAL TIPS

Limit time on the computer and watching TV.

Family activities which encourage exercise create good patterns, but don't force it! Have a family ball game.

Just 30 minutes brisk walking per week or its equivalent, eg swimming, cycling, football etc can produce a 7 % weight loss alongside dietary changes.

Physical education in schools has been reduced so much and most adolescents only receive one hour per week. Bear in mind demotivation and time spent changing etc and the real figure is even less!

Cycle together or go to the park or field and time them on circuits. This avoids unfair competitiveness as they are just improving their own performance. This way even an overweight child can take part and be praised for individual improvement.

Swimming together. There are so many theme pools now that they don't even realise how active they've been.

Indoor ball parks and activity centres for toddlers makes a good party outing.

Walk to school or park further away. Saves the parking hassles too! This can accumulate over a week.

Make an obstacle course in the garden using mats, wooden planks, ropes and balls.

Sporting activities after school or at weekends should be encouraged but remember that not all children enjoy this. Try martial arts as well.

Fresh air is important for bones, skin, heart and well-being.

Don't make exercise a chore, make it fun!

Teach them your old playground games. Buy skipping ropes.

Stretch some strong elastic between two posts or have someone hold two ends and introduce skipping rhymes.

Fit a basket ball ring to the side of the house.

Remember water intake is usually very low in children and you will certainly need to increase with exercise. Buy them a 'cool' sports bottle.

Accept that teenagers tend to become lazier. They have very real energy problems with accelerated growth.

Exercise will increase energy, but nagging will not! ∎

Eyes

SEE ALSO: CRADLE CAP, IMMUNE FUNCTION, CANDIDA, ALLERGY, HAYFEVER, INSOMNIA, INFECTIONS

Always seek medical advice if you suspect visual problems or infection. Rarely, can be linked to diabetic visual problems.

STICKY EYE
Bathing with boiled and cooled water is usually effective. Use separate cotton wool ball for each eye and wipe once only from the inner to the outer eye. Beware infection and conjunctivitis.

CONJUNCTIVITIS
Red, itchy and watery eyes. Usually due to infection and literally means inflammation of the conjunctiva (surface membrane of the eye). It is very contagious. Do not share towels and flannels.

WATERY EYES
May be due to allergic reaction to inhalants, eg dust, pollen, animal dander and feathers. Sensitivity to bright lights may indicate other problems such as adrenal stress or vitamin B2 deficiency. Contact irritants, eg soap, shampoo, chlorine may be factors. Also caused by blocked tear ducts in babies and toddlers. Occasionally surgery is required for this. See an optomotrist.

BLEPHARITIS
Often associated with cradle cap or infection. Eyelids become red and scaly as cradle cap flakes into the eyes. Bathing as for sticky eyes. Treat cradle cap. Bathe eyes in Eyebright and goldenseal solution. (HS) Consider fungal infections.

DARK CIRCLES UNDER THE EYES
Usually due to wheat intolerance, stress (adrenal glands), liver problems or fatigue/poor sleep, iron deficiency. Identify and address links such as candida, anxiety, leaky gut, toxicity.

PUFFY, SWOLLEN EYELIDS
Can be linked to allergy.
Nutrients to consider potassium ascorbate. (BC)

General dietary advice for eyes:

- Vitamin A, vitamin C / bioflavonoid and iron foods.
- Celery is good for fluid balance (makes soup for younger children).
- Increase potassium foods and water to help kidneys excrete toxins.
- Avoid salt, eg cheese crisps and breakfast cereals.
- No sugar or white flour.
- Increase antioxidants esp. purple coloured fruits.
- For Dark Circles, eliminate wheat and if no effects after a week try dairy exclusion.
- BENEFICIAL FOODS: Sweet potatoes, berries, kale, brightly coloured fruit and vegetables, carrots as juice, blackcurrants, blackberries, and leafy green vegetables, celery.

STYES

Caused by bacterial infection in an oil gland which presents as a spot on rim of eyelid. Raspberry leaf tea as an eyewash or hot compress and vitamin A one drop daily taken orally (BC) as deficiency is common if styes recur. Vitamin C for immunity

ITCHY EYES

Usually associated with hayfever and allergies. Homeopathic euphrasia can help or eyebright. (A) Opticrom eye drops. (Ch)

SHORT-SIGHTEDNESS (MYOPIA)

Research has linked high sugar and starch/low protein to some cases. Calcium and vitamin D deficiencies may also be connected. Vitamin C with bioflavonoids 500mgs 1-2 daily (BC,L). Incidence is estimated at 10-40% of junior age children.

GENERAL ADVICE

Visual problems such as long / short sightedness and squints should always be checked by an optician or opthalmologist.

Homeopathic euphrasia can help keep eyes healthy. Can use euphrasia tincture in eye washes.

Cooled chamomile tea can soothe and green tea can reduce dark circles. Make tea with a bag and use the cooled bag on the eyes for 15 minutes.

Boost immunity.

The Bates method is a system of eye exercises to improve long and short sightedness and improve squints.

Contacts:
The Bates Association for Vision Education
Tel: 0870 241 7458   ■

General nutrients to consider

● Anti-oxidants including vitamins A, C, E and minerals zinc and selenium; Se ACE one daily over 8 years (L); Vitamin C x 4 drops (BC) or children's capsule one daily. (BC)

● Colloidal silver drops into eye diluted. (HN)

● Chloride compound for redness. (BM)

● B vitamins for red-rimmed eyes; 10 drops daily (BC) or childrens capsule 5-12 years (BC) or B Vital one daily over 5 years. (HN)

● EFAs – Essential Balance Junior 1-3 tsps daily from weaning (HN) or Udo's Choice (Sa, HN) or CLO for EFAs and vitamin A, but beware dose in under 5 years as vitamin A toxicity possible.(BC)

● For Conjunctivitis,

   ● Eyewash (eyebright and barberry) add two drops to 25ml boiled and cooled water and bathe eyes twice a day. (HS)

   ● Chamomile or fennel tea bags applied warm or hot (bacteria dislike heat).

   ● Vitamin A is sometimes deficient if conjunctivitis is recurrent. one drop daily. (BC)

● For Dark Circles,

   Calendula under eye therapy Tel: 02890 662551 for stockists (contains marigold). Only for older children and teenagers. Floridix iron (HS) if iron deficient diagnosis by Salus House which is herbal iron with B vitamins and vitamin C (one drop per 6lbs body weight). (N)

E

FAINTING

SEE ALSO: BLOOD SUGAR, DIZZINESS, ANAEMIA, TEMPER TANTRUMS, DIABETES.

Not uncommon in children. Usually harmless and transient. May be preceded by pallor, sweating and dizziness. If recurrent, seek medical advice to rule out conditions such as anaemia and diabetes.

May even occur if standing for a prolonged period, eg having long hair dressed or assembly at school.

Also occurs on rising due to postural hypotension when blood pressure does not increase sufficiently on getting up to supply the brain with enough oxygen. Anxiety and stress can exacerbate this as the adrenal glands manage stress and blood pressure.

FACTORS TO CONSIDER

Anaemia.
Low blood pressure.
Musculo-skeletal problems.
Temper tantrums.
Breath holding.
Pain.
Bleeding.

GENERAL ADVICE

Check spine and particularly neck if problem is recurrent. May be slight occlusion of blood supply by out of place vertebrae. Osteopathic assessment can identify and correct problems. Cranial osteopathy can help children.

During temper tantrums children may hold their breath. This results in loss of consciousness. This is frightening to observe, but as soon as consciousness is lost, breathing recommences.

Ask GP to check iron levels.

During a fainting attack put him in a recovery position. On reviving, raise his legs above head for at least 15 minutes (feet up the wall or sofa, if comfortable). If recovery slow or any sign of blueness around lips dial 999.

Fresh air and reducing temperature can stop fainting.

Honey and water or fruit juice if conscious and low blood sugar suspected as the cause.

If energy, thirst and frequent urination are also involved ask GP to check for diabetes. ∎

Dietary advice

- Increase iron rich foods and eat them with vitamin C rich foods.
- Small regular meals (blood sugar guidelines).
- Clean water x 4-5 glasses daily.
- Ensure adequate protein, eg chicken, fish, seeds, nuts, pulses, milk and cheese – see Appendix.
- BENEFICIAL FOODS: Oily fish, seeds, fortified cereals, green vegetables, citrus fruits, blackcurrants, raspberries, bananas, eggs, wholemeal bread.

Nutrients to consider

- Vitamin C as magnesium ascorbate powder. (BC)
- B complex; drops or children's capsule. (BC)
- Gingko Complex for brain circulation; $^{1}/_{2}$tablet twice daily (BM) or tincture in older children. (N)

Fatigue

SEE ALSO: CFS, BLOOD SUGAR, ANAEMIA, ANXIETY, SLEEP PROBLEMS

Low energy levels can be linked to adolescence, depression, learning difficulties, anxiety, anaemia and may be due to lack of sleep, food intolerances, iron deficiency, blood sugar irregularities, and high sugar/ junk foods. If not improved by adequate sleep and dietary intervention seek further advice and investigation. See CFS for details of management. ■

Fever

SEE ALSO: CONVULSIONS, VIRAL AND BACTERIAL INFECTIONS, IMMUNE FUNCTION

Also known as pyrexia, fever is the body's natural way of addressing an acute infection (viral or bacterial). However in young children there is a real risk of febrile convulsion.

Temperatures of under 103(F or 38-9(C in children are rarely a risk unless a rapid rise occurs.

GENERAL ADVICE

NB: never give aspirin to a child with a fever or any child under 12 years.

Avoid iron supplements other than homeopathic if it is a bacterial infection and during the fever as iron feeds bacteria.

Tepid sponging. Remove clothing and gently bathe body with luke-warm/cool flannel. Use strokes away from the heart. This has been found in studies to be more effective than paracetamol.

Fanning can help.

Never wrap the child up even if shivering which is the bodys' way of controlling heat.

Homeopathic aconitum napellus and bryonia alba can be effective in controlling children's temperatures and therefore reducing risk of convulsions.

Catnip tea with blackstrap molasses can be given to infants and children to reduce fever.

See Appendix for homeopathic, herbal, aromatherapy and flower essences. ■

Dietary advice

- Fluids only, water or vegetable and fruit juices, during a fever to eliminate toxins, rehydrate and rest the digestive system.
- Watermelon and its juice are cooling.
- Avoid milk or formula until fever has gone.
- Increase protein after fever to assist rebuilding of body tissue and antibodies to fight infection.
- Lemon and honey in water can help replace sodium and potassium losses during fever.
- BENEFICIAL FOODS: Watermelon, fruit and vegetable juices, frequent sips of water.

Nutrients to consider

- Iron phosphate is a homeopathic celloid so it does not feed the bacteria. (BM)
- Zinc – can also be misused during a fever so wait until it subsides – 10 drops or 15mg capsule (BC) or sherbet flavoured powder $1/2$level measure under tongue alternate days over 8 years. (HN)
- Vitamin C – 4 drops (BC) or Bio C $1/8-1/4$tsp daily (AN, NC,R) or chewable. (L)
- Echinacea Complex contains echinacea, vitamins A, C, B6, honey and zinc; 5mls up to thrice daily. (Nu)
- E-Kid-Nacea from 2 years or E-Kid-Nacea Plus from 4 years to boost immunity. (K)
- B vitamins can stimulate appetite, energy and immunity after fever. (BC)
- Calcium, vitamin A and vitamin C may be depleted after fever.
- Bounceback Formula after fever for recuperation over 2 years chew 2-3 daily between meals. (BM)

FLATULENCE

Dietary advice

- Live natural yoghurts can help. Dairy alternatives to cows' milk are available if intolerant, eg sheep, goats' or soya.
- Avoid the cabbage family, sweetcorn, pulses and artificial sweeteners in diet drinks.
- Digestive enzymes in pineapple and papaya may help.
- Any possible intolerance should be eliminated (see food intolerances).
- Support digestion with celery and watercress soup
- Reduce raw foods (if any are eaten!) lightly steam or make soups instead.
- BENEFICIAL FOODS: Celery, watercress, pineapple, papaya, live yoghurt, parsley, pinch nutmeg.

Nutrients to consider

- Probiotics.
- Peppermint tincture (not in babies).
- Windy Pops is a herbal tincture safe from birth. (K)
- Kiddy Tum from 2 years. (K)
- Digestive enzymes. (see Appendix)

SEE ALSO: IRRITABLE BOWEL SYNDROME, BLOATING, FOOD INTOLERANCES, DIGESTIVE PROBLEMS, COLIC, EXERCISE, CANDIDA

Although young children find this very amusing, excessive wind can be uncomfortable and is a sign of digestive imbalance.

FACTORS TO CONSIDER

Bacterial or yeast overgrowth in the gut.
Poor digestion.
Inadequate chewing.
Stress.
Food allergies and intolerance.

GENERAL ADVICE

Encourage slower eating and good chewing
Sit down at the table to eat, not in front of the TV. This encourages good posture, conscious eating and conversation
Discourage eating whilst active
Peppermint and chamomile tea can soothe
Cinnamon, fennel and rosemary can relieve wind. Eat with offending foods or as herbal teas to reduce gas in older children.
Parsley is helpful for digestion, but not many children like it. Include some in cooking or juicing
Exercise (see IBS)
Food combining may help some children. (See appendix)
If candida or food intolerances are suspected see a qualified nutritionist. ▪

FLUORIDE

SEE ALSO: TEETH, GUMS, CANCER, AUTISM, THYROID FUNCTION

Calcium fluoride is said to be important for healthy teeth and bones. But artificial fluoride (hexaflurosilicilic acid) is added to water in some areas and this is toxic. It is an industrial waste product.

Pros:
Use of fluoride has reduced decay.

Cons:
Used to make rat poison and fertilisers.
Cumulative levels due to fluoridation of water, toothpastes, mouthwashes, medications and pesticides may affect children more than adults.
If using fluoride toothpaste, children often swallow it and in addition to fluoridation water this can be too much.
Fluorosis. (mottled colouring on the enamel)
Can affect thyroid function in some individuals.
May be involved in some cases of autism.
Encourages loss of the minerals calcium and phosphorus from the bones encouraging rickets and osteoporosis.
Alzheimer's linked to aluminium toxicity and fluoride increases aluminium retention. Aluminium toxicity, which is not uncommon in children, can be linked to fluoride poisoning.
Fluoride is more toxic than lead. Has been linked to cancer, birth defects and nervous system diseases. May be neurotoxic in unborn, developing child and in infants.
Cancer has been linked to fluoride exposure – may be due to oestrogens and thyroid depression.
Other signs of fluoride poisoning include muscle cramps.

GENERAL ADVICE
Filter water and increase intake to detoxify.
For details of a urine test for fluoride levels contact Good Health Keeping Tel: 01507 601655.
Avoid fluoride toothpaste/mouthwashes. Try Green People, Aloe Dent (HS) or Dentects. (BC)
Peelu is an ayuvedic herb available as a toothpaste which has antibacterial properties, removes plaque and whitens teeth. (HS)
Symptoms of fluoride toxicity can include headaches, leg pains and 'flu-like symptoms.
Sunlight provides vitamin D for healthy teeth and bones.
Xylitol gum after meals in children over 5 years is sugar free and can reduce plaque. ■

Dietary advice

● Organic foods are free from pesticides containing fluoride.

● Plenty of water (filtered) to detoxify.

● Dairy products are rich in calcium phosphate but low in magnesium. Increase magnesium foods.

F

FLUORIDE

FOOD INTOLERANCE/ ALLERGIES

SEE ALSO: ALLERGIES, IBS, IMMUNE FUNCTION, CANDIDA, EATING DISORDERS, LEAKY GUT, BLOATING, FATIGUE

True allergies are IgE reactions and are for life. These are the ones that can cause anaphylactic shock and sudden death, so scrupulous avoidance of all traces of offending foods need to be maintained for life. Sufferers often carry adrenaline with them in case of emergency.

Food intolerance is not an allergy, but a different response in the body's immune system. Involves IgG antibody. Usually develops during life, but often resolves with treatment.

The most common foods in children are milk, lactose, gluten, wheat, eggs, citrus, salicylates and additives.

FACTORS TO CONSIDER
Anxiety.
Gut infections especially candida.
Poor immunity.
Poor digestion.
Leaky gut.

GENERAL SYMPTOMS
Mental function – insomnia, learning difficulties, hyperactivity, autism.
Skin – eczema, rashes.
Chest – coughs, colds, bronchitis, asthma, infections.
Head – earache, dark circles round eyes, hayfever, rhinitis, sore throats, headaches.
Digestion – diarrhoea, bloating, tummy ache, wind, poor growth, colic, IBS, constipation.

COWS' MILK INTOLERANCE
Cows' milk intolerance is an allergic reaction triggered by a protein in cows' milk. Like any allergic reaction, it represents an abnormal response by the immune system to a specific protein. It is one of the most common allergies in babies; some studies suggesting that up to 7% of infants may suffer from it.

Cows' milk allergy should not be confused with lactose intolerance. Many babies who are allergic to cows' milk eventually outgrow the problem.

A baby with cows' milk allergy can usually tolerate breast milk, but when fed a formula containing cows' milk, it triggers a sequence of events that result in the allergic response. Some babies react to breast milk if the mother is eating lots of dairy foods. If the family has a history of suffering from allergies (atopy), a baby may have an increased likelihood of being allergic to cows' milk.

Symptoms of cows' milk intolerance in babies are diarrhoea, frequent vomiting, blood in stools, irritability, unexplained skin rashes, slow growth rate.

Symptoms of cows' milk intolerance in older children are itchy rash, headaches, diarrhoea, vomiting, breathlessness, coughing, wheezing, runny or blocked nose.

LACTOSE INTOLERANCE

A fairly common milk-related problem in which the sufferer may lack an enzyme needed to digest milk sugar. In most cases, it disappears on its own by the time the baby is 1-2 years old. If not it tends to worsen as children get older. Many babies develop it as a temporary condition lasting for just a few weeks after a bout of gastro-enteritis. Probably due to dysbiosis and high gut permeability (leaky gut).

Symptoms include diarrhoea, poor weight gain, vomiting, colic and wind.

Supplementing lactase enzymes is usually helpful (liquid form from Biocare) or Colief drops. (HS,NC)

CASEIN OR WHEY INTOLERANCE

Sometimes a factor and excluding whole milk may be unnecessary. Formulas are available to address these problems. Some paediatritions advise women to avoid drinking cows' milk both when they are pregnant and whilst breast feeding

Supplementation of a multi-vitamins and minerals plus calcium is important as well as foods, which are high in calcium if the formula is not fortified.

In addition to obvious milk-based products, cows' milk may be present in in condensed, fresh, dried, evaporated, skimmed milks and butter, margarine, cream, yoghurt, desserts, shakes, cakes, biscuits, some bread, cereals and soups, instant mashed potatoes, gravies, sauces, sweeteners, butterscotch,

F

Dietary advice

Some replacement foods for dairy intolerance:

● Babies under 6 months: replace cows' milk products with Nanny Goat Formula which is fortified.

● Over 6 months some babies can tolerate milk from other animals such as goats, eg Nanny Goat Formula (not if lactose intolerant). More often, the baby will be transferred to a Soya formula.

● There are formulas available with digestive enzymes such as Pregestamil and Neutramagen. which may therefore be less allergic. However they still contain cows' milk. A GP prescription is usually required. In 2002 Cow&Gate have introduced the first formula called Omneo Comfort with beneficial bacteria included to assist digestion.

● Over 2 year olds: replace cows' milk products with rice, fortified soya, pasteurised goats' milk, oat milks. Some children are also sensitive to goat and sheep milks, eg if lactose intolerant which leaves only soya, rice and oats! Too much soya in young children is thought to upset hormone balance and digestion. It is best to vary the source.

General Replacement Foods

- See appendix for more detail.
- Replace wheat products with: rye, oats, rice, barley, amaranth, millet, quinoa, corn and buckwheat.
- Replace gluten products with: rice, amaranth, millet, quinoa, buckwheat (which is not wheat) NB: Gluten is also in MSG.
- Replace sugar with: manuka honey (HS), blackstrap molasses, FOS. (HS, HN) See also appendix.
- NB: with anti-candida regimes there should be no sugar but FOS is okay.

milk chocolate and toffee. The key ingredients to look out for on food labels are casein, lactose and whey, although hydrolysed casein should not cause an allergic reaction.

Giving the baby only breast milk for the first few months of life can often prevent a cows' milk allergy from developing.

NB: Ordinary cows' milk, as opposed to formula milk containing cows' milk proteins, should never be given to babies under one year old. It contains high levels of sodium and potassium with which immature kidneys cannot cope. Ordinary cows' milk also contains proteins which infants are unable to digest so it should be boiled when first introduced.

Other allergens include peanut, gluten, eggs, wheat, citrus, salicylates, additives, fish, corn, soya, sugar

PEANUT ALLERGY

A true IgE allergy reaction which is becoming more common. Cause is not determined, but may be due to cheap peanut oil in processed foods, pregnancy sensitisation or during lactation. Even some eczema creams and lotions and zinc and castor oil cream contain peanut oil. Look on the ingredients for arachis oil, groundnut or peanut oil. Until 1996 some infant formulas contained arachis oil. Avoidance of other legumes, eg tree nuts and soya may be advisable, but more research is needed.

WHEAT / GLUTEN INTOLERANCE

Wheat farming has changed much faster than our bodies have evolved. Consequently, many children and adults find it hard to digest and may develop immune reactions to it. Confusion abounds over wheat and gluten. Wheat contains gluten as part of its protein molecules so if wheat free, you do not necessarily need to exclude gluten as well. However gluten free products are not necessarily wheat free as gluten is only part of the wheat.

Gluten is present in rye, oats and barley as well as in wheat. If gluten sensitive you need to avoid all four grains. Gluten free breads need something else to stick them together. Xantham gum is effective.

Buying gluten free products usually guarantee you will be excluding wheat. However, wheat protein could still be present if gluten is excluded. Buying wheat free products does not guarantee they are

118

gluten free as other grains may be present.

Symptoms include persistent digestive upsets, blocked nose, skin problems, bloating, wind, fatigue, joint pains, headaches, asthma, lack of concentration, learning difficulties and depression. Gluten sensitivity may also include failure to thrive and pale/foul stools.

Labels are misleading.

For wheat free avoid names including modified starch (unless source is specified), gluten (unless wheat free specified), MSG, semolina, pasta, couscous, some breakfast cereals, flour, gravy, soups, sauces, stuffing and malted bedtime drinks.

For gluten free avoid all four grains.

For gluten and wheat free this includes; cakes, biscuits, sausages, some cornflakes, baking powder, MSG, pepper, stock cubes, salad dressings, dry roasted nuts, communion wafers.

Beware baked beans, baking powder, sauces, crispbreads, breaded foods, eg fish fingers.

EGGS
Eggs are involved in a wide range of childhood illnesses including sleep problems, learning difficulties, eczema, behaviour problems, hyperactivity, asthma. Egg replacer available from General Dietary Ltd.

TESTING
Allergy is only a symptom so although testing helps identify offending foods the underlying cause is still unaddressed. Tests can be invasive for children. Also you need to be sure whether you are looking for IgG or IgE responses. A negative response from medical allergy testing can be misleading as IgG reactions which make up the majority of childhood allergies are rarely tested.

ALLERGY TESTING
Testing for intolerances by exclusion diets:

With children supervision is important. Never try with babies whose diet is limited anyway without advice from a qualified nutritionist. It is not what you exclude, but what you replace it with that is important. Consideration also needs to be given to the psychological aspects of implying that foods may be harmful. The seeds of an eating disorder are sometimes sown quite young.

Nutrients to consider
- Digestive enzymes which may help:
- Lactase enzymes – 4 drops to one pint milk. Refrigerate for 24 hours and the use normally. (BC)
- Prolactazyme Forte one with dairy food (BC). Useful when unavoidable or not sure, eg eating out.
- Children's digestaid – general support for digestion, over 4 years. (BC)

F

FOOD INTOLERANCE

York Labs best for children. Finger prick blood sample done by parent at home with kit provided. IgG for 40 foods – Very comprehensive food sensitivity guidebook. Cost £125, Inhalant, 90 food and vegetarian profiles also available.

Drs Laboratory – children's panel. Full blood test. Do many other tests. Costs approximately £60.

Kinesiology is a system of muscle resistance assessment and can be done via the mother in tiny babies. Scientific basis is not clear but seems to be helpful for some. Non-invasive and cheap at about £35.

Vega testing which uses electrodes on acupressure points may be a useful guide, but its scientific basis is unclear.

GENERAL ADVICE

Seek professional help for elimination diets in children.

There are many recipe books to support the approach recommended.

Most allergy exclusions require 3 months total withdrawal to be effective in a child.

Acute reactions may be relieved with the following: one tsp sodium bicarbonate plus ¹/₂tsp potassium bicarbonate in ¹/₂glass of warm water, sip slowly to help alkalise the system and reduce allergic reactions.

Keep a food diary for a few weeks and note the symptoms. With intolerance these may occur hours even days after eating, but allergic reactions are immediate and obvious.

Correct weaning with no fresh cows' milk, wheat, gluten or eggs before one year helps to reduce allergic reactions. Doorstep cows milk after one year should be full cream not skimmed or semi-skimmed and boiled to break down the fats.

Nut free chocolate is available from Marks and Spencer in their character ranges, eg Bob the Builder etc. and Cadbury. (Cadbury's Careline Tel: 08457 818 181)

Boosting immunity helps to balance immune function and prevent hypersensitivity.

Concerns about calcium deficiency when dairy free are unfounded if diet includes plant sources and fish. $^1/_2$ to 1 pint of calcium fortified soya milk will replace losses from no dairy.

Eating fortified breakfast cereals, marmite and meat should safeguard vitamin B2 (riboflavin) intake if dairy free.

Some research into links between pregnancy and lactation diet and atopic (familial) allergies. Results so far are inconclusive, but it seems sensible to reduce risks of sensitisation before birth with allergy free diets.

NB: Never give gluten to young babies and never give honey under one year.

Try homeopathic gentiana x 10 drops $^1/_2$ hour before a meal containing suspected foods especially good for wheat intolerance. (F, A)

Food sensitivity Remedies Ltd supply individual solutions, eg wheat to allow eating out when ingredients uncertain. Tel: 01242 890108 for advice. ▪

FUSSY EATERS

SEE ALSO: APPETITE, FOOD INTOLERANCES, EATING DISORDERS, DIGESTIVE PROBLEMS, ANAEMIA, CONSTIPATION

Dietary advice

- Add one tsp blackstrap molasses to cereals and yoghurts to increase minerals.
- Increase iron, vitamin C and zinc foods if possible.
- Offer iron and vitamin C foods together to increase iron absorption, eg boiled egg and orange juice.
- Reduce milk as a drink as it can fill her up.
- Increase water and juices.
- Fibre for constipation, eg oats, fruit and vegetables.
- BENEFICIAL FOODS: Eggs, lentils, sardines, wholemeal bread, oats, dried fruit, meat, beans, potatoes, oats, yoghurt, fruit, vegetables, fruit purees, shakes and sunflower seeds (to nibble).

Many young children seem to survive on thin air. Many parents worry endlessly over their finicky food habits and lack of variety in their diets. Optimally children should eat a wide variety of fresh, whole foods but many will eat only fish fingers and bread! If growth, development and general health are good then the least emphasis the better! Generally we worry too much but there are some conditions which should be eliminated as factors.

FACTORS TO CONSIDER

Anaemia.
Nausea.
Tummy ache.
Food intolerance.
Zinc deficiency.
Constipation.
Candidiasis.
Autism.

If the child is anaemic or just low in iron stores appetite will be low. If zinc is deficient appetite, taste and smell are affected. Food intolerances can cause cravings for those foods, nausea, bloating and discomfort. Keep a food diary and identify foods eaten frequently, eg wheat. Candidiasis can result in sugar and yeast cravings, food intolerances and tummy ache.

In rare cases food fear is severe and may be related to eating disorders, autism and Asberger's syndrome. If your child only eats dry food, wheat, certain shapes or sizes or an exact number of peas or grapes this could be an issue.

GENERAL ADVICE

Eliminate any of the possible physical causes.

Omnivorous babies often turn into picky toddlers. This may be an evolutionary protective method as the child begins to explore independently and there is not always someone there to screen harmful foods. The child self-selects. Unfamiliar foods are suspect until proven otherwise.

Try not to make a scene. Praise for good eating, ignore if not eating. Don't punish.

Offer interesting food, presented in an appealing way, eg porridge is less interesting than baby corn or mini ricecakes to some children.

If old enough ask her to write down what she likes and try to negotiate around that.

Involve her in choosing food, but within a limited healthy choice, eg flavour of yoghurt or a banana or grapes?

Avoid taking her shopping with you as marketing for children is very powerful!

Eat as a family at least once a day.

No TV dinner however tempting it is to distract them and shovel it in!

Only give tiny portions on tiny plates. There is nothing more daunting to a child than a huge pile of food.

Offer freshly squeezed juices of vegetables or fruit. This enables you to give concentrated nutrients You can even hide supplements in them!

If she only wants bread consider the possibility of wheat intolerance or candida (yeast cravings).

Let children learn to cook.

Don't diet. Children soon pick up on messages that food is somehow bad for you.

Supplement vitamins, minerals and oils.

Make sure she drinks enough.

Is she having too much milk, which suppresses appetite?

Have set meal times at regular intervals with no snacks so she is hungry.

Don't make mealtimes a battleground.

Insist on staying at the table until everyone has finished, even if she eats nothing. Re-instate the art of communication!

One doll or teddy can come to the table for some food – 'one for teddy, one for me'.

Don't link vegetables with healthiness as a subconscious link is made that if a bribe is needed they can't be very nice!

Constant nagging and over-emphasis can lead to an unhealthy relationship with food and may initiate eating disorders and food obsessions.

If she says she's full up believe her even if she's eaten one pea, but don't give her anything else except non-milk drinks until the next meal.

There are many psychological factors related to food including anger, independence and copying older siblings.

Small children are often very active and sitting still to eat can be a problem. Foods need to be easy to recognise, attractive and quick to eat.

Raw vegetables are often accepted, more than cooked.

'Food Dude' videos with Goodies fighting General Junk and his Junk Punks. Available for school or home. ■

Nutrients to consider

- MVM.
- Zinc citrate – 10drops (BC) or 15-25 mgs capsule (L, BC) or sherbet flavoured powder $^1/_2$level measure alternate days under the tongue for over 8 years (HN) alternate days.
- Probiotics.
- Fibre as apple pectin $^1/_4$tsp daily to soothe the gut and help constipation (S) orEliminex. (L)
- EFAs as oils – Essential Balance junior is butterscotch flavoured 1-3 tsps from weaning (HN) or Udo's Choice (HS, Sa) or Dricelle omegaplex powders. (BC)
- Vitamin C as magnesium ascorbate powder especially if constipated or children's capsule one daily (BC) or chewable from 4 years. (L)
- Easy Iron – 2-5 years sprinkle one capsule every 3rd day; 5-8 years one capsule alternate days; over 8 years daily (HN) or Floridix herbal minerals. (N)
- Iron phosphate contains homeo-pathic iron. (BM)
- Calcium phosphate is a constitutional strengthener. (BM)

G

GASTRO-ENTERITIS

SEE ALSO: BACTERIAL INFECTIONS, NAUSEA, VOMITING, DIARRHOEA, ALLERGIES, DIGESTIVE PROBLEMS, IMMUNE FUNCTION

This condition is potentially life threatening in babies due to rapid dehydration and electrolyte imbalances. Always seek medical advice if diarrhoea and vomiting lasts more than 24 hours in babies and small children.

Symptoms include diarrhoea, vomiting (not necessarily both), fever, drowsiness, abdominal cramps, headaches, fatigue and nausea.

FACTORS TO CONSIDER
Food poisoning
Bacterial infections.
Drug sensitivity and allergies.
There are many different types of bacterial infection with variable severity and duration. Diagnosis is usually on a stool test via GP. Common minor gastric upsets have many possible causes including poor eating habits, anxiety and school phobia.

GENERAL ADVICE
If symptoms do not resolve completely and medical advice has been followed consider allergic reactions. ▪

Dietary advice

- Liquids only, initially to rest the digestive tract.
- Gradually introduce diluted juices and then dilute milk.
- Food re-introduction with bland cereals first.
- Older children may start on toast, soup or yoghurt.
- Lots of water to detoxify and rehydrate.
- Ginger has anti-nausea properties.
- Honey has anti-bacterial qualities and is very effective if added to rehydration drinks especially for younger children but do not give honey to under one year olds as risk of botulism is higher.
- BENEFICIAL FOODS:
To prevent or rebalance: Chick peas, peas, corn, cucumber, asparagus, artichokes for prebiotics, live yoghurt, cottage cheese, soya.

Nutrients to consider

- If it is food poisoning that requires an antibiotic, always follow with a course of probiotics, eg ABC Dophilus. (S)
- Chamomile as tincture or tea. (N)
- Older children:
  - Charcoal at first signs to remove toxins from the colon and neutralise poisons. (HS)
  - Super Gar is antibacterial; one daily over 8 years. (HN)
  - Potassium as dehydration can mean it is depleted. 100mgs over 12 years. (BC)
  - Vitamin C and bioflavonoids – Bio C $^1/_4$tsp daily has beneficial minerals as well. (AN,R, NC) NB: vitamin C can cause diarrhoea so wait until subsided and add slowly.
  - Goldenseal tincture for 4-5 days only from the start. (N, NC,)
  - Kiddy Tum from 2 years to calm digestion and alleviate nausea. (K)
-

GLANDULAR FEVER

SEE ALSO: VIRAL INFECTIONS, CFS, IMMUNITY, CANDIDA, ANAEMIA, ALLERGIES

Also known as infectious mono-nucleosis, this is a herpes viral infection due to the Epstein-Barr virus (EBV). It can be confused with influenza. Occasionally occurs in young children, but mainly in adolescents. Infection is by saliva contact hence the alternative name of 'kissing disease'. Usually lasts around a month but can be for longer. It is diagnosed by a blood test for EBV antibodies. Incubation is 10 days in children and an average of 40 days in adults.

Symptoms include fatigue, fever, swollen lymph glands in the neck, axilla and throat, headaches, sore throat, sometimes a rash or jaundice. Complications include chronic fatigue and depression, which can last several months. Can affect the spleen and liver with possible jaundice. May appear to recover and then relapse.

GENERAL ADVICE

Boost immune system.
Keep towels and flannels separate.
Do not share crockery or cutlery.
Avoid kissing.
Frequent small meals to relieve digestion.
Bed rest in the acute phase.
Avoid constipation as straining can damage the spleen.
Lifelong presence of EBV in the body with no cure so diet and lifestyle especially important to balance the body.
Persistent cases can be linked to candidiasis, food allergies or anaemia.
Stress aggravates the condition as it often occurs in the 15-25 year age group, examination pressure can complicate recovery.
Rest and optimal nutrition as soon as diagnosed can help reduce the chance of protracted illness and chronic fatigue.
Homeopathy ailanthus Glandulosa 6c thrice daily for 10 days can relieve symptoms. (See a homeopath.) ■

Dietary advice

- Clean up the diet by sticking to natural wholefoods aiming for 40 –50% raw.
- Avoid sugar, cola, junk food, takeaways and fizzy drinks.
- Homemade, wholesome soups with parsley and added ginger and garlic for cleansing.
- Increase clean water.
- Fresh fruit juices for concentrated nutrients and live enzymes.
- Adequate protein from easily digested sources for the formation of immune antibodies.
- No alcohol due to liver involvement.
- Identify and eliminate potential allergens like wheat and dairy.
- Increase beta-carotene, vitamin A, magnesium, potassium and vitamin C foods.
- Live yoghurt daily.
- BENEFICIAL FOODS:
Water, wholefoods, soups, parsley, ginger, garlic, milk, shakes, fresh juices, chicken, fish, lentils, seeds and live yoghurt.

Nutrients to consider

- (doses for over 12 years)
- Elderberry extract has been shown to block replication of EBV and is an immune tonic. (S)
- Sambucol $1/2$tsp twice daily. Contains elderberry for immunity.(HN)
- Bounceback Formula for recuperation. (BM)
- Immuno Kid 1-2 tsp twice daily. (K)
- Probiotics, eg Bio-acidophilus one or two daily. (BC)
- Magnesium becomes low – try calcium, magnesium and zinc complex (S) or Bio Mg one daily (BC) or Mg solution $1/4$tsp 1-2 times daily (AR,NC,R) or Bio Mg with calcium, minerals, B6 one daily 6-12 years. (BM)
- Vitamin C 1-2g Bio-C $1/4$– $1/2$tsp daily (AN, R, NC) or Mg ascorbate powder. (BC)
- Super Gar 1 daily for over 8 years. (HN)
- Cats Claw daily with triple the dose in acute phase – suggest 1-2 gms for 14 year old.
- Evening primrose oil x 500mg 3 times daily. (L, HN, HS)
- MVM.

GROWING PAINS

SEE ALSO: SLEEP PROBLEMS

Nutrients to consider

- Manganese if deficient is a mineral associated with growing pains. Give 2 drops daily. (BC)
- Increase protein for mineral absorption and growth.
- EFAs for supple joints – Essential Balance Junior 2-3 tsps daily (HN) or Udo's Choice (Sa,NC,R) or dricelle omega plex. (BC)
- Magnesium and calcium are soothing minerals for muscles. Always give in combination 2:1 calcium:magnesium unless otherwise advised. (BC, S)

Growing pains are common in children; maybe 1 in 4 suffer with the most likely age range between 4-8 years and gone by 11-13 years. Manifests itself as pains in the legs, knees, back and other joints. Seems to be bone pain. Often wakes the child in the night as growth hormone (GH) is secreted more at night. The pain comes in spurts several times lasting for approximately 20 minutes.

GENERAL ADVICE

Sunlight and daylight encourage daytime secretions of growth hormone.

Exercise helps keep joints and ligaments supple, but too much can aggravate.

Plenty of fluids to avoid dehydration and stiffness.

Try to avoid painkillers as it will pass within half an hour.

Massaging the area with diluted lavender oil can relax the area. 2 drops of oil to 10ml of almond oil.

If pain is severe or longer lasting consult the doctor to eliminate arthritis or lymphatic problems.

Physiotherapy usually by GP referral may be helpful if persistent with no other cause. ■

GROWTH PROBLEMS

SEE ALSO: CANDIDA, LEAKY GUT, ANXIETY, PARASITES, THYROID PROBLEMS, OBESITY, DIGESTIVE PROBLEMS

Dietary Advice

- BENEFICIAL FOODS: Fresh fruit juices, shakes, protein from meat, fish, eggs, pulses, wholegrains, nuts especially almonds and seeds.
- Alternative approaches: see a qualified nutritional therapist to:
  - Identify any candida, parasites, bacterial infections in the gut and treat;
  - Improve absorption / digestion;
  - Remove any allergic foods as these aggravate absorption of vitamins and minerals;
  - Assess leaky gut;
- Increase protein.

Children grow in spurts. From birth to 6 months most double their weight despite low protein intake. There are accelerations in growth at 5 years, 7 years and 12 years. Most growth is completed by 16 years.

Height and shoe sizes are linked.

Double birth height by 5 years old and $^2/_3$ of adult height by 6 years old. Children generally increase one shoe size per year between 5 and 10 years old.

Too much emphasis on scales can be misleading. Need to account for head circumference and activity level too, eg at 9 months-1 year babies become mobile and growth will slow as energy is diverted for activity.

At 18months-2 years children are extremely

lively and may even lose weight. This is a time when interest in food can also wane temporarily and children become selective.

Growth hormone rises 8-9 times daily lasting for 20 minutes usually at night.

Failure to thrive is a term applied to children whose growth falters and is usually associated with ill health. These children need to be referred to a paediatrician and the family may need support/ assessment to see what, if any, psychological factors are involved relating to food, meal times, nursery school etc.

FACTORS TO CONSIDER

If growth is a concern or suddenly slows or stops, consideration needs to be given to the following:

See a GP for possible investigations to eliminate coeliac disease, diabetes, growth hormone deficiency, cystic fibrosis, heart or kidney problems, pituitary abnormalities and thyroid imbalance;

Poor absorption may be due to lack of beneficial bacteria especially if antibiotics are used frequently;

Candidiasis or parasites may affect absorption;

Nutrient deficiencies, eg zinc, EFAs and iron;

Food intolerances may induce unhealthy cravings and aversions and are linked to 'leaky gut';

Stress, anxiety and emotional problems (not usually under 18months).

Causes of low growth hormone: pituitary gland damage; thyroid insufficiency; genetic; problems with hypothalamus; and rarely, pituitary tumour or leukemia treatment.

Effects of low growth hormone: obesity as hormone controls fatty tissue under the skin; short stature; failure to thrive .

Excessive growth, eg very tall, can be linked to medical conditions such as adrenal tumour and overactive thyroid. Seek paediatric advice.

Contacts:
Child Growth Foundation, 2 Mayfield Avenue, London, W41PW. Send an SAE with four x 1st class stamps stating sex of child for an information pack. ■

Nutrients to consider

● Zinc to stimulate GH and appetite – 10 drops daily (BC) or sherbet flavoured powder $1/2$ level measure alternate days under the tongue for over 8 years (HN)

● Vitamin A deficiency has been implicated in growth faltering; one drop Vitasorb A. (BC)

● Arginine and orthonine are two amino acids (proteins) linked to GH. Give Solgar's combined supplement or Amino Sport which delivers protein to build muscle and strength, $1/2$ to 1 capsule 1-3 times daily over 2 years (BR, NC, R) under supervision if underweight. NB: Avoid if there is cold sore or herpes problem.

● Probiotics. (age specific)

● Calcium phosphate is a constitutional strengthener (BM)

● MVM, eg Get up and Go (HN) can be added to shakes or Aqueous Multi Plus one tsp daily (BR). Spray vitamins/minerals. (NW)

● Digestive enzymes: see Appendix.

G

GUMS

SEE ALSO: FLUORIDE, TEETH, IMMUNE FUNCTION

Dietary advice

- Filtered water 4 –5 glasses daily.
- Avoid or minimise fizzy drinks, sugar, and sweets and only eat at meals times rather than in between.
- Offer fruit such as apples after a meal to neutralise acidity and reduce bacterial growth.
- Fibre foods such as fruit and vegetables which help to remove plaque.
- Vitamin C foods for immunity.
- BENEFICIAL FOODS: Vegetables and fruit especially peaches, citrus fruits, cherries and apples.

Nutrients to consider

- Vitamin C with bioflavonoids Childrens capsule (BC) or chewable one daily over 4 years. (L) NB: some chewables have sugar.
- MVM.
- Vitamin A , 1 drop Vitasorb. (BC)
- B2 and B3 also helpful (always support with a B complex) – 10 drops daily or children's capsule for 5-12 years. (BC)
- Vitamin E – pierce a capsule and apply to sore gum for healing.
- EFAs are anti-inflammatory – Essential Balance Junior is butterscotch flavoured from herbs and not sugar $^1/_2$-3 tsp daily. (HN)
- Probiotics can help immunity especially if antibiotics are taken often.

Inflammation of the gums is less common in children than in adults, but some may have a genetic predisposition to form tartar.

FACTORS TO CONSIDER IN BLEEDING GUMS

Too vigorous brushing.

Vitamin C deficiency.

Lack of fibre.

Rarely bleeding gums may indicate leukaemia if accompanied by pallor, easy bruising and tiredness.

GENERAL ADVICE

An electric toothbrush can be fun and cleans the backs of teeth and gums gently and thoroughly.

Aloe Vera gel topically.

Beware mouthwashes. Some contain sugar, fluoride and additives. Mouthwash with one drop of tea tree oil in a full glass of water to cleanse mouth and reduce bacterial growth. Not in young children as they might swallow it.

Most toothpaste contains sodium laurel sulphate, a potentially harmful chemical. Try AloeDent (HS) or Green People.

Avoid fluoride supplements as they are already in most toothpaste and water supplies.

Natural sugar free licorice sticks can clean gums.

Sugar free gum sweetened with Xylitol has been shown to protect gums by removing plaque and reducing bacterial activity. (HS, NC)

NB: Gum is not safe for under 5 year olds and at any age when active due to risk of choking.

Supplementing Co Q10, good for gum health, is not recommended in children, but toothpaste is available. (HS, NC)

Refined and processed foods require too little chewing. ▪

Hair Loss

SEE ALSO: ANXIETY, ANAEMIA

Medical term is alopecia. Sparse, thin hair can be genetic in origin and the hairs are widely spaced, small in diameter or short. Unless there are also problems with nails, skin and teeth, this should rectify itself as the child grows.

Hair loss is quite unusual in children but causes vary.

Factors to consider

Genetics.
Friction on bedding – mostly in babies.
Pulling and twisting hair.
Auto-immune disease (patchy hair loss: areata).
Impaired circulation.
Iron deficiency.
Thyroid disease.
Low protein diet.
Stress/anxiety.
Drugs especially antibiotics, chemotherapy or contraceptive pill in teenagers.
Heavy metal toxicity, eg lead or aluminium.
Hormonal changes at puberty.
Pregnancy.
Dysbiosis.

General Advice

Hair *is* protein and minerals.
Avoid fine-toothed combs and hair dryers.
Comb gently when dry.
Use natural PH balanced hair products, eg Jojoba products. (try Green People)
Effects of supplements on hair growth can take 4 months to be noticeable so persevere.
Aloe vera oil applied topically at night may help.
Apply a mix of wheatgerm, brewers yeast, dulse powder and ground pumpkin seeds or their oil to hair and leave half an hour before rinsing (or leave overnight).
Anxiety/stress cause constriction of blood vessels in scalp and hair loss.
Alternate hot and cold water rinses to stimulate circulation. Scalp massage daily can stimulate circulation.
Ask GP to test for iron deficiency. If proven supplement short term and increase Vitamin C.

Dietary Advice

- Increase biotin and silica foods.
- Decrease salt, sugar, caffeine, eg in cola.
- Avoid sugar and processed foods.
- Drink 4-5 glasses of water daily.
- As hair is protein, ensure each meal contains a third protein.
- BENEFICIAL FOODS: Brown rice, lentils, soya, oats, sunflower seeds, walnuts, couscous, pulses, oily fish, eggs, peas, leafy green vegetables, beetroot, parsley, garlic, onions, carrots, peppers, cucumber, apricots.

Nutrients to consider

- Amino acids especially L cysteine and L lysine. Amino Acid Quicksorb under professional guidance, one drop thrice daily. (BR)
- Children's B complex – 10 drops (0-5 years) or 1 capsule daily over 5 years (BC) or B Vital (especially good for anxiety) one daily over 5 years.
- Biotin as part of children's B complex. (as above) Biotin can be adversely affected by dysbiosis. Consider acidophilus (1 L).
- Vitamin C – chewable C (L), children's C and bioflavonoids 4 drops or 1 capsule. (BC)
- Zinc stimulates hair growth by enhancing immune function. 10 drops

H

or 15mg capsule BC or sherbet flavoured powder. $^1/_2$level measure under tongue alternate days over 8 years. (HN)

- Vitamin E 100 ius 1 drop or capsule. (BC)

- Brewers yeast. (HS)

- EFAs – Essential Balance Junior, $^1/_2$-3 tsp from weaning, (HN)

- Gingko biloba tincture over 8 years (N) or gingko complex. $^1/_2$tablet twice daily (BM) for circulation.

- Iron – Nutrisorb iron – 10 drops daily (BC).Easy iron (taken 3 months maximum) 2-5 years 1 capsule every third day sprinkled onto food, 5-8 years 1 capsule alternate days sprinkled onto food, over 8 years 1 capsule daily. Salus House Florivatal is a herbal form of easily assimilated iron. (N)

Encourage child to swing on bars or do head and hand stands to increase blood flow to scalp.

Consider a hair test for toxic metals. Although this means sending a sample of the diminishing hair, it could identify the cause!

Homeopathic sepia, lycopodium or phosphoric acid all at 6oC may help. (A)

Cayenne pepper, sage tea or apple cider rubbed into scalp as a rinse have been reported to stimulate cells to regrow hair. Be careful of eyes. ■

H

Halitosis (Bad Breath)

SEE ALSO: BODY ODOUR, CONSTIPATION, DIGESTION, GUMS, TEETH

Usually temporary in children and common when they are ill. This is due to acetone when dehydration affects kidney function. Consult GP if long term to eliminate diabetes, kidney disease or liver malfunction.

FACTORS TO CONSIDER

Poor digestion.

High animal protein diet, eg meat, dairy which slow bowel function.

Anxiety/ stress which depresses digestion.

Zinc deficiency reduces stomach acid and enzyme secretion.

Dysbiosis.

Heavy metal toxicity, eg mercury, lead.

Gum and dental disease (inadequate brushing/ flossing).

Food intolerances.

Poor digestion.

Constipation.

Sinusitis.

GENERAL ADVICE

Parsley, thyme, mint, dill and coriander chewed after meals can help but most children will refuse these herbs!

Encourage proper chewing.

Food combining can help but it is not easy or practical for children. Teenagers may manage this.

Avoid constipation.

Check with dentist for gum disease (gingivitis).

Teach children how to floss.

Clean toothbrush in citricidal. (HN)

Avoid mouthwashes as they can irritate membranes in mouth. Try one drop tea tree and peppermint in cooled, boiled water after meals in older children. Do not swallow.

Encourage exercise for healthy bowel function. ■

Dietary advice

- Animals eat grass when unwell digestively. Give green vegetables and alfalfa sprouts to provide chlorophyll for fresh breath and cleaner bowel function.
- Fresh fruit especially pineapple and papaya for bromelain which is a digestive enzyme. Eat after meals.
- Increase water intake to minimum 5 glasses daily.
- Reduce dairy and animal protein, especially if sinuses congested.
- Add 1 tsp cracked golden linseeds to cereals, soups or yoghurt daily. (HS)
- Avoid garlic, onions and spicy foods.
- Sugar and refined foods like cakes and sweets can result in poor gum/dental health.
- Increase raw foods for fibre to clean plaque.
- Fresh lemon and warm water on rising and before meals – can add honey to taste.
- BENEFICIAL FOODS: Fresh herbs, artichokes, live yoghurt.

Nutrients to consider

- Digestive enzymes in children old enough to swallow a capsule. (BC) See appendix.
- Vitamin C for gum health and immunity.
- Avoid chewable varieties.
- Kiddy Tum over 2 years. (K)
- Aloe Gold (HN) for digestion.
- MSM $1/4$tsp daily over 8 years. (HN)
- Probiotics to improve bowel function and immunity.

H

HAYFEVER

Dietary advice

- Quercetin is anti-inflammatory – present in onions and garlic.
- Increase anti-oxidant foods. See appendix.
- Wheat avoidance may help as it is a grass. Dairy sensitivity may also be a factor as cows eat grass and dairy also increases mucous secretions.
- Citrus fruits especially oranges may trigger attacks.
- Avoid sugar as it depresses immunity.
- 4-5 glasses water daily (min).
- Elderflower spritzer – see Helpful Information.
- BENEFICIAL FOODS
Onions, garlic, avocado, peppers, ginger, beetroot, carrots, fresh vegetables, sweet potato, sweetcorn, papaya, apples, black and blue berries, kiwi, live yoghurt, brown rice, oily fish, beans, seeds, lentils.

Nutrients to consider

- Vitamin C is anti-histamine – Bio C $^1/_4$tsp daily is alkalising (AN) or Immune C, 1 daily over 8 years. (HN) or Quercetin plus vitamin C – $1^1/_2$tablets daily for 5-12 years. (R)
- Nettle tincture may help desensitise. (N, HP)
- Anti-oxidants especially vitamins A, C, E and selenium and zinc. Try selenium ACE 1 daily over 12 years. (L)
- MVM.
- MSM sulphur as powder. $^1/_8$ to $^1/_4$tsp daily over 8 years. (HN)
- Super Gar 1 capsule daily over 8 years (HN) or liquid. (N)
- Sambucol – 1 tsp twice daily for immunity (HN) up to 4 dsps or 1 lozenge 3-4 times daily.
- Oralmat is rye grass extract which contains tryptophan and zinc to strengthen immune system and magnesium to relax muscles. It may also have a de-sensitizing effect. 1 drop under tongue thrice daily held for 15 seconds and then swallowed. (HS)

SEE ALSO: ECZEMA, ASTHMA, ALLERGIC RHINITIS, ALLERGIES, FOOD INTOLERANCES, IMMUNE FUNCTION

Allergic rhinitis is the correct term and is usually seasonal but can be perennial. Unusual under 5 years. Can be associated with asthma so see medical practitioner for diagnosis. Histamine is released in response to antibody production leading to itchy, watery eyes, nasal congestion, sneezing, coughing and headache.

FACTORS TO CONSIDER

Genetics.
Pollen sensitivity from grass or trees and shrubs.
House dust mite, mould and animal dander sensitivities.
Food intolerances.
Imbalanced immunity leading to over-reaction.
Stress and fatigue.

GENERAL ADVICE

Can add one drop each of chamomile, rose, lavender oils in Vaseline to nostrils 2-3 times daily.
Avoid stress and fatigue.
Boost immune function.
Regular hair washing/showering will remove residual pollen which is higher in afternoon and evening.
A stressful situation may precipitate an attack.
Mattress protectors and no carpets can reduce attacks if linked to house dust mite.
If severe it may be necessary not to dry clothes and bedding outdoors as pollen can attach to fabrics.
Research has shown that vitamin E may reduce leakage of histamine from cells and therefore reduce allergic reaction.
Homeopathic euphrasia, especially for itchy eyes, pulsatilla or allium cepa may help. Ainsworth do a combination hayfever remedy.
Acupressure useful. Press top of nose quite hard, hollow above centre of upper lip or underneath cheek bones beside nose to alleviate congestion.
Air filters or ionisers may clear air of pollens/toxins (Healthy House).
Preventative action should start 3 months before expected season. Give vitamin C and local honey daily.
Manuka honey can support immunity.
Skin prick testing can identify type of allergens. Needs GP referral.
Reishi tablets lower histamine. (Chinese herbalists or HS) ■

HEADACHES

SEE ALSO: MIGRAINE, FOOD INTOLERANCE, CONSTIPATION, BLOOD SUGAR

Up to 20% of children suffer recurrent headaches. There are several types of headache. Young children are not very good at describing symptoms. If accompanied by nausea, tummy ache and sensitivity to bright lights, it could be migraine. Always seek medical help if headache follows injury, eg falling off a bike, to eliminate concussion.

FACTORS TO CONSIDER
Fever/infections such as colds.
Anxiety/stress.
Constipation.
Misalignment of neck or jaw.
Dehydration.
Blood sugar imbalances which starve the brain of glucose.
Hunger.
Food intolerance especially wheat.
Fluoride toxicity.
Visual problems can create bilateral frontal headaches.
Sensitivity to perfumes, chemicals, smoke.
Anaemia.
Pre-menstrual syndrome.
Magnesium deficiency.
Dysbiosis.
Vitamin A toxicity.

GENERAL ADVICE
Check with an osteopath specialising in cranial osteopathy in children that there are no structural problems.
Feverfew in over 12 years may help but can take 3 weeks to work – 10 drops twice daily. (HP)
Have vision checked regularly.
Fresh air can alleviate.
A light snack if not nauseous may relieve.
Contraceptive pill can cause oestrogen-related headaches. Discuss with GP or Family Planning.
Avoid regular painkillers as this can create headaches.
A hot bath at first signs can increase circulation and prevent some migraine.
Iron and vitamins B3 and B5 are commonly deficient in headache sufferers.
Ginger may help.
Aromatherapy oils such as lavender or chamomile applied to the temples can relieve pain. ▪

Dietary Advice
● Add cracked golden linseeds – 1 tsp daily to cereals. (HS)
● Increase water intake to at least 5 glasses daily.
● Include soluble fibre daily for bowel function.
● Small, regular meals to balance blood sugar.
● Avoid sugar, caffeine, MSG, processed foods, soy sauce, ice cream, ice, salt, chewing gum, aspartame, preservatives (especially nitrites in cold meats).
● Consider a trial exclusion of wheat products (See Food Intolerance) for 2 weeks.
● Avoid tyramine foods, eg bananas, avocados, cheese, chicken, citrus fruits, peanut butter, fresh bread, and re-introduce one at a time.
● Add 1 tsp lecithin granules to cereals daily as preventative to provide choline for brain function.
● Increase magnesium foods to reduce throbbing pain.
● BENEFICIAL FOODS:
Oats, fruit, pineapple, cherries, vegetables, broccoli, pepper, blackstrip molasses, nuts, seafood, oily fish, turkey, ginger.

Nutrients to consider
● Boswellia serrata (S) – dilates blood vessels linked to muscular tension and is analgesic – only in over 12 year olds.
● Ginkgo complex $1/2$ tablet twice daily (BM) or tincture in older children. (N)
● Vitamin B6 and magnesium if PMS involved.
● Children's B complex – 10 drops or 1 capsule daily, 5 to 12 years (BC) or B Vital one daily over 5 years especially if stress related. (HN)
● Fish oils, eg cod liver oil 500mgs one daily over 8 years (HN) or Dricelle cod liver oil. (BC)
● Feverfew tincture 5-10 drops over 8 years. (HP)

HEADLICE

Nutrients to consider

● Neem oil shampoo and conditioner. (BF)

● Quassia shampoo (over 3 years) contains tea tree, lavender and quassia for nits, lice and fleas. (N)

● Nice'n Clear is a spray containing neem oil, orange, lavender, tea tree, thyme, nettle and citronella. Tel: 020 8875 9915.

● Massage scalp with 2 drops each of lavender and tea tree oil in 6 drops olive oil. Rinse off with vinegar.

Nits are the eggs of lice. They are very common in children, especially of nursery and school age. Nits look like white dots stuck to the hair shaft, most easily detected at nape of neck. They are attracted to clean hair. The adult lice are grey insects which move around the scalp and cause itching.

GENERAL ADVICE

Many over-the-counter treatments contain organ-phosphates linked to cancer.

Most over-the-counter tea tree shampoos contain minimal tea tree oil and are ineffective.

Daily combing with a fine-toothed comb helps control infestation.

Remove child from school to reduce cross infestation.

Treat the whole family.

Blow dry hair for 10 minutes daily for 10 days to destroy lice and remaining eggs (nits). ■

HENOCH'S SCHONLEIN PURPURA

SEE ALSO: FOOD INTOLERANCES, RASHES

Dietary advice

● Identify and eliminate food intolerances.

● Avoid red meat, dairy, sugar, soft drinks, white flour.

● 4-5 glasses of water daily.

● Reduce animal protein to relieve load on kidneys.

● Increase fresh fruit containing flavonoids for blood vessels.

● Vegetables are anti-inflammatory.

● BENEFICIAL FOODS: Oily fish once or twice per week, fresh fruit and vegetables, almonds, millet, amaranth and quinoa (all alkaline grains).

Nutrients to consider

● Pain relief for joint and abdominal pain may be necessary short-term.

● Probiotics to support digestion and reduce inflammation.

● Vitamin C for immunity and inflammation.

Henoch's Schonlein Purpura (HSP) is inflammation of the blood vessels which can result in clustered rashes, usually on legs and buttocks, and unexplained bruising. The cause is unknown but may involve auto-immune reactions or dietary triggers.

Usually occurs between 5-11 years of age and often starts in Spring following a cold or cough. It often begins with a spreading purple or pink rash on buttocks. In more severe outbreaks, 25-30% of cases indicate kidney disorders ranging from mild urinary problems such as frequent infections to dysfunction such as the more serious glomerulonephritis.

Joints may become inflamed and intestinal inflammation may cause tummy ache, blood in stools and indigestion. Most children make a complete recovery after several episodes. Medical treatment is usually steroids but alternatives would involve an anti-inflammatory approach. ■

Hiccups

SEE ALSO: WIND, COLIC

Spasm of diaphragm due to air swallowing in babies
usually follows breast or bottle feeding, but also occurs
in children if eating too quickly, laughing or taking fizzy
drinks. Best solution is prevention by regular breaks
and winding for babies and encouraging slower eating
in children. Avoidance of carbonated drinks is also
advisable.

General advice

There are many old wives tales to stop hiccups but the
safest solution for children is raspberry syrup. Use
pure raspberry juice and sugar or honey rather
than squashes and artificial sweeteners. It's only
occasional so sugar is not a problem.

Dosage: 1-6 months 2.5 – 5mls
6-12 months 5 – 10mls
Over 1 year 10 – 20mls ■

H

Hives

*SEE ALSO: CANDIDA, ANTIBIOTICS, FOOD INTOLERANCE,
ALLERGIES, IMMUNE FUNCTION*

A red, raised, itchy rash which appears suddenly. Can
cover significant areas of body. Also known as urticaria.
Some people call it nettle rash.

Factors to consider

Drug reactions, eg antibiotics.
Allergic reaction to contact irritants.
Food intolerance.
Candida albicans.
Viral infection, eg Epstein Barr Virus and Hepatitis B.
Bacterial infections.
Stress.

General Advice

Assess all household products for links with attacks of
hives, eg personal hygiene and cleaning products.
Some plants, eg strawberry leaves, can cause hives.
Check garden for potentially dangerous plants.
Hives can develop in mouth and throat. This can
become an emergency.
Cold compresses if area is localised may relieve.
Bathing in cool water with 1 drop each chamomile and
lavender oil can soothe irritation. (use non-slip mat)
Adding bicarbonate of soda to a bath can also relieve
itching. ■

Dietary advice

● Possible culprits
include meat, poultry,
dairy and processed
foods due to addition of
antibiotics or additives
or strawberries and
shellfish due to allergic
reactions.

● Avoid soft drinks.

● Consider yeast and
sugar (candida link).

Nutrients to consider

● Urtica is a herb
(stinging nettle) useful
for allergic rashes (BF,
HP) or in homeopathic
potency 30C. (BM)

● Aloe vera gel can
soothe. (HN)

● Vitamin C with bio
Flavonoids as
antihistamine – Bio C
$^{1}/_{4}$tsp daily is anti-
inflammatory. (AN, NC,
R)

135

Hyperactivity

SEE ALSO: *Attention Deficit Hyperactivity Disorder (ADHD)/Attention Deficit Disorder (ADD)*, *food intolerances*, *learning difficulties*, *toxicity*

This need not necessarily be ADD or ADHD but even mild hyperactivity and poor concentration should respond to the recommendations in that section.

Symptoms include restlessness, aggression, speech delay, lack of control, emotional, excitable, irritable.

Keep it simple to begin with as good effect can be achieved simply by removing additives and sugar from the diet. There may be a short healing crisis of a few days due to withdrawal symptoms and detoxification. The child may become more aggressive and agitated. Do not give up! It will pass.

Some hyperactive children, especially boys, may have thyroid hormone resistance, a genetic abnormality which prevents the proper use of thyroxine in cells. More common in boys and if there is a family history of thyroid disease.

Contact:
HACSG (Hyperactive Children's Support Group)

Booklet: *Findout* by Foresight Association

IMMUNE FUNCTION

1

SEE ALSO: ALLERGIES, FOOD INTOLERANCE, BACTERIAL/ VIRAL INFECTIONS, TOXICITY

For the first 6 months of life, a baby depends on maternal anti-bodies acquired in pregnancy. From then on the food she eats will influence her health. The immune system is included as many conditions involve immune dysfunction which is speculated as being a major cause of ill health.

The immune system is a complex defence system designed to protect the body from harmful enemies including bacteria, viruses, fungi, food, chemicals as well as defective body cells. It is a wonderful weapon. When under attack it has the capacity to produce many thousands of new immune cells every minute.

The role of the immune system ranges from a tiny cut on the knee to cancer. There are many different types of immune cells, the main types being white blood cells, B-cells, T-cells and macrophages. B cells are involved in antibody production which interfere with viral replication and protect from previously encountered infections, eg measles only once in a lifetime.

They can also remember reactions to food which causes a repeated response when the same food is eaten again. This is why a rotation diet (eating food only once in 4 days) is better than a little everyday. After 4 days anti-bodies are less likely to react as memory is short and new cells are formed initiated by the immune system. We are protected from other foods by physical reactions that stop us repeating the experience.

The immune system can over or under react or initiate auto-immune reactions when the body 'attacks' itself mistakenly.

Our first line of defence is healthy mucous membranes in the digestive tract and respiratory system.

Research has linked the immune system to the nervous and endocrine systems explaining complex interactions such as depression and hormonal disruption.

To describe the immune system fully requires a whole book in itself and here we concentrate on ways to boost immunity naturally.

The immune system comprises the lymphatic system, thymus gland, tonsils, spleen, lymph glands, bone marrow, intestines and liver. When lymph glands become swollen it is an indication that invaders and debris are being deposited there for destruction.

Two thirds of the immune system centres around the gut. The digestive system has its own immune antibodies in the intestinal tract. These are dependent on healthy mucous membranes so food allergies resulting from leaky gut would affect immunoglobulins reducing immunity still further.

FACTORS WHICH CAN INFLUENCE IMMUNE FUNCTION
Poor diet and stress are the main factors.

Stress – long term stress can depress immunity by up to 60%.

Sugar, additives, saturated fats, artificial sweeteners.

Vaccination.

Infectious illness.

Obesity.

Surgery.

Lack of sleep.

Rapid weight loss.

Anxiety and depression.

Low thyroid function.

Allergies.

Dieting and eating disorders.

Breast feeding enhances the developing immune system.

UV radiation.

Smoking, alcohol and marijuana.

Drugs such as chemotherapy and antibiotics.

SOME EFFECTS OF IMMUNE DYSFUNCTION
Frequent infections.

Poor hair, skin and nail condition.

Low energy.

Insomnia.

Fatigue.

Poor taste and smell.

Sore eyes.

Coated tongue.

Digestive problems.

Diarrhoea.

Consitpation.

Cancer.

Diabetes.

Candida.

Auto-immune disorders include some thyroid problems, juvenile arthritis, neurological conditions.

Dietary advice

● Sugar is the most potent immune suppressant. Avoid it. Check labels for hidden sources, eg flavoured yoghurts, squash and canned drinks, processed foods even savoury.

● Reduce saturated fats as they weaken the immune system and congest the lymphatic system, ie avoid crisps, chips, fried foods and too much dairy and red meat.

● Frying food increases saturated fats and produces free radicals. The only oil safe to heat is olive oil.

● Reduce mucous forming foods which clog up immune system, eg dairy, red meat, eggs, fats.

● Additives such as colourings, preservatives and aspartame can stress the immune system.

● Salt stresses the kidneys which results in magnesium loss. Avoid cooked meats, bacon, sausages, crisps and some breakfast cereals.

● Protein is required for constant replication of immune cells, but too much can use up vitamin B6 and suppress immunity. Vegetarians tend to have better immunity. Concentrate on vegetarian sources of protein and clean fish.

● Lots of fruit and vegetables for anti-oxidants, vitamins, minerals and fibre for digestion and elimination of toxins.

● Eat organic whenever possible.

● Eat a third of food raw. Fresh juicing is a good way to include concentrated fruit or vegetables. You can add spices and flax oil.

● Increase anti-oxidant, iron and B vitamin foods.

● Include EFAs daily.

● Garlic daily is a great immune booster having anti-fungal, viral and bacterial properties. Put into herbs, raw crushed into manuka honey or in cooking.

● Extra fluids to assist elimination of toxic debris. No caffeine.

● Live yoghurt 4-5 times weekly can maintain beneficial gut bacteria and may help to boost immunity.

● Low salt yeast extract provides B vitamins and minerals.

● BENEFICIAL FOODS:
Fresh fruit or vegetable juices especially carrot, tomato, orange or apple, all vegetables especially beetroot, carrots as a soup or a juice, tomatoes, sweet potatoes, squash, broccoli, leeks, peppers, mushrooms, onions, garlic, leafy green vegetables, all fruits especially oranges, berries, kiwis, apples and their juice, grapes, red and blackcurrants, rhubarb, water melon, apricots, strawberries, avocados, mangoes, bananas, fresh juices and shakes, cinnamon, ginger, oregano, parsley, sprouted seeds, eg alfalfa, grains, seeds especially sunflower seeds, nuts especially brazil, almonds, pecan and cashew, lentils, beans, brown rice, oats, raisins, flaxseed oil, wholegrains and cereals, wholemeal bread, tempeh, tofu, oats, quinoa, maiitake, honey especially manuka honey, low salt yeast extract, eggs, low fat live yoghurt.

● In Summary: balanced protein, low fat, lots of fruit and vegetables and EFAs.

I

Immune boosting nutrients

● Optimal vitamins/minerals especially vitamins A, Bs, C and E and minerals zinc, magnesium, iron and selenium are vital. Particularly important B vitamins are B6, B12 and folic acid. B vitamins help stress and immunity.

● Anti-oxidants can disarm the harmful free radicals produced by infections.

● Vitamin A and zinc are needed for healthy mucous membranes, our first line of defence. Vitamin E and selenium work together to protect cells. Beta carotene is converted to vitamin A in the body and is safer and more effective than vitamin A. Excess zinc and iron can depress the macrophages which literally eat bugs. Ideal adult dose is 20mgs zinc. Bacterial infections cause the body to store iron to prevent bacteria feeding on it so supplementation can lead to toxicity in active bacterial infection.

● Vitamin C is the king of immune nutrients with approximately 12 different immune functions. It is also an anti-histamine (histamine is involved in allergic reactions) and can reduce the stress effect on immunity by supporting the adrenal glands. The RNI for vitamin C is adequate to prevent scurvy but could be much too low to prevent infection. Vitamin C is non-toxic as it is water soluble with any excess being excreted. The only side effect of too much vitamin C is diarrhoea.

GENERAL ADVICE

Zinc deficiency increases colds and other infections in children.

Act at the first sign of illness to control, eg 'off colour', low appetite, sore throat.

Better still – prevent it!

The immune system works better in heat hence fevers. Less infections in summer due to the increased temperatures.

Summer is also a difficult time for the immune system with asthma worsening, hayfever, sinusitis, insect bites, pollution from crop spraying, city traffic, sun radiation etc.

Cancer cells hate oxygen so exercise which increases circulation of oxygen keeps cells healthy. Lack of oxygen means cells revert to primitive reproduction which needs to be faster – hence tumours. Depressed levels of immune cells in bone marrow and thymus means not enough are sent to tissue cells.

Adequate sleep enables the immune system to regenerate at night.

Sunshine boosts immunity via brain chemicals but excess unprotected sun increases cancer risks through radiation. See Sunburn.

Gorillas beat their chests to stimulate the thymus gland. Show your child how to tap the sternum with knuckles on rising each day. This makes a good game accompanied by a 'war cry' to wake everyone up!

Asthma, eczema, hayfever, food intolerances and diabetes are some of the conditions increasing in our children. Many feel this is partly linked to our obsessiveness with anti-bacterial cleaners and hygiene etc. Natural resistance from playing in the dirt is reduced.

Lactating mothers can take adult doses and pass on the benefit of nutrients to the infant.

Laughter boosts immunity. Have a good tickle! That lovely chuckle will boost your immune system too.

Reading:
Boost Your Child's Immune System by Lucy Burney is invaluable reading.

Eat for Immunity by Kirsten Hartvig ■

Herbs

- Echinacea is a great immune herb. If used continuously the effect is reduced so take for 2 weeks with one week off. It can be taken by lactating mothers to benefit infant. (BM)

- Grapefruit seed extract acts like an antibiotic but does not destroy beneficial gut bacteria.

- Aloe vera has antiseptic, anti-viral and immune boosting properties Also acts as a tonic and is anti-inflammatory.

- Elderberry extract prevents viral takeover.

- Garlic has anti-fungal, anti-viral, anti-bacterial properties.

- Tea tree oil for external use has antiseptic properties.

Miscellaneous

- Probiotics are beneficial bacteria which boost immunity via the gut. Supplement during a bacterial infection and after any antibiotics. Research has even shown specific probiotics to benefit children with HIV.

- Manuka honey is a pleasant way to take tea tree oil as the pollen from these New Zealand bushes is the source. Buy active sort, eg Comvita.

- EFAs especially omega 3 fatty acids can reduce inflammation and inappropriate immune reactions, eg allergies.

- Stabillum can help resistance – one daily for a 50lb child to a maximum of 3 daily. (AR) Can be given to infants at graduated dose under supervision.

Nutrients to consider

- MVM.

- E-Kid-Nacea over 2 years or E-Kid-Nacea Plus over 4 years or Immuno Kid over 2 years. (K)

- Echinacea ACE and Zinc has several vitamins/minerals as well as echinacea and garlic. One daily over 5 years. (BM) Echinacea tincture from 6-12 months 5 drops thrice daily, 1-6 years 10 drops thrice daily, 7-12 years 15 drops thrice daily. (Sa, HS) Children's echinacea complex with Plantago as a tincture. (BF)

- Immune C provides zinc, vitamin C and elderberry – one daily over 8 years. (HN) Bio C $^1/_8$-$^1/_4$tsp daily contains calcium, magnesium and potassium. (AN)

- Sambucol (elderberry extract) 1tsp twice daily under 5 years, up to 4 dessertspoons or one lozenge 3-4 times daily for older children, or echinacea and black elderberry and olive leaf extract 1-2 capsules over 5 years. (HN)

- Quercetin 300 1-2 times daily for 50lb child includes vitamin E and C is anti-histamine and supports immune system (AR) or Quercetin C for 5-12 years $1^1/_2$ tablets daily. (R)

- EFAs – high potency fish oil, one daily, (L) flax seed oil 1tsp to 1tablespoon in shakes or salad dressing. (AR) Dricelle linseed oil. (BC)

- B vital includes B vitamins and ginseng for stress. One daily over 5 years. (HN)

- Super Gar one daily over 8 years (HN) or liquid. (N)

- Zinc.

- Calcium/magnesium – one each chewable over 4 years. (L) Magnesium can reduce allergic reactions.

- Silver is natures antibiotic. (HN, Sa)

- Cytolog one spray twice daily boosts immunity. (AR)

- Galium Complex one daily for lymphatic support. One daily over 8 years. (BM)

- Bounceback formula for kids – chew 2-3 with meals thrice daily over 2 years. Designed to support immunity and speed recovery. (BM)

- Calcium phosphate is a constitutional strengthener. (BM)

- Wholly Immune is a complex with wide ranging immune nutrients. For serious immune dysfunction under supervision $^1/_4$ scoops daily. (AR)

- Immune Booster cocktail – see Helpful Information.

I

IMMUNE FUNCTION

IMPETIGO

Dietary Advice
● Avoid yeast and sugar as they promote fungal growth.
● Raw garlic in honey can be eaten or applied.
Nutrients to consider
● Vitamin C as Bio C. $^1/_4$tsp daily (AN, NC, R) or Immune C 1 daily over 8 years. (HN)
● Super Gar 1 daily over 8 years (HN) or liquid. (N)
● Vitamin A – 1 drop (BC) for skin healing.
● Zinc boosts immune system and aids healing.
● Probiotics.

SEE ALSO: *BACTERIAL INFECTIONS, IMMUNE FUNCTION, ANTIBIOTICS*

This is a streptoccocal or staphyloccal bacterial infection of the skin entering through a scratch or cut. Symptoms include sore, weeping, irritated patches which form blisters and crust over. Often situated on legs, but also face, scalp, neck and elbows. Worse in poorly nourished children. Usual treatment is antibiotics, but resistance is increasing.

GENERAL ADVICE

Twice daily, carefully remove crusts from all sores with a solution of warm boric acid using 1 tsp to $^1/_2$pint boiled water, cooled to body temperature. Apply tea tree oil or gel and cover.

Keep child's flannels and towels separate.

Pat on vinegar.

2 cups Epsom salts in warm bath.

Apply vitamin E from a capsule to site when crusts have gone to reduce scarring. (HS)

1 drop vitamin A to pustule may help. (BC) ▪

INDIGESTION

Dietary advice – Indigestion
● Pineapple contains digestive enzyme bromelain. Best raw but can use organic juices or occasionally canned in juice. Use in fruit salads, as a snack or in stir fries.
● Papaya is less acidic, rich in vitamin C and papain a digestive enzyme and may be more palatable for young children. Make into a sorbet, ice cream or fruit salad.
● Avoid fatty meats, sugar, salty snacks, citris fruits, peppers, onions, chocolate and fizzy drinks.
● Consider wheat intake. Often too high in children.
● For exclusion diets see food intolerance and consult a qualified nutritionist.
● Fresh juicing retains natural live enzymes if drunk immediately.
Nutrients to consider
● Peppermint Tea reduces muscular spasms in gastric, gall bladder and liver areas.
● Psyllium Complex (BM) contains milk thistle (for sluggish liver), dandelion (diuretic and liver/gall bladder support), garlic (immune booster and antifungal/ bacterial) and sodium sulphate for spasms.
● Flax Oil is an anti-inflammatory source of omega 3 fatty acids. (HN)
● Kiddy Tum or Kid Catnip over 2 years or Windy Pops from birth. (K)

SEE ALSO: *DIGESTIVE PROBLEMS, FOOD INTOLERANCES, NAUSEA, COLIC, IRRITABLE BOWEL SYNDROME*

GENERAL ADVICE

Offer smaller meals more often.

Consider food combining, eg protein and carbohydrates separately and fruit alone. NB not advised if blood sugar is imbalanced.

Maintain a healthy weight.

Encourage slower eating.

Do not drink with meals as this dilutes digestive enzymes.

Consider food intolerances if unresolved.

Ginger, cinnamon, fennel or catnip teas may help. ▪

INFECTIONS

SEE ALSO: IMMUNE FUNCTION, BACTERIAL OR VIRAL INFECTIONS, COLDS, COUGHS, LEAKY GUT, CANDIDA, VACCINATION, ANTIBIOTICS

A major cause of childhood illnesses ranging from a cold to meningitis. Infectious viral diseases such as measles, mumps and whooping cough are common in non-immunised children.

Involves invasion of bacteria, viruses, fungi or parasites via food, drink, skin lesions or respiratory tract. Defense is via the immune system.

Symptoms include sneezing, coughing, diarrhoea, vomiting, rashes, fever or swollen glands dependent on the type of infection. These are all ways in which the body eliminates toxins and defends itself. ∎

Dietary advice

- Lots of fresh fruit and vegetables, whole or as juices. Disguise onions, garlic and fresh vegetables in homemade pizzas, bologneses and soups to fight infection.
- Adequate protein for immune function. Protein losses are high during an infection.
- Avoid additives, crisps, chocolate, sugar, fizzy drinks and white flour.
- Increase water intake to 6 glasses daily.
- Increase Vitamins C, B and E, zinc and EFA foods.
- BENEFICIAL FOODS: Fish, chicken broth, eggs, fresh juices, broccoli, green peppers, carrots, onions, garlic, tomatoes, strawberries, kiwi, blackcurrants, lentils.

I

Nutrients to consider

- Elderberry extract as Sambucol for viral infections 1tsp twice daily under 5 years, or up to 4 dessert spoons 3-4 times daily in older children, or lozenges. (HN)
- Probiotics for bacterial or fungal infections.
- Caprylic acid as Mycopryl Junior for fungal infections, 2 daily. (BC)
- Grapefruit seed extract can address all three types of infection – 2-6 drops, 1-3 times daily over 8 years between meals. (HN) NB – Not if citrus sensitive. Can be given younger under supervision.
- Vitamin C (in short term, higher doses can inactivate viruses).
- Bounceback Formula for convalescence contains immune vitamins and minerals and winter cherry. 2-3 tablets daily chewed with meals thrice daily over 2 years. (BM).
- E Kid or Immuno Kid as a tonic from 2 years. (K)
- E-Kid-Nacea.
- Oralmat is rye grass extract which contains tryptophan and zinc to strengthen immune system and magnesium to relax muscles. It may also have a desensitizing effect. 1 drop under tongue thrice daily held for 15 seconds and then swallowed. (HS)

IRRITABLE BOWEL SYNDROME (IBS)

SEE ALSO: DIGESTIVE PROBLEMS, FOOD ALLERGIES/
INTOLERANCES, CANDIDA, BLOATING, FLATULENCE,
CONSTIPATION, DIARRHOEA AND PMS

This is a label encompassing a series of symptoms including fluctuations of bowel habits (diarrhoea or constipation), bloating and wind (burping or rectal). It is often acompanied by marked discomfort/pain in the lower abdomen. Common in adults, but not to be ignored in children. As young children are not very good at describing symptoms it is important to ask specific questions to identify the problem. Always rule out more serious digestive disorders such as Crohns/Coeliac disesase.

(Young children often describe all illness as 'tummy ache' when in fact it may be something else.) NB: acute abdominal pain may be appendicitis and should always be medically assessed.

FACTORS TO CONSIDER

Food intolerance.

Hormonal changes at puberty.

Inadequate chewing.

Lack of fibre and/or water.

Vitamin C deficiency.

Candida/Dysbiosis.

Parasites.

Anxiety/stress.

Sluggish liver.

The nervous system may be overreacting causing incorrect pain impulses.

GENERAL ADVICE

Encourage regular bowel habits, eg reading on the toilet after meals.

If candida is suspected consult a qualified nutritional therapist.

Chamomile flower tea is anti-spasmodic and calming.

Peppermint tea especially for upper digestive tract (you can combine the two teas for children, eg 1 tsp peppermint leaves and ¹/₂tsp Chamomile flowers infused in a cup of hot water and strained after 10 minutes.

Dietary advice

- Aiming to reduce inflammation in gut.
- Eggs, oranges and white flour may be implicated. Avoid white flour for 2 weeks and replace orange juice with pear, pineapple or apple.
- Fresh carrot juice twice weekly.
- Avoid processed, refined foods, sugar and salt.
- Increase soluble fibre from fruit and vegetables or oats.
- Decrease wheat and avoid wheat bran. Replace with oats, oatbran, rye, ricecakes bread and crispbreads. A wheat exclusion may be helpful (see Food Intolerance). Rice, corn or vegetable pasta is available. Gluten from rye, barley, oats may also be involved. Try wheat first. Dairy or lactose may cause inflammation and allergy. Consult a qualified nutritionist for help with exclusion diets and candida.
- Increase water.
- Add 1-2 tsp cracked golden linseeds to cereals. Follow with a glass of water.
- Increase magnesium and potassium foods.
- Avoid sausages, bacon, ham as preservatives may aggravate.
- Garlic in honey can stimulate digestive juices and correct bacterial imbalances.
- Pulses such as kidney beans and fruits such as grapes and raisins can exacerbate the pain.
- BENEFICIAL FOODS: Oats, ricecakes, lentils, millet, quinoa, amaraith, fish, alfalfa sprouts, brown rice, ground seeds, carrot juice, garlic, ginger, olive oil, sunflower oil, soya milk, apples, pineapple and apple juices, bananas, live yoghurt with added fruits.

Encourage slower eating and proper chewing.
Avoid drinks with meals.

Stress is a major factor. Identify source.

Encourage correct breathing and exercise.
Swimming helps to massage the
abdominal muscles for relief of trapped
wind and reduces stress.

Menstrual cycle can be linked with IBS for
some teenagers – magnesium and
vitamin B6 may help here with more
careful attention to possible imbalances
premenstrually.

Increased sensory nerve pain for unknown
reasons may respond to psychological
approach.

Acupressure – gently stroke abdomen in
clockwise direction.

If anxiety related try Bach or Bush Flower
Remedies.

Contacts:
Irritable Bowel Syndrome Network
Tel: 0114 261 1531

Nutrients to consider

- Charcoal tablets for wind and bloating (HS), not daily or in conjunction with other supplements as it also absorbs vitamins and minerals.

- Aloe Vera juice is anti-inflammatory, cleansing and healing. (HN)

- Vitamin C if constipation is a problem – Magnesium Ascorbate Powder $^1/_4$-$^1/_2$gram (BC) or chewable over 4 years (L) or 4 drops, or Bio C. (AN)

- Slippery Elm powder (BM) or Kiddy Tum, Kid Chamomile from 2 years or Windy Pops from birth. (K)

- Evening primrose oil if related to menstrual cycle in teenagers. (HS)

- Psyllium powder. (N)

- Liver support is important – Children B complex 1capsule 5-12 years or 10 drops. (BC) B Vital 1 daily overy 5 years is especially good if anxiety related (HN); Milk thistle $^1/_2$tablet twice daily, (BM) or 5-10 drops once or twice daily. (HP, BF)

- Probiotics. (BC or S)

- Magnesium/calcium. Low magnesium can cause cramping and constipation 1:1 ratio over 8 years, (HN, S) chewable calcium or magnesium 1daily over 4 years. (L)

- Garlic can help digestion and correct bacterial imbalances – Super Gar 1 daily over 8 years (HN) or liquid. (N)

- Digestive enzymes for children (BC) over 4 years if able to swallow a small capsule.

- L-glutamine powder to soothe and heal gut lining. $^1/_4$tsp between meals from 2 years 1-3 times per day, (HN) or Seacure 1-2 capsules sprinkled onto food (a fish derivative). (NC)

I

JAUNDICE

SEE ALSO: GLANDULAR FEVER, DIGESTIVE PROBLEMS, TOXICITY, FOOD INTOLERANCES, ANAEMIA

Caused by an accumulation of old red blood cells normally excreted in bile, jaundice is a symptom of underlying disease and requires medical advice.

Fairly common in newborns especially premature babies due to immature liver function. Usually clears by 2 weeks even in premature babies.

In older children, jaundice usually indicates a viral infection, eg glandular fever or hepatitis but rarely may indicate blockage of the bile duct. If accompanied by joint pains, rash and fever seek medical help urgently.

Occasionally mild jaundice may appear following Hepatitis vaccination.

Symptoms include yellowing of skin and whites of eyes, drowsiness, sometimes fever, fatigue, aching, bowel changes including greenish stools, nausea and vomiting, bright yellow urine, skin irritation, headache, bruising, anaemia.

FACTORS TO CONSIDER

Viral infection, eg hepatitis A or B or Epstein Barr virus.
Toxic overload in body putting stress on liver/gall bladder, eg allergies, blood sugar imbalances or heavy metal toxicity.
Malnutrition – lack of vitamins/minerals in diet.
Alcohol or drug abuse.
Haemolysis – abnormal destruction of red blood cells.

GENERAL ADVICE

(These recommendations are designed to aid recover y.)
In newborns contact GP or Health Visitor if jaundice persists more than 1 week, urine is dark and stools pale.
Identify cause – usually needs medical diagnosis as may be a sign of a more serious illness.
Consider seeing a medical herbalist as there are many herbs for liver support, but in children supervision is advised. Dandelion is a liver herb. Dandelion 'coffee' in older children.
Reflexology may help.
In teenagers be aware of risk of drug usage. Jaundice may occur from contaminated needles. Medical advice is vital.
No alcohol. This shouldn't be a problem but teenagers need to understand that apart from the legal aspect of underage drinking, it can cause liver problems and exacerbate jaundice. ■

Dietary advice

- Artichoke stimulates release of bile, but not many children like it. Try a soup.
- Avoid salt and fried foods.
- A good, clean diet of natural, unprocessed foods.
- Distilled or bottled water – 6 glasses daily.
- Identify allergens.
- Lemon juice in warm water on rising and before meals. Add manuka honey for immunity, as a sweetener.
- Add 1 tsp each of lecithin granules and brewers yeast to cereals, soups, yoghurt or shakes daily.
- BENEFICIAL FOODS: Artichokes, raw fruit and vegetables, fresh juices especially carrot, beetroot or cucumber, tofu, sprouted seeds and pulses.

Nutrients to consider

- Not for babies who always require medical attention.
- Milk thistle $^1/_2$ tablet twice daily (BM) or 5-10 drops 1-2 times daily. (HP, BF)
- Children's B complex 10 drops or 1 capsule over 5 years. (BC)
- Vitamins A, C E as part of anti-oxidant complex, eg Se ACE 1 daily over 12 years (L) or separately. (BC, L)
- Amino acid Quicksorb 1 drop thrice daily under supervision. (BR)

JOINTS

SEE ALSO: ARTHRITIS, RICKETS, FOOD INTOLERANCE, EXERCISE, GROWING PAINS, STRAINS AND SPRAINS

Pain in joints has several reasons. Most joints are synovial which reduces stress on the bones by absorbing shock.

FACTORS TO CONSIDER
Strains and sprains in babies and toddlers are rare as the joints and muscles are very pliable, but schoolchildren commonly injure themselves with usually rapid recovery.

Bursitis is inflammation of the liquid sac of joints restricting movement and creating friction. Often affects hips, shoulders, feet or elbows. May be known as frozen shoulder or housemaid's knee. Fairly rare in children.

Infection which creates inflammation in body and uses up vitamin C can result in joint pain.

Fever.

Food intolerance.

Nutrient deficiencies.

GENERAL ADVICE
Exercise is vital for flexibility but in an acute state of joint pain, rest is important.

Refer to Arthritis section. ■

Dietary advice

- Reduce animal protein as it acidifies the body causing inflammation. This means dairy and red meat.
- Add turmeric to water when cooking rice as it is anti-inflammatory. You also get yellow rice – a good way to disguise healthier, brown rice.
- Increase vitamin C and calcium foods.
- Avoid citrus fruits, rhubarb and cola drinks.
- BENEFICIAL FOODS: Oily fish, nuts, seeds, lentils, fresh non-citrus fruit, rye bread.

Nutrients to consider

- Vitamin C can thin the synovial fluid in joint spaces enabling freer movement – Bio C $1/4$tsp daily. (AN, NG, R)
- Vitamin A 1 drop daily. (BC)
- EFAs – Essential Balance Junior $1/2$–3 tsps from weaning. (HN)
- Bromelain – 100mgs twice daily, (BM) is anti-inflammatory.
- MSM – $1/4$tsp daily or as cream applied topically over 8 years. (HN)
- Children's B complex 10 drops or 1 capsule over 5 years. (BC)
- Elderberry and horsetail extract 5-10 drops 1-2 times daily. (HP)

J

LEAKY GUT

SEE ALSO: CONSTIPATION, DIGESTIVE PROBLEMS, IRRITABLE BOWEL SYNDROME, FOOD INTOLERANCES, AUTISM, ASTHMA, ECZEMA

This is not really a condition in its own right but an effect of other factors. The term refers to damage to the intestinal gut lining. Effects of this are to impair absorption of vitamins, minerals and other nutrients and increase the risk of food intolerances. Most people with food intolerances will have a leaky gut. When the intestinal lining is damaged, partially digested food particles came into contact with the circulatory system and the immune system, seeing them as foreign, initiates an immune response to protect the body.

FACTORS TO CONSIDER
Stress, which causes inflammation in the system.
Infections, especially candida, but also from parasites and bacteria.
Toxic accumulation in the intestines/bowel (of food, hormones, chemicals etc).
Poor eating habits.
Refined, processed foods.
Food intolerances.
Constipation.
Dysbiosis.
Conditions which may be linked to leaky gut include rheumatoid arthritis, autism, irritable bowel syndrome, eczema, asthma and acne.

Symptoms may include undigested stools, bloating/tummy ache, fatigue, weight loss or gain, failure to thrive, brain 'fog'.

GENERAL ADVICE
Seek professional help from a qualified nutritionist, as it is important to identify the causes and address these before attempting to heal the gut lining.
Manage anxiety/stress with exercise and breathing.
Encourage good eating habits.
Avoid constipation.

Dietary advice

- Strict exclusions may be required to reduce inflammation and allow healing to commence. Seek professional help.
- Gluten, dairy foods and sugar may need to be avoided. Fresh fruit and vegetables between meals, not after.
- 1 tsp cracked golden linseeds added to cereals or yoghurt daily to detoxify the bowel.
- Nuts and seeds ground onto salads and cereals (not in very young children).
- Inulin foods to support liver function and improve digestion, eg beetroot, artichokes.
- Use cabbage cooking water for soups, gravy, stews as rich in L-glutamine.
- BENEFICIAL FOODS:
Oily fish, chicken, linseeds, nuts, soya or rice milks, amaranth, artichokes, quinoa, brown rice and millet, nuts, seeds, live yoghurt, beetroot, papaya, pineapple, apples, bananas, apricots, garlic, ginger.

Nutrients to consider

- Permavite (AR), eg $^1/_2$tsp twice daily between meals for 3 years of age for 2 -3 months. (AR)
- Aloe Gold 1tsp daily over 5 years. (HN)
- L.glutamine powder (fuel for gut cells) $^1/_4$–1 tsp between meals 1-3 times daily from 2 years. (HN) This is in Permavite. (AR)
- Zinc for healing.
- Vitamin A – 1 drop daily, (BC) or betacarotene 1 capsule over 8 years. (HN)
- Essential Balance Junior $^1/_2$-3tsps from weaning. (HN)
- Dricelle Omega Plex contains fish oils and GLA for reducing inflammation. (BC)
- MVM, eg Nutribalance. (AR)
- Bio C to cleanse the bowel.
- Probiotics and digestive enzymes.

LEAKY GUT

LEARNING
DIFFICULTIES

SEE ALSO: DYSLEXIA, DYSPRAXIA, MEMORY,
ADHD, BLOOD SUGAR, STRESS, ANXIETY

Thought to be a problem for 1 in 10 school children. Encompasses dyslexia, dyspraxia, ADHD and several other learning difficulties. May result from obvious genetic disorders such as Down's Syndrome or phynylketonuria, but also linked to conditions such as autism, visual and hearing problems and brain damage. Developmental delay occurs in various degrees and each child needs to be assessed individually.

Please refer to relevant sections for details, but optimal diet, good levels of fluid intake and EFAs may help performance.

There have been several controversial studies over recent years suggesting that high levels of vitamins and minerals can raise IQ. Whether this is true or not the brain requires constant supplies of nutrients including oxygen, glucose and water as well as vitamins and minerals.

GENERAL ADVICE

Always check vision and hearing.
Specific exercises to stimulate circulation and wake up the brain. Read *Smart Moves for brain / body exercises*.
Bio-Education is becoming trendy, but ensuring adequate nutrition for brain function seems obvious.
Badger your child's school for water in lessons and especially during exams. Many children have one drink during the school day of 6 hours and that is often squash!
Involve your children in philosophical discussions to teach them to think laterally and independently – Why am I here? What is belief?
Exercise can decrease stress and increase oxygen and nutrients to the brain. ∎

Dietary Advice

● Increase water intake as dehydration is a common cause of poor concentration span and memory. Some studies have indicated as much as 8-15 glasses daily!
● Breakfast is vital as blood sugar levels are very low on waking. Some children have nothing until lunch time.
● The brain needs iron and levels have to be sustained for concentration and memory. Combine iron and vitamin C foods, eg boiled egg, wholemeal toast and orange juice.
● BENEFICIAL FOODS:
Cereals, orange juice, eggs, fruit especially bananas, nuts, seeds, oily fish.

Nutrients to consider

● Recent research (May 2002) by the Dyslexia Research Trust has achieved encouraging results with a particular balance of omega 3 fatty acids.
● Eye Q – start with 2 capsules per day building up to 6 per day for 3 months, then 2 per day maintainance. Contains preferable ratios of EPA / DHA /GLA (omega 3 and 6 oils) for memory, concentration and processing of information. (HS, NC) Alternatively Eskimo 3 has similar ratios. Give 5mls daily. (Nu) These are the best researched choices of EFAs at time of writing.
● Gingko Herbal Complex tincture for memory (N) or $^1/_2$tablet twice daily. (BM)
● Zinc – 10 drops or 15mg capsule BC or sherbet flavoured powder. $^1/_2$ level measure under tongue alternate days over 8 years. (HN)
● Magnesium for anxiety and sulphation 15mg per kilo of body weight. $^1/_2$ capsule daily for 1-3 year olds then 1 daily or chewable lemon 1 daily (L) or True Food Mg 1-2 tablets daily for over 8 years (HN) or magnesium solution $^1/_2$tsp 1-2 times daily (2.5mls) (AR)
● Ginseng for stress eg B Vital 1 daily especially during exams.
● L Glutamine for brain function and blood sugar balance $^1/_4$tsp over 8 years sprinkled onto cold food or into juice. (HN)

(See Over)

L

- Zen taken in anxiety-related brain dysfunction relaxes child whilst maintaining mental alertness. 1 daily over 5 years. (AR)
- Brain Food Formula has a complex of nutrients to improve concentration and learning and reduce anxiety. 1 per day over 12 years. (HN)
- Chocolate Memory is a delicious chocolate drink containing phosphatidyl serine to boost brain chemicals for memory. 10gms in milk or water at bedtime. (HN)
- Iron is an important brain nutrient. Easy iron – 2 to 5 years 1 capsule every 3 days, 5-8 years alternate days, over 8 years daily (HN) (1 tablet crushed) or Floridix by Salus House which is herbal iron with B vitamins and vitamin C (one drop per 6lbs body weight), (N) or Nutrisorb iron ascorbate 10 drops. (BC) Iron phosphate is homeopathic so does not feed bacteria (one tablet crushed). (BM)

L

Dietary advice
- Increase EFAs.
- Include plenty of foods rich in vitamin E, vitamin C, B vitamins and zinc.
- Increase water intake to 6 glasses daily.
- BENEFICIAL FOODS:
Eggs, milk, fresh vegetables especially green leafy variety, avocados, seeds and their oils, oily fish.

Nutrients to consider
- MVM to include above nutrients.
- Children's B complex 10 drops or 1 capsule over 5 years daily. (BC)
- Essential Balance Junior $^{1}/_{2}$-3 tsps from weaning. (HN)

Topicals
- Infant Starflower Cream.(N)
- Vitamin E Cream. (L)

LIPS

SEE ALSO: COLD SORES, MOUTH ULCERS

Cracked, sore lips and mouth corners often occur in winter and after a cold, but if persistant consider the following:
Deficiences of vitamin B2 or E.
Vitamin A toxicity – rare.
Dehydration especially if other areas of skin are sore.
Overuse of inhalers.
Glue sniffing – usually accompanied by sore, spotty areas around mouth and nose.
Smoking.

GENERAL ADVICE
Flavoured lip balms are available in chemists. They protect but rarely heal or address cause.
Protect lips before going out, after eating and at bedtime.
Identify any drug abuse or smoking in teenagers and address. NB. Sore lips in teenagers may indicate bulimia due to enforced vomiting. ∎

LUMPS

SEE ALSO: BITES AND STINGS, CANCER, INFECTIONS, HIVES, IMMUNE FUNCTION

Always see a doctor for diagnosis.

The lymphatic system is important in fighting childhood infections so swellings are fairly common.

Swollen glands are enlarged lymph nodes. Commonly occurs in neck during infection, but can also happen in armpit or groin. Common conditions associated are glandular fever, childhood infectious diseases or respiratory infections. Rarely it may indicate serious conditions such as Hodgekins Disease or other lymphomas.

Skin Lumps may be hives, bites, stings, cysts or lipomas (benign fatty cysts – not to be confused with lymphoma).

Cysts are usually fluid-filled sacks commonly occurring after an injury or infection. They themselves can become infected forming an abscess which needs treatment.

Allergic reactions may cause swollen glands and can also result in hives.

GENERAL ADVICE
A qualified homeopath may be able to help reduce cysts.

Exercise is vital to improve lymphatic drainage as unlike circulatory system which has the heart, the lymphatic system has no pump and requires movement for efficiency.

Massage can help.

Dry skin brushing (see Appendix) for lymphatic drainage and improved circulation. ■

Dietary advice

- Avoid dairy as it is mucous forming and clogs up the lymphatic system.
- Boost immune function.
- Clear system by removing all artificial food and increasing natural, wholefoods.
- Increase EFAs.
- Raw crushed garlic in honey boosts immunity and increases circulation.
- BENEFICIAL FOODS: Peppers, fresh fruit and vegetable juices (especially beetroot), carrot, cucumber, garlic and honey.

Nutrients to consider

- See Immune Function.

L

M

MEMORY

SEE ALSO: LEARNING DIFFICULTIES, BLOOD SUGAR, THYROID, ADDICTIONS, CANDIDA, FOOD INTOLERANCE

Memory is something we take for granted until it's less efficient. In children, memory loss or poor retention of information can be confused with inadequate processing or dyslexia.

Babies are thought to have accumulated memories from before birth and the rate of stimulation and new experiences in infancy is high.

Huge demands are made on children at school with exams and assessments seemingly ongoing and crisis times require optimum brain function.

FACTORS TO CONSIDER

Lack of glucose to the brain – blood sugar imbalances.

Poor circulation – blood is the transporter of oxygen, iron and glucose.

Neurotransmitters are brain chemicals which act like electrical switches which can 'short-circuit' if nutrients are unavailable.

Nutrient deficiencies especially B vitamins and EFAs.

Lack of protein.

Thyroid disorders.

Candidiasis – yeast overgrowth in gut.

Food intolerances especially wheat, can lead to brain 'fog'.

Drug abuse or alcohol in teenagers.

Heavy metal toxicity, eg lead or aluminium, can affect memory.

GENERAL ADVICE

Do not allow mobile phones at school and use a protective cover.

Efficient breathing.

Use it or lose it applies to all ages! Keep brain active on fun activities. Make a game out of counting backwards, doing codes, playing board games as a family, eg memory game of matching cards, doing crosswords. In the car, use number plates to encourage number work.

Don't allow too long on the computer or watching TV. Alternate activities.

Sport encourages co-ordination and uses different areas of the brain.

Consider a hair test to identify any toxic metals.

Dietary advice

● Add lecithin granules 1 tsp – 1 tablespoon to cereals, shakes, yoghurts daily for choline which provides acetylcholine for memory.

● Try a wheat exclusion for one month. Re-introduce if no improvement. (see Food intolerances)

● No sugar, cola, tea, coffee or chocolate as these stimulants can affect glucose supply to the brain and cause fatigue.

● Reduce carbohydrates as they can reduce brain function.

● Small, regular meals with some protein to regulate blood sugar levels.

● Adequate protein for choline, but avoid red meat.

● Increase EFAs, especially oily fish.

● Eat organic foods as much as possible.

● Filter all water to avoid fluoride.

● BENEFICIAL FOODS: Oily fish, poultry, eggs, live yoghurt, nuts, seeds, pulses, wheat germ, brown rice, grains, ginger, peppers, sweet potatoes, avocados, squash, parsley, sprouted seeds, citrus fruits, berries, blackstrap molasses.

'Rosemary for remembrance' – put 1 drop on a
tissue and allow child to sniff when doing
exams or homework or put in a room burner.
Rescue Remedy is a Bach flower remedy which can
help if anxiety is linked, eg in exams.
Fluoride free toothpaste.
Exercise for circulation especially inversion.
Encourage gymnastics, bar swinging, head and
hand stands and arm swinging when walking.
Plenty of sleep and fresh air.
Be alert for possible marijuana smoking. ▪

Nutrients to consider

● EFAs – Eye Q; start with 2 capsules per day building up to 6 per day for 3 months; then 2 per day maintainance. Contains preferable ratios of EPA / DHA /GLA (omega 3 and 6 oils) for memory, concentration and processing of information. (HS, NC) Alternatively Eskimo 3 has similar ratios. Give 5mls daily. (Nu) These are the best choices of EFAs at time of writing.

● Gingko biloba increases circulation to the brain. Gingko Herbal Complex (N) or $^{1}/_{2}$tablet twice daily. (BM)

● Children's B complex 10 drops or 1 capsule over 5 years (BC) or B Vital 1 daily over 5 years, if anxiety linked. (HN)

● L-glutamine is an important brain fuel. $^{1}/_{4}$–1 tsp over 8 years. (HN)

● MVM.

● Brain Food Formula – 1 daily over 8 years contains several brain nutrients. (HN)

● Chocolate Memory Drink – 10gms in milk at bedtime contains phosphatidyl, serine and phosphatidyl choline. (HN)

M

Migraine

SEE ALSO: HEADACHES, FOOD INTOLERANCES

Dietary advice

- Commonest food triggers are the 4 Cs – chocolate, caffeine, cheese and citrus fruits, but yeast, dairy, wheat and tomatoes may also be involved.
- Avoid tyramine foods (see Headaches) and peanuts.
- Eat small, regular meals to avoid swings in blood sugar level.
- No fizzy drinks, soy sauce.
- Increase vitamin C foods.
- Reduce saturated fats from red meat and dairy.
- Increase EFAs.
- Increase water to at least 5 glasses daily.
- BENEFICIAL FOODS: Almonds, nuts, seeds, watercress (as a soup), parsley, garlic, cherries, pineapple, oily fish.

Nutrients to consider

- Calcium/magnesium to control nerve impulses and muscular contractions.
- Bio Magnesium $-^1/_2$capsule 1-3 years (BK), Chewable magnesium or calcium one daily over 4 years (L), solution $^1/_4$tsp 1-2 times daily (AR), or 1:1 ratio Ca/Mg combined. (S)
- EFAs especially evening primrose oil or starflower oil 1-3 times daily in 4-12 year olds. (L)
- Children's B complex – 10 drops or 1 capsule over 5 years. (BC)
- MVM.
- Gingko Complex $^1/_2$tablet twice daily (BM) or tincture in older children. (N)
- Children's vitamin C capsule or 4 drops. (BC)
- Probiotics for digestion.
- Feverfew tincture 5-10 drops over 8 years. (HP).

Migraine tends to run in families and is more common in late childhood. Probably as common in children as adults but less well recognised.

Symptoms include severe one sided head/facial pain often accompanied by nausea, vomiting, tummy ache and pallor. Intolerance to bright light is another indicator.

If fever or neck stiffness are present, see a doctor urgently to eliminate meningitis. Persistent incapacitating headaches should be medically checked to rule out brain tumour which is extremely rare.

FACTORS TO CONSIDER

Genetics.
Food intolerances.
Toxic metals.
Leaky gut.
Dysbiosis.
Magnesium deficiency.
Triggers include too long on computer, skipping meals, stress, dehydration, irregular sleep pattern, citrus fruit, chocolate, cheese.

GENERAL ADVICE

Prolonged infant colic, frequent tummy aches or travel sickness may, in fact, be early migraine attacks which are only diagnosed later. If your child has a history of these problems his headaches may well be migraine.

Barometric pressure changes can affect migraine sufferers.

DMG improves oxygenation of brain. Under professional supervision.

Arrange a hair test to assess mineral imbalances and possible toxic metals.

Ask dentist to check for tooth grinding and misalignment of jaw. (TMJ)

Keep child in smoke-free environment.

Frequent use of painkillers can actually create attacks.

Accupressure: massage point between thumb and forefinger with palm uppermost.

Reflexology: apply pressure to inside base of big toe 3 times for 10 seconds each time.

In teenagers fearful of a migraine attack on exam

days, preventative medication is available from GP, but particular attention to diet, blood sugar levels and fluid intake is important too.
Keep a food diary.
Consider testing allergies with York Labs.
Regular exercise.

Contact:
Migraine Trust Helpline: 020 7831 4818

Migraine Action Association: 01932 352468 ▨

Moods

SEE ALSO: DEPRESSION, ANXIETY, BLOOD SUGAR, FOOD INTOLERANCES, PUBERTY, ADHD, PMS, EATING DISORDERS

From crying babies through toddler temper tantrums to adolescent angst, mood swings can try the most patient of parents. It is easy to contribute them to 'age' whether they are 2 or 12 years, but one should not overlook possible physical causes. In young children it is normal to experiment with how much you can get away with.

Symptoms include fluctuating moods ranging from elation and over excitability to depression, fatigue, poor sleep, attention seeking, varying appetite.

FACTORS TO CONSIDER

Blood sugar imbalances.
Nutrient deficiencies eg zinc or EFAs.
Hormonal disturbances in 9-16 year olds.
PMS.
Eating disorder.
Contraceptive pill.
Drug use.
Bullying.
Emotional issues such as jealousy, middle child syndrome, family disturbance like ill health or separation, loss of pet or friend, change of school, moving house.

GENERAL ADVICE

Identify causes.
Exercise.
Make time to be alone with her. Discuss anything she wishes, but try not to be direct about moods as she will clamp up – look for clues.
If this fails, ask sensitively what is wrong. Tell her you love her, are concerned and want to help. Give suggestions, eg are you worried about daddy, school etc.
Ignore bad moods, respond to good moods.
Keep a diary of when they occur. May be linked to foods or to menstrual cycle about which she may be embarrassed. ■

Dietary advice

- Small, regular meals (3 hourly longest gap).
- Avoid stimulants like sugar, coffee, tea, cola.
- Identify any food intolerances – keep diary as foods eaten frequently may be the culprit.
- Increase water intake.
- More soluble fibre.
- BENEFICIAL FOODS: Chicken, turkey, cottage cheese, brown rice, quinoa, fresh fruit and vegetables.

Nutrients to consider

- B Vital one daily over 5 years. (HN)
- B-complex including 50mgs each B vitamin over 12 years. (BC)
- Seretone 5HTP one daily over 8 years at bedtime to improve mood.
- Chromium one drop (BC) or 200mcgs over 8 years (HN) for blood sugar.
- EFAs – Einstein DHA 1-2 capsules daily (HN) or Eye Q – start with 2 capsules per day building up to 6 per day for 3 months, then 2 per day maintainance. Contains preferable ratios of EPA / DHA /GLA (omega 3 and 6 oils) for memory, concentration and processing of information. (HS, NC) Alternatively Eskimo 3 has similar ratios. Give 5mls daily. (Nu)
- Brain Food Formula – 1 daily over 12 years contains various nutrients to reduce stress, improve sleep and wellbeing and stabilise mood fluctuations. (HN)

M

Mouth ulcers

SEE ALSO: FOOD INTOLERANCE, IMMUNE FUNCTION, GUMS, TEETH

Often occurs following an infection or when mouth is bitten, but some children are very prone. Usually indicates temporary immune suppression.

Factors to consider
Food intolerance especially wheat.
EFA deficiency.
Vitamin A deficiency.
Dental problems.
Dysbiosis.
Leaky gut (mucous membranes in mouth can reflect health in whole digestive tract).
Fluoride sensitivity.

General advice
Boost immunity.
Use soft toothbrush or electric toothbrush.
Regular dental checks to identify any friction, misalignment of teeth or gum disease.
Toothpaste should be fluoride-free – Boots do one but it will have sodium laurel sulphate.
Avoid sodium laurel sulphate, a potentially harmful chemical in most toothpastes and mouthwashes as it may trigger mouth ulcers by eroding natural mucous secretions. Use Aloe Dent (HN) or ring Green People for a catalogue. Some health stores may stock SLS-free toothpaste. ∎

Dietary advice
- Identify any food intolerances. Possible culprits are tomatoes, oranges, strawberries, kiwi fruits, pineapple, wheat, peanuts, ketchup, sugar and vinegar.
- Reduce all white flour and refined foods.
- Avoid fizzy drinks.
- Crisps, cheese, processed meat and smoked fish are all salty so avoid.
- Use drinking straws.
- BENEFICIAL FOODS: Camomile tea, licorice, low acid foods eg brown rice, crushed seeds.

Nutrients to consider
- Children's B complex 10 drops or 1 capsule over 5 years (BC) for healing and immunity.
- Probiotics.
- E-Kid-Nacea from 2 years. (K)
- Vitamin E capsules placed onto ulcer. (L)
- Sodiphos for acidity. (BM)
- Make a mouthwash with 1 drop each tea tree and lavender oil in boiled, cooled water and use after meals.

M

NAIL PROBLEMS

SEE ALSO: CANDIDA, THYROID

Nails can reveal a lot about overall health. Conditions which may be reflected in nails include thyroid problems, anaemia, asthma, candida, kidney disease, circulatory problems, arthritis, heavy metal poisoning or diabetes. (Many problems are linked to nutrient deficiencies.)

Brittle/split/dry – may be due to vitamin A, iron and calcium deficiency. Low stomach acid may be involved. Also dehydration. Try zinc to correct digestion or short course digestive enzymes. Unlikely in very young children.

Ridges – horizontal and vertical ridges indicate vitamin A or B deficiency. Vertical ridges may also mean iron deficiency. Horizontal may indicate severe stress. Most likely in older teenagers.

Spoon-shaped, ie concave can mean iron, vitamin B12, zinc deficiency or anaemia, and, rarely, cystic fibrosis.

White spots or bands – zinc vitamin B6 or protein deficiency. Can also be thyroid or digestive dysfunction.

Fungal nails often indicates yeast overgrowth and fungal infections. Taking probiotics and addressing possible candida are recommended. Try applying either caster oil, tea tree oil, Citricidal, Aloe vera gel or MSM cream (HN) twice daily to nails and nail bed.

Slow growth – zinc, iron or protein deficiency.

Discoloured nails – can indicate allergy or stress. Apply fresh lemon juice to nail bed and take digestive enzymes.

Nail-biting – usually a nervous habit, but it weakens nails and encourages infection. Try dipping finger tips in lemon juice to cleanse and discourage biting nails. Paint with natural nail varnish in girls to encourage pride in her nails and ask her gently why she has bitten them.

GENERAL ADVICE

Nail polish can damage nails and skin as toxic dyes are absorbed and can cause allergic reactions. Use red henna powder as a paste with water. Pat on, dry naturally and rinse off for delicate pink nails!

Always see a doctor if no resolution after one or 2 months or if accompanied by other unexplained symptoms.

Homeopathic lilica 6c or horsetail may help. (A)

Exercise fingers by knitting, squeezing a stress ball, clenching and opening fingers to increase circulation.

Soak fingers in olive oil and cider vinegar for 10-20 minutes daily to strengthen nails.

A mixture of avocado, honey, egg yolk and a pinch of salt rubbed intothe nails and nail bed nourishes the nails.

Dietary advice

- Adequate protein.
- 6 glasses water daily.
- Calcium and phosphorous are rich in fresh carrot juice. Offer daily to strengthen nailes.
- Reduce or avoid citrus, salt and vinegar.
- Brewers yeast or wheat germ daily.
- BENEFICIAL FOODS: Oatmeal, seeds, nuts, lentils, sprouted seeds, green leafy vegetables, fresh raw fruit and vegetables, carrot juice, eggs, oily fish, chicken, turkey.

Nutrients to consider

(See appropriate nail problem for which is needed.)

- Zinc – 10 drops of 15mg capsule BC or sherbet-flavoured powder. $^1/_2$level measure under tongue alternate days over 8 years. (HN)
- Digestive enzymes.
- Aqueous amino acids – one drop thrice daily. (BR, NC)
- Vitamin A – one drop daily. (BC)
- B complex to include biotin – one children's capsule over 5 years. (BC)
- Floradix iron from Salus Haus contains B vitamins, vitamin C and natural source iron from herbs. (N)
- Flax seed oil (HN) and dricelle mega GLA powder. (BC).

NAIL PROBLEMS

NAPPY RASH

SEE ALSO: THRUSH, CANDIDA, ECZEMA

Known as *dermatitis gluteatis infantum*, most
babies get a sore bottom at some stage of their
average 2 $^1/_2$ years in nappies. Skin that is constantly
warm, humid and damp is prone to inflammation
and infection. The rash may be very short-lived, ie
gone by next nappy, or persistent, lasting a week.

The rash can be localised or extensive including
angry spots and even bleeding. Secondary bacterial
infections may occur in untreated nappy rash, but
candida (fungal) infection is more likely.

Risk factors include teething times when urine
becomes more acidic, diarrhoea, too few fluids or
food intolerance. Deficiencies of vitamins A and B
and of EFAs can contribute.

GENERAL ADVICE

Frequent nappy changes.

Leave bottom exposed to air and preferably filtered
    sunlight whenever possible.

Change from disposable nappies to terry towelling
    as many disposables contain chemicals
    including bleach.

Do not wash nappies in strong, biological
    detergents. Change to Eco Balls and forget
    Fabric Conditioner.

Dry nappies outside when possible.

Avoid baby wipes and use cooled, boiled water to
    cleanse.

Protect soreness from further damage with a paste
    of cornflour and zinc cream.

If mother had thrush in pregnancy, baby may be
    born with it. Occurs in mouth as well.
    Lactating mothers should avoid yeast and
    sugar and take probiotics. (see Candida)

Try Jurlique range of baby products.

Beware: some creams including zinc and caster oil
    may contain acharis oil derived from peanuts.
    In damaged skin absorption is increased and
    research is suggesting a link with peanut
    allergy, asthma and eczema. ■

Dietary advice

- If weaned, offer avocados for vitamin E (for healing).
- Flaxseed oil 1 tsp added to foods daily for healing and anti-inflammatory. (HN)

Topicals

- Infant starflower cream. (N)
- Vitamin E cream.
- Lightly beaten raw egg white to exposed skin can help neutralise acidity.
- Skin of an avocado applied gently promotes healing and prevents infection.
- Apply live yoghurt to buttocks.

N

Dietary advice

- Avoid fried, fatty, spicy, smelly foods.
- High carbohydrate foods such as oats, dry biscuits, toast and oatcakes can usually be tolerated better. Also vegetable soups, steamed vegetables, cottage cheese and fruit salads.
- Avoid fats, sugar, spices and citrus.
- Small amounts often rather than 3 big meals offered.
- Add fresh root ginger to warm water and honey (no honey under one year old). Alternatively use ginger in stir fries or homemade biscuits.
- A pinch of nutmeg added to rice pudding, cereals, yoghurt, shakes.
- BENEFICIAL FOODS: Bananas, fruit juices, sorbet, fruit salad, cucumber, vegetable soups, nutmeg, oatcakes, dry toast, ginger and honey, ginger biscuits, brown rice, porridge, live yoghurt, cottage cheese, milky drinks for some.

Nutrients to consider

- Kid Chamomile can reduce anxiety-linked nausea, over 2 years. (K)
- Kiddy Tum has some ginger, over 2 years. (K)
- Vitamin B6 deficiency can lead to nausea. 10 drops alongside B complex one capsule over 5 years. (BC)
- Probiotics.
- Do not give iron unless diagnosed as deficient. Easy Iron – 2 to 5 years one capsule every 3 days; 5-8 years alternate days; over 8 years daily, (HN) or Iron Phosphate one tablet crushed. (BM) Salus Haus Floradix liquid contains herbal sources of iron, C and B vitamins. (N)
- Vitamin C helps utilise iron – 10 drops or Bio-C $^{1}/_{4}$tsp. (AN, NC)

NAUSEA

SEE ALSO: DIGESTIVE PROBLEMS, GASTRO-ENTERITIS, BLOOD SUGAR, TRAVEL SICKNESS, ANXIETY, CONSTIPATION

Feeling sick is difficult for a young child to describe. In older children, anxiety and worry can cause 'butterflies' and nausea. **If nausea is accompanied by a fever or abdominal pain, seek medical advice.**

FACTORS TO CONSIDER
Stress and anxiety.
Middle ear infections.
Iron deficiency.
Travel sickness.
Sluggish liver.
Gall stones.
Infections.
Food intolerances.
Infections.
Blood sugar inbalances.
Pregnancy in teenagers.

Symptoms include loss of appetite, dizziness, fainting, vomiting.

GENERAL ADVICE
Favoured remedies for symptomatic relief are chamomile (calming) and ginger which can relieve indigestion and nausea. Researchers believe it neutralises toxins in the gut, balances acidity and directly affects the feedback centre for nausea in the brain.

Avoid large amounts of drink in one go. Sip regularly.

Nausea is often worse when empty, eg on rising in the morning.

Hot water, lemon and honey can refresh the system.

Discourage missing meals. Encourage a little food, however tiny.

Keep blood sugar levels even.

Homeopathic Ipecac 3C or Nux Vomica may help.

Herbs include chamomile, red raspberry, fennel and peppermint as teas or tinctures.

Ask GP for tests for iron deficiency. ∎

NIGHT TERRORS

SEE ALSO: SLEEP PROBLEMS, ANXIETY

These nocturnal disturbances can be very distressing for parents, but the child often remembers little or nothing about it in the morning. They usually start between 4-7 years but can continue until puberty. They may happen nightly for a few days and not recur for several weeks.

Symptoms include crying, shaking, hallucinations. He is often not actually awake so is, in effect, sleepwalking. Thought to be sudden awakening, but not always nightmares.

GENERAL ADVICE

Wake him up gently, remove from the scene and give him a good hug or take him into bed until calm.

Children's oil blend to massage or bath in before bed gives relaxed sleep. (N)

Identify any trigger, eg school problems, insecurities.

Avoid TV before bed and monitor what he watches. Do not allow TV in bedroom.

Take care with computer games; some can be quite violent.

Worm wood (artemesia) has been suggested for liver stress which may result in night terrors – see a herbalist.

Homeopathic chamomilla. (A) ■

Dietary advice
● Avoid cheese before bed.
● Milky drink improves sleep.

Nutrients to consider

● Calcium/magnesium are calming minerals, often deficient in growing children and in stress. 1:1 ratio one daily over 8 years. (S, HN)

● Serotone 5HTP, 1 at bedtime for serotonin, over 8 years. (HN)

● Milk thistle $^1/_2$tablet twice daily (BM) or 5-10 drops 1-2 times daily. (HP, BF)

● B complex for nervous system – B Vital over 5 years one daily, (HN) contains ginseng for stress.

● Magnesium Phosphate for nervous child. (BM)

● Kid Catnip or Kid Chamomile over 2 years for nerves. (K)

● Zen works in acute anxiety states in 20 minutes if taken at the first sign of attack. 1 daily over 5 years. (AR, R)

NOSEBLEEDS

Nosebleeds (Epistaxis) can be associated with underlying rare illness such as liver disease, anameia, haemophyllia or leukemia.

Fairly common in children as the mucous membranes are thinner and children are prone to 'picking' the nose. Sometimes spontaneous with no apparent cause or may be aggravated by stress, injury, hayfever or infection. Occasionally a foreign body like a bead or pea has been put into the nose.

For some children nosebleeds happen often and then subside for a few weeks only to recur. Capillaries, the fine network of blood vessels in the mucous membranes lining the nose are fragile.

GENERAL ADVICE

Sit upright or with head between knees and pinch hard on lower nostrils to encourage clotting. Do not tip head back or lie child down as choking may occur.

Refrain from blowing nose afterwards.

Ice packs can stop bleeding.

Fruit juice ice lollies or ice cubes sucked, may help. ■

Nutrients to consider
● Vitamin C with bilberry – one capsule daily (BC) to strengthen capillaries.

OBESITY/OVERWEIGHT

SEE ALSO: WEIGHT PROBLEMS, EXERCISE, GROWTH, FOOD INTOLERANCES, BLOOD SUGAR, THYROID, DIABETES

Recent research revealed that on average, 15% of British children are overweight. Figures are conflicting due to inconsistent diagnostic criteria but it seems there has been approximately a 50% increase over the last 10 years. This is a major cause for concern as future health is at stake – diabetes, heart disease and cancer have all been linked to obesity and children as young as 6 years have had increased blood fats like cholesterol.

Eating habits in childhood set a pattern for life. Fat cell size and number is determined in childhood. The age of non-insulin dependent diabetes is getting earlier and appears to be directly linked to diet, lifestyle and obesity. The immune function can be adversely affected by obesity. The main reasons for weight increases in our children are processed foods and inactivity. Stress also plays a part.

Sugar is the main offender hidden in snacks, drinks, breakfast cereals, 'healthy' bars, take away foods especially Chinese. Sugar should consist of a maximum of 10% of calorie intake as it contains no nutrients and contributes to tooth decay, diabetes and obesity.

FACTORS TO CONSIDER

Genetics, family/school worries.

Refined processed diets, blood sugar imbalances, early weaning, bottle feeding.

Lack of exercise, commercial weaning foods, incorrect diet in lactation and pregnancy, nutrient deficiencies, thyroid insufficiency, depression/anxiety.

GENERAL ADVICE

It is better to increase activity and slightly reduce portion sizes than subject children to weight loss diets.

Avoid meals in front of TV.

Change whole family to a healthier eating regime to reduce craving and break habits.

Alter focus to fitness rather than weight loss.

Increase exercise as a family.

Encourage child to help plan and prepare meals.

Increase variety of foods.

Concentrate on healthy foods rather than calories.

Low fat foods are often high in sugar and low in vitamins/ minerals.

Avoid constipation as this slows digestion.

Beware of commercial baby foods; many contain above the government recommendations for sugar.

Nutrients to consider

- EFAs especially GLA can control appetite and regulate hormones. Evening primrose oil 1-3 times daily 4-12 years (L)
- Chromium 1 drop (BC) or Bio Chromium Complex one daily over 12 years (BM) or CrGTF one alternate days over 8 years (HN)
- MVM to replace losses from junk diets and protect intake when reducing foods
- Digestive enzymes may help utilise calories efficiently during initial stages
- Children's B complex 10 drops or one capsule (BC) or B Vital one daily over 5 years (HN) if anxiety involved contains ginseng for burning calories
- One tsp lecithin granules to cereals, yoghurt or in shakes daily to help fat digestion
- Seretone 5HTP may help suppress appetite and improve self esteem, 1-2 daily (HN)

OBESITY

SHORT, SAFE DETOX FOR CHILDREN

If diet is full of junk foods, sugar and chemicals, a gentle clean up will relieve the digestive system, liver and hormones of the overload, allowing them to function more efficiently. It can also reduce cravings. The initial headache, fatigue and irritability is soon overcome with more energy and a positive outlook. Self-control is regained.

Avoid all processed, junk foods and red meat and dairy products which are hard to digest, for 3 days. Yoghurt is good.

First thing:
Lemon juice, honey or maple syrup and water or orange juice with acidophilus powder.

Breakfast:
Fresh fruit salad and live yoghurt.

Mid-morning:
Fresh carrot or vegetable juice with ¹/₄tsp vitamin C powder. (BC, AN)

Lunch:
Raw, crunchy vegetables with yoghurt dip or good salad with lemon/olive oil dressing.

Mid-afternoon:
Peppermint tea and honey, nuts and seeds.

Tea:
Avocado, carrot, kiwi salad.
Swiss bouillon drink.

Bedtime:
Chamomile and honey tea or shake with pineapple, mango, banana and apple juice.

NB: This is not a weight loss regime, but a short term detox for 3 days maximum, over a weekend or holiday.

Dietary advice

- Do not put your child on a diet without nutritional guidance.
- Introduce complex carbohydrates which also contain protein eg pulses, baked potatoes. Increase protein foods to control appetite.
- Consider food intolerances. Most likely to be wheat or dairy products.
- Grill, bake or steam instead of frying.
- Keep ready meals and take aways for emergencies – very rarely.
- Increase EFAs in favour of saturated fats. This means less cheese, red meat and processed foods and more oily fish, chicken, nuts, seeds and green vegetables. Fat is important for children but needs to be the right type.
- 6 glasses of water daily. No squash or fizzy drinks.
- Avoid caffeine in tea, coffee, cola, chocolate.
- Milk should be semi-skimmed from 5 years; never skimmed.
- Snacks are good but encourage plain popcorn, seeds, nuts, fruit, carrot sticks, yoghurt.
- Avoid pasties, cakes, biscuits, crisps, sugar.
- Offer shakes and fresh juices to cover the 5 portions of fruit and vegetables daily.
- No salt on the table or in cooking. There is more than enough in processed foods. Salt encourages fluid retention and weight gain.
- Avoid artificial sweeteners. They encourage sweet cravings.
- BENEFICIAL FOODS:
Most vegetables and fruits especially sweetcorn, celery, pears, apricots, prune puree, pineapple, raspberries, dried fruit, avocados, baked potatoes, beans, milk and fruit juices, blackstrap molasses, cracked golden linseeds, sprouted seeds and grains, plain popcorn, nuts, seeds, lentils, live yoghurt, brown rice, wholemeal bread and pasta, oat bran, olive oil, oily fish, shellfish, chicken and turkey.

O

Always encourage breakfast and eat regular meals with 2-3 snacks. Many children who skip breakfast eat sweets and crisps on the way to school.

Discourage artificial sweeteners. They are dangerous to health and encourage a sweet tooth.

The average child consumes its own weight in additives by teenage years and 1 $1/4$lbs sugar per week!

Lunch boxes can pose a problem as peer group pressure to conform is strong. Sneak some tomato or cucumber into sandwiches but leave out the mayonnaise. Increase fish fillings or replace butter with thin peanut butter or houmous. Include fruit, yoghurt or a seed bar. Avoid crisps and sugary drinks.

If breakfast, after school snacks and main meals are healthy then the lunch box may be the place to ease up a little!

Avoid overt parental dieting as this gives confusing messages about food.

The current fear of eating disorders is resulting in less attention for the much more common problem of overweight children. Obesity can create later eating disorders.

Walk to school (see Exercise). The risks of abduction and road traffic accidents are rapidly being overtaken by the risks of obesity.

Banning specific foods is counter productive. Keep as occasional treats but avoid food as rewards.

Campaign for healthier school meals and tuck shops, banning of drinks and chocolate machines in schools and the playground ice cream van and an increase in cycle paths, playing fields and PE in school.

TV advertising is full of junk foods aimed at children. Avoid commercial channels and reduce time watching. Choose specific programmes together and then turn the television off. Help them to make a weekly timetable of programmes to watch. This discourages channel-flicking and gives them some control.

Do not weigh. Go by clothes size.

Discourage snacks 2 hours before bed. However, some research indicates that milk and honey at bedtime can increase the quality of sleep and reduce appetite by raising serotonin levels.

Boost your child's self-esteem. Find activities he is good at and praise, praise, praise!

Some very obese children may need help from appetite suppressants. There are several natural herbs, but consult a practitioner. ▪

Obsessive Compulsive Disorder (OCD)

SEE ALSO: ANXIETY, LEARNING DIFFICULTIES, DYSLEXIA, DYSPRAXIA, DEPRESSION

Incidence is thought to be 1 in 100 young people, but 1 in 50 over all age groups. OCD is a manifestation of anxiety. It is a way of coping with worries. Many sufferers experience intrusive, obsessive thoughts which are very disturbing and develop strategies of compulsive behaviour to distract themselves. This 'secret' condition involves rituals, routines and habits which can take up large amounts of time each day.

OCD may be triggered by a change of school, death of a loved one, family stress etc. Most children develop little rituals which pass naturally, eg not stopping on the cracks or the bears will get you, but there are two main questions to be asked.

Does she become anxious if unable to perform the ritual?

Does the behaviour interfere with other aspects of her life, eg not being able to attend a sleep-over or go swimming or being late for school?

Typical obsessions are fear of contamination, causing harm to someone else, making mistakes or behaving unacceptably – there is excessive doubt and a need for symmetry and exactness.

Typical compulsions include excessive hand washing, tapping, counting, checking lightswitches or door locks, cleaning, collecting and hoarding, repeating actions or words and having very precise positions for objects. It is not possible to interrupt or ban these actions without increasing anxiety.

Factors to consider

Family history of OCD, high IQ, anxious disposition. Studies show that the part of the brain involved in managing threat is larger in OCD sufferers.
Also, seretonin deficiency is likely which is why medication seems to work for many sufferers by reducing anxiety, whilst a behavioural therapist gently addresses the rituals. It is slow and painful, but vital.
Professional help is imperative, but you may have to wait until she is ready to accept help. Co-operation is vital.

Dietary advice

- Avoid junk food.
- Include tryptophan foods daily to boost seretonin levels.
- Increase foods containing B vitamins, zincs and EFAs.
- Drink plenty of water.
- Avoid stimulants, eg caffeine, cola, sugar, chocolate.
- Wheat intolerance may be affecting brain function.
- Add 1 tsp lecithin granules to soup, cereals, shakes daily for choline for brain function.
- BENEFICIAL FOODS: Nuts, seeds, wholegrains, cereals, oily fish, shellfish, eggs, turkey, milk, cottage cheese, fruit and vegetables.

O

O

Nutrients to consider

- B complex – B vital one daily over 5 years.(HN)
- Eye Q – start with 2 capsules per day building up to 6 per day for 3 months; then 2 per day maintainance. Contains preferable ratios of EPA / DHA /GLA (omega 3 and 6 oils) for memory, concentration and processing of information. (HS, NC) Alternatively Eskimo 3 has similar ratios. Give 5mls daily. (Nu)
- MVM.
- Magnesium/Calcium in 2:1 ratio (S) or chewable separately over 4 years. (L)
- Bach Flower Remedies to suit individual – leaflets available. (HS/CL) See also Appendix.
- Australian Bush Flower Remedy Boronia is sometimes helpful.

GENERAL ADVICE

The first thing to do is to see a sympathetic GP for referral to a specialist experienced in child OCD.

This condition is all-pervasive affecting the whole family and requiring a lot of patience and understanding. Working together and not denying or resisting the problem helps the child immensely.

Sometimes an underlying learning difficulty will be involved, eg dyspraxia or dyslexia. The child is often bright with normal grades but the effort of attaining the expected results takes a heavy toll.

Consider psychometric testing for learning problems which may be increasing anxiety.

Fatigue is a common feature due to the inability to relax. Sleep is often disturbed by intrusive thoughts and nightmares.

Social life can suffer as normal situations like shopping or trips to the cinema can create fears of contamination.

One in 5 children suffers some sort of mental illness.

OCD has been described by sufferers as 'bossing you around, getting in the way of your life' or 'being like mental hiccups'.

Reassurance, love and support are vital. Parents need to accept the behaviour is an illness the child cannot control.

Sufferers often feel they are going mad! OCD may result in school/college failure or drop-out, difficulty with social relationships, yo-yo dieting, self harming, depression.

Get advice for the family and support. Young Minds are excellent for this.

It is not the child's or the family's fault. It is a medical illness. ▪

Contacts:
Young minds (see Appendix)

Obsessive Action. Tel: 020 7226 4000 – CD Rom available £5.

Maudesley Hospital run the only specialist OCD unit for children in Britain. Tel: 020 7740 5222

www.ocdresource.com has information and a children's club.

PANIC ATTACKS

SEE ALSO: ANXIETY, FOOD INTOLERANCES, BLOOD SUGARS

An acute episode of anxiety which may include palpitations, sweating, dizziness and tingling hands and feet due to hyperventilation, pallor, crying, shaking and a fear of choking.

It is the body's natural fight or flight response in overdrive at the wrong time which can result in increased pulse, blood pressure and breathing. It can occur day or night with no immediate trigger obvious. An attack may last a few seconds or longer.

FACTORS TO CONSIDER
Food intolerances.
Blood sugar.
Stress.
Phobias.
High caffeine intake.
Iron deficiency.
Other mineral imbalances.
Busy schedules.

GENERAL ADVICE
During an attack, stay calm, reassure and encourage breathing into a paper bag. (Keep one in pocket)
Bach Rescue Remedy is very useful during an attack.
After an attack, fatigue is common.
Avoid blood sugar fluctuations as a constant supply of glucose to the brain can reduce attacks.
Teach deep, slow breathing. Breathe in slowly to the count of 4, hold for 4, exhale for 4, hold for 4.
Exercise like swimming to encourage full breaths.
Food intolerances can be linked to panic attacks.
Consider wheat or dairy exclusions first.
Homeopathic ignatia or aconite may help.
The Flopsy Bunnies become sporific on lettuce!
Chamomile is calming.
Consider a hair test for mineral levels.
Take time to listen to your children, especially teenagers who are often not considered.
Cancel some after school and weekend activities. Is ballet, football, athletics etc necessary? Doing nothing is fine sometimes. **It will pass.** ■

Contacts:
No Panic – Helpline: 0800 783 1531 10am to 10pm

First Steps to Freedom –Helpline: 01926 851608 10am to 10pm

Dietary advice
- Avoid caffeine and sugar as stimulants can trigger attacks.
- Increase foods high in zinc, B vitamins, calcium, magnesium and vitamin C.
- Proteins with tryptophan can calm, eg turkey, cottage cheese.
- No aspartame, MSG or preservatives as they can trigger an attack.
- Reduce animal fats, salt and processed foods.
- BENEFICIAL FOODS: Sesame seeds, almonds, oatmeal, beans and wholegrains eg brown rice, couscous, low sugar cereals, quinoa, porridge, blackstrap molasses, asparagus, mushrooms, leafy green vegetables, broccoli, avocados, mashed potatoes, peppers, soya products, oily fish, yoghurt, chicken, turkey, milk, cottage cheese, apricots, bananas, kiwi, cherries, pears, lettuce.

Nutrients to consider
- B Vital contains ginseng as well as B vitamins for stress. One daily over 5 years. (HN)
- Calcium/magnesium in 2:1 ratio (S).
- Vitamin C – Bio C $\frac{1}{4}$tsp daily (NC, AN) contains minerals.
- Chromium – 1 drop daily, (BC) or Bio G Complex 1 daily over 12 years. (BM)
- Potassium Citrate 100mgs over 12 years. (BC)
- Seretone 5HTP – 50mgs at bedtime over 8 years. (HN)
- Chill Food Formula to calm, stabilise and support the nerves. 1 daily. (HN)
- Zen works in acute anxiety states in 20 minutes if taken at the first sign of attack. 1 daily over 5 years. (AR,R)

P

PARASITES

SEE ALSO: WORMS, CANDIDA, IMMUNE FUNCTION, LEAKY GUT, ANTIBIOTICS, BACTERIAL INFECTION

Parasites by definition are organisms which need a host to survive. This is something at which we all cringe but unfortunately they are very common and frequently are an underlying cause of ill-health. There are many varieties and after entering the body via the skin, mouth or nose they migrate to their preferred site and set up home. This is often the intestinal tract or lymphatic system but can be the brain, skin, liver or other organs. In some ways a virus is a parasite, being unable to survive without taking over a cell.

Children are particularly vulnerable due to immature immune system, poor hygiene and close contact with other infected children or adults. Premature infants are also prone.

Sources of parasites include food, water, soil, insects and stools.

Common parasites in children include threadworms (and in teachers!), scabies and headlice. But here we mainly discuss intestinal 'unseen' parasites.

Signs and symptoms to look for include anal itching, changes in bowel habits, irritability, tummy ache, fatigue, fever, headache, joint pains, weight loss and food intolerances.

It is important to seek medical/nutritional help to identify the exact problem and target effective treatment.

Diagnosis is usually by stool or blood test. This may be accompanied by bacterial infections as parasites often use bacteria as hosts and lowered immunity allows multiple infections. Addressing bacteria first is important with certain types of parasite, to weaken the parasite and make it easier to kill and eliminate.

Dietary advice

- Wheat may irritate gut and could become an allergen.
- Dairy food increases mucous encouraging parasites.
- Increase vegetable protein from beans, pulses, soya and reduce animal protein from dairy foods and meat.
- Beware of sources of fish and cook thoroughly.
- Avoid all refined foods such as white flour, sugar, processed foods as these provide ready food for the parasite.
- Increase soluble fibre to improve elimination, eg wholegrains and vegetables.
- Include lots of anti-oxidant foods, eg brightly coloured fruit and veg. NB – if candida also involved, fruit restriction may be necessary initially.
- Go organic to reduce load on immune system from toxic chemicals. However careful hygiene in preparation is involved as more soil and 'bugs' are present.
- Filter all water or use bottled.
- Boil all milk; preferably use organic.
- Add garlic to food daily or give in honey.
- Pumpkin seeds are anti parasitic. Use ground in cereals and add 1 tsp oil to foods.
- Papaya juice or crushed seeds have cleansing properties.
- Fresh juices especially cucumber, beetroot and carrot.
- Avoid processed, cooked meats like ham or chicken slices.
- Avoid soft and cream cheeses.
- BENEFICIAL FOODS: Quinoa, oats, oat bran, pumpkin seeds and their oil, papaya, amaranth, brown rice, all vegetables, especially peppers, carrots, beetroot, garlic, berries.

GENERAL ADVICE

Treatment protocol should include gentle cleansing of bowel (eg Elminex), dietary modification, herbal nutritional remedies and probiotics. Follow with leaky gut repair and immune support.

NHS tests are restricted by funding and are not always sensitive enough to identify all parasites as ideally a 3 day culture is required.

Conditions which may be associated with parasites include ADHD, autism and learning difficulties.

Children re-infect themselves and others readily by scratching bottoms, sucking thumbs, holding hands.

Scratching, though not always a feature, often occurs at night when parasites migrate to the warm moist anus to lay their eggs.

Keep fingernails short and clean.

Pyjamas or pants at night rather than a bare bottom.

Change linen/nightwear/towels frequently and use hot water. Dry outside.

Wash anal area gently after the toilet with one drop tea tree oil dissolved in small bottle of boiled, cooled water.

Probiotics after a course of antibiotics to reduce risks of infection.

A course of probiotics prior to foreign travel to reduce risks of infection.

Frequent handwashing with nail brush especially after the toilet and before meals.

There may be food intolerances as a result of a damaged gut lining.

Homeopathic ipecac for cleansing.

Epsom salts 2 tsps at bedtime in water.

Testing is important to identify exact infection, but sensitivity is not usually possible for parasites as they are general dead in the stool. ∎

Nutrients to consider

- MVM eg Aqueous Multi Plus (BR) or Nutribalance. (AR)
- Probiotics are vital to prevent re-colonisation during treatment.

Anti-parasitic treatments under supervision:

- Colloidal Silver is effective against many bacteria, parasites and yeast. (S, HN, AR) Tasteless and colourless. Easy to use.
- Black walnut tincture (Uva orsi) 5 drops twice daily (age specific). (N, BF, HP)
- Olive leaf extract or Uva Ursi. (AR)
- Paraclens one capsule thrice daily over 8 years. (HN)
- Wormwood (artemesia) cloves or euphorbia complex (BM) or Artenesinin one capsule daily over 4 years. (AR)
- Citricidal 2-6 drops 1-3 times daily in water or juice. (HN)

Digestive support /cleansing:

- Slippery Elm $^1/_4$tsp in water with honey and nutmeg, (N) Kiddy Tum from 2 years. (K)
- Aloe Gold 1 tsp daily. (HN)
- Eliminex is prebiotics which feed 'good' bacteria and gently cleanse bowel $^1/_4$–$^1/_2$tsp to cereals. (L)
- Vitamin C powder. Bio C $^1/_4$tsp daily (AN) or Magnesium Ascorbate. Short term increased doses to induce temporary diarrhoea, eg 250mgs or $^1/_4$scoop. (BC)
- MSM $^1/_8$–$^1/_4$tsp daily (HN)
- Sodium phosphate helps alkalise the system after infection. (BM)
- Bounceback formula as immune tonic afterwards. (BM)
- After eradication, consider re-testing before healing gut lining.

P

PENIS AND TESTICULAR PROBLEMS

SEE ALSO: CANDIDA, IMMUNE FUNCTION, BACTERIAL INFECTION

Balanitis is a bacterial infection of the head of the penis and foreskin. Poor hygiene or incontinence can also contribute. Symptoms include swelling, inflammation, difficulty passing urine, white discharge and soreness.

Phinosis is a tight, unretractable foreskin. Normal in under 2 year olds and some boys cannot retract the foreskin until 4 years. After this age, secondary infection may occur due to hygiene difficulties. Do not force the foreskin back. Sometimes circumcision is required.

Hypospadias is a malformation where the urethral opening is situated on the underside of the penis. This can lead to a mis-shapen penis and usually requires surgery to prevent urine infections and sexual problems later.

'Jock Itch' is irritation of the scrotum and sometimes penis often caused by infection of yeast (candida), bacteria or sometimes scabies or pubic lice.

Undescended testicles Testes fail to drop into the scrotum. This usually occurs before birth and should be detected at newborn paediatric examaniation. Surgery may be required around 2-3 years to prevent infertility.

Hydrocele Fluid filled sac in scrotum around testicles which usually resolves by 6 months of age. Can be associated with an inguinal hernia in the groin. Causes in older boys include inflammation, infection and injury. Occasionally requires local anaesthetic to allow drainage of fluid.

GENERAL ADVICE

Most of these conditions are either self-limiting or require medical or surgical intervention. Nutritional therapy may help to improve immune function, circulation and identify and address factors such as candida.

Loose cotton pants and shorts increase circulation/ reduce genital temperature.

Avoid strong detergents and fabric conditioners.

Use organic, fragrance-free personal hygiene products. Contact Green People.

Teach good personal hygiene from an early age.

Bathing foreskin in warm saline solution after urination can reduce risk of bacterial infection. ■

Nutrients to consider

- Immune nutrients.
- Super Gar 1 daily over 8 years. (HN)

Topicals (external use):

- Infant Starflower cream. (N)
- Vitamin E cream to soothe or heal. (L)
- Tea tree cream – try Dermasorb. (BC)

P

PERIOD PROBLEMS

SEE ALSO: PUBERTY, PMS

Menstruation usually starts around 12-13 years of age, a year after breast development begins, but the of onset can range from 9-16 years. Onset of periods can be delayed by being underweight, exercising a lot, or stress. **NB. It can take 2–3 cycles for these recommendations to be effective whilst the hormones readjust. So be patient.**

Irregular periods This is normal at the start of menstruation but if it persists, malnutrition and vitamin deficiencies may be involved. Maintain correct weight and reduce stress.

Period pains Mild cramping is nature's way of expelling the uterine lining each month. Some girls experience pain on ovulation in one side of the abdomen or in the back. This happens around week 2 after the last period. Period pains are often due to deficiencies of calcium and magnesium.

Heavy periods Unlikely at early adolescence but need to rule out thyroid or liver problems or nutrient deficiencies.

Bloating and fluid retention Can occur pre-menstrually and cease when period starts. May affect breasts or abdomen. Reducing salt and fluids immediately prior to period may help. Vitamin B6 is a natural diuretic. Take 50mgs for a few days prior to period. (BC) ■

General Dietary advice

● Ensure adequate protein; needs to eat a palmful with each main meal and include a little with snacks.

● Increase iron rich and vitamin C foods.

● BENEFICIAL FOODS:
Seeds, nuts, brown rice, wholegrains, fortified cereals, fruit especially kiwi, strawberries, oranges, pineapple, vegetables especially peppers, green leafy eg broccoli, kale or spinach, pulses, olive oil, dried fruits.

General Nutrients to consider

(doses for over 12 years)

● Vitamin C 200-1000mgs daily can improve menstruation generally.

● MVM – eg Teenage pack containing MVM, vitamin C and cod liver oil, (HP) or Premtis with higher magnesium.

(See Over)

Nutrients to consider Irregular Periods

● MVM and B complex, zinc preferably with vitamin B6, one daily (HP)

Nutrients to consider Period Pains

● Calcium taken hourly at onset of period. Give magnesium as well for muscle function, eg chewable calcium (L) or calcium/magnesium ratio 2:1. (BC)

● Pre-mens 1-3 daily for a few days prior to period. These contain relevant minerals, vitamin C and B6. (HN)

● Vitamin C Buffered – contains calcium, magnesium, potassium and vitamin C (AR) or Bio C $^1/_2$tsp, (AR) or mixed ascorbates for vitamin C and calcium/magnesium ratio 2:1. (BR)

● Clary sage as a massage oil on abdomen may help. (A, HS)

● See doctor to eliminate endometriosis or polycystic ovaries if problem is severe and persistent.

Dietary advice Heavy Periods

● Increase manganese foods eg tea, pineapple, nuts, seeds, wholegrains.

Nutrients to consider Heavy Periods

● Vitamin E 100-400 ius daily can reduce clotting and associated cramps. Take 100 ius daily as part of a MVM and add in 200 ius for a week prior to period and during.

● Vitamin C may help blood flow Premtis 1-2 daily. (L)

P

- Calcium/magnesium ratio 2:1 or 1:1. (S, BC)
- Zinc and B6, one daily. (HP)
- Female Complex tincture for cramps. (K)
- Evening Primrose or starflower oil 1-2 daily to balance hormones.

NB: It can take 2-3 cycles for these recommendations to be effective whilst the hormones readjust. So be patient.

Dietary advice

- Avoid citrus, tomatoes white flour.
- Increase fibre.
- Reduce salt.
- Drink 6-8 glasses water daily.
- BENEFICIAL FOODS:
Nuts, seeds, oats, live yoghurt, dried fruits, fresh non-citrus fruit especially berries, apples, prune juice.

Nutrients to consider

- Vitamin C.
- Zinc for healing – 10 drops or 15mg capsule (BC), or sherbet flavoured powder $^1/_2$ level measure under tongue alternate days over 8 years (HN), zinc citrate 15mgs daily. (L).
- Slippery elm powder $^1/_4$tsp. (N)
- Aloe Gold 1 tsp daily over 5 years. (HN)
- Homeopathic horse chestnut for circulation.

Topically

- Vitamin E cream. (L)
- Calendula cream. (N)
- Witch hazel.

PILES

SEE ALSO: CONSTIPATION, ANAL FISSURE

Rare in children as usually due to prolonged constipation but may occur in teenage years if this has been a problem.

There may be fresh blood streaks on toilet tissue or pants. Main approach is to correct constipation.

GENERAL ADVICE

Epsom salt baths, 2 cups to a bathful, 3 times a week can soothe or apply topically in 1:6 ratio with water.
Swimming can exercise abdominal and pelvic muscles.

P

THE PILL (CONTRACEPTIVE)

SEE ALSO: LEAKY GUT, CANDIDA, PERIOD PROBLEMS, PMS

It is illegal under 16 years to have sexual intercourse, but some girls are given the 'pill' for irregular cycles or they seek it as a contraceptive.

Doctors are bound by confidentiality so a parent may not be aware. Additionally a child may attend a family planning clinic. Underage users are always advised to discuss with their parents. If a child is sexually active, she needs to be aware that the pill will not protect her from disease.

Some problems associated with taking the pill include weight gain, dysbiosis, leaky gut, candida, bloating and for some, increased risks of cancer and blood clots, deficiencies of vitamins A, C, E and B and minerals zinc, magnesium and calcium. However an unwanted pregnancy may present with far worse consequences. It is a fine balancing act.

GENERAL ADVICE

When stopping the pill there can be rebound deficiencies of vitamin A and C as liver stores are depleted.

Smoking whilst taking the pill greatly increases risks of heart disease in later life.

Long term use of the pill may affect fertility later.

Some people suffer from more thrush when on the pill.

Progesterone-only pills are sometimes prescribed to delay a period for exams, holidays etc. If used frequently they may interfere with the normal cycle.

The 'morning after' pill is emergency contraception after unprotected sex. Most teenage girls will be aware of this 'solution'. However it can encourage promiscuous sex and sexually transmitted diseases. In some situations it can prevent a pregnancy, but can cause marked nausea and irregular cycles.

Encourage free and open discussion about sexual development and behaviour so your daughter feels able to approach you when concerned.

Contacts:
Women's Nutritional Advisory Service: Tel 01273 487366 ■

Dietary advice

- To offset risks of the pill, reduce sugar, refined foods, meat, salt, saturated fats and dairy products. This is good round nutritional advice for anyone, but especially if on the pill.
- Increase brown rice, oats and other whole grain cereals for B vitamins.
- Vitamin C foods, eg berries, kiwi.
- Regular, live, plain yoghurt to replace beneficial bacteria in gut which can be depleted by the pill.
- Fish three times weekly.
- Sunflower and pumpkin seeds for zinc.
- BENEFICIAL FOODS: Cherries, kiwis, cantaloupe melon, apricots, peppers, broccoli

Nutrients to consider

- Premtis 1-2 daily as a MVM and for hormonal balance. (L)
- Vitamin C 200-500 mgs daily. NB – higher dosage not advised on pill as 1000mgs can increase oestrogen efffect of the pill.
- Milk thistle one tablet daily (BM) or 10 drops twice daily (BF, HP) to help liver deal with oestrogens.
- Zinc 15-20 mgs daily. (BSC)

P

POISONING

SEE ALSO: TOXICITY, FOR FOOD POISONING — SEE GASTRO-ENTERITIS

This can occur from garden plants, medications, contraceptive pill, vitamins, minerals and chemicals.

Always seek urgent medical advice.

Salt water is not a safe way to induce vomiting in children as failure to vomit can result in dangerously high sodium levels, eg one tablespoon salt for a 3 year old and 1 teaspoon to a baby, can be fatal.

Use syrup of ipecac (BM) but remember that with some poisons it is not advisable to induce vomiting, eg drinking of bleach, when milk can help to neutralise acidity and burning.

Poison Ivy A red intensely irritating rash that develops oozing blisters. Scratching can spread rash. This can last up to one week.

- Vitamin C 250mgs per 38 lbs of body weight. Additionally mix to a paste with water and apply topically. Relieves in 24 hours.

- Apply cornstarch, epsom salts, baking soda or oatmeal. One tsp to 3 tsps water.

- Tofu or water melon applied to the rash can soothe, but not many people have these to hand!

- Aloe vera gel. (HN)

GENERAL ADVICE

If sensitive to sunlight, reactions to poison ivy will be worse.

Keep cool.

Strip child and place in warm bath of epsom salts. Then shower. Only effective if within 10 minutes.

Wash all clothes.

PRE-MENSTRUAL SYNDROME (PMS)

SEE ALSO: PUBERTY, PILL, MOODS, PERIOD PROBLEMS, BLOOD SUGAR

PMS is the current term for a series of symptoms accompanying the menstrual cycle. It has also been known as pre-menstrual tension (PMT) but this fails to encompass symptoms not related to mood.

This section may help mothers as well as their daughters. Younger teenagers do not tend to suffer PMS, although mood changes may be heightened at this time with increased irritability.

Symptoms include bloating, headache, breast tenderness, fatigue, backache, irritability, depression, sugar cravings.

GENERAL ADVICE

Chocolate cravings are quite common pre-menstrually, but should be avoided if possible as sugar and caffeine content can increase irritability.

Regular exercise to balance hormones.

Bloating may be linked to food intolerance or candida especially if it persists during the month.

Stress is likely to increase PMS, eg exams.

Consider candida if PMS is unresponsive to diet and supplements.

Reading:
Natural Solutions to PMS Marilyn Glenville ■

Dietary advice

● Maintain even blood sugar levels, with frequent meals of natural fibre rich foods and complex carbohydrates such as cereals, pasta.
● Reducing protein immediately prior to a period may help.
● Limit salty snacks if fluid retention a problem.
● Avoid fatty foods but increase EFAs.
● Walnuts and bananas for vitamin B6.
● No caffeine, eg cola, coffee, tea as this increases PMS.
● Add 1 tablespoon cracked linseeds to cereals, yoghurts or soup daily.
● Increase calcium foods for depression, fluid retention and pain.
● Drink 6-8 glasses filter water daily.
● Encourage vegetables rather than fruit in short term.
● Organic dairy and meat reduce the artificial oestrogen load which can imbalance hormones.
● BENEFICIAL FOODS:
Cereals, wholemeal pasta, oats, wholegrains, pulses, nuts especially walnuts, sunflower and pumpkin seeds, brown rice, bananas, papaya, tomatoes, avocados, vegetables, tomatoes, potatoes, oily fish, yoghurt, cottage cheese, chicken, soya bean foods, eg Tofu.

Nutrients to consider

(over 12 years)
● Premtis 1-2 daily as a MVM with high magnesium and agnus castus which re-balances hormones. (L) Only additions – GLA as evening primrose or starflower oil 2 daily and 200mgs extra calcium for 2 weeks up to due period. (HN, BC)
OR:
● Pre-mens 1-3 daily for a few days prior to period. This contains the relevant minerals plus vitamin C and B6. (HN)
● These two are the most comprehensive, but following choices may be used instead:
  ● Calcium 400mgs 1 daily increasing to 2 daily for 2 days before period starts. (S)
  ● Magnesium 200mgs daily for tension and fluid retention. Included in Premtis.
  ● Vitamin B6 50mgs (BC) over 14 years with B complex. 1 daily. (BC, L)
  ● Chromium GTF 1 daily over 12 years (HN, HP) or Bio Chromium Complex 1 daily. (BM)
  ● Vitamin A 1 drop daily (BC). Be sure pregnancy is not a risk.
  ● Vitamin E 200 ius daily for breast tenderness. (BC, L)

P

PRICKLY HEAT

Dietary advice

- Avoid hot or spicy foods. Not many children like these, but teenagers may.
- Increase water for detoxification.
- BENEFICIAL FOODS: Avocados, apples, apricots, papaya, mango, carrots, broccoli, onions, garlic, oily fish, nuts, seeds.

Nutrients to consider

- Vitamin C is an anti-histamine – 250mgs per 28lbs body weight, short term.
- Nettle liquid formula. (N)
- Starflower cream.(N)
- Aloe vera gel topically. (HN)

A very itchy rash of tiny, inflamed pimples. This develops when excessive sweating eg under a nappy, after sport, if overweight.

It is thought to be related to an enzyme which controls sweat glands and may be triggered by fatigue and stress, antibiotics and standing for too long.

Food intolerances may be involved.

GENERAL ADVICE

Cornstarch mixed to a paste and applied topically.
Nettle tea may cleanse.
Homeopathic Sol 30 for older children.
Contact Green People for organic personal hygiene products.
Plenty of hypo allergenic sunscreen in the heat.
Consider allergy testing if persistent. ∎

PSORIASIS

SEE ALSO: ECZEMA, VEGETARIAN/VEGAN FOOD INTOLERANCES, NAIL & SCALP PROBLEMS

Dietary advice

- Clean up diet – eliminate all junk food, sugar.
- Vegan or vegetarian diet may help to reduce inflammation, but fish may be beneficial.
- Reduce dairy products as this creates inflammation.
- Avoid citrus fruits, red meat, saturated fats and alcohol.
- Psoralens is a compound in celery which can alleviate psoriasis. Offer as juices or soup – but it is best as raw, fresh juice.
- Carrots for beta carotene.
- Add one tablespoon cracked golden linseeds (Flax) to cereals, yoghurts or soup daily.
- Increase zinc, selenium and folate foods.
- Increase fibre to cleanse bowel.
- Add lecithin granules –1tsp–1 tablsp daily (cereals or drinks).
- BENEFICIAL FOODS: Celery, carrots, broccoli and other green leafy vegetables, oily fish, mangoes, apricots, cranberry or apple juice, blackstrap molasses, flax seeds, brazil nuts, turmeric.

Rare in children, but may manifest in adolescence with hormonal influences often around 15 years old. The growth of epidermis cells (the surface skin cells) is 4 times faster in psoriasis, resulting in encrustations and inflamed elevated patches covered in silvery scales. May cause dandruff. It is very different skin condition to eczema but may respond to some advice. The main sites are legs, knees, elbows, back, neck, ears and scalp. Nails may also be pitted and ridged.

FACTORS TO CONSIDER

Genetics.
Toxicity/poor liver function.
Candida.
Digestive disturbances.
Stress.
Food intolerances.
Dysbiosis which lowers immunity, encourages mercury toxicity and increases inflammation.
Magnesium toxicity.
Drugs and alcohol.
Folic acid deficiency.
Excess weight.

GENERAL ADVICE

Natural therapies for skin may take several months, so persist and be patient.

Psoriasis often improves in the sun or salty water, so go on holiday!

Expose skin to early morning sun most days.

Recent research has indicated that Pycnogenal or anti-oxidant can reduce the overactive genes in psoriasis.

Exercise to increase circulation is beneficial.

A combination of cod liver oil or flax oil with homeopathic berberis aquifolium (psoriaflora) showed significant improvement in 3 months in a trial. A cream is available. (V)

Several herbs can help – see a herbalist.

A combination of 7 herbs for 2-3 months has shown benefits. Contact Andean Medicine Centre (Tel: 020 7510 4825) regarding children and adolescents.

Nettle tea can help to gently detox the liver.

Can be associated with arthritis, ie psoriatic arthritis in adults.

Detoxifying the colon may help, eg Elminex. (L)

Add 2 tsps ginger and lavender to bath water.

Thallasotherapy (salt bath therapy) may help.

Vitamin D cream is available on prescription and may help.

A new drug Dovobet, can give rapid relief for short term events, eg holiday, but it is still a steroid plus vitamin D. Not for long term use

More susceptible to staph bacterial infections and herpes outbreaks. ■

Nutrients to consider

- EFAs – especially flax and evening primrose or starflower oil. (HN, N, BC)
- Vitamin A one drop daily, or beta carotene 15mgs daily over 12 years. (L, HP)
- Zinc citrate 25mgs daily (BC) to increase healing, as zinc loss is high in psoriasis.
- MVM.
- Milk thistle one tablet daily (BM) or 10 drops twice daily (BF, HP) to support liver.
- Magnesium phosphate. (BM)
- Silica number 12. (R)
- Vitamin B complex daily.(BC)
- Probiotics.

Topically

- Aloe vera gel. (HN)
- Tea tree oil solution.
- Starflower cream. (N)
- Ginger and lavender baths.
- Vitamin E cream (L,K)
- SK cream is natural and often very effective for psoriasis or eczema. Try for 1 month. (Green People)
- Golden Emu oil. (Green People)

P

PUBERTY

SEE ALSO: PERIOD PROBLEMS, PMS, PILL, MOODS, ACNE, OBESITY

Dietary advice

● Increase of calories overall requires careful balancing. Encourage nutrient dense foods from natural wholefoods.

● Snacks can comprise upto a quarter of adolescent intake. Make available healthy choices.

● Avoid fizzy drinks as the phosphorus can leech calcium from bones.

● Offer honey or blackstrap molasses instead of sugar and avoid artificial sweeteners.

● Iron, zinc, calcium, magnesium rich foods.

● Encourage seeds as snacks or ground onto cereals for zinc and EFAs. Adding ground seeds to packets of cereal and shaking well overcomes laziness or contrariness! But best to encourage good eating.

● Fruit instead of sweet/ salty snacks are obviously preferable. Sometimes juices are better accepted, but these can lack fibre. Juicing their own is 'cool'.

● BENEFICIAL FOODS: Hard boiled eggs, dairy products, peanut butter, green leafy vegetables, fish, chicken, turkey, nuts, seeds.

This is not a health problem but a natural progression which may be accompanied by problems if nutrition is inadequate.

It is earlier in girls than boys by about 2 years. Overall, puberty appears to be getting earlier with some girls as young as 9 years starting menstruation. One in 6 girls enter the early stages of puberty at 8 years old but the average age range is 10-15 years.

Boys tend to start with a deepening voice, enlarging genitals and shoulders, growth of pubic and facial hair and a rapid increase in height. They reach physical and sexual maturity at 18-21 years.

Girls commence with enlarging breasts and periods usually start about a year afterwards. Accompanied by pubic hair, changing shape, ie narrower waist and wider hips and increased weight as normal. Both sexes may be affected by acne, oily hair, mood swings, anxiety which may indicate nutritional stress.

Adolescence is accompanied by a growth spurt and extra nutrients/calories are required to supply adequate minerals for development. Peak bone mass is determined at this stage.

Factors to consider in the age of onset of puberty include step families, pesticides, increased soya intake, being overweight or underweight, eating disorders, thyroid dysfunction.

GENERAL ADVICE

This is a time when eating disorders are most likely to develop but equally obesity may become more apparent. Eating habits now can 'shape' the future.

Don't nag about food, but make available the right choices and set an example.

Do not diet overtly. This gives wrong messages.

Expect some conflict. Adolescents are finding their independence. Be consistent, fair and try to discuss and compromise even if she won't!

If periods are delayed until 15 years old, see your GP.

Shop and cook together sometimes.

Brain and liver size are out of ratio so glucose

stores are often inadequate – frequent meals are needed.

Requirement for calories especially protein and minerals are equalled only by pregnancy and lactation.

Try to eat as a family most days.

Nutritional needs from 14 years are the same as an adult.

Adults have less control over food choices now so educating your child on healthy eating from an early age is important.

Skin and hair problems can often give an 'entry' into changing diet and lifestyle. Vanity often wins!

Remember peer group pressure is high. They need to be the same. Healthy food options may need to be kept to home.

Sports performance can be another acceptable approach if he moves at all!

Remember it is actually very tiring being a teenager.

Contacts:
www.teenagehealthfreak.com for older children. Covers sexuality and health problems.

www.parenttalk.co.uk

www.NetDoctor.co.uk for online medical advice regarding puberty. ■

Nutrients to consider

MVM eg Teenage Pack containing MVM, vitamin C and cod liver oil. (HP)

● Zinc citrate 15mgs daily (L) especially for boys.

● EFAs especially GLA as evening primrose or starflower oil. Take 3 daily 10-12 years. (L, HS)

● Vitamin B complex – Children's capsule or adult from 12 years 1 daily. (BC)

● Minerals to include calcium and magnesium. Bio-minerals $^1/_2$ tablet twice daily (BM) or Concentrace 10-15 drops (weight specific) daiily. (HN)

● Bio Magnesium 1 daily 6-12 years, or 2 daily over 12 years, contains manganese, vitamin B6 and calcium as well. (BM)

PUBERTY

RASHES

SEE ALSO: LIVER, ECZEMA, PSORIASIS, IMPETIGO, RINGWORM, ATHLETES FOOT, NAPPY RASH, HENOCH'S PURPURA, PRICKLY HEAT, FOOD INTOLERANCE, ALLERGIES, DIGESTIVE PROBLEMS, LEAKY GUT, COLD SORES, SCABIES

The skin is the body's largest organ. It is an excretory organ filtering toxins from the body.

Rashes have many different causes and are very varied in their presentation.

FACTORS TO CONSIDER
Childhood infectious diseases, eg measles.
Allergic reactions to food or contact irritants.
Skin infections, eg impetigo, nappy rash.
Eczema.
Vaccinations.
EFA deficiency.
Drug reactions, eg antibiotics.
Sun and wind burns.
Stress.

The commonest causes in children are infectious diseases and food allergies especially eggs, peanuts and milk.

Please refer to the above sections and seek medical diagnosis if in doubt. Identifying the type of rash and its cause is fundamental to resolving it.

GENERAL ADVICE
External skin problems sometimes indicate internal problems like mouth ulcers, leaky gut, digestive problems.

Roseola Infantum is caused by a type of herpes virus. Sudden fever and a flat rosy rash which turns white on contact. Duration is 24-48 hours and one child in 3 will succumb usually during spring or summer. Treat the fever and soothe the rash.

Urticaria is short-lived intermittent irritating rash often caused by contact irritants such as plants, detergents or by medicines. Relieving the irritation with bicarbonate of soda mixed as a paste is often all that's needed.

Nettle rash may respond to vinegar, baking soda or homeopathic nettle. ■

Dietary advice

● Consider dairy intolerance.

● Lots of fruit and vegetables to alkalise the body.

● Increase vitamin E, vitamin A and zinc foods for healing.

● Vitamin C foods can reduce allergic reactions..

● Avoid cola, salt, sugar and saturated fats eg cheese, crisps, chips.

● Increase water intake to 5-6 glasses daily.

● BENEFICIAL FOODS: Brightly coloured fruit and vegetables, seeds, oily fish, pulses, wholegrains.

Nutrients to consider

(This depends of the type of rash. Some are irritating and can be soothed with the following.)

Topicals:
● Aloe vera gel. (HN)
● Infant starflower cream. (N)
● Rescue Remedy cream. (CL and HS)
● MSM cream to detoxify.

Supplements:
● Vitamin A and zinc are needed for skin healing.
● EFAs eg Essential Balance Junior $^1/_2$-3tsps from weaning. (HN)
● MVM with lots of anti-oxidants. (vitamin A, C, E, zinc, selenium)

Raynaud's Syndrome

SEE ALSO: BLOOD SUGAR, CHILBLAINS, EXERCISE

More common in females and unlikely in young children. Teenagers however may suffer from this circulatory disorder which causes sudden restriction of the blood vessels in fingers and toes. They become white or bluish, very cold and numb. It can be linked to migraine in some cases.

Triggers include emotional stress, smoking, temperature changes. Nutritional factors include EFA and iron deficiency.

GENERAL ADVICE

Ask GP to do blood test for iron and B12 levels.

Aggravated by smoking and alcohol which may be relevant for some older teenagers.

Exercise can increase circulation, eg walking, cycling, rebounding.

Prevention is better than cure. Warm socks and gloves.

Massage and lymphatic drainage may help.

Poor digestion can affect calcium, iron and vitamin B12 levels. Check stomach acid levels by taking one tsp bicarbonate of soda in a glass of water $1/2$ hour before a meal and monitor the burps! If no burping occurs then hydrochloric levels are probably low. See a nutritionist.

Aromatherapy massage using black pepper, cinnamon or rosemary can stimulate circulation. Massage into affected areas in a carrier oil like almond or jojoba.

Magnetic therapy is reported to help by some sufferers.

Contraceptive pill and migraine medications may aggravate the symptoms.

Ask GP for iron tests.

Contact:
Raynaud's and Scleroderma Assocation. Tel: 0800 917 2494

Homedics. Tel: 0161 798 5876 for shoe inserts etc ■

Dietary advice

- Reduce saturated fats such as cheese, crisps, butter, red meat.
- Add one 1 tablespoon cracked golden linseeds (flax) to yoghurt, cereals or soup daily for omega 3 fatty acids.
- Increase EFAs.
- Have homemade soups and stews to warm the system.
- Avoid salt, caffeine, frozen and cold foods and drinks. No ice in drinks.
- Add garlic to food daily.
- Natural wholefoods rather than processed.
- Increase magnesium, vitamin E and C foods.
- Maintain even blood sugar levels as a drop in blood sugar can restrict blood vessels.
- Add root ginger to stir fries, hot water or cereals to stimulate circulation
- BENEFICIAL FOODS:. Oily fish, nuts, seeds, wheatgerm, citrus fruits, berries, apples, ginger, cabbage, avocados, sweet potatoes, broccoli, onions, garlic, eggs, cinnamon.

Nutrients to consider

- Adult doses as usually over 12 years.
- EFAs as GLA to encourage right balance of prostaglandin hormones. Try Mega GLA 1-2 daily. (BC)
- Multi-mineral complex. (HP, BC)
- Gingko biloba for circulation; Seredrin 120mgs daily. (HS)
- Vitamin E can thin the blood and increase circulation; 200 ius twice daily. (BC)
- Vitamin C 1000mgs with bio flavonoids to strengthen blood vessel walls. Take 2 daily. (L, HS)
- Magnesium can dilate blood vessels; BioMg 1-2 daily. (BC)
- Super Gar one daily. (HN)
- Vitamin B3 (niacin) 50mgs (C, HS). Always take with food to reduce the natural flushing effect. Add a B complex.

RICKETS

SEE ALSO: EXERCISE, JOINTS, ARTHRITIS, CRAMP

Dietary advice

- Adequate fat as very low levels decrease bile needed for vitamin D absorption.
- EFAs especially from oily fish containing vitamin A and D.
- One teaspoon lecithin granules to cereals daily.
- Increase calcium rich foods.
- Olive oil for cooking instead of solid fats.
- Avoid fizzy drinks, sugar and junk foods.
- Foods fortified with vitamin D include cereals and margarine.
- BENEFICIAL FOODS: Green leafy vegetables, raw fruit and vegetables, low fat dairy products, cottage cheese, live yoghurt, sesame seeds, nuts, seeds, canned sardines, pineapple juice, tahini.

Nutrients to consider

- Vitamin C – Bio C $^1/_8$-$^1/_4$tsp daily.(AN)
- Calcium phosphate to promote calcium and phosphorus absorption. (BM)
- MVM containing vitamin D in its active form of D3.
- Cod liver oil (HN or BC dricelle). NB – Ensure a clean source as many products contain toxins.
- Zinc for calcium absorption – 10 drops daily (BC), 15mg capsule (L) or sherbet flavoured powder under the tongue $^1/_2$level measure alternate days over 8 years. (HN)
- Vitamin D – 2 drops daily. (BC)

A childhood illness linked to vitamin D, calcium or phosphorous deficiency.

Rickets appears to be increasing again especially in the Asian community who often cover their skin, and premature babies and children due to too little exposure to sunshine, which creates vitamin D in the body. Our fear of skin cancer is justified, but some sunlight daily is important.

Playing outside has reduced due to safety fears, computers and television. Some babies may be born deficient in vitamin D if the mother had little sunlight and a poor diet. Growth is usually normal.

Other factors to consider include malabsorption, low milk intake, some medications, kidney disease, vitamin C deficiency, prolonged exclusive breast feeding over one year.

Symptoms include nervousness, profuse sweating, irritability, softening of skull, bow leggedness, spinal curvature, swollen painful joints, knock knees, numbness in hands and feet, cramps (tetany), tooth decay, enlarged head in babies, delayed weight bearing and walking.

GENERAL ADVICE

Regular short-term exposure to sunlight. The use of sunscreen may diminish the skin's ability to make vitamin D.

Early diagnosis and treatment results in bone healing and no long term damage, but untreated may necessitate surgical correction of bone/joint deformity.

It is normal for babies to have slightly bowed legs when held vertical. Ask your Health Visitor.

Regular shoe fitting can identify incorrect posture and unusual specific wear on shoes, eg inside edge. This may be due to knock knees or bow legs which in turn may indicate rickets.

If in any doubt about your child's development, ask GP for referral to a paediatric orthopaedic specialist.

Consider a hair test for mineral deficiencies.

If child has allergies, asthma, coeliac disease or bronchial problems, absorption problems are more likely. As growth and weight are usually normal, diagnosis of malabsorption can remain undetected. ∎

R

RICKETS

Ringworm

SEE ALSO: IMMUNE FUNCTION, RASHES, HAIR LOSS, CANDIDA, BACTERIAL INFECTIONS, ATHLETE'S FOOT

This is an infectious rash with a distinctive circular lesion. There is a ring of tiny red, raised, scaly spots about 1/2 inch diameter which is irritating and infectious. Most common sites are groin area, face, arms or scalp where it may result in patchy hair loss.

It can be spread easily due to scratching and also passed to other children and adults. Can also be caught from cats.

Contrary to its name the cause is a fungal infection and not a parasitic worm.

More common if on the contraceptive pill or antibiotics, if overweight or have candidiasis.

GENERAL ADVICE

Dispose of hairbrushes and combs.

Use separate towels and flannels from family ones.

Recurrent fungal infections may indicate immune suppression or diabetes – see GP.

Secondary bacterial infections may occur if sites do not clear.

Manuka honey is useful for boosting immune function.

Cotton underwear to reduce perspiration.

Wear flip flops at swimming pools.

Add one drop of tea tree oil to a few tsps of milk, mix well and add to a bath. Make sure it is fully dispersed before the child enters.

Tea tree shampoo if scalp affected. Many commercial shampoos are very low in active ingredient. Try Green People.

Ringworm of scalp can cause hair damage and loss if not treated promptly.

Homeopathic sulphur can help cleanse the body.

Epsom salts – 2 cups added to a bath for 20 minutes can help. ■

Dietary advice

- Reduce grains ie rice, wheat, oats, rye whilst healing.
- No sugar, cola, fried foods.
- Increase raw foods and garlic.
- Include zinc, vitamin A and vitamin C foods daily.
- Reduce yeast or follow anti candida diet under supervision.
- Reduce mucous forming foods like cows' milk products and red meat.
- BENEFICIAL FOODS: Carrot or celery sticks, raw baby corn cobs, garlic, honey especially Manuka honey, fish.

Nutrients to consider

- Probiotics.
- Immune nutrients, eg zinc, echinacea, Vitamin C.
- MSM sulphur $1/4$ tsp over 8 years. (HN)

Topicals

- Apply tea tree or thuja oil directly to affected lesions.
- Raw, crushed garlic applied to the site and loosely covered with gauze has a strong anti-fungal affect.
- Aloe vera gel to soothe irritation, as an anti-fungal and healer. (HN)
- Vinegar topically may help.
- Black walnut tincture to the site. (Nu,BF,HP)

R

S

SCABIES

SEE ALSO: IMMUNE FUNCTION, RASHES

This is a persistent, highly infectious itchy rash which can develop into dry, scaly, red lumps. These may have fine, dark, wavy lines emanating from them giving the appearance of an insect. Most common sites are wrists and forearms, between fingers and toes and around genitals. Caused by a parasite mite which burrows under the skin to lay its eggs. Scratching can initiate bacterial infection. Children under 15 years mainly.

Diagnosis is usually by skin scraping for microscopic examination. Treatment usually consists of benzyl benzoate cream/paste applied to the whole body.

GENERAL ADVICE

After treatment use aqueous extracts of horsetail (equsetum) in ratio 2:1 with chamomile to wash affected area 4-5 times daily.

Itching can last for 1-2 weeks even after treatment. Oatmeal baths may soothe skin.

Whole family needs treating simultaneously.

Hot wash linen seperately and tumble dry at high temperature.

Useful aromatherapy oils are lavender, rosemary, tea tree and peppermint. Use very diluted for children.

Homeopathic sulphur 6c may help.

See appendix.

Dietary advice

● Diet is insufficient to cure scabies, but include immune boosting foods to assist the body in fighting back. Avoid fizzy drinks, sugar, chocolate and processed foods.

● BENEFICIAL FOODS: Sunflower seeds, blackstrap molasses, soya, yeast, wheat bran.

Nutrients to consider

● Boost immunity.

● Vitamin C as an anti-histamine – drops or children's capsule (BC) or chewable (L) over 4 years.

● Super Gar as an anti-parasitic one daily over 8 years (HN) or oil. (N)

● Zinc for immune system.

Topicals

● Peru balsam is an anti-parasitic plant remedy available as tincture or ointment. (N,HS)

● EPO to heal skin. Try infant starflower cream for all ages. (N)

● Aloe vera gel to soothe itching and heal. (HN,X)

● Colloidal silver solution to prevent secondary infection. Can also be sprayed on topically.(HN, Sa)

● Calendula cream for itching. (N)

● Vitamin E cream to heal afterwards. (L,X)

Scalp problems

SEE ALSO: ACNE, CRADLE CAP, SCABIES, RINGWORM, HEADLICE, IMPETIGO, CANDIDA, FOOD INTOLERANCE

Dandruff (dry scalp) A lack of sebum (oil) produced by sebaceous glands around hair follicles can result in dry, flaky skin accumulating.

Factors to consider include candida, EFA deficiency, food intolerances, dehydration, poor digestion, stress.

GENERAL ADVICE

Massage rosemary oil in olive oil into scalp and leave overnight. Wash and rinse well in lemon juice solution.

For a range of natural hair care products try Green People or Jurlique.

Raw, beaten egg white to hair can improve texture.

Greasy scalp Opposite of dandruff when sebaceous glands are over active. Common in teenagers and may be accompanied by acne.

GENERAL ADVICE

Don't be tempted to wash hair more often than every 3 days as over-stimulation of the sebaceous glands will exacerbate the problem and alter the pH.

Use pH balanced hair products and rinse in lemon juice or vinegar solution.

Exercise can reduce sebum by balancing hormones.   ■

Dandruff Dietary advice

- Increase EFA foods.
- Include vitamin E and B foods.
- BENEFICIAL FOODS: Brown rice, nuts, seeds, oily fish, pineapple, papaya, avocados, live yoghurt, wheatgerm.

● Nutrients to consider

- (Adult doses as usually occurs over 12 years)
- Vitamin E 200 ius twice daily. (BC)
- Vitamin B complex one daily over 5 years. (BC,L,HS)
- Udos Choice 1-2 tsp or add to salads, rice, vegetables, shakes, juices. (S, HS)
- Vitamin A x 1 drop daily. (BC)

Greasy scalp Dietary advice

- Avoid sugar, cola, white flour, caffeine, fizzy drinks.
- Reduce red meat.
- Incrase EFAs and vitamin E foods.
- Add one tablespoon cracked golden linseeds to cereal, soup or yoghurt daily.
- Drink 6-8 glasses water daily.
- BENEFICIAL FOODS: Soya products eg tofu or milk, avocado, wheatgerm, fish, seeds, nuts, broccoli, pulses.

● Nutrients to consider

- Biotin 500mgs x 3 daily over 12 years and a B complex over 5 years. (L)
- Udos Choice as above.
- Vitamin A x one drop daily. (BC)

SEASONAL AFFECTIVE DISORDER (SAD)

SEE ALSO: DEPRESSION, ANXIETY, FOOD INTOLERANCE, BLOOD SUGAR, THYROID

This occurs during winter when daylight is less. It can affect children as young as 7 years old, but more commonly a problem between 12-16 year olds. Three successive winters of depressive symptoms which clear in spring, are required for diagnosis. Deficiency of serotonin and excess of melatonin due to the pineal gland not receiving enough light to cease production are thought to be involved.

Symptoms include fatigue, anxiety attacks, weight gain, food cravings (usually for carbohydrates), low self esteem, depression, poor sleep, weight gain.

FACTORS TO CONSIDER
Food intolerances.
Blood sugar imbalances.
Low thyroid function.

GENERAL ADVICE
Try to take a winter holiday especially in snow. The beneficial effects can last for 3 to 4 weeks after returning home.

Encourage outside play especially if a brighter day or snowing.

For teenagers, walking to school and back can provide much needed light.

Light therapy machines are available to boost seretonin levels. 2-3 hours of full spectrum light daily can offer 35% reduction in symptoms in one week.

Use full spectrum fluorescent lights.

Make sure underlying depression is not an all year factor.

Weight gain can occur due to a combination of carbohydrate cravings and low levels of brain neurotransmitters that help control appetite.

Contacts:
SAD Association (SADA) Tel: 01903 814942 for information pack and details of Light Therapy Equipment.

Dietary advice
- Increase tryptophan foods to encourage serotonin production.
- Protein with every meal to stimulate dopamine for alertness.
- Identify likely food intolerances and exclude.
- Avoid sugar, caffeine, alcohol, white flour to balance blood sugar.
- No saturate fats but plenty of EFAs.
- Eat fish for EFAs and vitamin D which can increase serotonin levels.
- Increase vitamin C and D foods.
- BENEFICIAL FOODS:
Oily fish, nuts, roasted pumpkin seeds, dried sunflower seeds, beans, wheatgerm, peanuts, lentils, oats, brown rice, soya products, chicken, turkey, lean meat, milk, cottage cheese, potato skins, eggs, avocados, raw fruit especially bananas, apricots, pears and citrus fruits; vegetables especially green, leafy variety and sea vegetables.

Nutrients to consider
- (Adult doses as most are over 12 years)
- L-tyrosine 500mgs daily. (L)
- Serotone 5HTP – 50mgs at bedtime. (HN)
- B complex daily for nervous system especially folic acid to raise serotonin levels. (BC)
- Cod liver oil for vitamin D and omega 3 fatty acids. (HN) NB: ensure from a clean source as some are from polluted waters.
- Zinc 15mgs twice daily (HP, L, Nu) or 30mgs once a day. (S)
- Bio Magnesium 1-2 daily. (BC)
- Ginseng as a tincture or capsules for adrenal stress. (N) or take B Vital which includes B vitamins and ginseng. (HN)

S

Seizures/fits

SEE ALSO: TOXICITY, BLOOD SUGAR, FOOD INTOLERANCES, IMMUNE FUNCTION, VACCINATION

Fits or convulsions are other terms for seizures. Usually due to fever (febrile convulsions). One in 50 children under 5 years are likely to experience one. Usually the rapid rise in temperature rather than its eventual level is what causes overactive brain function. It is not harmful and is usually outgrown by 5 years old. Rarely, some develop epilepsy.

Fits can range from loss of concentration and visual awareness (petit mal) to grand mal attack where consciousness is lost and the body jerks and twitches.

Prevention includes immune support, avoidance of immunisation when unwell or having been in contact with someone ill and control of fever during infection. Always report to a doctor.

Factors to consider
Fever.
Meningitis or epilepsy.
Deficiencies of B vitamins.
Immune deficiency.
Toxic metals, especially aluminium in seizures (a hair test can determine this).

Seizures refers to a period of sub-consciousness sometimes resembling a mini-fit. Investigations often show no obvious cause and discount epilepsy. Symptoms range from a moment's vagueness to becoming floppy and semi-conscious. The child often has no recall afterwards.

Factors to consider
Maternal deficiency of B6 in pregnancy.
Blood sugar irregularities.
Food intolerance.
Toxic metals especially aluminium.
Mineral or vitamin D deficiencies.
Calcium/magnesium imbalances.
Dysbiosis.
High taurine (a protein) in the brain may rarely be involved.

General advice
Nutritional therapists are not permitted to treat epilepsy but identifying nutritional deficiencies

---

Dietary advice

- Identify possible food allergens – possibly wheat, but may be others.
- Balance blood sugar levels to ensure adequate glucose to the brain.
- Increase yoghurt, cottage cheese and other tryptophan foods.
- No aspartame as it can be neuro-toxic.
- Include wholegrains and increase fibre.
- No colourings, preservatives or additives such as MSG.
- Filtered water only to avoid contamination with toxic metals.
- Organic diet to avoid toxins.
- Avoid caffeine and refined foods sugar and white flour.
- Add 1tsp–1tabsp lecithin granules daily to cereals, yoghurt or drinks for choline which supports liver and brain function.
- Increase calcium, magnesium and mineral foods.
- Salicylates may be contra-indicated. Exclude if other recommendations are ineffective.
- BENEFICIAL FOODS: Oily fish, green leafy vegetables, tofu, yoghurt, milk, dried fruit, cottage cheese, bananas, baked potato skins, brown rice, soya products, lentils.

S

SEIZURES

(NB – if epilepsy has not been ruled out do not give GLA or EFA found in evening primrose, borage or starflower oil.)

- MVM.
- Milk thistle $^1/_2$ tablets twice daily (BM) or 5-10 drops 1-2 times daily. (HP, BF)
- Aloe gold 1tsp over 5 years daily. (HN)
- Flax or fish oils has no GLA. (HN, BC)
- Probiotics.
- Manganese as part of trace minerals 4 drops daily, (BC) or Concentrace 5 drops per 30lbs body weight. (HN)
- Vitamin D x 2 drops daily. (BC)
- Zinc especially if taurine is found to be elevated.

and optimising diet may help in non-epileptic seizures. Consult a nutritional doctor.

Consider a hair test for mineral ratios and toxic poisoning.

Identify sources of metals in the home, eg aluminium foil, deodorant sprays, water supply.

Test the water with supplier for toxic metals.

Beware of flashing lights from the television, computer, videos or disco lights which can trigger a seizure.

2 cups of epsom salts in the bath twice weekly is calming and provides magnesium through the skin.

Cranial osteopathy may help. ■

Sinusitis

SEE ALSO: CATARRH, FOOD INTOLERANCES, ALLERGIC RHINITIS, HAYFEVER, BACTERIAL AND VIRAL INFECTIONS, IMMUNE FUNCTION, EARS

Sinuses are small cavities in the skull behind the nose and eyes which should be air filled, but can become blocked with mucous and become infected. Can be caused by a viral or bacterial infection or an allergy.

Identifying whether sinusitis is due to infections or allergy is important. If infectious, antibiotics may be prescribed. If mucous is thick and yellowy-green, infection is likely, but if clear, allergy is more likely. Sometimes chronic sinusitis may be linked to asthma.

Reducing inflammation is a key strategy.

Symptoms include headaches, hearing loss, facial pain, earache, congestion (like a permanent cold), sleep disturbances, snoring, loss of appetite and taste impairment. Mild fever may accompany a secondary bacterial infection.

GENERAL ADVICE

See Immune Function section.

Tiger Balm on chest or bedclothes for younger children. (HS)

Avoid fumes, pollution, smoke and chemicals.

Teenagers could try a solution of ¹/₂tsp sea salt, a pinch of bicarbonate of soda and a glass of warm water into the nostrils 3 times daily to relieve blockages. Use a nasal dropper or spray bottle. (Ch)

This is one occasion when sniffing and spitting discreetly into a tissue is preferable to strained nose blowing.

Lemon juice, hot water and manuka honey can relieve congestion.

Steam inhalation with chamomile. NB: take care with hot water and young children.

Aromatherapy burner with eucalyptus oil. Keep out of reach of children. ■

Dietary advice

- Eliminate all cows' milk products for one month. See food intolerances for details. Dairy is mucous forming.
- Eggs and white flour products can also be mucous forming. Have protein from fish, nuts, tofu and grains. Quinoa is a full protein grain.
- Increase vitamin C, zinc and vitamin A foods.
- Hot drinks can increase mucous flow. It may help or worsen symptoms so experiment.
- Increase raw foods as snacks.
- Avoid sugar as it suppresses immunity.
- Regular fresh vegetable juices for anti-oxidants to fight inflammation.
- Drink 6-8 glasses water daily.
- BENEFICIAL FOODS: Quinoa, nuts, sesame and sunflower seeds, brown rice, tofu, ginger, cinnamon, strawberries, papaya, berries, citrus fruits, soya milk, fish, garlic, onions, baby corn, celery and carrot sticks, cherry tomatoes, vegetable juices.

Nutrients to consider

- Quercetin as an anti-histamine and anti-oxidant. Esterol with vitamin C – 1 to 2 capsules sprinkled onto food daily, or Quercetin 300 1-2 daily for 50lbs body weight, (AR) or Quercetin C 1¹/₂tablets daily over 12 years. (R)
- Bio C ¹/₄tsp daily to reduce inflammation, boost immunity and act as a natural anti-histamine. (AN)
- Super Gar 1 daily over 8 years (HN)or liquid. (N)
- Probiotics to follow any antibiotics prescribed.
- Sambucol Complex to boost immunity. (BM,HN)
- B Complex one daily over 5 years, as often low in inflammatory sinusitis. (BC)
- Beta-carotene – 1 tablet between meals over 8 years, (HN) or 15mg with meals over 12 years. (HP,L)
- Zinc – 10 drops or 15mg capsule BC or sherbet flavoured powder. ¹/₂level measure under tongue alternate days over 8 years (HN) for immunity.

S

SLEEP PROBLEMS

SEE ALSO: BLOOD SUGAR, ANXIETY, FOOD INTOLERANCES, NIGHT TERRORS, DEPRESSION, SNORING, GROWING PAINS

Dietary advice

- Increase tryptophan foods at evening meal to improve serotonin levels.
- Lettuce made the Flopsy Bunnies soporific as it contains a sedative called lactucarium!
- Balance blood sugar levels. Low blood sugar often wakes child up around 2-3am.
- Young children are better eating their main protein meal at lunchtime with more carbohydrates for tea, eg fish and vegetables for lunch, pasta and banana for tea.
- Identify any food intolerances.
- No caffeine in the evening, ie coffee, tea, cola.
- Foods containing tyramine, a brain stimulant, should be avoided close to bedtime. These include tomatoes, bacon, cheese, potato, chocolate, sugar, sausages and marmite.
- BENEFICIAL FOODS:
In afternoon/evening: lettuce, turkey, bananas, milk, yoghurt, tuna, peanut butter, wholegrain crackers, baked potato, sunflower seeds, pasta, brown rice, celery, oily fish, sunflower and sesame seeds.

This can be more harmful for the parents than the child but long term problems can lead to poor sleep patterns in later life, learning difficulties, irritability, fatigue and recurrent infections. One fifth of children from 1-3 years refuse to settle at night or wake repeatedly.

A specific cause like teething or urine infection should pass, but may create bad habits.

Babies can vary in their sleep requirements from 18 to 20 hours daily to as little as 4 or 5 hours. Teenagers can sleep the clock round!

AVERAGE SLEEP REQUIREMENTS

2 years old	12 hours
3-5 years old	11 hours
6-12 years old	9-10 hours
13 years-16 years	8-12 hours
Adult	7-8 hours

Generally speaking primary school age children, ie up to 12 years, need be in bed by 9pm on school days.

FACTORS TO CONSIDER

If long term seek medical advice to eliminate thyroid problems, diabetes, depression, anaemia or urinary problems. Blood sugar imbalance. Anxiety, food intolerances, serotonin deficiency., snoring and hunger, night terrors, growing pains, bad dreams, need to urinate.

GENERAL ADVICE

Children need routine. Always have a regular pattern before bed.

Address cause if possible, eg depression, anxiety or fears.

Make sure adequate daylight is achieved daily. 20-30 minutes is the minimum.

Regular exercise earlier in the day.

Avoid TV and computer for 1-2 hours before bed and keep these machines out of the bedroom. Encourage quiet games, reading, talking.

For over one year olds, add Children's Oil Blend which contains calming herbs to the bath or as a massage. (N)

Put your baby in his cot when awake rather than rocking him to sleep.

Some babies prefer background noise to silence. For 9 months during pregnancy she could hear bodily sounds and external noises like music and talking. Try playing quiet CDs like ocean sounds.

In babies whose main dietary component is milk there may be an intolerance. Milk contains calcium which is calming and tryptophan to increase seretonin for sleep, so granny's hot milk at bedtime was true unless the child has a dairy allergy! Adding honey and brewer's yeast increases the effect.

Avoid sleeps in the afternoon if possible. The toddler who falls asleep on the way home from day nursery will be up all evening.

Some children attending day nursery are encouraged to rest/sleep in the afternoon. If you have a 'sleepless' child, discuss this practice with the staff.

Prevent over-tiredness.

If you have got into the habit of taking your child into your bed you will need to wean off gently. Start by staying in his room whilst he goes to sleep, maybe on a spare bed. Then stroke his head, then sit on the stairs, etc, etc. It will work if you are consistent and patient.

Sleep problems become more difficult when a child goes into a bed. Put the stair gate across his open door rather than the stairs. If he wants to play quietly, let him for a while.

Once the child reaches 2-3 years and daytime sleeps get later in the day, discourage a nap but encourage a quiet time of reading, cuddling or drawing together followed by an outside activity together to 'wake him up'. Bring bedtime forward

If bad dreams or night terrors are a factor, try Bach Flower Remedies, herbs, homeopathy and aromatherapy.

Passion flower is a relaxing herb safe for children over 4 years. Always get alcohol-free. (R)

Homeopathic Coffea Cruda can calm an overexcited child.

Catnip and chamomile can calm. See appendix.

Referral to a sleep clinic by your GP or health visitor is possible in most areas if the above recommendations are ineffective.

KEY POINTS TO CHANGING SLEEP PROBLEMS

Ensure wide range of foods.

Establish routines all day.

Regain control with crying, ie gradually extending time left to cry.

Consistency – same 'rules' applied by each carer and every night. ∎

Nutrients to consider

● Kid Catnip over 2 years can have a calming, sedative effect in anxiety. (K)

● Older children can suck a zinc lozenge at bedtime to aid sleep. (L)

● Calcium/magnesium are natural calmers. Take 2:1 ratio in favour of calcium (S) or if magnesium deficient, give 2 Ultra Food Form at bedtime over 8 years. (HN)

● Seretone 5HTP 50mgs at bedtime if over 8 years. (HN)

● Vitamin B complex for anxiety/stress if relevant, over 5 years. This supports the nervous system.

● Ginseng in the morning may help older children Try B Vital one daily for B vitamins as well (HN) or 10-20 drops ginseng daily (depends on weight) for up to 8 weeks. (N)

● Chill Food Formula one at bedtime contains GABA – a calming nutrient over 12 years. (HN)

● Liv Calm – Sleep Deep contains herb Stephania Rotunda that has been shown to produce a rapid calming effect with improved sleep, comprehension, anxiety and learning ability. Doses need to be tailored to the individual, some are better taking 1 capsule 3 times per day others all at night. For children under 5 years start with $^1/_3$ of a capsule 6 hourly building up to 1 capsule thrice daily. May need 2 for bedtime. Needs professional supervision.

● Stabilium one daily for a 50lb child to a maximum of 3 daily. Can be given to infants in graduated dose under supervision. (AR)

SMOKING

SEE ALSO: ADDICTIONS, BLOOD SUGAR, ANXIETY, COUGHS

If you have discovered your child is smoking (and many do), the following measures may help to offset damage and reduce addictive tendencies. Peer group pressure is high in early teens and although you should obviously discourage the habit, teenagers are notoriously independent, contrary and secretive.

Blood sugar imbalances are often involved. A packet of 20 cigarettes deprives the body of 500mgs vitamin C. Most teenagers do not eat even half that amount daily. Smoking also depletes vitamin B6 and vitamin B12.

GENERAL ADVICE

Do not permit smoking by anyone in the house.

Discuss the dangers with your child. Girls are particularly at risk of thrombosis if also on the 'pill'.

Nagging will drive it underground.

Concentrate on providing a healthy diet with lots of anti-oxidants and setting a good example.

Most smokers start out socially to impress or experiment and become addicted quite quickly. Early intervention is the key.

Offer to pay for a nicotine replacement programme if addicted.

Exercise can provide an outlet.

Temporarily alter the habits linked to smoking, eg clubs, coffee, pubs etc.

Chewing natural licorice can reduce cravings and discourage smoking.

Tell your son that his penis will be smaller and he may have trouble maintaining an erection if he smokes. This is true and is usually a very effective approach !!

A smoker's cough can be relieved but not cured until the habit has stopped.

Contacts:
No Smoking Helpline: 020 7487 3000

Dietary advice

- Avoid all stimulants, eg tea, coffee, cola, sugar, alcohol to regulate blood sugar.
- Reduce meat and dairy to protect lungs.
- Increase alkaline foods such as vegetables, millet, fruits.
- Anti-oxidants can offset some damage to cells by free radicals. See appendix.
- If your child wants to give up the habit suggest 1-2 days on fruit and vegetable juices and seed oils to remove nicotine residues and boost hormone function.
- One papaya or similar daily would provide adequate vitamin C to offset losses from nicotine.
- Garlic, onions and eggs contain sulphur to help detoxify the body.
- Increase chromium, B vitamins, vitamin C, A and E and magnesium foods.
- Isothiocyanates are present in broccoli and may reduce carcinogenic effects of smoking.
- BENEFICIAL FOODS: Green leafy vegetables, carrots, parsley, watercress, broccoli, onions, garlic, celery or carrot juice, asparagus, sprouted seeds and pulses, brown rice, oats, nuts, seeds, licorice, plums, apricots, citrus fruits, papaya, avocadoes, melon, apples, oily fish, cloves, ginger.

(All for over 12 years)

• Vitamin C 1-2gm daily. (BC, L, HS)

• B complex 1 daily (L, BC) extra 50mg niacin (B3) with food (C, HS) may help cravings and circulation. B Vital also has ginseng 1-2 daily. (HN)

• Ginseng as tincture 30-50 drops or 1-2 gms just for 2 months (N).

• Anti-oxidant formula – Se ACE one daily (L) or Nutriguard Plus one daily. (BC)

• MSM sulphur 1-2 capsules or $^1/_2$tsp powder daily. (HN)

• Chromium GTF for blood sugar 1 daily. (HN)

• L tyrosine can reduce nictone cravings. Take 500mgs daily. (L)

• Magnesium – Bio Mg capsule whole or sprinkled onto food or drink; chewable 1 daily from 4 years (L); $^1/_4$tsp Mg solution in glass water daily over 4 years (AR) or Bio magnesium with calcium, minerals, B6, one daily 6-12 years. (BM)

• L-glutamine can help. (see Addictions)

SNORING

SEE ALSO: ADENOIDS, SLEEP PROBLEMS, FOOD INTOLERANCE, OBESITY, EARS, ALLERGIC RHINITIS, DIGESTIVE PROBLEMS, SINUSITIS

Snoring in children is not usually harmful but may disrupt the sleep pattern resulting in fatigue, headaches and concentration problems. Can be caused by an abnormality of the septum at the back of the nose, but most commonly caused by enlarged adenoids.

Can occur in babies if they have a cold or allergy but mainly in school age children

FACTORS TO CONSIDER
Obstruction of airways.
Food intolerances.
Poor digestion.
Throat infections.
Otitis media.
Excess weight.
Smoking.

GENERAL ADVICE
Open the window at night if safe. Air the room well in the day.
Elevate the head – put big books under the top legs of the bed or cot.
Add an extra pillow if old enough, but be sure not to cause neck 'crick'.
Earlier bedtime may help.
Address weight if child is heavy.
In teenagers, smoking and alcohol will aggravate.
Chewing xylitol gum can open up eustachian tube between ear and throat.
Try a room ioniser to control negative particles in atmosphere. (Healthy House)
Avoid feather bedding. Consider mattress and pillow protectors. ∎

Dietary advice
• Avoid cows' milk products for 2-4 weeks as they can increase mucous and congestion. Monitor effects.

• Sugar, fizzy drinks, junk foods and white flour can increase inflammation and exaggerate any swelling.

• Identify any food intolerances.

• Lots of fresh, whole foods rather than processed.

• Increase water intake to 5-6 glasses daily.

Nutrients to consider
• Magnesium to relax muscles and improve sleep quality.

• Probiotics.

• MVM.

• Digestive enzymes.

SOILING

SEE ALSO: BED WETTING, TOILET TRAINING, UTI, CONSTIPATION, ANAL FISSURE, PILES, FOOD INTOLERANCE, ANXIETY

Known medically as encopresis, this condition of soiling beyond the usual age is sometimes, but not always, accompanied by delayed 'dryness', ie eneuresis.

It may occur occasionally, restart with after being 'clean' for some time or be constant with the child never attaining bowel control. 'Normal' age for bowel control is approximately 3-4 years but may be earlier or later and is often later in boys. If your child is not clean at 4-5 years, or if he has relapsed, seek medical advice to eliminate any bowel abnormality.

If constipation is a factor, he may have experienced pain on one occasion and now withhold faeces to prevent a distressing experience. Soiling may occur due to liquid 'overflow'.

FACTORS TO CONSIDER
Constipation.
Diarrhoea.
Dysbiosis.
Emotional problems.
Bowel obstruction.
Anal fissure.

GENERAL ADVICE
Bowel control is usually later than bladder control and day continence comes before night.

Look at the diet and adjust times of laxative foods, ie don't give them near bedtime or to cause problems at school.

Discuss with the school and give clean pants to the school nurse or equivalent person. A spare pair in his bag may save him the embarrassment of asking for help.

Teach him to clean himself well after an accident. A smelly child will not gain friends. Include a small pack of baby wipes with his spare pants/trousers.

Try to avoid laxatives as these can make the bowel lazy.

Psychological support/assessment may be necessary if emotionally induced.

Do not scold but sympathise, support and help him to address the cause. He is not naughty! At worst he is seeking attention which needs to be addressed. Fear of reprisal will encourage him to squat behind the sofa or hold on as long as possible.

Homeopathy, aromatherapy and Bach flower remedies may be useful. See appendix.

Contacts:
ERIC produces a booklet *Childhood Soiling. A Guide for Parents*. Leaflets are also available. ■

Dietary advice

- Identify cause and refer to appropriate section.

- If constipation involved increase soluble fibre and water and reduce refined foods adding 1tsp–1tabsp cracked golden linseeds to cereal daily.

- If diarrhoea, avoid sugar, increase soluble fibre and water.

- If food intolerance suspected seek nutritional help to identify and eliminate safely.

- Increase magnesium foods to help muscular function and anxiety.

Nutrients to consider

- See constipation/diarrhoea section if appropriate.

- Probiotics may normalise stool consistency.

- Magnesium/calcium for anxiety. Bio Mg capsule whole or sprinkled onto food or drink; chewable 1 daily from 4 years (L); ¼tsp Mg solution in glass water daily over 4 years, (AR) or Bio magnesium with calcium, minerals, B6, one daily 6-12 years. (BM)

SOLVENT ABUSE

SEE ALSO: ADDICTIONS, SMOKING, BLOOD SUGAR, ANXIETY

Sometimes a passing phase but can be very dangerous. The heart, brain, kidneys and liver can all be damaged. Choking on vomit is also a risk.

Spraying aerosols into the mouth can result in swelling of the throat and asphyxiation. Butane gas can lead to heart failure.

Products used are often readily found in your home. It is not just glue sniffing. These may include petrol, polish, correction fluid, adhesives and glues, nail varnish remover, marker pens, most aerosol cans and nasal sprays for colds.

Lock away all suspect products if you are in any doubt.

Symptoms include dilated pupils, vomiting, loss of appetite, mood changes, sore lips/nose, bloodshot eyes, flushed skin, poor co-ordination, slurred speech, frequent infections, effects like drunkenness and loss of inhibitions are common.

More seriously accidents whilst under the influence include road traffic accidents and drowning. Malnutrition can result.

See Addictions for specific advice.

Contacts:
National Drugs Helpline Tel: 0800 776600 ■

Sore Throats

SEE ALSO: INFECTIONS, IMMUNE FUNCTION, SNORING, FEVER, ANTIBIOTICS, CROUP, EARS, CATARRH, BACTERIAL AND VIRAL INFECTIONS, CANDIDA

Usually the first sign of impending infection, which subsides as a cold develops. Can be viral or bacterial and precede colds, coughs, glandular fever and childhood infectious diseases such as scarlet fever.

Recurrent, persistent sore throats indicate immune suppression or tonsillitis.

For first 3 years of life, tonsils trap germs to protect the body but once the immune system is better developed this process can result in infection due to trapped toxins.

NB: persistent sore throat in teenagers may indicate bulimia due to forced vomiting.

Laryngitis is inflammation of the voice box resulting in hoarseness, pain, loss of voice and sometimes fever. Usually caused by a viral infection but may also be due to allergic reactions.

Tonsillitis is swelling of the tonsils either side of the throat which can be very painful. Usually accompanied by fever, white coating or redness on tonsils and feeling unwell. Can be felt as earache and is common in children 3 years and over due to contact at nursery and school, but if recurrent, consult a doctor who may decide to refer to an ENT specialist.

However modern practice is no longer to remove tonsils unless they are blocking the airway or are cancerous as they provide a vital lymphatic immune defence. It is better to boost immunity to prevent infection in the first place. Diet, allergies and deficiency may also be involved in recurrent tonsillitis.

Quinzy is a more serious version of tonsillitis in teenagers and young adults possibly with an abscess. This requires more urgent medical intervention as choking can occur.

FACTORS TO CONSIDER
Immune suppression.
Fatigue.
Candida.
Infection.
Lymphatic stress.
Allergies if persistent.

Dietary advice

- Liquids best in an acute phase. Aim for 6 glasses of water/juice daily.
- Avoid dairy products if catarrh and mucous are a problem.
- Ice cubes or home-made sugar free lollies to soothe.
- Keep fluid intake high. Drinking straws may help and regular sipping rather than gulping is easier.
- Warm or cold drinks depending on preference.
- No sugar, white flour, cola or processed foods.
- Increase fresh fruit and vegetables.
- Licorice can soothe.
- BENEFICIAL FOODS: Milk shakes, fresh fruit and vegetable juices, chamomile tea, fruit juice lollies, blackcurrants, soups, ginger, garlic and honey, thyme.

GENERAL ADVICE

Immune suppression is indicated by recurrent sore throats.

Ears can be affected if recurrent sore throats as eustachian tube links ear and throat. Chewing Xylitol gum may open up eustachian tube.

Gargling with solution of cooled, boiled water with one drop tea tree oil can help in older children. Do not swallow.

Do not overload the child with after school activities. It is important to have rest as well as extra curricular activities. Children need to 'just be' as well. Too much stimulus strains immunity.

Manuka honey is great for immunity as it comes from New Zealand tea tree pollen.

Clean toothbrush regularly in Citricidal. (HN)

Humming like Winnie the Pooh can reduce swelling!

Epsom salts 2 cups in a bath for 20 minutes may detoxify and relax.

Allergy to wheat or dairy may be linked.

In more serious but rare conditions, sore throat may indicate chronic fatigue syndrome or diptheria.

Tickling and chronic coughing may indicate food allergies.

Humidify atmosphere by placing a bowl of water in room near the radiator or fire or use a room burner for bergamot, lavender and eucalyptus.

Chamomilla, aconite and lycopodium are some of the homeopathic remedies which may help.

Inhalations of eucalyptus in older children. NB – beware hot water/steam. ■

Nutrients to consider

- Zinc lozenges if old enough to suck and chew. (L)
- Vitamin C – 4 drops or one children's capsule (BC) or chewable 1-2 daily over 4 years. (L)
- E-Kid-Nacea over 2 years and E-Kid-Nacea Plus over 4 years (especially good for catarrh). (K)
- Calcium phosphate as a tonic and strengthener. (BM)
- Bounceback formula for kids. Chew 1-3 tablets with meals daily in over 2 years for convalescence. (BM)
- Probiotics after any antibiotics.
- Immuno Kid from 2 years to build resistance and as a tonic. (K)
- Elderberry extract. (HN)

Dietary advice

- Optimise hearing and conduction of sounds by avoiding cows' milk products. This reduces mucous build-up.
- Include plenty of fresh fruit and vegetables which contain bio-flavonoids.
- Raw garlic in honey can clear passages.

Nutrients to consider

- Herbal aloe ear drops. (HN)
- Xylitol syrup for under 5 years or gum for older children can open ear passages. (HS, Ch)

AEE ALSO: EARS, AUTISM, ADHD, LEARNING DIFFICULTIES

The number of children with language problems is estimated as one in ten. Speech delay is very common and causes are varied. The most likely is partial hearing loss often as a result of repeated ear infections and mucous build up.

Communication difficulties can result in behavioural problems and tantrums due to frustration.

Stammers, stutters and lisps are usually psychologically triggered. A psychotherapist may help to address underlying causes.

See GP or health visitor for a referral to a speech therapist and audiologist.

FACTORS TO CONSIDER
Hereditary hearing loss.
Cleft palate.
Too much background noise.
Being a twin.
Large families.
Bilingual household.
Only child.
Anxiety.
Mucous build-up.
Food intolerance.
Autism Spectrum Disorders (rarely).

'NORMAL' SPEECH DEVELOPMENT IN BRIEF
Sounds and babbling 4 months to one year, eg baba, dada, ta.

Names familiar objects and echoes like a parrot 12-18 months. Understands simple requests.

There is often a pause at 18 months – 2 years whilst ingoing information is processed. It may come all in a rush at 2 years so don't worry until 2 years. An average 18 month old has 10 words, answers 'what's this?' and may link 1-2 words at 18 months–2 years, eg me go, more drink.

Short sentences and phrases 2–2 $^1/_2$ years.

By 3 years most children are using sentences of 3 or more words and ask 'why?'

By 4 years whole adult sentences. Asks lots of questions.

GENERAL ADVICE

If there are other developmental delays a referral to a paediatrician is required for a full assessment.

Turn off the TV and radio!

Have quiet times together.

Speak at eye level.

Use signs to reduce frustration.

Some children attain 'normal' speech and occasionally forget words. This is usually normal but may indicate a speech development problem.

If hearing is affected, Hopi ear candles can remove wax. (HS, NC)

Contacts:

Michael Palin Centre for Stammering Children offers assessment and advice for 2-18 years. Tel: 020 7530 4238

I CAN is a charity running 5 specialist nurseries for pre-school children with speech and behavioural difficulties not linked to obvious ADHD, dyslexia or autism. It aims to avoid statementing for special needs. Tel: 0870 010 4066

Hanen System offers detailed guidance and support for parents to improve the way they communicate with the child. Tel: 0141 946 5433

Royal College of Speech and Language Therapists. Tel: 0131 4762666 Helpline: 0870 2412068 ■

SPRAINS AND STRAINS

Dietary advice

- Avoid inflammatory foods such as dairy products and red meat for a week.
- Increase anti-inflammatory foods like fish, almonds and fresh fruit and vegetables.
- Drink lots of water.
- Add seed oils to food or shakes, eg Udos Choice. (Sa, HS)
- No fizzy drinks.
- Lots of fresh fruit juices especially pineapple which contains anti-inflammatory bromelain.
- Increase magnesium, vitamin C and silicon foods.
- BENEFICIAL FOODS: Wholegrains, beans, nuts, oats, brown rice, green vegetables, grapefruit, pineapple.

Nutrients to consider

- Vitamin C is vital for connective tissue, growth and repair. Childrens capsule 1 daily. (BC)
- Calcium/magnesium help muscles function. Try 1:1 ratio. (S, HN)
- MVM.
- Zinc for tissue repair. Try zinc lozenges (L) or drops. (BC)
- Bromelain to reduce swelling and pain 100mgs daily. (C,NO)

Muscles are very flexible in children and it takes quite a hard injury to cause damage.

Always be sure there is no fracture to bones. Your doctor or casualty department may recommend an x-ray.

Time is the best cure but a nutritional approach can speed the process.

Strains result in knotted or over-stretched muscles with spasm pain, swelling and bruising. Common sites are ankles, wrists and knees in children.

Sprains affect joints due to ligament damage.

GENERAL ADVICE

RICE stands for:

R – rest to allow for healing and prevent further stress.

I – ice to lower inflammation.

C – compression, ie supportive bandage to reduce swelling.

E – elevation, ie raise the affected area to reduce swelling and improve drainage.

If your child is prone to injuries, assess his vitamin/mineral status with a nutritionist and identify any underlying factors such as ADHD.

STRESS

SEE ALSO: ANXIETY, SLEEP PROBLEMS, LEARNING DIFFICULTIES, EATING DISORDERS, DEPRESSION

Stress is necessary for survival but modern day stress tends to be more insidious and the body does not return to normal as it would after fighting a sabre-toothed tiger! The stress continues having cumulative effects on the body.

Stress is an underlying factor in the large majority of ill health and children are no exception. The adrenal glands are the organs which manage the way our body deals with stress, and if children start to overload them the chances of ill health later can be increased. Short term stress can depress immunity and digestion resulting in frequent colds and coughs and tummy ache.

Nowadays children are exposed to a less carefree life with school and home pressures and media pressure to grow up too soon. Childhood is becoming shorter. Stress creates anxiety and there are several ways in which children will attempt to control anxiety. Adolescence is a time of stress on the body without external stresses like alcohol and smoking!

Symptoms to watch out for include sleep disturbances, appetite changes, mood swings, weight increase or loss, headaches, fatigue, frequent illness, missing school, withdrawal from friends, bedwetting, resumption of thumb sucking, declining performance at school

Some typical stressors include marital break-up/ new step families, a new baby, TV influence, parental pressure to do well, busy parents, exams (children are now tested in infant school), chemical-laden diets, bullying or being bullied, peer group pressure, extra curricular activities, loss of freedom due to safety fears, loss of a pet, relative or friend and moving school.

Contacts:
Childline produce a leaflet *Exam Stress and How to Beat it*. Tel: 0800 1111

Please refer to 'Anxiety' section for details and management.■

Dietary Advice

- Several nutrients are used up rapidly during stress and extra amounts may be needed, eg magnesium, B vitamins and vitamin C. Increase these food sources.
- Diet needs to be varied and rich in starchy carbohydrates like pasta, bread and cereals.
- Plenty of fresh fruit and vegetables.
- Reduce foods which are hard to digest such as meat, dairy products and saturated fats.

Exams and acute stress

- Stress can affect achievement at school and exam results.
- ZEN can be taken before an exam, flying etc and has a deeply relaxing effect in 20-30 minutes whilst maintaining mental alertness. One daily over 5 years. (AR)
- Stabilum one daily for a 50lb child to a maximum of 3 daily. Can be given to infants at graduated dose under supervision. Can also work for the above situations. (AR).
- Gingko Herbal Complex may help memory and stress for exams – $1/2$tablet twice daily (BM) or tincture in older children. (N)

S

SUNBURN/SUNSTROKE

SEE ALSO: BURNS, FEVER

Dietary advice

- Rehydrate urgently. Sips of water, ice cubes, ice lollies.
- Increase anti-oxidants, ie brightly coloured fruit and vegetables, especially orange coloured by beta carotene which can protect skin.
- Extra water in sun and heat and especially once problem has occurred.
- Extra protein to speed skin healing.
- Avoid sugar to promote healing.
- BENEFICIAL FOODS: Apricots, carrots, mangoes, sweet potatoes, eggs, pulses, chicken, fish.

Nutrients to consider

- (See Burns section)
- Beta carotene – one tablet between meals over 8 years, (HN) or one 15mg capsule with meals over 12 years. (HP, L)
- Anti-oxidant complex to reduce damage to cells and reduce inflammation. Se ACE one daily over 12 years. (L)
- Zinc for healing – 10 drops or 15mg capsule BC or sherbet flavoured powder $^1/_2$ level measure under tongue alternate days over 8 years. (HN)
- Vitamin C and bioflavonoids as calcium ascorbate to promote healing. (HS)
- Minerals to nourish the skin – Concentrace minerals 1 drop per 6lbs body weight (HN) or mixed ascorbates $^1/_2$ scoop daily (BC) to alkalise the system and provide minerals and vitamin C.

All children need a certain amount of sunshine for the production of vitamin D to strengthen bones, but children are more susceptible to sun damage as their skin is thinner and production of the tanning hormone, melatonin, is less efficient.

Sunstroke is a serious condition which can be life threatening due to dehydration. Symptoms include fever, drowsiness, irritability, headache, nausea and shaking.

Sunburn is avoidable and should not happen if proper preventative care is taken. Your child is dependent on you to protect her. Skin can be damaged in the shade, just playing in the garden or out shopping. Burning is more likely on holiday, early in the year or by the sea when cool temperatures often mislead us about the strength of the sun, between 11am and 3pm, in fair skinned, blonde or red-haired blue-eyed, freckled children, in younger children and in those with nutrient deficiencies.

Symptoms include red, sore, hot skin, irritability and sometimes blisters.

GENERAL ADVICE

A cool bath or dip in the sea at first signs can reduce burning. Add oatmeal, baking soda or vinegar to bath water.

Sunburn is not always obvious at the time but may develop a few hours later.

Excess exposure to ultra violet light from the sun is an increasing concern for skin cancer later in life due to the thinning of the protective ozone layer above the earth.

Some medications are contra-indicated in the sun eg St John's Wort increase sensitivity to the sun. Most children will not be old enough to take these but some teenagers may be affected.

If tissues are adequately nourished with vitamin A (as beta-carotene), vitamin C, vitamin E and B vitamins, the chances of sunburn are greatly reduced.

Calamine lotion is still a good remedy for relief.

Homeopathic remedies may help.

Bach flower rescue remedy as drops or cream.

S

PREVENTION

Always use highest natural SPF sun cream before exposure. (Green People)

Use waterproof suncream or reapply regularly if by the sea or pool.

Canopies on pushchairs/prams are *de rigeur* and make sure they are adjusted as you change dierection.

Hats with neck and face protection at all times.

Plenty of water before and during exposure.

Increase beta carotene intake prior to and during exposure, eg carrot juice or supplement.

Protect lips with aloe vera and vitamin E stick. (HS)

■

Topicals

- Aloe vera gel to soothe and heal. (HN)
- Colloidal silver solution sprayed onto area to prevent infection. (Sa,HN,HS)
- Mix baking soda into a paste and apply to burn immediately.
- 5% tea tree oil cream. (HS)
- MSM sulphur cream. (HN)
- Soak clean handkerchief in comfrey tea and apply to site. Do not take internally.
- Chamomile or comfrey cream. (N)

S

SUNBURN

TEETH

SEE ALSO: FLUORIDE, GUMS, FEVER, NAPPY RASH, HALITOSIS, TOXICITY

TEETHING

Milk teeth – 20 milk teeth emerging from birth to 3 years. Average first tooth 4-6 months old and then approximately monthly. Breast fed babies tend to be later due to different sucking action and later weaning.

Associated problems include sore bottom, chapped chin due to dribbling, fever and irritability.

Adult teeth – children are typically 'gappy' from 5-7 years with front teeth falling out first and can be in teens before a full set of 32 is acquired.

Wisdom teeth – 4 at the rear usually late teens and into adulthood. Sometimes difficult to erupt.

GENERAL ADVICE

Apply a little peppermint oil.

Fennel or chamomile tea can soothe.

Waleda Chamomilla 3, just a few granules from 6 months, but liquid form only from one year due to minute amounts of alcohol suspension. (N)

Apply infant starflower cream to sore chin from dribbling. (N)

Vitamin C and bioflavonoids – one drop vitamin C and honey in cooled water. (BC)

Apply barrier cream to chin, eg petroleum jelly.

Carrot sticks are hard and cold for a child over 6 months. Always supervise.

Chill teething rings in the fridge for comfort.

Homeopathic chamomilla calms.

DECAY

Tooth decay is a bacterial disease aggravated by sugar. See Dietary Advice panel.

GENERAL ADVICE

Use of fluoride has reduced dental caries but there are problems with fluoride including fluorosis (mottled colouring on the enamel) and toxicity. There are still a third of children under 4 years with decay.

If using fluoride toothpaste, children often swallow it and in addition to fluoridated water this can

---

Dietary Advice

- Beware of baby foods and children's biscuits both of which can be very high in sugar.

- Increase raw fruit and vegetables.

- Dairy products are rich in calcium and phosphorus but low in magnesium. Increase magnesium foods.

- Yoghurt is a good source of probiotics and calcium.

- If offering occasional sweets as a treat, give after a meal. Constant sweet nibbling increases decay.

- Avoid sugar and eat honey, sweets and molasses only at mealtimes.

- Milk and cheese after a meal can help restore pH (acidity). Casein in dairy can reduce erosion of tooth enamel and provide a source of calcium and phosphorus.

- Apples after meals help to clean plaque.

- Increase fibre to clean teeth.

- Dried fruit between meals is better than other sugary snacks, but beware sugar levels.

- Citrus fruits and some fruit juices contain corrosive citric acid. Stick to diluted grape, pear or tomato juices.

be too much. Children's toothpaste contains a reduced level, but fluoride free pastes are also available. (try Boots or Green People)

Gum health is also important.

Take your child with you to the dentist when you go so they can be familiar with the chair, noise and smells. Once he is happy, take him for 4 monthly check ups.

Visit the dentist 4 monthly from an early age.

Start brushing 'teeth' even before they appear to stimulate good circulation. Encourage flossing when old enough.

Sunlight provides vitamin D for healthy teeth and bones.

Xylitol gum after meals in children over 5 years can reduce plaque.

Avoid sodium laurel sulphate (SLS) in toothpastes and mouth washes as they can be toxic. Try Aloe Dent (HN) or ring Green People.

Many commercial mouthwashes contain sugar and artificial additives. Mouth wash with one drop citricidal (HN) or tea tree oil in children old enough not to swallow.

Avoid chewable vitamin C as this may erode enamel. Vitamin C orally is fine.

Aromatherapy for tooth related ear ache. See appendix.

MERCURY FILLINGS

Mercury is a toxic metal which can leach from fillings. Some adults have health problems which may be linked to mercury toxicity, eg multiple sclerosis, chronic fatigue. Other sources of mercury are from foods and the environment but dental fillings are the main ones. Children under 6 year olds are thought to be more sensitive to mercury overload. If your child needs a filling, ask for composite fillings and definitely not mercury, especially if there are kidney problems. Start his life with a clean slate.

Maintaining good levels of beneficial bacteria in the gut and adequate selenium can protect against mercury toxicity.

You may need to contact a specialist mercury free dentist (Tel: British Society for Mercury Free Dentistry – 020 7373 3655). ∎

- Fizzy drinks which contain phosphoric acid erode teeth. Keep to a minimum.
- Using a straw reduces contact of fruit juices and soft drinks with tooth enamel.
- Increase vitamin C and folic acid foods.
- Papain in papaya is anti-bacterial.
- BENEFICIAL FOODS: Fruit and vegetables, papaya, apples, peaches, cherries, green leafy vegetables, brown rice wholegrains, seeds, seafoods (not under 2 years), milk, and cheese.

T

TEMPER TANTRUMS

SEE ALSO: ADD/ADHD, SPEECH PROBLEMS, LEARNING DIFFICULTIES, FOOD INTOLERANCES

Young children take time to master self control over their emotions. The 'terrible twos' is a generic term applied to toddler tantrums. Whole books have been devoted to the subject and various 'gurus' over the years have advised us how to manage them, ranging from constant attention to ignoring the child.

Few, however, have addressed possible physical causes. Biochemical factors may be aggravating the situation.

FACTORS TO CONSIDER

Blood sugar imbalance.
Hunger or thirst.
Toxic metal poisoning.
Food intolerances.
Pain.
Mineral deficiencies especially calcium,
        magnesium, chromium.

GENERAL ADVICE

Do not laugh at him. His frustration is very real.
Do not rely on reason with a child under 3 years.
        They lack maturity for rational thought.
Ignoring the tantrum is usually most effective as it
        is often an attention seeking device.
Persistent, severe or frequent tantrums over the
        age of 4 years may indicate a problem such as
        ADD, hearing loss or autism. ■

Dietary advice

● Follow blood sugar recommendations. An irritable child will be more stable with a constant supply of glucose to the brain.

● Increase fluids. Dehydration increases irritability and fatigue.

● Increase soluble fibre to sustain blood sugar levels.

● Avoid sweets, crisps and sugary drinks.

● Identify food intolerances.

● Increase calcium, magnesium and chromium foods.

● BENEFICIAL FOODS: Oats, fruit especially bananas, dried fruits, vegetables, seeds, nuts, wholegrains, fortified cereals, soy products, honey, canned salmon, tuna or sardines, egg yolk.

Nutrients to consider

● EFAs eg Essential Balance Junior 1-3 tsps. (HN)

● MVM eg Nutribalance Childrens Formula. (AR)

● Chromium one drop or trace minerals x 4 drops which includes chromium for blood sugar levels. (BC)

● Probiotics to improve absorption and maintain B vitamins for nervous system.

● Children's B complex x 10 drops. (BC)

● Calcium/magnesium 2:1 ratio (S) or chewable separately over 4 years. (L)

● NB Nutribalance contains all the above – 20gm scoop per 50lbs body weight. (AR)

Thirst

SEE ALSO: DIABETES, ADD/ADHD, BLOOD SUGAR, UTI

Thirst is the body's way of preventing dehydration which can lead to serious imbalances of minerals and electrolytes and a fall in blood pressure.

Thirst is a symptom controlled by a part of the hypothalamus in the brain and is linked to blood volume and kidney function. It may be a symptom of hyperactivity, probably linked to EFA deficiency.

If the child is drinking excessively he may have diabetes.

OTHER FACTORS TO CONSIDER

Deficiency of EFAs, ADHD/ADD, squash drinking syndrome, dehydration, blood sugar imbalances, kidney problems and dry throat due to the use of asthma inhalers.

See Useful Information for approximate daily fluid requirements.

GENERAL ADVICE

See GP who may test for diabetes.

Squash drinking syndrome is usually linked to ADHD, ADD or hyperactivity. Addiction to food additives, artificial sweeteners or sugar may be linked. Offer only diluted fruit juice or water.

Monitor the frequency of urination. Too often may indicate diabetes or urinary infections; too little may indicate dehydration.

Conversely if your child is a poor drinker, reduce amount of milk in diet and increase fruits, vegetables and activity levels.

Mix fruit juice with sparkling mineral water as a treat.

Offer straws and novelty cups or beakers.

Buy him a 'cool' water bottle and have one yourself. ∎

Dietary advice

- Include plenty of water-based foods like fresh fruit and vegetables.
- Water is best for thirst.
- Reduce all salt especially in cheese and snacks like crisps, peanuts and processed foods.
- Increase EFAs.
- Avoid sugar, caffeine (which dehydrates) and fizzy canned drinks high in phosphorous.
- Filter all water or buy bottled.
- Additives and artificial sweeteners may affect thirst mechanisms.
- BENEFICIAL FOODS: Oily fish, nuts, seeds, green vegetables, fresh fruit, diluted fruit juices.

Nutrients to consider

- EFAs – 1g daily of fish or flax oil. Try these:
  - 1) Eye Q – start with 2 capsules per day building up to 6 per day for 3 months, then 2 per day maintainance. Contains preferable ratios of EPA / DHA / GLA (omega 3 and 6 oils) for memory and concentration (HS, NC) or use Eskimo 3 x 5 mls daily. (Nu)
  - 2) Biocare do various combinations of omegas as Dricelle powders (contains citrus).
  - 3) Einstein's DHA (omega 3 fish oils only) – under 3 years take 1-2 daily squeezed onto food; 3-12 years 2-3 capsules daily. (HN)
  - 4) Essential Balance Junior which provides Omega 3 and 6 in natural butterscotch flavour. Can be used when Omega 3 levels are improved, $1/2$–3tsps from weaning. (HN)
- Chromium – one drop daily, (BC) or Chromium GTF – one alternate days over 8 years (HN) for cravings and any blood sugar imbalance. NB – Do not use if diabetes is suspected.

T

THRUSH

SEE ALSO: CANDIDA, VAGINAL PROBLEMS, NAPPY RASH, IMMUNE FUNCTION, TONGUE PROBLEMS

Thrush can be in the mouth or vagina and is a yeast/fungal infection. Nystatin is the usual medical treatment.

Infants can contract oral thrush during a vaginal birth or via the nipple during breast feeding, if the mother has candida. Babies and those with depressed immune function are most susceptible. Some nappy rashes are linked to yeast infections, most often in bottle fed infants.

In older children, thrush may be linked to antibiotics, contraceptive pill, asthma inhalers, high sugar diets and perfumed toiletry products and can cause vaginitis and vulvitis (itching and discomfort in the genital area). Boys can get thrush too, but it is more common in girls.

Symptoms include itching, white spots in mouth and on tongue or white curdled vaginal discharge or a sore nappy area. If the infection affects the urethra, urinary frequency may occur.

GENERAL ADVICE
Live yoghurt as a vaginal douche in older children.
Cotton underwear.
Leave nappies off during the day.
Treat lactating mothers simultaneously with infant to prevent re-infection. Treating the mother can help the infant. NB: anti-candida regimes require supervised care during lactation.
Rinse mouth after using asthma inhalers, but allow a few minutes for the medication to be absorbed first.
Re-sterilise all bottles, teats, spoons, cups and dishes.
Clean toothbrushes regularly in citricidal (HN) and replace frequently.
Change washing powder if vaginal thrush is regular.
Occasionally a white coated tongue, if accompanied by illness, can indicate scarlet fever.

Dietary advice

- Anti candida diet recommended – mainly avoid yeast and sugar, but consult a nutritionist.
- Live yoghurt daily.
- Re-alkalise the body with potassium foods.
- Avoid cows' milk products in children for a month and monitor symptoms.
- BENEFICIAL FOODS: Soya milk, potatoes, bananas, dried fruits, vegetables, cranberry juice, garlic, live yoghurt.

Nutrients to consider

- Vitamin C.
- Galium Complex contains echinacea and calendula which are gentle on digestion to boost immunity. (BM)
- Probiotics.
- MVM.
- For oral thrush apply tincture of myrrh with a cotton bud to affected areas.
- Colloidal silver can be sprayed or painted onto oral thrush.
- Cervagyn cream for vaginal thrush in over 12 year olds. (BC)

THYROID PROBLEMS

SEE ALSO: GROWTH, WEIGHT LOSS, ALOPECIA, DEPRESSION, OBESITY, IMMUNE FUNCTION

The thyroid gland in the neck produces thyroxine hormone. Too much or too little can affect health. Most important roles of the thyroid gland in children is to control growth and development, calcium metabolism and sexual development.

Ultimately the thyroid gland is controlled by a series of feedback mechanisms linked to the hypothalamus in the pituitary gland of the brain. All hormonal glands work together as an orchestra. If one gland is out of tune the whole 'orchestra' can be imbalanced. Hence the thyroid may be affected by stress-linked adrenal gland problems. The thyroid gland may be under-active (hypothyroidism) or overactive (hyperthyroidism). Thyroid hormone levels can be affected by food, activity level, age and time of day. Diagnosis is usually by blood tests. The heel prick test performed on all newborns for PKU also detects hypothyroidism preventing cretinism. However problems can occur subsequently due to environmental factors including diet.

Thyroid problems should be treated by a specialist in endocrinology but nutrition may help to identify linked problems and to support the body holistically.

FACTORS TO CONSIDER
Genetics.
Auto-immune disorders.
Maternal use of thyroid medication in pregnancy.
Antibodies from mother crossing placenta.
Fluoride toxicity.

Nutritional factors include iodine deficiency, stress and anxiety, liver overload, chemical toxicity, food intolerances. Thyroid imbalances can affect calcium and vitamin D metabolism.

SYMPTOMS OF HYPOTHYROIDISM (UNDERACTIVE)
Poor growth, fatigue, poor appetite, hair loss, constipation, dry skin, excess weight gain and sensitivity to cold. Treatment is usually with artificial thyroxine for life.

Dietary advice for all thyroid imbalances

- Avoiding wheat may help if antibodies are present as cross-reactive immune processes can occur.
- Identify food intolerances. Start with wheat, but allergy testing may be indicated.
- If underactive thyroid, avoid peanuts, soya beans, millet, cabbage family and pine nuts as they contain goitregens which can depress function. Cooking inactivates goitregens, eg cabbage is alright, but coleslaw is not.
- If overactive thyroid, increase the above foods.
- No stimulants, ie tea, coffee, cola, sugar, chocolate, alcohol.
- Avoid fluoride in tap water as it can disturb thyroxine levels.
- Add lecithin granules 1tsp–1tabsp daily to cereals, shakes or yoghurt to provide iodine and support the liver.
- Increase potassium, selenium, magnesium, zinc and B vitamin foods.
- Increase protein if overactive thyroid.
- Add 1-2 tsp blackstrap molasses to cereal, yoghurts, shakes or fruit daily for minerals.
- BENEFICIAL FOODS to balance thyroid:
Seafood (no shellfish under 2 years), eggs, milk, poultry, asparagus, garlic, onions, mushrooms, peppers, watercress soup, carrots, dark green vegetables, avocados, pineapple, citrus fruits, berries, blackstrap molasses, sesame seeds, tahini, wheatgerm, rice bran, brazil nuts, pinto and lima beans, wholegrains, sea vegetables including kelp.

T

THYROID

Nutrients to consider

- (Consult a nutritionist who may recommend some of the following.)
- General thyroid support:
- Children's B complex 10 drops or one capsule daily (over 5 years) (BC), B Vital which also contains ginseng to support adrenals (HN) one capsule daily.
- Vitamin C.
- Selenium with vitamin E one daily over 12 years (L) or vitamin E 100 ius capsules or one drop. (BC)
- Concentrace minerals one drop per 6lbs body weight (HN) or Trace Minerals x 4 drops (BC) or Bio-Mineral Complex $^1/_2$tablet twice daily (includes iodine and potassium). (BM)
- Zinc – 10 drops or 15mg capsule BC or sherbet flavoured powder. $^1/_2$level measure under tongue alternate days over 8 years. (HN)
- If thyroxine is low:
- Beta carotene as it will not be well converted from vitamin A. One tablet daily over 8 years (HN) or one x 15 mg capsule over 12 years. (L,–HP)
- Iodine 150 mcgs daily over 12 years. (L)
- L Tyrosine 500mgs daily over 12 years. (L)

SYMPTOMS OF HYPERTHYROIDISM (OVERACTIVE)

Irritability, rapid pulse, flushed skin, prominent eyes, poor growth / weight gain, sleep problems. Antibodies crossing the placenta in pregnancy can cause this usually temporary condition. Nutrients including protein are used up at a rapid rate due to increased metabolism.

In older children, diagnosis is less easy with symptoms including hyperactivity, sudden growth spurts, bulging eyes, sweating, anxiety, poor progress at school, depression. Medication is sometimes needed but may be temporary.

GENERAL ADVICE

Thyroid levels affect children's IQ. Studies show IQ reduction in children born to mothers with low thyroids or who suffer themselves.

Temperature testing can be more precise in adults than blood testing as it detects minor deviations from normal. Its efficiency in children is less proven, partly due to more variable body temperature, differing ages and problems with accuracy in taking. It needs to be taken immediately on waking without moving for three consecutive days under the arm with a mercury thermometer.

Nutrient deficiencies, eg selenium, B vitamins and zinc can affect conversion of thyroid hormone to its active form.

The liver is involved in the utilisation of the thyroid hormone so if other stresses like blood sugar imbalances, digestive problems or toxicity, the liver may be less efficient.

Puberty, especially in girls can temporarily affect thyroid function due to fluctuating oestrogen levels. PMS and heavy periods in teens may indicate low thyroid function. Conversely, thyroxine deficiency may delay onset of periods.

Teenagers with thyroid imbalances who experiment with cigarettes or alcohol can increase problems.

Identify stress and support the adrenal glands by balancing blood sugar, exercising and taking ginseng.

Fluorescent lighting can deplete vitamin A needed for thyroid function.

Fluoride in tap water and toothpaste can depress thyroid function by interfering with iodine, a chemical relation.

Good circulation is important for hormone function. Encourage daily exercise.

Sea water may help by absorption of iodine through the skin.

Calendula cream applied to the throat twice daily for a month has shown improvements in thyroxine level. (N)

Homeopathy has helped some people but see a practitioner for children. It may rebalance hormones and homeopathic armour thyroid may occasionally avoid the need for thyroxine. ■

TONGUE PROBLEMS

SEE ALSO: MOUTH ULCERS, THRUSH, FOOD INTOLERANCES, GUMS, DIGESTIVE PROBLEMS

A healthy tongue is smooth and red. Some naturopaths believe the state of the tongue can diagnose illnesses.

Sore tongues in absence of obvious causes usually indicates deficiencies of iron, vitamin B2, B6 and folic acid. Folic acid deficiency results in ulcerated lips, mouth and tongue.

Coated tongue – bacterial infection or thrush (candida).

Geographical tongue occurs in a prolonged deficiency of B vitamins due to clumping of the taste buds. Also food allergies, iron deficiency or infection may be involved.

Discoloured tongue – Purplish due to vitamin B2 deficiency, bright red due to vitamin B3 deficiency.

Smooth tongue – Indicates vitamin B12 and folic acid deficiency.

Enlarged tongue – Usually due to vitamin B5 deficiency.

Loss of taste – The taste buds are situated on the surface of the tongue. Any infection can affect taste but so can zinc deficiency, ear infections, food intolerances, sinusitis and hayfever.

FACTORS TO CONSIDER
B vitamin deficiencies.
Dysbiosis.
Liver stress.
Bacterial or yeast infection.
Zinc deficiency.
Dehydration.
Food allergies.
Digestive problems.

GENERAL ADVICE
Assess digestion and check nutrient status – see a nutritionist.
A teenager with a coated tongue may be smoking.
Detoxification is often recommended for adults with children, avoiding sugar and 'junk' and maybe yeast should be sufficient to relieve digestion.
Homeopathic pulsatilla for taste loss. Check age first. (A)
Herbs which may help include myrrh topically. ■

Dietary advice

- Identify any food intolerances.
- Reduce/avoid dairy products.
- Increase foods rich in B vitamins, vitamin A, vitamin C and zinc.
- Avoid irritants such as caffeine, vinegar, pineapple, citrus, spices, junk foods.
- BENEFICIAL FOODS:
Sunflower and sesame seeds, live yoghurt, fruit and vegetables, wholegrains, ginger, garlic and onions, celery, beetroot.

Nutrients to consider

- Zinc picolinate 15mg daily includes 60gms vitamin C. (Nu)
- Vitamin C.
- E-Kid-Nacea Plus especially if catarrh involved. (K)
- Children's B complex x 10 drops or one capsule over 5 years. (BC)
- Super Gar 1 daily over 8 years. (HN)
- Digestive enzymes.
- Milk thistle ¹/₂tablet twice daily, (BM) or 5-10 drops tincture 1-2 times daily. (HP, BF)
- Refer to relevant problem for specific nutrients.

TOXICITY

SEE ALSO: HYPERACTIVITY, ADD/ADHD, LEARNING DIFFICULTIES, CFS, MEMORY, TEETH, VACCINATIONS, FLUORIDE, IMMUNE FUNCTION

This section is mainly connected to heavy metal poisoning which affects many children and is often an underlying cause of ill health and behavioural disorders. Pesticide poisoning is also included.

A toxin is something which is harmful to the body. It may be produced by the body or be external.

Modern processed food is lower in healthy minerals like selenium and magnesium, making our children susceptible to an overload of toxic minerals. Toxicity can occur from a wide range of sources affecting the air we breathe, the water supply, food, homes and schools. Children are at vehicle exhaust level in the street and their immune systems are less mature especially under 5 years. One of the main effects of heavy metal poisoning is immune suppression.

FACTORS TO CONSIDER
Food intolerance.
Medications and drugs including vaccinations.
Poisoning.
Infections.
Nutrient toxicity.
Pollution.
Heavy metals/ toxic minerals.
Infections.
Fluoridated water.
Maternal toxins crossing the placenta.

Possible effects of toxic overload include Chronic Fatigue Syndrome, thyroid disorders, ADHD/ADD/ hyperactivity, learning problems, cancer, autism, immune suppression, liver and kidney overload.

POSSIBLE SYMPTOMS
Poor memory and concentration.
Sleep disturbances.
Irritability.
Fatigue.
Loss of appetite.
Nausea.
Hyperactivity.

Dietary advice – general
- Increase mineral rich foods.
- Eat organic as much as possible to reduce pesticides and other chemicals.
- No tap water. Filter all water or buy bottled to reduce chemical input.
- Keep diet clean and natural by avoiding processed, refined and take-away foods.
- Avoid additives, sugar and artificial sweeteners.
- Identify and eliminate possible food intolerances.
- Add 1tsp lecithin granules to cereal, soup or yoghurt daily to support liver function.
- Increase eggs, onions, garlic and beans for sulphur.
- Soluble fibre can help carry metals out of the body.
- Discard outer leaves of vegetables.
- Remove meat fat before cooking (pesticides tend to accumulate in fatty tissue).
- Wash all fruit and vegetables in water with 1tablespoon vineger added. Better still, use Citricidal in the water. (HN) See glossary.
- Strawberries contain ellagic acid which can help neutralise chemical pollutants.
- Apples contain pectin – a soluble fibre to aid elimination of toxic metals.
- BENEFICIAL FOODS: Organic fruit and vegetables, especially strawberries, raspberries, peppers, citrus fruit, apples, onions, eggs, garlic, legumes.

Nutrients to consider
(Needs professional guidance)
• Liver support, eg milk thistle $^1/_2$ tablet twice daily (BM), or 5-10 drops tincture 1-2 times daily (HP,BF), or Thiodox one per day for 50-60 lbs body weight. (AR)
• Livrotrit $^1/_2$ tablet per day over 6 years or Lipoic Acid one capsule per day over 4 years to support detoxification (BR) under supervision.
• Anti-oxidants, eg Se ACE one daily over 12 years (L), or as part of a good MVM.
• Appropriate nutrients for specific metals (see below).
• MSM sulphur to assist detoxification in gut $^1/_8$-$^1/_4$ tsp per day. (HN)

PESTICIDES

Research into organophosphate poisoning has indicated that children are more susceptible to the cocktail of chemicals in the environment. This is due to their relative weight, restricted variety of foods, increased metabolism and immature kidneys and liver. Poor nutrient status, is common in children. Fruit, vegetables and grains are the most affected foods but dairy products and meat are part of this food chain.

Effects are aggression, irritability, brain dysfunction, nausea, co-ordination problems, multiple chemical sensitivity including food intolerances especially to wheat and dairy products. NB – many headlice preparations contain OGPs.

GENERAL ADVICE

Consider a hair mineral analysis test to identify deficiencies and any toxic metals.

During detoxification, liver support is important to help with mobilised toxins.

Eat organic whenever possible.

Filter water or buy bottled water.

Avoid living under power cables to reduce electro-magnetic radiation.

Limit time on computer and use a filter shield.

Refuse x-rays unless absolutely necessary, eg fractures or scanning. Dental x-rays are not often needed for children.

Do not buy produce grown or sold near roads.

Do not allow your child to use a mobile phone without a protective shield.

Keep children away from microwave ovens.

Avoid aluminium cookware, foil, talc and deodorants.

Exercise regularly to increase oxygen to body cells. Avoid polluted areas.

No secondary cigarette smoke.

Ask water board to test your water. This should be free.

Prospective parents with toxic lead levels often fail to conceive or miscarry due to damage to the foetus and mineral deficiencies.

Use aluminium-free toiletries, eg Pitrok or Trust anti-perspirant. (Ch) Contact Green People.

T

TOXICITY

214

Individual Toxic Metals

Most common toxic metals found in the hair of children are lead, antimony, arsenic, aluminium and mercury.

Lead – exposure increased and tolerance decreased. Stored in the bones, liver, central nervous system, brain and hair.

Sources: drinking water (pre 1986 water pipes had lead solder even if copper pipes), some pottery, petrol fumes and exhaust emissions and some calcium supplements containing bonemeal which can be contaminated. Used to come from paint and pencils. Even though lead pollution in the air is less, deposits in soil last much longer and enter the food chain. Lead can cross the placenta affecting growth and development of the foetus.

Effects: Headaches, depression, sleep problems, irritability, learning problems, hyperactivity, blue gums, anaemia, diarrhoea, colic pain, joint pain. NB – toxicity can be present long before onset of symptoms.

Aluminium – Sources: kitchen foil, talc, deodorant, toothpaste, saucepans, baking powder, cheese and white flour.

Effects: Iron deficiency, memory problems, hyperactivity, irritability, dizziness.

Arsenic – Sources: are chemicals in carpets and wall paper, shellfish, water, fruit and vegetables from contaminated soil.

Effects: Often asymptomatic, but learning problems and hyperactivity commonly involved.

Dietary advice (Lead)
- Increase calcium foods. Include kelp for alginic acid which carries lead out of the body.

Nutrients to consider
- Calcium can reduce lead absorption in the gut.
- Vitamin C can speed its elimination.
- Vitamin B1 plus a B complex. (BC)
- Amino acids liquid. (BR)

Dietary advice (Aluminium)
- Increase calcium, zinc and magnesium foods.

Nutrients to consider
- Apple pectin stops absorption and increases excretion. (S)
- Super Gar 1daily over 8 years (HN) or liquid. (N)
- Magnesium and vitamin C as magnesium ascorbate $1/4$gm 1-2 per day. (BC)
- General advice: Use an aluminium free deodorant. (HS,X)

Dietary advice (Arsenic)
- Increase selenium and sulphur foods

Nutrients to consider
- MSM sulphur $1/8$–$1/4$tsp over 8 years. (HN)
- Charcoal tablets over 12 years. (Ch)
- Super Gar a daily over 8 years (HN) or liquid. (N)
- Anti-oxidants especially selenium, eg Se ACE 1 daily over 12 years.

T

Toxicity

Dietary advice (Antimony)
● Increase calcium and magnesium foods, soluble fibre and protein.
Nutrients to consider
● Calcium/magnesium each chewable from 4 years (L) or 1:1 ratio over 8 years (HN)
● MSM sulphur $^1/_8$–$^1/_4$tsp over 8 years. (HN)
● Selenium as trace minerals 4 drops (BC) or Se /Vit E combined 1 daily over 12 years. (L)

Dietary advice (Mercury)
● Increase eggs, onions, garlic, beans for sulphur.
● Fish also contain chemicals to control mercury levels so moderation is the key word. Cooking by broiling so juices are drained off reduces Hg whilst retaining benefits.
● Increase iron, selenium and zinc foods.
Nutrients to consider
● Iron, selenium and zinc, eg Concentrace minerals 5 drops per 30lbs body weight. (HN)

Dietary Advice (Copper)
● Increase zinc, vitamin C and E foods.
Nutrients to Consider
● Vitamin C and zinc are helpful in controlling copper levels.

Antimony is found more often in children's hair over recent years.

Sources: fire retardants in sofas, mattresses and carpets which are all places where children spend a lot of time. Wood treatments often used when renovating a house prior to having a baby can give off chemicals later. Plastic toys are another source and young children 'mouth' a lot.

Effects: Behavioural and brain dysfunction. Often found in hair of autistic and hyperactive children.

Mercury has no useful purpose in the body and settles mainly in the brain. It is more toxic than lead.

Sources: large fish, eg cod, pesticides, dental fillings (see Teeth section), water, some cosmetics, fabric softeners, some medicines, plastics and wood.

Effects: diarrhoea, zinc deficiency, fatigue, skin irritation, headache, irritability, visual/hearing loss, learning problems, immune suppression, hyperactivity and depression.

Copper is needed in small amounts. Excess can occur from;

Sources: cookware, swimming pools, water supply, contraceptive pill and certain foods.

Effects may include diarrhoea, colic, nausea, hyperactivity, zinc deficiency, autism and depression.

Chlorine is used to disinfect water. If your child swims often external contamination of a hair sample can distort results.

Effects: destroys vitamin C and E which are important anti-oxidants

Cadmium – Sources: cigarettes, exhaust fumes, refined foods, tea and coffee.

Effects: Can effect blood pressure, cause cancer, kidney and liver disorders and depress zinc levels.

Contacts:
Pesticides Action Network UK. Tel: 020 7274 8895 ▓

Dietary advice (Cadmium)
● Increase fibre, pumpkin seeds, zinc foods.
Nutrients to consider
● Apple pectin $^1/_4$tsp daily onto food. (S)

T

TOXICITY

TRAVEL SICKNESS

SEE ALSO: NAUSEA, VOMITING, DIGESTIVE PROBLEMS

Motion sickness is usually linked to the ears which control balance. Unfortunately it can also become a vicious circle due to anxiety about feeling sick!

GENERAL ADVICE

Sea bands are non-invasive and work on acupressure points. Wear at start of journey until your arrival. (Ch)

If you can encourage sleep, nausea is avoided.

If old enough, the front seat is often better as the eye can look ahead.

Drive for short stretches with frequent breaks. On boats stay on deck.

Keep a window open.

Chewing Xylitol gum or peppermints may help.

No reading or writing in the back seat. Offer story tapes instead.

Bach Flower Rescue Remedy if anxious.

Most travel pills are effective but best to avoid medication whenever possible. Homeopathic travel pills are available. (Ch, A)

Individual homeopathic remedies such as petrol or cocculus (to balance ears) may help, but see a homeopath.

Homeopathic travel pills are available. (Ch, HS) ∎

Dietary advice

- Day before eat only light meals such as fruit, soup, yoghurt, salad.
- A light meal 3-4 hours before a journey.
- Avoid food during the journey.
- Frequent sips of water.
- Ginger biscuits or rice cakes may be tolerated.

Nutrients to consider

- Ginger – 5 to 10 drops in a drink sipped regularly, over 5 years. (HP,BF)
- Kid Catnip. (K)
- Magnesium is a natural tranquilliser. Bio Mg $1/2$capsule 1-3 years, one capsule 3-12 years. (BC)
- Kid Chamomile (K) or Waleda Chamomilla 3 x a few granules under one year or liquid after one year. (N)
- Children's B complex x 10 drops for nervous system if anxiety involved. (BC)
- Passion flower tincture is calming. (R)control balance. Unfortunately it can also become a vicious cycle due to anxiety about feeling sick!

TUMMY ACHE

SEE ALSO: DIGESTIVE PROBLEMS, PERIOD PAINS, COLIC, FOOD INTOLERANCES, CONSTIPATION, BLOOD SUGAR, IBS

Young children cannot differentiate parts of the body very well and 'tummy' may refer to anywhere between the neck and legs!

'Tummy ache' is often used to describe feeling unwell and may not necessarily mean abdominal pain.

In older girls it may be linked to period pains. Anxiety can cause colitis, literally inflammation of the colon. See a doctor.

FACTORS TO CONSIDER
Migraine.
Colic.
Wind.
Infectious diseases, eg measles.
Food intolerances.
Infection.
Constipation.
Anxiety.
Stitch.
Colitis.
Low blood sugar.
School phobia.

However, it may herald more serious conditions especially if accompanied by vomiting. Appendicitis, intestinal obstruction, inflammatory bowel disorders, eg Crohn's Disease, coeliac disease obviously require medical intervention urgently.

GENERAL ADVICE
Never delay seeking medical advice if pain is sudden and accompanied by vomiting.
If pain, cramping or nausea is a factor offer only light foods and drinks until it subsides.
Address constipation.
See Aromatherapy in appendix. ■

Dietary advice
- Identify food intolerances.
- Avoid rhubarb, citrus fruits, sugar, beans, pulses.
- Increase calcium and magnesium foods for muscle function and to calm nerves and relieve muscle pain.
- Potassium foods may help cramping pains.
- Increase EFAs.
- Increase clear fluids.
- Also refer to appropriate sections.
- BENEFICIAL FOODS: Oily fish, berries, nuts, seeds, green leafy vegetables, onions, potatoes, bananas, apricots, blackcurrants, raisins.

Nutrients to consider
- (See appropriate sections)
- Aloe vera gold 1tsp daily. (HN)
- Calcium/magnesium ratio 2:1 to calm cramping. (S, BC)
- Slippery Elm powder – a pinch to $^1/_4$tsp daily. (N)
- Kiddy Tum, Kid Chamomile, Windy Pops or Kid Catnip can all help tummy aches. (K)
- Probiotics.

URINARY TRACT INFECTIONS

SEE ALSO: CANDIDA, ANTIBIOTICS, IMMUNE SYSTEM, BACTERIAL INFECTIONS

Dietary advice

- Raw garlic in honey or add garlic to meals.
- Plenty of water.
- Increase potassium foods.
- Avoid too much meat, dairy, eggs and wheat as they can create acidity.
- Diluted cranberry juice. Some include aloe vera (HN). Try cranberry juice $^1/_2$ & $^1/_2$ with sparkling mineral water.
- Barley water with no sugar (see Helpful Information).
- Avoid yeast, sugar, salt and processed foods like biscuits.
- Some fruits are high in sugar, eg melon, grapes, mango and should be avoided initially.
- Live yoghurt daily to replenish beneficial bacteria.
- Celery is diuretic helping to flush out the system.
- BENEFICIAL FOODS: Blueberries, cranberries, papaya, celery, salads, vegetables, garlic, live natural yoghurt, oats.

Nutrients to consider

- Avoid iron during bacterial infection and give low dose of zinc afterwards to boost immune system.
- Garlic, vitamin C with bioflavonoids.
- Probiotics especially after a course of antibiotics.
- Potassium citrate from the chemist $^1/_4$ to $^1/_2$ tsp in water between meals 3 times daily.
- Uva Ursi tincture (HP) or as Uva complex. (BM)
- Sodium phosphate to regulate acidity of urine. (BM)
- Colloidal silver is natures antibiotic. (Sa, HN)
- Cranberry – one capsule over 8 years. (HN)

In babies, more common in boys, but later girls are 20 times more likely to suffer as bacteria pass from the rectum to urethra more easily. Always see a doctor taking with you a specimen of urine. E coli is a common urinary bacterium. If recurrent, identify possible underlying factors. Persistent infections may indicate kidney involvement or diabetes.

FACTORS TO CONSIDER
Dehydration.
Poor hygiene.
Candida.
Dysbiosis.
Acidity.

SYMPTOMS:
Lassitude.
Strong offensive urine.
Tummy ache.
Irritability.
Sometimes fever.
Frequency but poor result (cystitis).
Burning on passing urine.
May be accompanied by vaginal discharge in girls (suspect candida).

GENERAL ADVICE
Cotton underwear reduces perspiration and cools genitals.
Teach your daughter to wipe bottom from front to back to reduce transfer of rectal bacteria to vagina and urethra. Supervise young children.
Use bidet if available.
Avoid constipation as this can restrict flow of urine.
Advise counting to 20 after passing urine and then trying again.
Cranberries and blueberries contain a polymeric compound, which prevents E coli adhering to urinary tract. ∎

Vaccination/immunisation

SEE ALSO: IMMUNE FUNCTION, VIRAL INFECTIONS, FEVER, TOXICITY

This is a very controversial issue and a book in its own right!

Vaccination is a state programme to immunise the nation. It bears little resemblance to individual care. However over the years vaccination has been very successful, virtually eradicating some diseases such as smallpox, diphtheria and tuberculosis (TB is increasing particularly in ethnic minority groups. Ethnic babies are usually tested after delivery).

Common childhood diseases like measles and whooping cough are much reduced but very serious when they do occur which is usually in epidemics.

Parents are encouraged to immunise their children, but many are increasingly concerned about the possible individual effects on their children. Every time there is a media scare, take-up declines and infections rise. There are several pending legal actions regarding suspected vaccine damage. Conditions suspected as being attributed to vaccine damage range from minor fits to autism and growing evidence is linking vaccination to auto-immune and degenerative diseases.

Overall the majority of children have no adverse effects but artificial initiation of an antibody response depletes the immune system and may increase susceptibility to the very diseases we are trying to avoid!

Live vaccines introduce a small dose of the virus to activate the body's own immune response, so if in contact later with the disease, anti-bodies are ready to defend the child.

Problems with live vaccination include a minor bout of the disease, eg measles rash and temperature 7-10 days later. If the immune system is low and this is not always obvious, the effect may overwhelm the child

Passive vaccines introduce the antibodies 'ready-made', eg whooping cough. The problem with passive immunity is a tendency to suppress the immune system making it lazy.

Mercury preservatives in vaccinations Fear also surrounds thiomersals which is almost 50%

mercury and used as a preservative in some vaccines. MMR does not contain mercury but DPT and Hib do. Some people think this is the problem when rare reactions do occur. Mercury free alternatives are not yet approved and may be less effective.

Theoretically an accumulation of mercury from earlier immunisations could lower immunity so that the MMR vaccine could be the last straw leading to brain dysfunction such as speech and language delay and autism. The Food and Drug Administration in America estimates that safe mercury levels are exceeded by up to 100% during the vaccination programme in the first 6 months of life and are phasing out the use of thiomersal. Levels in the UK may be lower.

Multiple vaccines
Diptheria, whooping cough, tetanus (DPT) are given in 3 doses alongside oral polio, Hib (a flu strain) and meningitis C at 2, 3 and 4 months. Generally well received with low side-effects if precautions are followed.
Measles, mumps and rubella (MMR) is given at 13-15 months.
Boosters of diptheria, tetanus, polio and MMR are given before starting school. Tetanus requires a 10 yearly booster.

Separate vaccines The Department of Health (DoH) discourages doctors from offering single jabs on the basis that infection is possible between doses, take-up may be interrupted by illness or holidays and that the individual components in triple vaccines work at different rates. The DoH insists that the immune system is capable of resisting many viruses at once. Other research suggests that only one antibody reaction at a time is possible.

A complete course of MMR separately would require 180 days to complete as a 30 day gap is advised.

Fears surround the MMR (introduced in 1988, but with 30 years of use worldwide) in particular since research in 1998 indicated a possible link with autism and bowel disorders. The research was small and has not been replicated but many parents are now nervous. Measles and mumps vaccines are not licensed separately in the UK.

Contra-indications/precautions These vary according to who advises but erring on the side of caution:
Previous egg allergy. (measles vaccine contains egg white)
Epilepsy or close family history of epilepsy.
Unwell on the day.
Recent antibiotics can inactivate some vaccines and indicate lowered immunity.
Diarrhoea. (especially for polio as given by mouth)

GENERAL ADVICE
Ultimately a personal decision.
Assess each disease for potential life-threatening effects and compare with risks of each vaccine. Hepatitis, TB and meningitis are the main killers. See Reading below.
Vaccination is mainly for the whole population to reduce cross infection rather than for the individual. Assess your child's risks.
A wholesome diet full of nutrients and low in additives and sugar should support the immune system allowing it to resist infection.
Some diseases, eg measles, seem to continue to rise and have epidemics despite vaccination, whereas smallpox has been mainly eradicated.
Microbes continually evolve and resist the vaccines, eg polio.
There are wide variations in the effectiveness of vaccinations.
Whooping cough (petussus) vaccine accounts for about half of the reactions, especially fits. Asthma and allergies are 50% more likely later in life.
For 6 weeks after the polio vaccine is given a baby's stool can transmit polio to unvaccinated subjects (adult or child).
Immune programming may be disturbed.
Babies have maternal antibodies until 6 months especially if breast fed and slightly less if not, as long as the mother was not vaccinated.
Increasing numbers of babies and very young children attend day nurseries, toddlers often go to playgroup from 2 years instead of 3 years

What are the alternatives?

- The best route is to boost the child's immunity to enable the body to fight childhood diseases naturally. Naturally acquired immunity like this is now thought to be lifelong whereas artificially acquired immunity through vaccination may be temporary, eg rubella as a child may be ineffective by the time of conception, most girls are now vaccinated at 13 years.
- Drink plenty of water.
- Eat a wholefood diet with plenty of anti-oxidants.
- Reduce early exposure to infection - avoid day nursery/early school as much as possible.
- MVM to provide the nutrients to boost immunity.
- EFAs can reduce inflammation.
- Probiotics to protect the gut.
- B complex 10 drops daily to replace deficiency caused by the vaccine. (BC)
- Vitamin C for immunity and as an anti-histamine to reduce allergic responses –
- Vitasorb x 4 drops. (BC)
- Selenium, zinc, and iron are important for controlling mercury in the body – Trace minerals x 4 drops (BC), or Concentrace 1 drop per 6lbs of body weight. (HN)
- Quercetin short term as an anti-oxidant and for anti-allergy effects in reactions.

and school starts as young as 4 years instead of 5 years. All this increases exposure to infections whilst the immune system is still less active.

Supplementation has been shown to reduce a serious illness to a mild, temporary illness.

Diptheria is only present in the former USSR states.

Polio is 90% asymptomatic in a healthy child.

Medical advice is to give Calpol after vaccination. This could compound problems for some children as paracetamol cannot be detoxified if the child already has sulphation problems in the liver (suspected in some autistic children). Added to the load is sugar and colouring. Fever is the body's way of dealing with infection (see Fever section for natural ways to safeguard against sudden temperature rises and convulsions).

Children with immune-suppressing or medical conditions such as diabetes, asthma and cancer are recommended by the Department of Health to have a flu vaccine. This is an additional onslaught but in some cases may be worth it. Ask health visitor and GP.

DPT affects the thymus gland, the main immune centre and according to Food and Drug Adminstration, has been implicated in some cases of brain damage.

Vaccines also contain aluminium, formaldehyde and several other chemicals.

Granny used to actively encourage children to contract childhood diseases to strengthen the immune system! Granny was right in a lot of things.

Even Louis Pasteur felt the 'host', ie individual body, was more important than his original germ theory.

Other possible effects of vaccination include activation of eczema, asthma, hayfever, food allergies, epilepsy, ADHD and childhood arthritis. Some now believe that the increase in leukaemia and other cancers, other auto-immune diseases and cerebral palsy may be linked to immune dysfunction affected by up to 30 vaccinations by the age of 5 years.

Virus particles are more likely in the gut of a child with sulphation problems. Could this lead to vaccine reactions in susceptible children? Or did the research show sulphation problems rather than vaccine damage?

Reading:

Boost your Child's Immune System (chapter 4) Lucy Burney

An Educated Decision by Christina Head (homeopathic approach) Tel: 020 7978 4579

The Vaccination Bible Lynne McTaggart

Should I have my child vaccinated? Dr W Goebel (booklet)

Mass Immunisation: A point in question by Trevor Gunn (booklet) - send £3.50 to Alive Health Club, 25-27 Castle Street, Brighton, BN1 2HD

Dispelling Vaccination Myths Alan Phillips Tel: 01892 537254 (booklet)

My Healthy Child (What Doctors Don't Tell You)

Contacts:

Direct Health 2000 Tel: 020 8859 1511 for single dose vaccines.

JABS (Justice, Awareness and Basic Support Group www. argonet.co.uk/users/jab for doctors providing single measles vaccine as opposed to MMR.

The Informed Parent Tel: 020 8861 1022 for guidance on whether to vaccinate or not.

Association of Parent of Vaccine Damaged Children 2 Church St,. Shipton-on-Stour, Warwickshire, CV36 4AP ■

Homeopathic options

- Some herbalists and homeopaths claim to provide the same protection as vaccination against common diseases. Seek professional guidance.

- I am not a homeopath but as I understand it, homeopathic philosophy is not interested in herd immunity, but in individual susceptibility to disease. Homeopathy can be used to 'vaccinate' by stimulating the immune system to produce its own anti-bodies.

- Homeopathy can also be used constitutionally to manage the normal progress of a disease, eg measles, supporting the immune system to help itself and aiding a safe recovery.

- Homeopathic vaccinations, eg petussus, may give whooping cough for one day and then the child is immune.

- For vaccination side effects:

    - Homeopathic thuja at 30c twice daily for one week before and one week after vaccination.

    - Homeopathic vitamin A in potency especially for measles.

    - Homeopathic silica for adverse reactions.

VAGINAL PROBLEMS

SEE ALSO: THRUSH, CANDIDA, UTI, WARTS, IMMUNE FUNCTION, BACTERIAL INFECTIONS

The main problem is vaginitis or vulvitis, an inflammation of the delicate mucous membranes lining the vagina or the external area (the vulva).

Vaginosis is a bacterial infection of the vagina which can lead to pelvic inflammatory disease in adulthood if not treated. This usually requires antibiotics.

FACTORS TO CONSIDER
Candida albicans overgrowth.

Frequent use of antibiotics.

Foreign body inserted or forgotten tampon (this can be very dangerous).

Masturbation.

Improper use of tampons.

Vitamin B deficiency.

Worms,.

Sexually transmitted diseases in sexually active teenagers

Sensitivity to personal hygiene or laundry products.

Rarely, sexual abuse may be involved.

Diabetes or contraceptive pill may increase risks of vaginitis.

Symptoms include itching, soreness, discharge, rash, urinary frequency and/or pain. Vaginosis may have a white discharge with a fishy smell. Vulvitis may result in vulval blisters. Candidasis usually involves a white, cheesy discharge smelling of beer or bread but may be asymptomatic.

GENERAL ADVICE
Reducing itching is important but identifying the cause and addressing it is more effective in the long term (refer to appropriate section).

Boost immunity.

Bathing in weak saline solution, ie one cup sea salt to a bath may control infection and inflammation.

Mix one drop of tea tree or chamomile oil in baby oil and mix well into bath.

Add 2 cups of apple cider vinegar to bathwater.

Older children can douche after toilet or in the bidet with 2tsp baking soda, 1tsp honey and

---

Dietary advice
- Fresh, whole foods.
- Anti-candida diet if amalgamated as a yeast overgrowth.
- Live yoghurt daily.
- Avoid sugar, red meat, processed foods, chocolate, cola, coffee.
- Increase soluble fibre.
- Lots of bottled or filtered water (6-8 glasses daily).
- BENEFICIAL FOODS: Live yoghurt, onions, garlic, manuka honey, cranberry juice, wholegrains, vegetables, fish, chicken, turkey, fruits, oat bran, brown rice.

Nutrients to consider
(see also Candida)
- Super Gar 1 daily over 8 years (HN) or liquid. (N)
- Vitamin B complex can prevent itching. Make sure it is yeast free. (BC)
- Vitamin A one drop daily.
- Fish oils – Dricelle omega 3 or Mega EPA over 12 years. (BC)
- E-Kid-Nacea. (K)
- Other immune nutrients.
- Cranberry complex 1-5gms. (L)
- Probiotics after any antibiotics.

VAGINAL PROBLEMS

1pint water or ¹/₄tsp acidophilis powder in small bottle of cooled, coiled water.

Discontinue all personal hygiene products and change to organic, perfume-free and pH balanced products. Try Green People.

Change washing powders and fabric conditioners to Eco Balls. (Green People)

Use only cotton underwear. Encourage loose trousers/shorts or dresses to encourage air flow and reduce perspiration.

Avoid tights.

If she is sexually active, partners may need to be treated. This is a very sensitive issue and you should take your daughter to the Family Planning Clinic or Genito-urinary clinic at the hospital if concerned.

Poor feminine hygiene especially during menstruation may be to blame.

Remove wet swimming costume quickly.

If problem persists, ask GP to take a swab. ∎

Topical
● Calendula cream externally in over 12 years. (N)
● Infant starflower cream to vulva. (N)
● Vitamin E cream to soothe and heal. (L)
● Tea tree cream – try Dermasorb. (BC)
● Cervagyn cream for over 12 years. (BC)

VEGETARIANISM/VEGANISM

This is not a health condition but it is included briefly as more teenagers especially girls, are becoming vegetarian and prevention of deficiencies is important. Some parents, of course, choose to rear their children as vegetarian or vegan.

Vegetarians and vegans are often healthier with reduced rates of heart disease, cancer, obesity and digestive illnesses, but only if the diet is a 'good' vegetarian diet.

Just cutting out meat is not healthy. It must be replaced with other proteins and care taken to include adequate minerals and B vitamins. Children's nutrient requirements are high and eliminating a whole food group may pose problems. A vegetarian diet can be positively beneficial in some health conditions, notably those involving inflammation.

Nutrients which may become deficient include protein, iron, zinc and B vitamins especially B12. These are particularly important for children at any age but mainly during puberty.

Vegan children may need to supplement vitamin B12, vitamin D and possibly iron at puberty but a

Dietary advice
● Calcium should be sufficient if nuts and seeds and other plant sources are consumed regularly. Soya also provides calcium.
● Protein sources:amino acids are protein particles. Eight are essential as we cannot make them in the body, often low in vegetarian sources of protein. Lysine is present in butter beans which combined with brown rice, provide a complete range of amino acids. Nuts, seeds and their oils, wholegrains, pulses, eggs and dairy products (soya milk and tofu if vegan). Quinoa has all 8 essential amino acids so provides an almost complete protein.
● Iron – sources include grains, apricots and green leaf vegetables, eggs for vegetarians.

V

- Vitamin B12 – fortified spreads, cereals, eggs for vegetarians.
- Increase iron, zinc, calcium and B vitamin foods from list. (Appendix and below)
- Dark chocolate is usually vegan or Expressions by Planil for treats.
- BENEFICIAL FOODS: Quinoa, fortified breakfast wholegrain cereals (beware sugar!), yeast extract, soya products, tahini, apricots, green vegetables, especially broccoli, lentils, nuts, raisins, quorn, butter beans, marigold yeast flakes, sea vegetables.

Nutrients to consider

- Vegan/vegetarian MVM is recommended. (S)
- EFAs – use oils as capsules are often gelatin.
- Green food supplements, eg Progreens in mango juice or shakes. (AR)
- Manganese can be deficient as animal protein is required for its utilisation. Take as part of Trace Minerals 4 drops daily. (BC)

Healing foods

- Raspberries contain tannic acid thought to be anti-viral.
- Garlic is anti-viral and supports immunity.
- Apple juice can kill viruses.
- Spinach soup or raw leaves.
- Natural licorice.

Supplements - Anti-viral

- Elderberry extract as Sambucol. (HN)
- Echinacea complex.
- Vitamin C – Bio C $^1/_4$tsp. (AN)
- Cod liver oil (HN) – ascertain a clean source as it can come from contaminated waters.
- Horseradish complex contains antispasmodic euphorbia, a bronchiole-dilator. (BM)

'good' vegan diet is closer to government recommendations than carnivorous diets with lower fat and higher fibre levels, so is theoretically healthier. Even vegetarians can ingest too much fat if dairy products are the main source of protein.

GENERAL ADVICE

Infants should be exclusively breast fed for 4-6 months.

Weaning should not include meat until 8-9 months anyway and for vegetarian and vegan babies, pulses, lentils, seed oil, etc can be substituted.

Ascertain enough calories for energy by including avocados, smooth nut butter, seeds, vegetable oils and pulses.

Beware iron levels from 6 months as stores are now depleted.

Growth rates in vegan children may be slower but most catch up by 10 years.

Some vegetarian foods, eg sausages and burgers are high in saturated fats.

Contacts:
Vegan Society Ltd Tel: 01424 427393

Vegetarian Society Tel: 0161 928 0793

Further reading:
Pregnancy, Children and the Vegan Diet Michael Klaper

Optimum Nutrition for Babies and Children Lucy Burney (p46-48) ∎

VIRAL INFECTIONS

SEE: COLD, IMMUNE FUNCTION, FEVER

Viruses are like parasites in that they need to 'occupy' a cell to survive. They do not respond to antibiotics. Specific immunity is acquired following infection with a virus.

80-90% of respiratory infections are viral. Also cause mumps, rubella and chicken pox (herpes virus) and glandular fever (Epstein-Barr virus).

Boost immunity to help the body heal itself. ∎

VOMITING

SEE ALSO: NAUSEA, BACTERIAL/VIRAL INFECTION, GASTRO ENTERITIS, TRAVEL SICKNESS, MIGRAINE, POISONING, FOOD INTOLERANCE

Can be serious in infants due to dehydration, especially if accompanied by diarrhoea.

Always seek medical advice if vomiting lasts more than 24 hours (12 hours in babies). Most children are sick at some stage and usually recover spontaneously. Babies often posset small amounts after feeds but persistent vomiting needs medical advice, especially if failing to thrive. Projectile vomiting may indicate pyloric stenosis in young babies and often requires surgery.

About half cases of vomiting in under 5 year olds are due to viruses.

FACTORS TO CONSIDER
Food poisoning.
Gut infestation.
Childhood infections, eg whooping cough.
Fever.
Colic.
Migraine.
Anxiety.
Motion sickness.
Food allergy.
Over-eating.
Bulimia nervosa.
Vitamin and mineral deficiencies, eg vitamin B6, magnesium, zinc or iron.
Anaemia.
Poisoning.
Drug side effects, eg antibiotics.
Recurrent bouts may indicate coeliac disease, cystic fibrosis or food allergy.

Symptoms which may be associated with vomiting and may give clues to cause include visual disturbances, tummy ache, bloating, flatulence (wind), 'butterflies', loss of appetite.

Almost all cases are preceded by nausea but vomiting can be quite spontaneous. Young children can be sick one minute and happily eat a meal the next!

GENERAL ADVICE
If due to nutrient deficiencies, symptoms will be

Dietary advice
- Fast for few hours until the vomiting has ceased. Offer frequent sips of water.
- Vitamin B6 foods may help.
- Increase magnesium and iron foods.
- Avoid citrus fruit and its juices.
- No coffee.
- Identify food intolerances.
- BENEFICIAL FOODS: Bananas, mashed potato, live yoghurt, vegetables steamed or made into soup, wheatgerm, yeast, dry crackers or toast, wholegrain cereals, brown rice, ginger, peppermint tea.

Nutrients to consider
- Kid chamomile or Kid Catnip. (K)
- B Complex to calm digestion and support the liver. (BC)
- Probiotics when vomiting has ceased.

VOMITING

V

229

more insidious and take longer to resolve.
See a nutritionist.

May be due to candida or parasites which may
cause a leaky gut and disturb digestion.

The digestive system needs to rest so food is not
necessary for 24-48 hours. Slowly re-
introduce after vomiting has stopped and
nausea subsides.

After this, an empty stomach can increase nausea
and although it is often difficult to start
eating again, it can help if introduced slowly,
eg dry biscuit 2 hourly, slowly increasing
variety and amount.

Make sure all meats, eggs and fish are thoroughly
cooked.

Chewing natural licorice when vomiting has
ceased may alleviate symptoms.

Homeopathic ipecac or nux vomica may alleviate
nausea. See a homeopath for individual
suggestions.

Peppermint or ginger oils on a tissue sniffed in
older children to reduce nausea. ▪

W

Occuring singly or in groups, warts are usually caused by human papilloma virus (HPV) of which there are sixty varieties. They are contagious.

There are 4 types:

Common warts are mainly found on the hands, knees, face or arms. They can be dry or moist, flat or raised with little black dots in the centre. They can spread very easily.

Plantar warts are common in children. Small, flat-topped, pink warts often in a line on hands and face.

Veruccas are a type of Plantar wart and are usually found on the soles of the feet and under the toes. Less likely to spread, but are infectious to other people and are commonly contracted at swimming pools or anywhere where bare feet is usual.

Genital warts are soft, moist growths around penis, vagina or general groin area. They are sexually transmitted but infants can contract them during vaginal delivery.

FACTORS TO CONSIDER
Antibiotics.
Vitamin A and mineral deficiencies.
Viral infection.
Vaccination.
Immune suppression.

GENERAL ADVICE
Most common warts disappear in 1-2 years without treatment.
Encourage flip flops at pools and beach.
Do not pick, trim or cut.
Rumour has it that a piece of overripe banana or papaya skin or raw potato cut and strapped with the inside skin next to the verucca can magic them away! I have only anecdotal evidence for this but what have you got to lose!
Crushed garlic onto wart, covered with a dry dressing for 24 hours will produce a blister which should then fall off in a week.
Apple cider vinegar on a plaster reapplied daily can eliminate in 2-3 weeks.
Caster oil and baking soda applied each night may remove it in 3-6 weeks.

Dietary advice
- Immune boosting foods.
- Increase eggs, broccoli, garlic and onions for sulphur.
- Increase vitamin C, vitamin A and zinc foods.
- Include live yoghurt daily to enhance immunity.
- BENEFICIAL FOODS: Eggs, garlic, onions, peppers, broccoli, asparagus, leafy green vegetables, parsley, kiwi, citrus fruits, melon, apples, apricots, tomatoes, oily fish, millet.

Nutrients to consider
- (see also immune nutrients)
- Lypsine is zinc and lysine both of which are anti-viral (BM) or L-Lysine 1-2 daily. (HN)
- Zinc 15mgs daily. (BC)
- Vitamin C children's capsule 1 daily, (BC) or chewable C, (L)
- Vitamin A – one drop daily, (BC)

Topicals
- Thuja tincture and caster oil applied twice daily is anti-viral. (BM, N)
- Silver solution applied topically is 'nature's antibiotic'. (Sa, HN)
- Aloe vera gel. (HN)
- Tea tree or black walnut tincture. Apply one drop 2-3 times daily directly to wart.
- Calendula ointment.(N)

Lemon juice, sea salt, onion juice and vitamin E oil (squeeze a capsule) mixed and applied.

For genital warts teenagers should attend the local hospital genito-urinary clinic and avoid sex for 3 months until healed. Cervical cancer may be linked to genital warts.

Salicylic acid applied to warts may encourage immune system to fight HPV and prevent recurrence.

Wear verucca socks at swimming pools until gone.

Various homeopathic remedies for different types especially homeopathic thuja orally as well as topically just until the wart has gone. See appendix. ▪

WEIGHT LOSS

SEE ALSO: GROWTH, DIARRHOEA, ANAEMIA, LEAKY GUT, ANXIETY, EATING DISORDERS, ANOREXIA NERVOSA, APPETITE, CANDIDA, PARASITES

(For overweight see Obesity.)

Underweight
Weight fluctuates in childhood with the first year of life and puberty being growth peaks. Ascertain whether the child is in fact underweight. Do not compare with other children as most are overweight! Some children are actually underweight for which there are many reasons covered in the above sections. Always see a doctor to rule out diabetes, cancer, bowel disease, thyroid problems or eating disorders.

FACTORS TO CONSIDER
Gut infections.
Poor digestion.
Dysbiosis.
Anaemia causing loss of appetite.
Zinc deficiency affecting growth and taste.
Low calorie intake, ie just not eating enough!
Malabsorption/leaky gut.
Nutrient deficiencies.
Anorexia nervosa.

Dietary advice
- Increase protein
- Avoid sugar.
- Increase shakes and juices to give concentrated nutrients.
- Complex carbohydrates and wholegrains.
- Toss vegetables, rice or pasta in oils after cooking.
- BENEFICIAL FOODS: Oily fish, chicken, turkey, lentils, nuts/seeds and their oils, beans and pulses, milkshakes, fresh juices, jacket potatoes, wholegrains, bananas, wholewheat bread, blackstrap molasses.

GENERAL ADVICE

Update child's baby book and check the growth
charts there. Ask your health visitor for
guidance here.

Do not be tempted to increase saturated fats, but
encourage EFAs.

5-6 small meals daily.

Milky snack, eg cereal or warm milk and blackstrap
molasses before bed.

Identify reasons for any appetite problems such as
anaemia or zinc deficiency. See a nutritionist.

Address anxiety if relevant.

Consider testing for gut infections or leaky gut with
a nutritionist.

Ask GP to do blood tests for iron deficiency, thyroid
etc.

An underweight teenager is often labelled as
anorexic which can be very distressing as this
is often not the cause. Ask GP for
investigations.   ■

Nutrients to consider

(Need to be well absorbed)

● EFAs – Essential Balance Junior $^1/_2$-3tsp from weaning. (HN)

● Ultra care for kids under supervision given in addition to full diet. Can be added to water or milk for children up to 12 years. Will act as a MVM as well. (Nu)

● Amino acid Quick Sorb 1 drop daily (BR), or Amino Sport $^1/_2$-1caps x3 daily over 2 years. (BR, NC)

● Zinc 15-25mgs daily. (BC)

● MVM - Aqueous multi plus 1-2 tsps daily. Adult dose over 12 years 1 tabsp. (BR)

● Probiotics.

● Aloe Gold to soothe digestion 1tsp daily. (HN)

● Consider digestive enzymes.

WHEEZINESS

*SEE ALSO: COUGHS, ASTHMA, BRONCHITIS, BACTERIAL/
VIRAL INFECTIONS, ALLERGIES, HAYFEVER, CROUP,
ALLERGIC RHINITIS*

Characterised by a whistling noise on breathing,
wheeziness in children is very common and often
diagnosed as asthma. There are many reasons for it.
Always see a doctor to diagnose cause and eliminate
serious conditions.

FACTORS TO CONSIDER

A cold or upper respiratory infection.
An inhalant allergy, eg house dust mite or pollen.
Hayfever.
Bronchitis.
Croup.
Childhood infectious diseases, eg whooping cough.
Foreign body in nose.
Asthma.

Although many causes of wheezing are not due to
asthma, the recommendations in that section may
be particularly useful.   ■

Worms

SEE ALSO: PARASITES, CANDIDA, IMMUNE FUNCTION, LEAKY GUT

Dietary advice

- Increase fibre from oats, vegetables and wholegrains.
- Only filtered or bottled water.
- No sugar, pork, refined foods or fizzy drinks.
- Reduce fruit intake except pineapple and figs.
- Cook all meat and fish thoroughly.
- All food to be nutrient dense as malabsorption can be a problem.
- Pumpkin seeds ground or as oil have anti-parasitic qualities.
- Cayenne pepper and senna mixed into yoghurt and eaten can immobilise the worms and speed expulsion.
- BENEFICIAL FOODS: Garlic, onions, pumpkin seeds, sesame seeds, turmeric, asian melon.

Nutrients to consider

- Malabsorption means high levels of vitamins and minerals are required. Use a high potency MVM.
- Slippery elm powder.(N,K)
- Aloe gold 1tsp daily. (HN)
- EFAs, eg Essential Balance Junior $^1/_2$-3 tsp from weaning to protect the gut lining.
- Citricidal 2-6 drops 1-3 times daily between meals is anti-parasitic.
- Sodium Phosphate one thrice daily to alkalise body. (BM)
- MSM sulphur one tablet or $^1/_4$tsp daily over 8 years, (HN) or Eliminex 1-2 tsps daily (L) to detoxify bowel.
- Artemesia (wormwood) or black walnut or cloves, only under supervision.

Types of worms in children commonly include threadworms and pin worms. They are present as little 'threads of cotton' around the anus, mainly at night when the worms migrate to the warm moist anal area to lay their eggs.

Treatment is usually a one dose capsule from chemist and the whole family must be treated. Repeat the treatment after about 2 weeks to address any eggs now hatched.

Less commonly and also known as parasites are tapeworms, hookworms and roundworms.

Some varieties of worms can migrate to other parts of the body. Pneumonia, jaundice or gum disease may result in rare cases.

GENERAL ADVICE

Bathe area after using the toilet with tea tree – one drop in a small bottle with cooled boiled water.

Petroleum jelly at night to relieve itching.

Vacuum carpets frequently especially around beds and where children play to remove eggs.

In older children wrap a small piece of garlic in sterile gauze and gently insert into the anus at night. Remember to remove it in the morning!

Infant starflower cream to reduce itching. (N)

Make children wear shoes if paddling in rivers, ponds etc.

Homeopathy may help.

Wounds

SEE ALSO: BURNS, BRUISING, IMMUNE FUNCTION, BITES AND STINGS

Cuts, bruises, blisters and grazes are all part of being a child but sometimes healing is slow.

Factors to consider
Diabetes.
EFA deficiency.
Mineral or protein shortage.
Suppressed immunity.

General advice
Cayenne tincture can stop bleeding.
Back Flower Rescue Remedy drops on tongue for shock.
Many homeopathic remedies for different types of wound but hypericum and calendula for general cuts.
Herbs include tea tree to prevent infection.
See appendix for more details of homeopathy, herbs, aromatherapy and flower remedies. ■

Dietary advice
- Increase foods rich in vitamin C and E, zinc, iron and EFAs.
- Plenty of protein to aid healing.
- Avoid sugar and junk foods as they suppress immunity.
- BENEFICIAL FOODS: Manuka honey, pineapple, blackcurrants, citrus fruits, green leafy vegetables, avocados, sprouted seeds, oily fish, chicken, eggs, flaxseed, wheatgerm.

Nutrients to consider
- Zinc for healing up to 30mgs daily short term. (S)
- Evening primrose oil 1-3 daily 4 -12 years. (L)
- Minerals, eg Concentrace 5 drops per 30lbs body weight. (HN)
- Vitamin A x 1-2 drops daily for 7 days only. (BC)

Topically
- Aloe vera gel. (HN)
- Witch hazel compresses; hot and cold alternately.
- Manuka honey as antiseptic but ordinary honey will do.
- Calendula ointment. Heals quickly so use when deep cut has begun to heal to prevent abscess forming in the centre. (N)
- Hypercal ointment. (BM)

W

APPENDIX

Supplements

(Nutrients to Consider)

This is a potential minefield!
- Supplements often need to be dairy, wheat, additive, citrus and egg free.
- Under 4 years is especially difficult due to doses, administration, formulation, taste.
- Powders, drops, liquids are best. Some supplements, eg digestive enzymes, are difficult due to necessity for capsule.
- Some children need quite extensive programmes initially so try to get multiple formulae whenever possible.

Always introduce very slowly one at a time to monitor any reactions such as diarrhoea.

An alarming number of supplements contain sugar, colouring, artificial sweeteners and citrus flavourings.

With the best will in the world the diet is not likely to be 100% perfect. Also you often cannot tell until too late when short term extra nutrients are required, eg an impending cold. Pollution, genetically modified ingredients, fussy eaters, allergic children, eating out, holidays and stress all affect nutrient requirements.

Ensuring adequate nutrients at all times by giving a children's multi vitamin is a sensible preventative approach, but where to start and how to choose?

A word about quality. Supplements are prime examples of 'you get what you pay for.' The ingredients of some cheaper 'off the shelf' products are often inferior in terms of bio-availability and absorption. Nutrients work both together and against each other. Doses are often too low.

Regular supplementation is also important. It's not much help to take a few when you remember.

The time of day affects absorption, eg minerals are mainly absorbed better in the evening, whilst B vitamins are good in the morning. Some vitamins are water-soluble meaning excess will be excreted in urine, eg all your vitamin C at once is a waste of money. However, ideal times for taking may have to be foregone in order to get the 'whole lot down in one' but vitamin C powder for instance can be added to drinks throughout the day.

Others are fat-soluble and can lead to overdosing if they accumulate in the body. Children are more susceptible to vitamin toxicity especially vitamin A and D.

Calcium and magnesium are often too low in MVM as they are too bulky to include in a reasonable sized tablet or capsule. This is where powder may be better. Also including ground nuts and seeds daily will boost calcium and magnesium.

For parents wanting a health insurance product, I have listed separately types of MVM for different ages. Also probiotics and digestive enzymes are separately listed.

For practitioners needing therapeutic ranges for a treatment programme suggestions are also listed under each condition.

Doses

Doses are linked to ages and body weight. Reference Nutrient Intakes (RNI) are adequate for prevention but not treatment.

Approximate calculations also depend on age and type of health condition.

During growing years and especially at growth spurts (first year, 5 years and 12 years) extra calcium, magnesium, zinc and vitamin D are required.

Under 3 years   25% (or $1/4$) of adult doses

3 – 6 years   50% (or $1/2$)

6 – 12 years   65% (or $2/3$)

12 – 14 years   75% (or $3/4$) Many 12 year olds can have adult doses if normal weight.

14 – 16 years   adult doses, but some nutrients are required in higher doses, eg calcium, zinc, vitamins A, D, biotin, and B6

Abbreviations

mls	millilitres
mg	milligram
mcg	microgram
ius	international units
tsp	teaspoon
tabsp/tblsp	tablespoon

NB: An oral syringe is an easy, accurate way to give small doses of liquid to small people (Ch). Graded 0-5mls in 0.5ml increments. Usually 1ml = 2mg.

Supplement Companies

Most have a nutritionist to answer queries

Key   DP = DIRECT TO PUBLIC
PO = PRACTITIONER ONLY

KEY	COMPANY	Phone/Contact	Details	DP/PO
A	Ainsworths	020 7935 5330	Homeopathic supplier. Can advise on remedies and Bach Flower Essences	DP
AN	Advanced Nutrition	01892 515927	Nutritional supplements including BioScience, Lamberts and Biocare	DP
AR	Allergy Research	01626 205417	Also available from NC	PO
AR	Ancient Roots	020 8421 9877	Australian Bush Flower Remedies	DP
BC	Biocare	0121 433 37270	Good selection of children's supple -ments with helpful technical back-up. Ask for leaflet *Supplements for Kids*.	DP

KEY	COMPANY	Phone/Contact	Details	DP/PO
	Bach Flower Remedies		Also NC, A, R, HS, Ch	
BF	BioForce	01294 277344	Herbal tinctures including echinacea complex and skin care products. Also Child Essence – see flower remedies	DP
BM	Blackmores	020 8842 3956 www.blackmores.com	Good selection of children's supplements. Ask for *Kids Range Consumer Leaflet* or website (also available at NC or R)	
BR	Biotics Research	01626 205417	Selected range from NC	PO
C	Cytoplan	01684 310099	Also from R, NC/Linked to Nature's Own	DP
Ch	Chemists	01491 834 678		
F	Farmacia	020 7404 8808	Homeopathic, herbal, skincare and nutritional products and professional advice on products	DP
HN	Higher Nature	01435 882880	Good selection of children's supplements and allergy tests. Helpful technical backups	DP
HP	Health Plus	01323 737374	Several MVMs for children, aromatherapy, skin care and herbal tinctures	DP
HS	Health Shops			
K	Kinetics	020 7435 5911	Herbal complexes specifically for children from birth	DP
L	Lamberts	01892 554312	Public sales as 'Nature's Best' or contact NC	DP
N	Napiers	0131 553 3500	Herbalists and nutritional supplements	DP
NO	Nature's Own	01684 310022	Bromelain 100mgs and also a MVM as a cereal bar. Several varieties, some G/W/F. Contain a little sugar	DP
	Neals Yard	0161 831 7875	Organic herbalists, homeopathy, aroma therapy, Australian Bush Remedies, Bach Flower, skincare, mother and baby	
Nu	Nutri	0800 212742	Eskimo 3 (DP), Echinacea and UltraCare for Kids (PO)	DP/PO
NC	NutriCentre	020 7436 5122	Sell wide range of nutritional supplements, personal hygiene, homeopathic remedies, books, accessories, ear candles, flower remedies etc. These include Epsom salts cream, Nature's Plus children's range, Herbal Actives children's range	DP
NW	Nutrition Works	01803 867440	Spray vitamins and minerals for children. Good for allergy sufferers	DP
S	Solgar	01442 890355	Ring S for nearest stockist (also from NC)	PO
Sa	Savant	08450 606070	Nutritional supplements, juicers, water filters, laundry capsules, personal care, books and pet foods	DP
R	Revital	0800 252875	Wide range supplements, health foods, ear candles, juicers etc	DP
RT	Rio Trading	01273 570987	Variety of products	DP
V	Victoria Health	0800 413596	Variety of products	
X	Xynergy	01730 813642	Skin care, natural deodorants, Spirolight energy bars	DP

Multi-Vitamin and Mineral Suggestions

Most of these products are free of gluten, yeast, wheat, milk, salt, artificial additives including sweeteners and are often vegan. Always check the label.

Some products in younger age ranges may be suitable in adjusted doses for older children, eg if a liquid or powder is required. After 12-14 years, adult products are usually suitable. Doses are not always given, eg if age range is wide.

From birth to 6months MVM are not usually required as breast milk from a healthy mother on an adequate diet or supplementing herself should be adequate. Bottle fed infants on fortified formula should also be okay. From 6 months or at weaning if earlier, zinc and iron levels are depleted.

Most conditions would benefit from a general MVM but in some cases, specific recommendations are made. Otherwise refer to the following list.

Multi-Vitamins and Minerals

Age and dosage	Product	Type	Company
From 4 years (2 years if opened)	Children's MVM recommended by HACSG	Small capsule or open onto food	BC
From 1 year	Vitaforte Banana MVM includes probiotics. Sprinkle onto cereals or fruit or add to drinks	Powder	BC
10-14 years	Vitaguard MVM	Capsule	BC
From 6 months–4 years 7-15 drops twice daily	Vitasorb Multivitamins	Drops	BC
From 6 months 4 drops	Nutrisorb Trace Minerals	Drops	BC
From 8 years 1-2 per day	Supernutrition Plus. 'True Food' product requires lower doses as better absorbed. Gentler iron	Tablet	HN
5-11 years 1 per day 11-14 years 2 per day	Optimum Nutrition Formula is a higher dose than Supernutrition Plus	Tablet	HN
Over 4 years 1 for each 2-3 years, eg 3 years = 1, 5 years = 2	Dinochews naturally sweetened, citrus free	Chewable. Can crush onto food	HN
4-10 years 1 per day, 11-14 years 2 per day	PlayFair includes calcium:magnesium in 2:1 ratio. Sugar and citrus fruit	Chewable	L

Age and dosage	Product	Type	Company
From 6 months	Salus House Kindervital	Liquid	N
From approx 2 years	Aqueous Multi Plus – an adult product but age specific doses possible, ie 50lb body weight = 1 tsp	Liquid	BR
From 2 years 20gms per 25lbs body weight	Nutribalance Children's Formula includes excellent levels calcium, magnesium, B vitamins and probiotics, EFAs and gut healing nutrients. Does not mix in drinks due to EFAs but add to mashed potato, yoghurts, cereals or with honey	Powder	AR
From 4 years One capsule per 10lbs body weight	Children's MVM – lower dose than above No probiotics	Capsules can be opened onto food	AR
2-11 years ¹/₂tablet per year of age, eg 8 year old has 3 per day	Supermouse orange and lemon flavoured, but citrus free!	Chewable	HP
11-13 years	MVM (3 varieties with or without iron/vitamin A)	Tablet	HP
13-14 years	Teenage Pack – a daily sachet containing 3 products	Tablet/Capsule	HP
From 10 years	Get up and Go. Some dislike the taste. Mix with milk or juice or in shakes	Powder	HP
3-10 years = ¹/₂bar per day 10-16 years = 1 bar per day	Nature's Own have a new cereal bar which contains a wide range of vitamins/minerals. Acts as a MVM with good levels of antioxidants. Some sugar. Good for teenagers who skip breakfast!	Cereal bar	NO
3-12 years	Ultra Care for kids via nutritionists only. A high dose beverage drink good for allergy sensitive children	Powder	Nu
4-12 years	MVM for Kids natural strawberry and orange flavour. May contain citrus	Chewable	BM
4-12 years	Vitamist Kid's Multi	Spray into mouth	NW
8-14 years	Vegetarian multiple	Capsule or open onto food	S
From 4 years 1 per day	Vitakid wafer	Wafer	S
4-12 years	Children's Everyday MVM	Capsule	Kirkman from NC

Nature's Plus from Nutricentre do a range of MVM for children including teenagers

Probiotics

The new born arrives with a sterile gut and needs to develop a healthy population of beneficial bacteria to protect from infections.

The balance of bacteria living in the intestinal tract varies with age; any anti-biotics, feeding method, weaning, type of delivery and pollution. Breast feeding is the best way to initiate correct intestinal balance.

Recently Cow and Gate produced the first formula milk fortified with probiotics called Omneo Comfort.

There are billions of healthy bacteria in an individual gut and many varieties, all preferring certain areas according to acidity and oxygen levels.

Infants and children require different species to adults so products must be 'age specific'.

Most should be kept under refrigeration. Many conditions would benefit from probiotics. Occasionally specific products are suggested, but otherwise refer to the following suggestions.

NB: Lacto does not refer to milk. Most probiotics are dairy free.

Suggested Prebiotics/Probiotics

Age/Dosage	Products	Type	Company
Birth to weaning and up to 4 years	Bifidobacterium Infants: ¹/₄tsp is 1 gm and delivers 4 billion friendly bacteria	Powder	BC
18mths–12 years (¹/₂tsp 2-4 years)	Strawberry or Banana Acidophilus ¹/₂tsp delivers 1 billion lactobacillus acidophilus and Bifidobacterium	Powder in a drink or on food	BC
From 4 years	FOS (a prebiotic) 10gms/1 tablespoon sprinkled onto cereal, fresh fruit or yoghurt or in juice. Can be used as a sweetener	Powder	BC
From 12 years	Acidophilus – 1 gm in drink once or twice daily delivers 4 billion lactobacillus acidophilus	Powder	BC
From 12 years	Bio-acidophilus – one capsule delivers 4 billion lactobacillus acidophulus and bifidobacterium bifidus	Capsule	BC
From 6 months One twice daily up to 12 years then 2 twice a day	Enterogenic Concentrate	Capsule	Nu
Birth – 4 years ¹/₄–¹/₂tsp	ABC Dophilus ¹/₂tsp delivers one billion. B bifidum, S thermophilus and B infantis	Powder	S
From 5 years ¹/₂–1 thrice daily	Super 5 Acidophilus is raspberry flavoured. Delivers 5 different species of organisms	Chewable tablet	Sa
From 2 years	Acidophilus/Bifidus		BM
Birth to 2 years	Infant acidophilus		BM
8-11 years one alternate days then 11-16 years one daily	Acidophilus – no fridge required/lower dose. Delivers 40 million acidophilus	Capsule – can open	HP
From 8 years 1-2 daily	Lacto-gest especially for digestion of proteins, eg allergy problems and after antibiotics. Delivers 150 million lacto-sporongenes	Tablet	HN
From 4 years ¹/₄tsp per day	Acidobifidus after infection or antibiotics. Delivers millions of bifidus, longum and brevis strains	Powder in drink or on cereals	HN
From 5 years One level tsp	FOS as a prebiotic and to sweeten drinks or in baking	Powder	HN
From 8 years One per day	Probiogest between meals or before bed with cool drink. Many millions of L-salivarias rapidly multiply. Good for allergy or digestive problems	Capsule	HN
From 5 years ¹/₄tsp	FOS as prebiotic	Powder	AR
From 8 years 1 level tsp per day	Symbiotics contains nine strains of bacteria and FOS delivering 4 billion organisms	Powder	AR
From 5 years ¹/₄tsp twice daily	Biodophilus – FOS supplying 3 billion per day	Powder	AR

Digestive Enzymes

Digestive enzymes are a problem for children as they usually need to be encapsulated to protect the enzymes from stomach acid. If put onto food they will digest it before your very eyes. A nice trick, but ineffective! Here are a few suggestions. Only use in the short term and get professional advice if problems persist.

- Beano is a carbohydrate digestive enzyme. Capsules for older children. (NC)

- Children's Digestaid small capsules with meals.(BC)

- Enzyme Complete powder. (NC)

- Digestive Aid – over 8 years chew one with meals.(S)

- Lactase enzyme. Add 4 drops to one pint of milk, yoghurt etc and leave for 24 hrs. Use as normal. For lactose intolerance. (BC)

- Bromelain 100mgs per day. (NO)

- Easygest one capsule with each meal. (HN)

Vitamin/Minerals/Food Sources

* = anti-oxidants

VITAMINS

Vitamin A* — Pumpkin seeds, cashew nuts, beans, fish liver oil, dairy products, eggs

Beta caroteneCarotenoids* — Dark green vegetables, eg kale and broccoli; courgettes, carrots, corn cobs, tomatoes, sweet potatoes, squash, mangoes, apricots, water melon. Beta carotene is converted to vitamin A in the body

Vitamin C* — Vegetables, especially greens, broccoli, tomatoes, peppers, parsley; fruits especially citrus, blackcurrants, apples, strawberries, kiwi, papaya, mangoes. Sprouted seeds and beans have increased levels

Bioflavonoids* — Lemons, blackcurrants, cherries, grapefruit, buckwheat

Vitamin E* — Green leafy vegetables, avocados, eggs, butter/margarine, sunflower oil, oil of nuts/seeds, rice, oats, oatmeal, wholegrain cereals, soy beans, legumes, eg nuts, chick peas, peanuts; wheatgerm, wholewheat, sprouted wheat

Vitamin D — Eggs, dairy products, oily fish especially mackerel or canned salmon; fortified cereals. Daily sunshine too

Vitamin K — Egg yolks, fish oils, honey, soya beans, leafy green vegetables, sea vegetables, potatoes, tomatoes, yoghurt. Also made by beneficial bacteria in gut

B Vitamins — Marmite, brown rice, wholegrains, nuts, wheat, bran, cereals, soya products, legumes, pulses, brewers yeast, milk/milk products, eggs, bread, meat, poultry, some fish, green vegetables, potatoes

Best Individual sources B Vitamins

B1 – Brown rice, egg yolk, fish, wholegrains, breakfast cereals, meat, nuts

B2 – Milk, cheese, egg yolks, wholegrains, yoghurt, poultry

B3 – Potatoes, eggs, wheatgerm, milk, red meat, breakfast cereals, fish, wholemeal bread

B5 – Brewer's yeast, eggs, legumes, fresh vegetables, nuts, mushrooms, rye flour, wholewheat bread

B6 – Brewer's yeast, chicken, carrots, eggs, walnuts, wheatgerm, sunflower seeds, peas

B12 – Sea vegetables, eggs, brewers yeast, oily fish, soya beans, milk, cheese, yoghurt

Folic acid – leafy green vegetables, brewers yeast, chicken, root vegetables, mushrooms, wheatgerm, wholegrains, wholemeal bread, fish

Biotin – Brewer's yeast, eggs, milk, poultry, soybeans, wholegrains

Choline – egg yolks, lecithin, legumes, milk, soybeans, wholegrain cereals

MINERALS

Calcium
Blackstrap molasses, milk, cheese, eggs, fortified bread, canned fish especially salmon; nuts, seeds, dark green leafy vegetables especially broccoli, parsley, cabbage, root vegetables

Magnesium
Nuts, seeds, dark leafy vegetables, wholegrains, brewers yeast, wheatgerm, cereals, lentils, soya beans, meats, poultry, fish, seafood, peas, garlic, potato skin, apricots, raisins, dried figs, bananas

Zinc*
Seafoods especially oysters, shellfish (not under 2 yrs old); canned fish, lean red meat, green leafy vegetables, mushrooms, potatoes, nuts especially pecans; seeds especially pumpkin seeds; cereals, rice, rye, oats, lentils, pulses, wholegrains, blackstrap molasses, brewers yeast, cheese, wholemeal bread, eggs

Iron
Shellfish (not under 2 years old), lean red meat, fish especially sardines (best absorption of animal iron); cocoa, green leafy vegetables, wholegrains, fortified cereals, nuts especially almonds; seeds especially sesame; peas, lentils, parsley, spices, egg yolk, yeast, wheatgerm, wholemeal bread, dried fruits, figs, blackstrap molasses

Selenium*
Nuts, especially Brazil nuts, fish/shellfish (not under 2 years old); dairy produce, cottage cheese, poultry, fruit, vegetables, broccoli, cabbage, mushrooms, onions, garlic; yeast, cereals, seeds; wholegrains

Chromium
Egg yolks, cheese, blackstrap molasses, nuts, wholegrains, wheatgerm, brewers yeast, fruit/fruit juices, honey, oysters (not under 2 years old) vegetables, potatoes, parsnips, thyme, chicken

Manganese
Root vegetables, leafy vegetables, spinach, wholemeal bread, eggs, nuts, beans and pulses, cereals especially oatmeal; fish, meats, tropical fruits, berries, pineapple juice, dried fruit, eg raisins

Potassium
Dried fruits especially apricots, bananas, fish, sunflower seeds, potatoes, vegetables, wholegrains and blackstrap molasses

Phosphorus
Lean meat, dairy products, eggs

Sulphur
Eggs, garlic, onions, fish, legumes, cabbage, dried beans, wheatgerm

Essential Fatty Acids (EFAs)
Green leafy vegetables, nuts, seeds and their oils, fish oils and flax (linseed),

Omega 3
Oily fish especially herring, tuna, mackerel, salmon, pilchards, sardines; flaxseed oil (linseeds), pumpkin seeds, green leafy vegetables especially spinach/cabbage

Omega 6
Sunflower/sesame/safflower oils and seeds, walnuts, soya, corn, evening primrose oil, breast milk

Proteins

HIGH PROTEIN FOODS

Fish – cod, plaice, salmon, tuna, haddock, mackerel (not smoked), bass, sardines etc.

Soya – tofu, soya cheese, soya yoghurts (sugar-free), tempeh, soya mince/chunks.

Sprouts – (seeds, legumes) alfalfa, mung, green lentil etc, aduki, chick pea.

Dairy and eggs (organic) – cottage cheese, natural yoghurt.

Meat (organic) – chicken, any lean cut.

LOWER PROTEIN FOODS

Nuts – almonds, walnuts, cashews, Brazils, pecans, hazelnuts, pine nuts.

Seeds – sunflower, sesame, pumpkin, flax seeds (linseed).

Pulses – kidney beans, mung beans, aduki beans, red, green, yellow lentils etc, soya beans, butter beans, chick peas (houmous).

Grains – quinoa, buckwheat, millet, amaranth.

Helpful Information/ Recipes

GENERAL TIPS TO ENCOURAGE HEALTHY EATING

- No salt in cooking. Use herbs, lemon, vinegar and spices to flavour meals.
- Feed your child the best quality food you can afford.
- Try not to take children shopping. They are likely to select unhealthy foods due to intense marketing. Instead, ask them to help plan meals and shopping lists from a selected healthy range, eg satsuma or banana, fruit or plain yoghurt, rather than crisps versus fruit. This will help them to feel involved and in control whilst teaching them about costs, nutrition and choices.
- Leave healthy snacks and leftovers for 'fridge-raiding', eg home made pizza, rice, fruit salad, home made popcorn.
- After school snacks can include carrot and houmous, cereals, fruit smoothies.
- Don't buy biscuits and crisps except as occasional treats.
- Make your own chips with scrubbed potatoes sliced into wedges and tossed in 1-2 tablespoons olive oil with a pinch of rosemary and baked in the oven. You can also use parsnips, sweet potatoes, squash etc for brightly coloured variety.
- Good natural food does not need additives.

SPROUTING SEEDS

A good source of protein, vitamins and minerals.

- Put one tablespoon of seeds, eg Alfalfa, sunflower or pulses (red, green or brown lentils, dried peas) in an empty jam jar.
- Half fill with water.
- Leave to soak overnight.
- Rinse and drain well in the morning.
- Place in a dark cupboard.
- Each evening and morning, rinse the beans and drain them well. Placing a piece of muslin over the neck of the jar with an elastic band makes this easier
- After a few days (depending on the bean) you should have a crop of sprouts. Once they are the right size for eating (about 2cm) put them in the fridge to stop them from growing further. Add to salad/stirfries or use as a snack.

Barley water

High in anti-oxidants and useful for infections especially urinary tract infections. Boil 2 tablespoons pearl barley in one pint water for 10 minutes. Strain and add barley to a fresh pint of water. Boil for further 10 minutes and serve with fresh lemon and honey.

Immune booster cocktail
One cup of hot water (not boiling).
- Juice of $^1/_2$ lemon.
- 1tsp honey (Manuka is especially good).
- Vitamin C powder – a pinch for a toddler, up to 500mgms for over 8 years
- $^1/_4$ cinnamon stick or pinch ground cinnamon (optional).
- Echinacea tincture – one drop for toddler, up to 15 drops from 8 years.
- All mixed together and drunk twice daily for 4 or 5 days until symptoms clear.

Elderflower spritzer
Good for immunity.
- Put one head of fresh elderflowers and a slice fresh lemon in a bowl with 100mls boiling water and one tsp honey. Cover and leave to stand for 1-2 hours until cool. Strain into a glass and add sparkling mineral water and ice and drink immediately. A straw and a sprig of mint makes it fun.

Popping corn
This is a healthy snack when not sugared or salted. Add some corn kernals to a little olive oil in a pan and cover. Wait until the popping stops and shake periodically. You can add one tsp molasses when popped. Fun and healthy!

Fluid requirements

Dependent on weight, activity, weather and health:

Approximately 500mls or $^1/_2$ litre daily from birth;

1000mls or 1 litre daily at one year;

2-2$^1/_2$ litres daily for older children.

Ways to encourage adequate fluid intake include increasing fruit and vegetables, using a water filter to improve taste, novelty ice cubes (also from filtered water), drinking straws, themed cups/glasses, 'cool' water bottles to impress friends, provide water by the bed at night, fresh home made juices.

5 PORTIONS FRUIT AND VEGETABLES

What does this mean for a child? eg 2 year old; half an apple or pear, half a satsuma, a tomato, 3 or 4 slices cucumber and a tablespoon of peas. Stewed fruit and raisins are also good suggestions. Introduce salad as a small garnish even if not eaten!

EFAs

Ground seeds/nuts are better assimilated. Put a selection in a small grinder (an old coffee grinder is ideal). Keep in the fridge and sprinkle onto cereals or salads. Also add oils to cooked rice or vegetables before serving.

DRY SKIN BRUSHING

Useful for detoxification and is calming and fun for children. Special soft bristle brushes are available from chemists and health stores, but you could use a natural dry sponge or flannel. Start from the feet and work towards groin in smooth, firm, stroking movements. Then from hands to shoulders and down the chest. Finally, gentle clockwise circular movements on the tummy (from right to left). Don't forget the back of the body. Best done before a shower or bath and is good for anxiety, toxicity, constipation and hyperactivity.

Replacement Foods

DAIRY ALTERNATIVES
(See also 'Food intolerance' and Mail order foods)

Nanny Goat Formula	Tel: 0800 328 5826 for stockists but health shops and some chemists stock it.
Babynat Organic Formula	Tel: 020 8340 0401. (HS)
Mead Johnson	Tel: 028 1754 3764 for formulas free of either lactose, casein or whey.
St Helen's	Tel: 01430 861715 for goats' butter, yoghurts, cheese, milk.
Goats' products	Including a cheese spread – Delamere Dairy – Tel: 01565 632422
Mill milk	is an oat milk. (HS)
Lactolite	has only 5% lactose in whole cows' milk – Tel: 0845 6006688 or supermarkets.
Evernat	organic oat drink. (HS)
Chocolate	Kinnerton confectionery for guaranteed nut-free chocolate in novelty ranges. Tel: 020 7470 1914 Also do a chocolate cake stocked by Sainsbury which is egg, nut, soya and dairy free.
	D&D Chocolates – dairy free – Tel: 01509 216400
Ice cream	Eskley Sheep or Winner Swedish Glace or Lolly Tots – Tel: 01270 589311.
Plamil	Veeze cheese is soya. Also do egg free mayonnaise.
Sheep milk	Eskley Sheep Milk – Tel: 01981 510294 – dried, skimmed sheep milk powder, bottled milk, cheese and ice cream.
Soya milk	Information Bureau – Tel: 01295 277777 (fact pack and recipes).
Spreads	Vitaquell, soya spread, Granose, hummous.

NB – Vegan products will be dairy free
All major supermarkets have nutritional advice services
regarding their products and will often send lists on request.

WHEAT/GLUTEN ALTERNATIVES
(See also 'Food Intolerance', Information file and Mail order foods)

Wheat free alternatives — Corn, crispbreads, poppadums, rice noodles, oatcakes, amaranth crispbreads

Gluten free/wheat free alternatives Ryvita, pumpernickel, rice cakes

Suggested substitutes for one cup of wheat flour can be:

3/4 cup corn starch	7/8 cup corn flour	3/4 cup coarse cornmeal
1 scant cup fine oatmeal	3/4 cup potato flour	3/4 cup potato starch
1 1/2 cup sago flour	7/8 cup buckwheat	7/8 cup rice flour
1 1/3 cup ground rolled oats	3/4 cup soyabean flour	

Rather than using one substitute, use a mixture to provide a greater variety to your diet.

Bread and mixes
General Dietary Ltd – Tel: 020 8336 2323 for gluten free bread and mixes, pasta and recipes.

Stamp Collection – supermarkets/health food shops – Tel: 01621 819596 for flour, pasta, bread mix, pizza bases.

Gourmet Gluten Free Imports Ltd – Tel: 02392 647572 for alternative flours and Xanthan gum.

Barbara's Kitchen – Tel: 01443 229304.

Glutafin – Tel: 01225 711801 or Juvela Nutrition Centre Tel: 0151 228 1992 for gluten free bread mixes.

Flours
Potato, grain (chick pea), soya, brown rice, tapioca. Spelt and kamut flours are early forms of wheat sometimes better tolerated for occasional use.

Ready meals
Dietary Specialities – Tel: 07041 544044 for ready meals for allergy sufferers.

Breakfast cereals
Nature's Path – rice and millet (like bran flakes), Mega Sunrise and others are wheat/gluten free. NB – some of their varieties contain spelt or kamut wheat – www.naturespath.com

Wheat free muesli mixes. (HS)

Oat bran by Mornflake for fine, wheat free porridge – supermarkets and health food shops.

Ice cream Cones
by Barkat – major supermarkets or GF Foods

Pancakes
Wheat free mix by Orgran Tel: 020 8450 9411 or major supermarkets.

Pasta
Corn, buckwheat (this is not wheat), millet and rice pastas from health food shops and supermarkets.

Sainsbury's
have a wheat/gluten free section next to dry organic goods.

Sausages
Try Locks for gluten free. Also some local independent butchers will make up a batch for your freezer and Iceland are very good for gluten free products.

Xanthum gum
adds strength to bread from Gourmet Gluten Free Imports, Suma and Barbara's Kitchen

SUGAR SUBSTITUTES

Raw, natural sugar beet is a mineral rich food, but after processing and refining all that is left is a concentrated form of sweetener which provides empty calories. Even worse for health are artificial sweeteners especially aspartame which has been linked to cancer.

Healthier substitutes include:

Blackstrap molasses	it is the last extraction of sugar cane and very rich in minerals, high in calcium, iron, potassium, B vitamins, magnesium and vitamin E. Good, natural source of iron. One tsp daily gives readily available nutrients. Use on cereals, in rice puddings or stewed fruit, in warm milk or water or as a spread.
Honey	natural, raw, untreated honey is a good source of minerals, vitamins and enzymes with anti-bacterial properties. It can aid healing and is a good substitute for sugar. **Do not give to babies under one year due to small risk of botulism.**
Manuka honey	all the benefits of honey with additional anti-viral properties. Comes from tea tree pollen, usually from New Zealand. Buy active form for a potent immune booster. One tsp daily keeps the bugs away. Suitable as a spread or sweetener. **Not for babies.**
Fructose	useful for baking when less is needed.
Fruit juice concentrates	diluted with 10 parts water make a healthier alternative to squash or ice lollies.
Dried fruit puree	eg date puree instead of sugar in baking.
FOS	a powdered prebiotic for use on cereals, yoghurt, fruit etc with the benefit of 'feeding' the beneficial bacteria in the gut. Very sweet so only need a pinch.

NB: Only FOS is suitable for candida sufferers
All major supermarkets have nutritional advice services regarding their products and will often send lists on request.

SALICYLATE FOODS

There are many healthy foods here so only exclude if other exclusions are ineffective. Exclude for 4-6 weeks, eg in ADHD, hyperactivity.

- Almonds
- Apples
- Apricots
- Artificial colours and preservatives, MSG
- Berry fruits
- Coca cola
- Cucumbers
- Dates
- Dried fruit
- Fruit juices
- Gherkins
- Grapes
- Green peppers
- Herbs and spices
- Honey
- Liquorice
- Marmite
- Nectarines
- Olives (including olive oil)
- Oranges
- Peppermints
- Pineapples
- Potato skins
- Prunes
- Raspberries
- Stock cubes
- Tea
- Tomatoes
- Tomato sauce
- Worcestershire sauce
- NB – Aspirin

Mail order foods

(Some companies are only mail order; others will give you the nearest stockist)

Allergy Care	Tel: 01823 325022/3 – specialist allergy foods
Allergy Free Direct	Tel: 01865 722 003 – allergy free foods, some organic
Barbara's Kitchen	Tel: 01443 229304 – wheat, gluten, egg, sugar, yeast-free foods, recipes and gluten replacements
British Goat Society	Tel: 01626 833168
Clara's Kitchen	Tel: 020 8953 4444 for pasta, snacks, biscuits, bread and mixes, stuffing, cereals, crumb coating
D&D Chocolates	Tel: 01509 216400 – dairy free chocolate
Doves Farm Foods Ltd	Tel: 01488 684880 – gluten/wheat free flours
Foodwatch International Ltd	Tel: 01258 73356 – for wide range of allergy and sugar/yeast free books, water filters and household cleaning products
General Dietary Ltd	Tel: 020 8336 2323 – Ener G cookies (gluten, wheat, egg, milk and soya- free) bread, pasta and recipes. Also sell egg replacer
Gluten Free Foods Ltd	Tel: 020 8952 0052 – includes gluten/wheat free ice cream cones, porridge flakes
Goodness Direct	Tel: 01327 871655, www.goodnessdirect.co.uk – allergy free foods
Green and Organic Ltd	Tel: 01420 520838/520530 – organic, allergy free foods, personal hygiene and household products – www.greenandorganic.co.uk
Innocent Ltd	Tel: 020 8600 3939 for 5 fruit puree drinks (nothing else added) – major supermarkets also stock
Lifestyle Healthcare Ltd	Tel: 01491 570000/411767 gluten free foods
Lock's Sausages	Tel: 01623 822200 – gluten free
Mrs Leepers	Tel: 01932 334501 – wheat/gluten, egg, soya and milk-free pasta
Nutricia	Tel: 01225 711801 – allergy free range
Organics Direct	Tel: 020 7729 2828
Pamela's	Tel: 01932 334500 – wheat/gluten free cookies
Simply Organic	Tel: 0845 1000 444
Suma	www.simplyorganic.net for wide range of allergy free products, health foods, some supplements and skin care and baby foods Tel: 01422 345513
Trufree Foods	gluten/wheat free flours – Tel: 020 8874 1130
Wellfoods	Tel: 01226 381712 – ready made loaves, gluten free flour etc

Other Therapies

HOMEOPATHY

Usually needs professional supervision in children,
but these are recommended for children.

Remedy	Complaint
Aconite	Acute earache, sore throat, fever, croup, chicken pox, shock, night terrors
Allum cepa	Hayfever
Ant tart	Night terrors, rattly cough
Arnica	Arthritis, bruising, sleep problems
Arsenicum	Frequent colds, rhinitis, mouth ulcers, fatigue, diarrhoea
Belladona	Bedwetting, earache, sore throat, fever, cough
Borax	Thrush
Bryonia	Constant crying, asthma, thirst, dry cough
Calcium Phosphorus	Teething
Calendula	Cradle cap (M), minor burns
Causticum	Bedwetting
Chamomilla	Teething at night, hyperactivity, earache, period pains, diarrhoea, sleep problems, colic
China	Food intolerance, digestive problems
China	Diarrhoea, wind, irritability, worms
Cina	Parasites, worms
Coffea Cruda	Overactive, unable to sleep, hyperactivity
Colocynthis	Constant crying, watery diarrhoea
Corallum rubrun	Coughs, asthma
Equisetum	Bedwetting
Euphrasia	Conjunctivitis, hayfever
Hep Sulf	Acute ear ache
Hypercum	Sunburn
Kali mur	Swollen glands, glue ear, catarrh
Kresotun	Bedwetting
Lycopodium	Cradle cap, deafness, catarrh, cold sores, sore throat, flatulence
Mecurias	Glue ear discharge
Mercuricus	Swollen glands, ear ache, oral thrush
Natrum Mur	Cold sores, cradle cap, colds
Nuxvomica	Irritability, halitosis, diarrhoea, vomiting
Phosphorus	Thirst, mood swings, croup
Plantage	Bedwetting
Pulsatilla	Clinging, sticky eyes, hayfever, cough, colic
Sepia	Panic attacks, period pains
Spongia	Croup
Sulphur	Acne, eczema, cradle cap, halitosis, sweet cravings, nappy rash

Ainsworths do a children's kit with essential remedies for children for around £30

HERBALISM

(Always seek professional guidance, but these are recommended for children)

Remedy	Complaint
Black root	Acute earache
Buchu	Nappy rash/acid urine at teething
Burdock	Cradle cap, acne, chicken pox
Butternut	Cradle cap
Cat mint	Distressed child, fever, croup, colic
IChamomile	Sleep problems, anxiety, pain, colic, teething, conjunctivitis, fever, croup
Cleavers	Swollen glands
Comfrey	Chicken pox
Comfrey	Congestion, coughs
Echinacea	Conjunctivitis, infection, immune system, thrush
Elderflower	Catarrh, fever, eczema
Elderflower	Chicken pox
Euphrasia	Catarrh
Eyebright	Conjunctivitis
Garlic oil	Earache (on cotton wool)
Golden rod	Catarrh
Goldenseal	Conjunctivitis (W), earache (D)
Heartsease	Impetigo
Hops	Sleep problems, acute earache/pain
Horsetail (equestum)	Bed wetting
Lavender	Impetigo, oral thrush
Lemon balm	Anxiety, bedwetting, oral thrush, colic
Limeflowers	Sensitive, nervous child, colic
Lyssop	Catarrh
Marigold	Nappy rash (ointment)
Marshmallow root	Teething, colic, vomiting
Meadowsweet	Cradle cap
Meadowsweet	Vomiting
Motherwort	Crying due to fear
Mullein	Ear acheT, DMyrrhEar ache
Oats	Hyperactivity
Passiflora	Earache, sleep problems
Peppermint	Immune system, oral thrush, chicken pox (crushed leaves)
Raspberry leaf	Conjunctivitis
Rosemary	Colds, sinusitis
Skullcap	Anxiety, hyperactivity
Taraxacum	Fever
Thyme	Coughs
Valerial	Hyperactivity, sleep problems
Vervain	Sedates reluctant sleeper, hyperactivity, cradlecap, anxiety
Wild cherry	Croup, coughsWild indigoImmune system

Please refer to *Healing Remedies* by Norman Shealy for method of use

Kinetics stock Nature's Answer products which are excellent herbal products in powder or drops, specifically for children. Tel: 020 7435 5911; East/West Herb shop stock GAIA herbal products and a booklet, specifically for babies and children. Tel: 0800 092 8828

AROMATHERAPY

With babies and children it is usually advisable to see
a qualified aromatherapist, but certain oils are safe
for general use. Lavender, chamomile and mandarin
are the safest. Always dilute first, even in the bath.

Remedy	Complaint
Tea tree	Impetigo, earache, sinusitis, colds, coughs, immune system, nappy rash, headlice
Lavender	Teething, croup, colic, eczema, sinusitis, headache, coughs, chicken pox, sleep problems, hyperactivity, cradle cap, earache (on cotton wool), minor burns, nappy rash, headlice
Chamomile	Sleep problems, hyperactivity, colds, colic, skin problems, bedwetting, headache, asthma, chickenpox, teething, earache, teething, eczema
Geranium	Chilblains, skin problems, minor burns, sunburn
Rose	Hyperactivity, colic, nappy rash
Neroli	Hyperactivity
Niaouli	Congestion, colds, catarrh
Sandalwood	Hyperactivity, acne, asthma, coughs, sinusitis
Lemon	Cradle cap, insect bites, headaches, veruccas
Mullein	Earache
Eucalyptus	Glue ear (M), colds and coughs, croup, headlice
Bergamot	Depression, eczema, cold sores, urinary infections, psoriasis, chicken pox
Fennel	PMS, wind, indigestion, colic
Ginger	Colds, nausea including travel sickness, arthritis, sinusitis
Peppermint	Indigestion, headaches, migraine
Rosemary	Concentration, memory and learning, fatigue, acne, headaches
Cinnamon	Colds, catarrh, coughs, croup
Thyme	Colds, coughs, thrush
Pine	Colds, coughs, croup
Myrrh	Coughs
Clove	Teething (oil)
Oregano	Thrush, candida
Black pepper	Worms

FLOWER ESSENCES

Good for emotionally related problems. Generally, mix 2 drops in a glass of water or juice. The following are safe for children:

Remedy	Complaint
Rescue Remedy	Calming in distress, cradle cap, earache, colds, coughs. For thrush, teething and nappy rash use the cream
White Chestnut	Overactive mind so can not sleep, unwanted thoughts
Rock Rose	Night terrors, cradle cap, panic, pain, croup, colic, fear
Aspen	Unidentifiable fears/anxieties, night terrors
Walnut	For change, eg new baby, house, school, divorce, teething
Mimulus	Fear of the dark, bed wetting
Larch	Lack of confidence
Vervain	Hyperactivity
Impatiens	Hyperactivity, temper tantrums, irritability
Cherry Plum	Loss of control/temper tantrums, hyperactivity
Wild Rose	Bedwetting, depression
Chestnut Bud	Bedwetting, learning difficulties
Star of Bethlehem	Shock, trauma
Olive	Recuperation, fatigue
Centaury	Bullying, lack of confidence
Gentian	Depression, moods
Mustard	Fatigue
Gorse	Depression

Bio Force make Child Essence, a combination of flower remedy similar to Rescue Remedy but specifically for children. Includes cherry plum, chamomile, larch, pink cherry, walnut and chicory. Try it for hyperactivity, fears, tantrums, anxiety. Promotes security and peacefulness.

Doses	2-5 years	4 drops 2-3 times per day
	6-12 years	8 drops 2-3 times per day
	Over 12 years	15 drops 2-3 times per day

Contact: 01491 834678 for register of practitioners and advice.

AUSTRALIAN BUSH REMEDIES

They are all safe for children. 7 drops under the tongue on rising or resting or mix in 30mls spring water and sip through the day. 66 individual essences are made and 14 combination essences, 5 mists and 5 creams.

There are so many uses for different ones – the following are just a few examples:

Five Corners	Eating disorders
Billy Goat Plum	Eating disorders, growth problems
Dog Rose	Fear, anxiety
Emergency essence	Night terrors, panic attacks, shock, trauma, bereavement, anxiety
Black-eyed Susan	Stress, hyperactivity, anxiety
Boronia	OCD, anxiety, eating disorders, sleep problems
Jacaranda	Poor concentration, hyperactivity
Croyer	Tension, anxiety, pain
Grey Spider Flower	Night terrors
Kangaroo Paw	ADHD
Waratah	Depression
Monga Warratah	Clinging, dependent child, insecurity
Green	Anxiety about skin disorders or IBS

Combinations are also made, eg Confid for anxious, tense child.

Face, hand and body cream for young girls and teenagers.

For more information and to order contact Ancient Roots – Tel: 020 8950 7822 and for reading *Australian Bush Flower Essence* by Ian White.

How to find a Practitioner

Nutritionists
British Association of Nutritional Therapists (BANT)
Tel: 0870 6061284 E-mail:theadministrator@bant.org.uk

Institute of Optimum Nutrition (ION) – Tel: 020 8877 9993

Yellow Pages hold BANT adverts and individual nutritionists.
Always check credentials. Registered with BANT?

Nutritional Doctors
British Society for Allergy and Environment Medicine –
A society who recognise the broad principles of nutrition and
treat patients accordingly. PO Box 28, Totton, Southampton,
Hampshire SO40 2ZA Tel: 023 8081 2124.

Homeopaths
Society of Homeopathy – for qualified homeopath Tel: 01604
621400.
British Homeopathic Association and Faculty of Homeopathy
– for new patient booklet and list of practitioners
Tel: 020 7566 7800 / 7810

British Homeopathic Society – for a medically qualified
homeopath Tel: 020 7935 2163

Homeopathic Medical Association – Tel: 01474 560 336

Herbalists
National Institute Medical Herbalists (NIMH)
Tel: 01392 426022

Acupuncturists
British Acupuncture Council (BAC) – Tel: 020 8735 0400

British Medical Acupuncture Society for doctors
Tel: 01925 730727

Chinese Medicine
Tel: 07000 079 0332

Naturopaths
British College of Naturopathy – Tel: 0207 4335 7830

British Naturopathy Association – Tel: 01485 840072

Counsellors
British Association of Counsellors – Tel: 01788 578328

UK Register of Counsellors (UKRC) – Tel: 0870 443 5232

Aromatherapists
Aromatherapy Organisations Council (AOC)
Tel: 020 8251 7912

Cranial Osteopathy
General Osteopathic Council (GOC) – Tel: 020 7357 6655

Bach Flower Practitioners Tel: 01491 834678

Various
Complementary Medical Association (CMA)
Tel 020 8305 9571

Information/Resources

AD-DISS offers support and information for ADHD – Tel: 020 8905 2013

Allergy Induced Autism (AIA) – Tel: 01733 321771 or 0121 444 6450

American Peanut Information Office – Tel: 020 7631 3434

Anaphylaxis Campaign – Tel: 01252 542029

Aquathin UK – Tel: 01252 860111 for reverse osmosis water purifiers

Auditory Integration Training (AIT) – Tel: 01483 579500 or Hale Clinic, Tel: 020 7631 0156

Autism File – Tel: 020 8979 2525 – diet, nutrition, GF/CF quarterly magazine including recipes, research, support or www.autismfile.com

Autism Research Unit, Sunderland University – Tel: 0191 510 8922

British Allergy Foundation – Tel: 020 8303 8525/8583

Citizens Advice Bureau – see local directory. They have a wealth of information on wide ranging issues.

Coeliac Society – Tel: 01494 437278 gluten free lists on GP request

Dietary Card – Tel: 01506 430251 for personalised 'credit' card depicting sensitivities in any language (£10). Useful for holidays

Eating Disorders Association – Tel: 01603 621414 or Helpline for under 18 years – Tel: 01603 765050

Eco-Balls – Tel: 020 8662 7200

ERIC – The Eneuresis Resource Centre – Tel: 0117 960 3060 (Helpline)

Food Commission – independent food watchdog Tel: 020 7837 2250

Foresight – Tel: 01483 427839

Fresh Water Filter Company Ltd. – Tel: 020 8597 3222

Fresh Water Company – Tel: 020 8558 7495 for plumbed in water filters

Green People – Tel: 01444 401444 for catalogue of chemical free products (personal, home laundry etc)

The Healthy House and Office – Tel: 01453 752216

Herbal Information Centre – www.herbalinfo.org.uk. Also has an email reply service for individual queries

Hyperactive Children's Support Group – Tel: 01903 725182

Hopi Ear Candles – from Revital – Tel: 0800 252 875 for mail order

The Inside Story – Tel: 020 7722 2866 – for allergy sufferers. Produce a very helpful newsletter loaded with contacts and suppliers (subscription required)

Jurilique Baby Products – Tel: 020 8842 3956

Justice Awareness and Basic Support (JABS) for information on vaccinations – Tel: 01942 713565

Medivac Healthcare – Tel: 01625 539401 vacuum cleaners that reduce circulation of dust and house dust mite

Migraine Trust – Tel: 020 7831 4818

National Asthma Campaign – Tel: 020 7226 2260 / 0845 701 0203

National Autism Society – Tel: 020 7833 2299 and for helpline that runs 'Early Bird' pre-school education programme – Tel: 0870 600 8585

National Eczema Society – Tel: 020 7499 7822 or 020 7388 3444

National Society for Research into Allergy – PO Box 45, Hinkley, Leicestershire, LE10 1JY

Overload network for facts about ADHD medications – Tel: 0131 555 4967

Sunflower Trust – Tel: 01483 428141 – recorded message for information on dyspraxia, dyslexia, autism, ADHD, hyperactivity and learning difficulties (Tel: 01252 703116 Monday and Tuesday 5-7pm helpline)

Think Natural supply natural products and accessories including ionisers and kinetics herbal products (K) – Tel: 0845 6011223

The UCB Institute of Allergy – Star House, 69, Clarendon Road, Watford, HERT, WD1 1DJ

The Vegan Society – Tel: 01424 427393

The Vegetarian Society – Tel: 0161 928 0793

What Doctors Don't Tell You – Tel: 020 8944 9555

Young Minds – mental health for children – Tel: 0800 018 2138 – extensive resources, books, tapes etc and very supportive

Testing Companies

DP	York Nutritional Labs – Tel: 01904 401410 – food intolerance test
DP	Higher Nature – Tel: 01435 882880 – allergy test
PO	Health Interlink – Tel: 01664 810011 – digestive, gut infection, hair and leaky gut tests
PO	Mineral Check – Tel: 01622 630044 – hair mineral analysis
DP	Foresight – Tel: 01483 427839 – hair mineral analysis
PO	Dr's Laboratory – Tel: 020 7460 4800 – wide variety blood tests including thyroid, allergy, iron, etc.
DP	Autism Research Unit – Tel: 0191 510 8922 – urine test for gluten and casein

Key

DP – Direct to public

PO – Practitioner only

Reading List

A selection of some of the most useful references for topics covered in the book.

Allergies and the Hyperactive Child Doris Rapp

The Allergy Bible Linda Gamlin

Allergy Free Cookbook Maggie Pannell

Alternatives to Antibiotics Dr John McKenna

Anxiety, Phobias and Panic Attacks; Your Questions Answered Elaine Sheenan

Asberger's Syndrome Tony Attwood

Beat Candida Cookbook Erica White

The Body Book Claire Rayner (explains puberty in pictorial form)

Boost Your Child's Immune System Lucy Burney

Complete Book of Food Combining Jan and Inge Dries

Complete Guide to Healing Foods Amanda Ursell

Complete Guide to Food Allergies and Intolerance Dr J Brostoff and Linda Gamlin (covers chemical, environmental, inhalant and food sensitivity and has comprehensive lists of foods)

Cooking Without Barbara Cousins

Diet and Arthritis Gail Darlington and Linda Gamlin – good section on types of JCA

Diet and Intervention in Autism Marilyn Lebretton – practical guidance for implementing casein/gluten free diets

E for Additives Maurice Hanssen

FINDOUT - Pocket sized booklet index of E numbers on a traffic light system. Available from Foresight Association Tel: 01483 427839

Food for Thought Maureen Minchin (especially colicky babies and breast feeding)

Food - Your Miracle Medicine Jean Carper

Foresight Wholefood Cookbook Available from Foresight Association Tel: 01483 427839

*From Thoughts To Obsessions – OCD in children and adolescent*s Jessica Kingsley

Homeopathic Remedies for Children Speight from Ainsworths

Illustrated Encyclopaedia of Healing Remedies C Norman Shealy

I'm Worried Brian Moses

The LCP Solution – Nutritional Treatment for ADHD, Dyslexia and Dyspraxia J Stordy and M Nicholl

Mental Health: The Nutrition Connection Patrick Holford and Dr C Pfeiffer (includes addictions, depression, insomnia, fits, anxiety etc

My Healthy Child – What Doctor's Don't Tell You Tel: 020 8944 9555

The Night Scary Beasties Popped Out of my Head Daniel and David Kamish for 4-8 year olds – about a boy who overcame his nightmares.

Nutritional Therapy Cookbook Linda Lazarides

Optimum Nutrition for Babies and Young Children Lucy Burney

Overcoming Candida – Xandria Williams (not specifically children)

Over It Carol Narmandi and Lauralee Roake (teenagers' guide to food obsessions)

Preventing Childhood Eating Problems Jane Hirchmann and Lela Zaphiropoulas

Safe Natural Remedies for Babies and Children Amanda Cochrane

Safe Shopper's Bible D Steinman and S Epstein

Smart Medicine for a Healthy Child Janet Zand and Rachel Watton

Solve Your Skin Problems Natalie Savona and Patrick Holford

Total Health for Children edited by David Belliman and Helen Bedford

The Vaccination Bible Lynne McTaggart (see also Vaccination section)

What Shall I Feed My Baby? Suzannah Olivier

Index